# Private Enterprises and China's Economic Development

Private enterprises have contributed significantly to China's recent economic growth, and will play a key role in achieving China's goal of building a comprehensively flourishing society. But how can private enterprises help China mitigate its macroeconomic problems such as unemployment, income inequality, financial disintermediation, and an unhealthy boom–bust cycle? And what are the main obstacles to private enterprise development? *Private Enterprises and China's Economic Development* answers these questions by identifying the range of cultural, political, and financial challenges confronting China's private enterprises, and assessing their performance and potential. Contributors also analyze the experiences and lessons of other countries, and propose strategies and policies to help China promote private enterprise development.

Using the most up-to-date research on private enterprises, including detailed econometric analysis and national representative data, the authors, including economists, policy-makers, and academics from the USA, China, Singapore, and Canada, comprehensively address the most important aspects of China's private enterprise development. This book will appeal to students, scholars, and policy-makers with an interest in the Chinese economy, economic growth, comparative economics, and transitional economics.

**Shuanglin Lin** is the Noddle Distinguished Professor of Economics at the University of Nebraska, Omaha, Director of China Center for Public Finance, and Chair of the Department of Public Finance at Peking University. He has served as the President of the Chinese Economists' Society. His research interests include public finance and economic development.

**Xiaodong Zhu** is Professor of Economics at the University of Toronto and Special Term Professor at Tsinghua University. He is an editor of the *China Journal of Economics* and serves on the editorial boards of several other international economics journals. His research interests include economic development and macroeconomics.

# Routledge Studies in the Growth Economies of Asia

# Private Enterprises and China's Economic Development

**Edited by Shuanglin Lin and Xiaodong Zhu**

LONDON AND NEW YORK

First published 2007
by Routledge
2 Park Square, Milton Park, Abingdon, Oxon, OX14 4RN

Simultaneously published in the USA and Canada
by Routledge
711 Third Avenue, New York, NY 10017

*Routledge is an imprint of the Taylor & Francis Group, an informa business*

First issued in paperback 2011

Typeset in Times New Roman by
Prepress Projects Ltd, Perth, UK

*British Library Cataloguing in Publication Data*
A catalogue record for this book is available from the British Library

*Library of Congress Cataloging in Publication Data*
Private enterprises and China's economic development / [edited by] Shuanglin Lin and Xiaodong Zhu.

p. cm. – (Studies in the growth economies of Asia; 72)

ISBN 978-0-415-77147-4 (hardback: alk. paper) 1. Business enterprises – China. 2. Privatization – China. 3. Government business enterprises – China. 4. Government ownership – China. 5. China – Economic conditions – 2000– 6. China – Economic policy – 2000– 7. Business enterprises – China. I. Lin, Shuanglin. II. Zhu, Xiaodong.

HD4318.P75 2007

338.6'10951–dc22

2006037797

ISBN10: 0-415-77147-1 (hbk)
ISBN10: 0-415-66644-9 (pbk)
ISBN10: 0-203-96091-2 (ebk)

ISBN13: 978-0-415-77147-4 (hbk)
ISBN13: 978-0-415-66644-2 (pbk)
ISBN13: 978-0-203-96091-2 (ebk)

# Contents

# Figures

# Tables

# Contributors

**Gene Hsin Chang** Department of Economics, The University of Toledo, Toledo, OH, USA

**Baizhu Chen** Department of Finance and Business Economics, Marshall School of Business, University of Southern California, Los Angeles, CA, USA

**Vivian W. Chen** Department of Economics, Virginia Polytechnic Institute and State University, Blacksburg, VA, USA

**Xiao-yuan Dong** Department of Economics, University of Winnipeg, Winnipeg, Manitoba, Canada

**Yi Feng** School of Politics and Economics, Claremont Graduate University, USA

**David F. Gates** Consultant, Markets and Countries, PFC Energy, Washington, DC, USA

**Haizheng Li** School of Economics, Georgia Institute of Technology, Atlanta, GA, USA

**Shuanglin Lin** Department of Economics, College of Business Administration, University of Nebraska, Omaha, NE, USA; and School of Economics, Peking University, Beijing, China

**Hong Lu** Department of Criminal Justice, College of Urban Affairs, University of Nevada, Las Vegas, NV, USA

**Jing Lu** Executive Director, Internal Audit & Corporate Securities, CIBC World Markets, New York, NY, USA

**Kerk L. Phillips** Department of Economics, Brigham Young University, Provo, UT, USA

**Wei Rowe** Department of Finance, Banking and Law, College of Business Administration, University of Nebraska, Omaha, NE, USA

**Yi Sun** Department of Economics, University of California, Santa Cruz, CA, USA

**Aselia Urmanbetova** China National Statistical Bureau, The Statistical Yearbook of China, 2005

**Xiaozu Wang** School of Management, Fudan University, Shanghai, China

**Bin Xu** China Europe International Business School (CEIBS), 699 Hongfeng Road, Pudong, Shanghai, China

**Lixin Colin Xu** Development Research Group, The World Bank, Washington, DC, USA; and Guanghua School of Management, Peking University, Beijing, China

**Yingfeng Xu** Department of Economics, University of Alberta, Edmonton, Alberta, Canada

**Dennis Tao Yang** Department of Economics, Virginia Polytechnic Institute and State University, Blacksburg, VA, USA; and the Center for China in the World Economy, Tsinghua University, China

**Jason Z. Yin** Stillman School of Business, Seton Hall University

**Xiaochuan Zhou** The governor of The People's Bank of China, China

**Tian Zhu** China Europe International Business School (CEIBS), Shanghai, China; and Division of Social Science, Hong Kong University of Science and Technology, Clear Water Bay, Hong Kong

**Xiaodong Zhu** Department of Economics, University of Toronto, Canada; and School of Economics and Management, Tsinghua University, China

# Acknowledgments

We thank all the participants of the International Symposium on Private Enterprises and China's Economic Development, organized by the Chinese Economists Society and the Chinese Academy of Social Sciences in Beijing on 18–20 June 2004, for contributing their high-quality research. We gratefully acknowledge the generous financial support from the Ford Foundation, the Center for International Private Enterprises, the First Data Corporation, LG Electronics, the Huaxia Yingcai Foundation, the Chinese Academy of Social Sciences, Northwestern University in China, and other institutes. We would like to thank Robert Lucas Jr. at the University of Chicago, James Mirrlees at Cambridge University, Jeffrey Sachs at Columbia University, Wei Zhang at Cambridge University, Wing Thye Woo at the Brookings Institution, Gang Yi at the People's Bank of China, Zhengzhong Wang at the Chinese Academy of Social Sciences, Young-Rok Cheong at Seoul National University, Jason Yin at Seton Hall University, Wei Yu at Stanford University, Shunfeng Song at University of Nevada, and Aimin Cheng at Sichuan University for their significant contributions to the conference and the publication of this book. We also thank Catherine Co, Miaomiao Yu, Xiangrong Yu, Alicia Tan, and Jing Wu for their excellent assistance in editing the book. We greatly appreciate the anonymous book reviewers for their helpful comments and the editorial staff at Routledge for their efficient editorial work.

# 1 Introduction and overview

*Shuanglin Lin and Xiaodong Zhu*

## Background

Markets have existed in China for thousands of years. However, on entering the modern era, the road to a market economic system has been painfully bumpy for the Chinese. In 1957, China completed its socialist economic transformation, eliminated all private enterprises, and established state-owned and collective enterprises. In the following year, China established collective farms in rural areas. Since then, China has become a centrally planned economy dominated by a large state sector. The socialist economic system relied on political propaganda to motivate workers and managers. In 1958, China launched the "Great Leap Forward" movement in an effort to catch up with Britain and the US in a short period of time. The whole country was mobilized in a military way, and food and steel were called the two "generals" by Chairman Mao. Lakes were filled to make more land, grassland was plowed to grow crops, and woods were destroyed in an attempt to make steel in farmers' backyards. Farmers in the people's communes worked together and ate together without paying anything. Soon, food reserves were used up, followed by three years of bad harvest. Many people starved and died. The steel made on farmers' backyard stoves was completely useless. To find a way out of the economic crisis, a group of pragmatic leaders in China introduced some incentive mechanisms to rural areas, such as allowing farm households to have a private plot of land to grow food for themselves, and letting a farm household have a fixed amount of land and keep the surplus after submitting a fixed amount of grain to the people's communes. These economic reforms improved productivity dramatically, and economic prosperity came to China in the middle of the 1960s. However, these reforms were criticized by the left-wing officials as revisionism and, in 1966, Chairman Mao launched the Movement of the Great Cultural Revolution to prevent China from going on the "capitalist road." Everyone was forced to participate in the movement. Farmers' private plots were taken back by the communes, free farmers' markets were forbidden, and factories in urban areas were paralyzed. Endless political struggles, insufficient incentives to work, and inappropriate and rigid planning brought the national economy to the edge of collapse in the middle of the 1970s. In 1978, China started market-oriented reforms and began to open up to the western world. After nearly three decades of economic reforms, the economic landscape of China has changed dramatically.

## Resurgence of private enterprises

Individual enterprises were revived at the end of the 1970s as a way of responding to the mounting pressures of unemployment and economic stagnation. They were treated as a "supplement" to the socialist planning economy. In the early 1980s, the people's communes were abolished in rural China, and the household responsibility system was established. Under the new system, a farm household has freedom to grow whatever they want on their assigned land and can sell the surplus of grain after submitting a fixed amount to the government. Agricultural productivity improved enormously, farmers' living standards were greatly improved, and they looked for opportunities in non-farming sectors. In this period, the private sector consisted mainly of individual entrepreneurs, street vendors, and private merchants. At the end of the 1980s, the government passed an amendment to the constitution and legalized the private economy. This spurred an increase in private enterprises. In 1992, Deng Xiaoping traveled to the south and called for further reforms. The government decided to establish a socialist market economy. The number of private enterprises increased rapidly. At the end of the 1990s, the private sector was recognized by the government as an important component of the economy. A new era for private enterprise development began.

The domestic private sector today has become equally as (if not more) important than the state sector in terms of contribution to the gross domestic product (GDP). In 2004, enterprises outside the state sector produced 65 percent of the economy's industrial output, employed 64.8 percent of the non-agricultural work force, and made 64.5 percent of the economy's investment in fixed assets (China National Statistical Bureau, 2005). The domestic private sector plays an important role in contributing to output, and a larger role in creating new jobs. The development of private and non-state-owned enterprises is fundamental to the impressive growth performance that China has enjoyed over the last two and half decades. If other non-state sector economic activities are included, the total non-state sector contributes about two-thirds in terms of GDP. Private sector growth has been especially dynamic, with an average increase of 71 percent per year in terms of output and 41 percent in terms of new employment since 1980 (see Tables 1.1.and 1.2).

At 1978 constant prices, per capita GDP was 2,880 yuan in 2004, 7.6 times as large as that in 1978. Figure 1.1 shows per capita GDP in 1978 constant yuan. It can be seen that the Chinese economy is growing at an increasing rate. From 1978 to 1992, the annual growth rate of real per capita GDP was 7.57 percent, while from 1992 to 2004, the annual growth rate of real per capita GDP was 8.01 percent. For a while, it was suspected that China had exaggerated its GDP growth figures. However, it turned out that the growth figure was under-reported, and the government has had to adjust the GDP figures upward recently. With a large,

*Table 1.1* Industrial value-added of all state-owned enterprises and non-state-owned enterprises above a designated size

| | 1985 | | 1990 | | 2000 | | 2004 | |
|---|---|---|---|---|---|---|---|---|
| | *Billion yuan* | *% of total* | *Billion yuan* | *% of total* | *Billion yuan* | *% of total* | *Billion yuan* | *% of total* |
| Gross industrial output value | 971.65 | 100 | 2,392.44 | 100 | 8,567.37 | 100 | 18,722.07 | 100 |
| Of the total: | | | | | | | | |
| State-owned and state-holding enterprises | 630.21 | 64.9 | 1,306.38 | 54.6 | 4,055.44 | 47.3 | 6,597.11 | 35.2 |
| Of the total: | | | | | | | | |
| Collectively owned industry | 311.72 | 32.1 | 852.27 | 35.6 | 1,190.79 | 13.9 | 1,058.64 | 5.7 |
| Shareholding cooperative enterprises | | | | | 289.73 | 3.4 | 394.32 | 2.1 |
| Shareholding enterprises | | | | | 2,367.44 | 27.6 | 8,078.58 | 43.2 |
| Foreign enterprises and enterprises with funds from Hong Kong, Macao, and Taiwan | | | | | 2,346.46 | 27.4 | 5,884.71 | 31.4 |
| Of the total: | | | | | | | | |
| Private enterprises | | | | | 522.04 | 6.1 | 3,089.86 | 16.5 |

Source: China Statistical Bureau, *The Statistical Yearbook of China*, 1991, 2005.

Note
Output for state-owned and state-holding enterprises in 1985 and 1990 only includes output of state-owned enterprises.

Table 1.2 Employment by various types of enterprises in urban areas

| Year | 1984 | | 1990 | | 2000 | | 2004 | |
|---|---|---|---|---|---|---|---|---|
| Number of employed persons | (10,000 persons) | % of total | (10,000 persons) | % of total | (10,000 persons) | % of total | (10,000 persons) | % of total |
| Urban employed persons | 12,229 | 100 | 14,690 | 100 | 23,151 | 100 | 26,476 | 100 |
| State-owned units | 8,637 | 70.63 | 10,346 | 70.43 | 8,102 | 35.00 | 6,710 | 25.34 |
| Urban collectively owned units | 3,216 | 26.30 | 3,549 | 24.16 | 1,499 | 6.47 | 897 | 3.39 |
| Cooperative units | | | | | 155 | 0.67 | 192 | 0.73 |
| Joint ownership units | | | | | 42 | 0.18 | 44 | 0.17 |
| Limited liability corporations | | | | | 687 | 2.97 | 1,436 | 5.42 |
| Shareholding limited corporations | | | | | 457 | 1.97 | 625 | 2.36 |
| Private enterprises | | | | | 1,268 | 5.48 | 2,994 | 11.31 |
| Units with funds from Hong Kong, Macao and Taiwan | | | | | 310 | 1.34 | 470 | 1.77 |
| Foreign-funded units | | | | | 332 | 1.43 | 563 | 2.13 |
| Self-employed individuals | 339 | 2.77 | 671 | 4.57 | 2,136 | 9.23 | 2,521 | 9.52 |
| Others | | | | | 8,162 | 35.26 | 10,024 | 37.86 |

Source: China Statistical Bureau, *The Statistical Yearbook of China*, 1991, 2005.

Note
Self-employed individuals were not treated as urban employees in *The Statistical Yearbook of China*, 1991. In calculating the percentage in total employment, we adjusted the data.

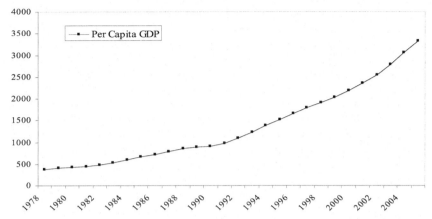

*Figure 1.1* China's per capita GDP 1978–2005 at the 1978 constant price. From China National Statistical Bureau (2006).

relatively well-educated labor force and a high national savings rate, the growth potential of the Chinese economy is enormous.

However, the development of private enterprises and the rate of regional economic growth are far from even across the regions. Table 1.3 shows regional investment in different enterprises and per capita gross regional product in 2004. It can be seen that the share of investment in state-owned enterprises is still very high in some regions. For example, in 2004, the investment shares of state enterprises were 84 percent, 61 percent, and 58 percent in Tibet, Gansu, and Guizhou, respectively, while the investment shares of state enterprises were 25 percent and 26 percent in Shandong and Zhejiang respectively. In 2004, the per capita gross regional product was 55,307 yuan in Shanghai, but only 4,215 yuan in Guizhou.

## Challenges

The Chinese economy faces unprecedented challenges. First, the unemployment rate remains high. Many state-owned enterprises (SOEs) and collectively owned enterprises (CVEs) are losing money and have had to lay off workers. Disguised and hidden unemployment problems could be much worse in the rural sector. As China gradually opens its markets to foreign competition, there will be more layoffs by SOEs and in rural areas. Second, income inequality is widening. Income gaps between rich and poor and between rural and city residents are growing. Third, the banking sector is burdened with large non-performing loans, and the non-banking financial sectors are underdeveloped. It is difficult to channel large amounts of savings to investment, and the threat of a potential financial crisis still exists. Fourth, China faces the challenge of maintaining healthy economic growth. Official Chinese statistics show that the growth rate is still as high as 10 percent. The high growth rate was achieved with high investment in state enterprises and government deficit spending. The influence of government command-and-control

Table 1.3 Regional investment in fixed assets by ownership[a] and per capita gross regional product in 2004

| | Investment share of enterprises with different ownerships (%) | | | | | | | |
| Region | State-owned units | Collectively owned units | Individual economy | Joint enterprises | Shareholding enterprises | Foreign-funded enterprises | Enterprises with funds from Hong Kong, Macao and Taiwan | Per capita GDP (yuan) |
|---|---|---|---|---|---|---|---|---|
| Beijing | 29.05 | 9.49 | 6.58 | 0.10 | 38.79 | 7.53 | 7.92 | 37,058 |
| Tianjin | 38.85 | 9.33 | 6.66 | 0.12 | 26.19 | 10.43 | 4.01 | 31,550 |
| Hebei | 32.02 | 21.02 | 13.63 | 0.80 | 23.79 | 3.06 | 3.74 | 12,918 |
| Shanxi | 38.56 | 8.27 | 13.17 | 0.84 | 37.26 | 0.80 | 0.73 | 9,150 |
| Inner Mongolia | 48.72 | 2.54 | 12.04 | 0.01 | 34.21 | 0.56 | 1.5 | 11,305 |
| Liaoning | 31.23 | 10.96 | 17.57 | 0.2 | 29.89 | 6.35 | 2.93 | 16,297 |
| Jilin | 39.04 | 4.58 | 13.81 | 0.09 | 32.19 | 7.31 | 2.05 | 10,932 |
| Heilongjiang | 44.85 | 3.34 | 15.31 | 0.02 | 30.89 | 1.69 | 0.76 | 13,897 |
| Shanghai | 29.81 | 10.12 | 8.30 | 0.87 | 21.07 | 20.51 | 6.32 | 55,307 |
| Jiangsu | 30.55 | 23.76 | 13.70 | 0.09 | 16.86 | 9.17 | 5.56 | 20,705 |
| Zhejiang | 26.21 | 28.53 | 10.77 | 0.08 | 26.34 | 4.70 | 2.76 | 23,942 |
| Anhui | 37.03 | 9.44 | 20.79 | 0.05 | 26.67 | 2.50 | 2.29 | 7,768 |
| Fujian | 30.21 | 12.44 | 15.40 | 0.29 | 17.84 | 10.26 | 12.65 | 17,218 |
| Jiangxi | 42.26 | 9.38 | 18.83 | 0.21 | 22.08 | 3.00 | 3.80 | 8,189 |
| Shandong | 25.11 | 23.22 | 13.81 | 0.69 | 27.74 | 5.68 | 2.79 | 16,925 |
| Henan | 35.26 | 13.17 | 19.9 | 0.18 | 24.99 | 2.92 | 2.55 | 9,470 |

| | | | | | | | |
|---|---|---|---|---|---|---|---|
| Hubei | 40.97 | 8.00 | 14.5 | 0.67 | 26.44 | 3.40 | 3.53 | 10,500 |
| Hunan | 40.34 | 12.95 | 17.5 | 0.37 | 23.72 | 1.97 | 2.24 | 9,117 |
| Guangdong | 29.29 | 15.30 | 14.41 | 0.42 | 16.98 | 7.96 | 15.14 | 19,707 |
| Guangxi | 43.33 | 3.70 | 22.47 | 0.18 | 22.71 | 3.53 | 3.40 | 7,196 |
| Hainan | 31.67 | 4.40 | 8.74 | 0.50 | 34.68 | 15.08 | 4.03 | 9,450 |
| Chongqing | 40.19 | 7.29 | 18.02 | 0.20 | 26.70 | 4.12 | 2.71 | 9,608 |
| Sichuan | 35.57 | 13.27 | 15.81 | 0.09 | 31.26 | 1.43 | 1.85 | 8,113 |
| Guizhou | 58.27 | 4.43 | 15.50 | 0.24 | 19.48 | 0.92 | 0.95 | 4,215 |
| Yunnan | 46.99 | 4.87 | 19.34 | 0.06 | 24.95 | 0.56 | 1.76 | 6,733 |
| Tibet | 84.41 | 0.71 | 5.92 | 0.04 | 5.43 | 0.07 | 0.00 | 7,779 |
| Shaanxi | 53.72 | 4.72 | 14.24 | 0.34 | 23.50 | 0.86 | 1.43 | 7,757 |
| Gansu | 60.86 | 6.56 | 12.64 | 0.11 | 16.66 | 1.01 | 1.45 | 5,970 |
| Qinghai | 51.51 | 3.64 | 9.86 | 0.06 | 31.39 | 2.00 | 1.11 | 8,606 |
| Ningxia | 36.65 | 10.21 | 20.65 | 0.27 | 29.88 | 2.04 | 0.31 | 7,880 |
| Xinjiang | 45.26 | 4.75 | 12.26 | 0.02 | 35.86 | 0.52 | 1.11 | 11,199 |

Source: Calculated by the authors based on data from the China Statistical Bureau (2005).

Note

a   The percentage of investment in fixed assets made by other enterprises is small and is not reported here to save space.

on the economy is still strong, and the economy has periodically experienced the cycle of decontrol–overheating–control–slump. Fifth, China has joined the World Trade Organization (WTO) and must honor its commitments, including the opening of a number of crucial markets. The state enterprises in these markets lack competitiveness. In implementing the future agenda of economic reforms and development, the private sector is important in employment and output growth, in government revenue collection, in poverty reduction, in narrowing the income gap between the interior and the coast, in technical innovation, and in raising China's international competitiveness.

Despite their importance to China's economic development, private enterprises still face many obstacles. They are still discriminated against by state-monopolized banks in borrowing and are subject to numerous taxes, fees, and levies from local governments. The legal system to protect private property is still weak. Private enterprises in China also face many other challenges, such as lack of credit, technical and information support, management experience, international trade and investment experience, and long-run planning. In addition, they must deal with competition from the SOEs, enterprise management disputes, contract violations, and corruption of government officials. How can private enterprises overcome these obstacles? What measures should be taken to promote private enterprise development? What lessons can China learn from other countries in promoting private enterprise development and privatization?

## Overview of the book

This book attempts to answer these questions. Most of the chapters in this book are selected from the papers presented at the three-day international symposium, "Private Enterprises and China's Economic Development," which was organized by the Chinese Economists' Society and the Chinese Academy of Social Sciences in Beijing, China, on 18–20 June 2004. The chapters can be divided into four parts, each focusing on a particular aspect of private enterprise development.

### Part I:  Financial reforms and enterprise development

One of the major obstacles that private enterprises in China face is the difficulty in getting access to credit. Despite some major reforms in the last decade, most banks in China are still state owned and have a strong bias toward large and state-owned enterprises in their lending behavior. The chapter by Xiaochuan Zhou, the governor of China's central bank, discusses how private financial institutions may first be introduced in rural areas. Zhou first argues that the development of healthy rural financial institutions is an integral part of rural development. He then discusses in detail how the reform of rural credit cooperatives should be carried out. He argues that many problems that rural credit cooperatives have had stem from the policy burdens they shouldered, and that rural financial reform should start with the separation of the policy and commercial functions of the rural financial institutions. He suggests that government aid should only be used to relieve rural financial institutions from historical burdens, and the future development of these institutions should depend primarily on private capital.

One way in which the Chinese government has tried to diversify enterprise ownership is by converting large SOEs into joint-stock companies and allowing some of them to raise capital from the equity market. In the second chapter, Xiaozu Wang, Lixin Colin Xu, and Tian Zhu examine the impact of public listing on enterprise performance using a panel of financial and ownership data from all the companies listed on the Shanghai Stock Exchange and the Shenzhen Stock Exchange from 1990 to June 2000. Their study shows that ownership reform through public listing has not worked well: the performance of enterprises in the post-listing years is considerably lower than their performance in both the pre-listing year and the initial public offering years.

Most private enterprises in China are small and medium enterprises (SMEs). Yingfeng Xu argues in his chapter that the difficulties that these enterprises have in accessing credit are common difficulties that SMEs have faced in other countries as well. Xu suggests that further financial sector reforms are needed to remedy these difficulties. In particular, he argues that bank lending rates should be liberalized to better reflect the risk associated with lending to SMEs, and that new financing vehicles, such as risk-taking equity capital, should be introduced.

As China's banks become more commercialized, they will be exposed to similar types of risk that banks in market economies often have to deal with: market, credit, and operational risk. How to manage risk properly is an important challenge faced by the Chinese banks. In the developed countries, bank regulation and supervision is an integral part of financial risk management. Jing Lu's chapter discusses the US experience in commercial bank regulation and supervision and the implications for China.

### *Part II: Private enterprise, efficiency, and economic growth*

Using new data (1997–2001) from 31 Chinese provinces, Shuanglin Lin and Wei Rowe have identified several factors that are related to the profitability of China's regional SOEs. They show that both the investment share of non-state enterprises and openness, measured by either export share in GDP or import share in GDP, were positively related to the profitability of SOEs. Moreover, they show that both the ratio of unhealthy assets over equity and the debt ratio were negatively related to SOEs' profitability. Finally, they found that SOEs in provinces with larger government size (a higher ratio of government spending in the GDP) had lower profitability. They suggest that, to improve the profitability of China's regional SOEs, Chinese provinces should encourage investment in non-state enterprises, promote exports as well as imports, reduce SOEs' debt ratios and unhealthy assets, and reduce local government size.

Kerk L. Phillips and Baizhu Chen apply the cross-country regression methodology of Levine and Renelt (1992) and Sala-i-Martin (1997) to analyze regional growth in China. There is a large literature on China's regional growth. One of the most robust results in this literature is that growth is negatively related to the size of the state sector. Phillips and Chen confirm this result in their study. Furthermore, they find that provinces with more innovation capital and with higher bank deposit to GDP ratios tend to experience higher economic growth.

Yi Feng and Yi Sun also analyze China's growth using regional data, but focus on the impact of investment sources on growth. Again, they find that the share of SOEs' investment is negatively related to growth, while the share of investment in collective and private enterprises is positively related to growth.

### Part III: Openness, legal protection, and private enterprise

China's exports have grown rapidly in the last decade and attracted much international attention. In his chapter, Bin Xu studies the impact of exports on enterprise productivity. He finds that exports are a key driver of productivity growth in private Chinese firms: private firms that did not export in 1998 but became exporters after 1998 experienced the highest total factor productivity (TFP) growth rate during the period 1998–2000. He also finds that research and development (R&D) investment is an important factor for the TFP growth of these private exporting firms. In contrast, R&D investment is found to be negatively related to productivity growth for state-owned firms.

The impact of China's growing demand for energy has also attracted much international attention. The chapter by David Gates and Jason Yin provides a timely study of this issue. Energy is one of the few sectors that is still monopolized by the state (others include telecommunications and banking). Gates and Yin begin with an overview of recent changes in energy demand and supply in China, including a discussion of the reasons for the recent surge in demand. Using a traditional demand elasticity approach, they analyze the elasticity of each of four major energy end uses and the potential for adjustments in these relationships. They then discuss the fundamentals that underlie energy supply and what these imply for the sustainable growth of China's economy and its efforts to protect its environment. The chapter concludes with suggestions for public policy to meet the challenge of growing energy demands and a discussion of the implications for the private sector, including both private and foreign investments.

One of the significant legal developments in the era of economic reforms was the passage of the 1994 Administrative Law. This was designed to mediate and adjudicate in disputes between private entities (e.g., individuals, private enterprises) and various governmental regulatory agencies (e.g., taxation, licensing, finance, environmental protection, and employment-related regulations). Using administrative court cases adjudicated in the 1990s, Hong Lu examines the claims and counter-claims and the courts' rulings on disputes between private enterprises and governmental administrative agencies in areas including: (1) licensing; (2) issues involving environmental protection; (3) issues related to employment (e.g., discrimination, workers' compensation, employment mobility); (4) business transactions; (5) taxation and fines; and (6) disputes in administrative certification. The chapter concludes with discussions of the symbolic and practical values of the Administrative Law in regulating the relation between the state and private enterprises.

### *Part IV: Private enterprises, employment, and earnings*

As China was at a very low level of development when economic reform started in 1978, the transformation of the centrally planned economy to a market economy is intimately related to the structural transformation from an agrarian society to a modern society. Most of the private enterprises in China started in rural areas. Dennis Tao Yang and Vivian Chen use household data to study the impact of labor market barriers on private enterprise development in rural areas. They find that the relaxation of controls on labor mobility induced farm households to reallocate productive inputs from agriculture to non-agricultural activities, which accounted for 43 percent of their total household income growth.

The poor efficiency of the SOEs is well established. However, privatizing these enterprises will cause transitional unemployment problems as many of the workers in the SOEs may not have the marketable skills that are required to work in private enterprises. Gene Hsin Chang provides a theoretical analysis of the trade-off between efficiency gains and employment losses from privatization. He argues that the increase in efficiency from privatization will have a trickle-down effect that will eventually generate more jobs and therefore have a positive effect on employment. He also argues that this positive effect can be better realized through some expansionary fiscal policy.

The chapter by Haizheng Li and Aselia Urmanbetova also studies China's rural labor market. They find that the marginal returns to middle school education relative to elementary school education are very low, in contrast to what has been found in the urban labor market, where the marginal returns to education are much higher and have been increasing since the early 1990s. Their results suggest that there are still substantial barriers to labor mobility between rural and urban areas that prevent the marginal returns to education being fully realized in rural areas.

China's rural inductry underwent radical property rights reforms with millions of township and village enterprises (TVEs) being privatized in the late 1990s. The privatization of TVEs was achieved mainly through the transfer of ownership rights from local governments to enterprise insiders, i.e. managers and employees. In her paper, Xiao-yuan Dong examines the impact of privatization of TVEs on earnings inequality using a unique data set from Jiangsu and Shangdong Provinces. It is found that the privatization of TVEs was associated with a sharp increase in earnings inequality over a short period of three years. Unequal distribution of share ownership has been an important source of the rise of earnngs inequality after privatization. Looking at other causes of the increased income disparity, she finds increased returns to education, increased returns to experience for mid-aged workers, a widened gender wage gap, and enlarged regional disparity.

All the industrialized countries are based on a market economic system and rely on private enterprises. China should be no exception. Market-oriented economic reforms, which have stimulated China's economic growth and improved people's living standards for more than a quarter of a century, are irreversible. It is expected that private enterprises will continue to grow rapidly and eventually become the dominant force in the Chinese economy.

### *This book's contributions*

This book is the first of its type focusing on the role of domestic private enterprises in China's economic development, and it represents a timely contribution to the current discussion on the private sector in China. The book provides urgently needed policy recommendations to the government, and suggests that government should play a role in providing a rule-based system through commercial legislation, regulation, and macroeconomic policies. It also recommends that, at the business operational level, the government should interfere less, continue to remove discriminatory barriers based on ownership, and provide a more conducive environment for private sector development. The state-owned financial institutions, which also play a role in private sector development, need to have more incentives to serve the private sector under the framework of a level playing field. In the past, the banks have lent primarily to the state sector because of lending directives, the perceived lower risks of state-owned companies, and the informal nature of the private companies. The financial institutions need to develop their abilities to assess private sector risks and improve their expertise in lending to the private sector.

The book offers advice to Chinese private enterprises on how to expand their businesses in China. Domestic private enterprises need to adapt to the best international business practices. Private entrepreneurs should change their previously informal status, opaque organizational structure, and non-transparent ways of doing business. The book is also useful to foreign investors in understanding China's market-oriented reforms, government policies, and development potential.

Moreover, the book reflects the most current and highest quality research on China's private enterprise development and its impacts on the Chinese and the world economy. It covers a variety of interesting research topics on the Chinese economy and employs numerous contemporary research methods. The book is an indispensable reference for scholars of private enterprises and China's economic development.

### References

China National Statistical Bureau (1991, 2005) *Statistical Yearbook of China*, Beijing: China Statistical Publishing House.

China National Statistical Bureau (2006) *China Statistical Abstract*, Beijing: China Statistical Publishing House.

Levine, R. and D. Renelt (1992) "A Sensitivity Analysis of Cross-Country Growth Regressions," *American Economic Review*, 82: 942–63.

Sala-i-Martin, X. (1997) "I Just Ran Two Million Regressions," *American Economic Review*, 87: 178–83.

# Part I

# Financial reforms and enterprise development

# 2 Some thoughts on financial reform in rural areas

*Xiaochuan Zhou*

The subject of this book, *Private Enterprises and China's Economic Development*, is a topic deserving significant discussion during the development of China's economy. As far as Chinese finance is concerned, most banks are still state owned. Although we have several joint-stock commercial banks, the diversity of the joint-stock system has developed gradually; therefore, we still cannot call them private enterprises. Our future rural financial institutions may be most similar to private enterprises. Rural finance is a relatively fundamental microeconomic issue. I would like to present some thoughts on rural financial reform.

## The fundamental categories of financial reform in rural areas

China's rural financial reform can be classified into broad and narrow categories. The broad rural finance reform includes rural policy finance, commercial finance, capital turnover guided by government, the creation and development of rural financing media, how to arrange continuous positive incentive mechanisms to stimulate the development of rural financial institutions, the exit system of rural financial institutions and contracts of agricultural products, agricultural products in future markets, development of agricultural insurance, etc. The broad rural financial reform has been coming for many years. After the national financial meeting in 2002, the State Council established a special working group to examine the development of rural finance and rural credit cooperatives. This special working group initiated by the People's Bank of China includes representatives of the Ministry of Agriculture, the Ministry of Finance, the Bank of Agriculture, the Bank of Agricultural Development, etc. After much discussion and research, the special working group submitted a special report to the State Council during the fourth quarter of 2003. This report provided many suggestions and ideas from the rural finance reform perspective.

Specifically, narrow rural finance reform refers to contemporary reform of rural credit cooperatives. On 27 June 2003, the State Council passed a "Notice of the Draft on deepening reform of rural credit cooperatives." The deepening of reform of rural credit cooperatives was supervised and implemented by the Control Commission of the People's Bank of China. Local government exerts four functions, namely management, consultancy, coordination, and services. The People's Bank of China is responsible for designing, regulating, and testing financial support schemes. Based on the principles of cooperation and voluntary participation, the selection of the experimental unit is reported by various provinces (municipalities, counties) on a voluntary basis. The Control Commission of the People's Bank of China compiles all the information and then reports to the State Council. Since July 2003, the financial reform of rural credit cooperatives has been carried out experimentally in eight provinces. Based on the spirit of finance reform, the experimental provinces provide specific advice that is first audited by the Control Commission and then implemented after receiving permission from the State Council. The Control Commission, local government, and the People's Bank of China carry out their responsibilities to improve reform of rural credit cooperatives in terms of the supervision management system. This system stresses that the central government controls and adjusts at the macro level, province governments take responsibility and manage based on the law, and credit cooperatives show self-restraint and control self-assumed risks. The reforms have made some progress so far.

## Three cognitive bases of rural finance reform

### The relationship between agriculture, farmer, and rural area and rural finance: coexistent or supporting and being supported?

As opposed to the previous rural finance reforms, this special group formed a new understanding of the relationship between agriculture, farmer, and rural area (AFR) and rural finance. Previous ideas were focused on the rural finance system supporting AFR, and hoped to provide more sources of rural finance while the capital price was cheaper. To some extent, AFR was supported by coercing rural finance. Now, the old concepts have been substituted for new concepts, which recognize that the development of AFR is coexistent and has mutual benefits with the development of rural finance. If we compare AFR to the body of a human being, rural finance would be similar to an important organ of the body. Rural finance takes from AFR, and gives back to AFR as well. It is not a supporting apparatus outside the body (AFR), which can be used but does not need to be fed. In the past, rural finance institutions were criticized when a problem related to agricultural capital emerged, and then these institutions were asked for more loans to solve the problems. Less attention, however, was paid to the health and continuous development of these institutions. Thus, many problems appeared in rural financial institutions, and their finances were not consistent and needed to be rescued. Under such circumstances, rural financial institutions were not able to make further contributions to the development of AFR.

Specifically, there are more than 32,000 rural credit cooperatives in China today. In the past, they shouldered half commercial and half policy duties, i.e., as the government kept stressing the importance of agriculture, the rural credit cooperatives were assigned many policy tasks, and the capital price was relatively low all the time. The poor performance of rural credit cooperatives may be due to the insufficient management of the operating position; however, it may be more attributable to the administration involved. With a mixed goal, an organization can hardly improve its financial quality by following commercial principles. In practice, the problems showed up as a high percentage of bad loans and severe losses. If classified by a rigid loan standard, the percentage of bad loans in rural credit cooperatives in general reached as high as 50 percent within two or three years after the Asian financial crisis. As a whole, the net value of rural credit cooperatives is a very large negative number. This negative amount is twice or three times as large as the previous book value of capital in rural credit cooperatives. With such a high negative net value and a high percentage of bad assets, rural credit cooperatives lacked the capacity to serve agriculture.

Meanwhile, the Agricultural Bank of China is undergoing reforms towards a commercial bank. As no profit was earned and agricultural business became a great burden, agricultural banks gradually retreated from rural areas to the county level. Their services gradually shifted to the cities. Another division of rural credit cooperatives is postal savings. There are many postal saving stations that absorbed lots of saving deposits. These postal savings cannot be used for loans. The saving deposits are not used in agriculture, but in other areas. The competitiveness of postal savings in attracting saving deposits is mainly due to their policies and systems. But some believe that the weak competitiveness of rural credit cooperatives is also a critical reason for their poor performance. Compared with postal savings, rural credit cooperatives lack competitiveness; thus, capital notably flows out of rural areas. Many people have likened postal savings to a water pump that pumps capital from the rural areas.

Under such circumstances, in order to guarantee basic services for AFR, the main measure for increasing capital is that the central bank supports rural credit cooperatives, using reloan at lower interest rates. In a sense, reloan capital has expanded total loans for AFR after the Asian financial crisis, especially since 1999. It is well known that the central bank's reloans cannot be applied in principle to such usage; moreover, it is also difficult to estimate the return on such reloans. Therefore, using reloans from the central bank for rural finance is a type of "outside" support, not a permanent, persistent, and problem-solving solution.

If we consider policy finance as a type of "outside" support, the relationship between commercial rural finance and AFR is interdependent and coexistent. This relationship requires us to run rural commercial financial institutions well, and change them into healthy and continuously developing financial institutions. In 10 percent or more of China, commercial finance cannot survive because of extreme poverty, and policy finance is needed. Most rural areas in China, however, are capable of supporting the development of continuously increasing, financially healthy, and dynamic commercial finance.

### Capital price: open or controlled

There are two opinions regarding capital price. One is the traditional idea, which believes that both grain and agriculture are important and, to the more important, the more credit will be given. So the loan interest rates for AFR are relatively low. But the numbers of small loans are large and costs are high, yet violation rates are not low according to some statistical data. If loan interest rates are priced by administration rather than by conformity with the market principle, rural financial institutions cannot cover risk premium via interest rates, and it is difficult to maintain high financial quality and continuous survival. The other opinion is gradually breaking up the traditional model. It agrees with giving up control and carrying out flow range for interest rates. In this round of rural finance reform, the most important aspect is to implement the market-oriented interest rate faster in the rural areas than in cities, i.e., the flow range of interest rates in rural areas is wider than in cities; thus, it enables rural financial institutions to survive and then gradually expand their business, and both AFR and rural finance are able to develop. However, some people may not agree. They argue that the current interest rates of rural credit cooperatives are too high to demonstrate their characteristics of supporting AFR.

### Thoughts on the cooperative system

The cooperative system was previously pursued in rural areas. Agricultural production is by a cooperative; the purchasing and commercial system is by supply and sale cooperative; and the rural finance system is a credit cooperative. These three cooperative organizations form a cooperative system. Owing to price fluctuation, organizational format changes, and high net losses and bad assets in rural credit cooperatives, through many years of their development, local farmers gradually paid little attention to rural credit cooperatives and did not consider them to be organizations that were established by the cooperation of the public to serve the public. During this period, the government considered rural credit cooperatives as quasi state-owned financial institutions. Once these rural financial institutions are exposed to conversion risk, the government will give succor and not permit any credit cooperative to go bankrupt as a result of conversion. They guarantee the disbursement and full amount of principal and interest compensation for depositors. They support rural credit cooperatives in the same way as they do state-owned financial institutions. However, without the restriction of bankruptcy, the ultimate restriction, it leads to "reverse selection" and "ethical risk."

Although differences in cooperative systems exist in various regions throughout the country, credit cooperatives are in good shape in some regions. But in general, this reform does not address the cooperative system outlined above, but reforms credit cooperatives according to the model of successful enterprise reform, and the form of joint-stock system and the joint-stock with cooperation system.

In a traditional view, a cooperative system is established in communities and then serves those communities. The requirement of a current capital adequacy ratio that is implemented in a commercial bank cannot be used to control a community organization. However, what needs to be stressed is that the capital adequacy ratio is not only a self-restraint to a commercial institution, but also a reflection of its anti-risk ability. It is a metric to measure whether a financial institution is able to develop continuously and healthily. According to the requirements of a joint-stock system, contributed capital should be sufficient and in place. A certain percentage of contributed capital should be used to resist risks. There are some successful examples of cooperative systems existing in other countries. Therefore, no one will object to a rural credit cooperative system as a format for rural financial institutions. We need to emphasize that, as far as the current rural credit cooperative reforms are concerned, no matter whether a joint-stock system or a cooperative system, they are subject to the same requirements of capital sufficiency, anti-risk capability, and unfavorable assets solutions. Thus, with regard to the form of rural financial institutions, we should allow exploration and innovation rather than sticking to one model as in the past.

## Some thoughts on the financial support of the central bank to rural credit cooperatives

Based on the above ideas, there are two levels of action that have been taken in China's rural finance reforms. The first level is the rural credit cooperative reform that has been experimental in eight provinces since the beginning of July 2003. In the summer of 2004, this reform was extended to the majority of provinces. The role the central bank plays during the process of reform can be summarized into three points: "face and relieve the historical burden on rural credit cooperatives, provide consecutive positive incentive mechanisms, and prevent from going downhill and ethical risk." The second level is mainly focused on broad rural finance reform, including policy finance orientation, postal savings reform, development of order agriculture, agricultural insurance, future agricultural products, etc. It is also necessary to form a policy gradually and then develop it step by step.

### *Face and relieve historical burden*

As noted above, the bad assets generated previously in rural credit cooperatives were caused by administration involvement and administrative order, by over-drafted funds owed to rural credit cooperatives for filling the financial breach in villages and towns, and by poor self-operating and price mechanisms. These loans were scattered over the basic unit level. Although administration departments have some power at the basic unit level, it is limited. In a sense, in order to prevent ethical risk, rural credit cooperatives should be forced first to disaggregate the risks produced by their self-operation. Those with non-returnable loans must be punished in order to lay a solid ethical foundation for later reform. However, there exists no effective means in practice to identify historical responsibilities. There exists no effective operating organization to supervise return losses either.

They depend on support from the government, which puts rural credit cooperatives at a new starting point in the hope that they can provide a finance service for AFR to grow up gradually. As the bad assets are scattered and the possibility of returns is low, any returns, if possible, rely on local personnel who get returns and can benefit from them. The historical burden on rural credit cooperatives, which was engendered during the transition to reform and on account of previously mixed functions of government and enterprise and incorrect prices, needs to be addressed. It requires the rapid development of rural finance reform. Only if these historical burdens are faced and relieved can another new starting point be created.

Why should we pay attention to this problem? Because some people are avoiding this problem. Some people believe that rural credit cooperatives have made great progress in recent years, and are effective in supporting farmers with small loans. If the central bank continuously provides reloans, rural credit cooperatives may eliminate their historical burden gradually within 20 or 30 or even 50 years; however, 20–50 years is too long.

There are two means of eliminating historical burden: one is the issuance of reloans at lower prices, which will help rural credit cooperatives to eliminate the historical burden by depending on the interest differences between deposits and loans; the other is the usage of notes from the central bank. The Policy Department of the People's Bank of China designed this means. The government covers 50 percent of net loss, and the rural credit cooperative covers the remaining 50 percent. Meanwhile, in order to increase the ability to clear up bad assets, the government will not take away returned bad assets. With capital support from the central bank, rural credit cooperatives should depend on their own capacity to increase capital and expand shares. They can increase contributed capital through utilizing a joint-stock system format, modifying corporate administrative structure, and improving internal control management.

### Provide a consecutive positive incentive mechanism

An example would be that B+ or A– students are easily targeted by incentive mechanisms while students who always get Ds are difficult to target. We hope to broaden the scope of incentive mechanisms, which can cover a range from relatively poor to good organizations, and meanwhile to continue the positive incentive mechanisms. If financial reforms rise to a new level, rural credit cooperatives should be stimulated to advance several levels consecutively. At the first level, if they choose to seek help from the government to eliminate historical burden, provinces, regions, municipals, counties, all the way down to rural credit cooperatives that participate in reform, should first promise their commitment to the reform plan before they can obtain financial support and incentive policy on bad assets. At the second level, rural credit cooperatives should try their best to eliminate bad assets on their own. Meanwhile, they should try to increase capital and shares to make the capital adequacy ratio grow from previously negative numbers to the zero level.

You may think that it sounds ridiculous but, as I said before, as their net value is an extremely large negative number, it is not easy to make ends meet. After reaching zero with great effort, the central bank can use its special note to replace their bad assets, meanwhile reimbursing special note interest to rural credit cooperatives. Thus, the note from central bank has become the healthy asset. The rural credit cooperatives, which received the special note, can improve their balance sheet but, as the note is not cash, it cannot be used to issue loans. Because it is prohibited to exchange the note in markets, it partially offsets the impact on monetary policy because of the issuing of reloans. At the third level, as the note is valid for just two years, the capital adequacy ratio should increase to 2 percent after the second year[1] [Basel Accord I (1998) requires 4 percent for core capital adequacy ratio and 8 percent for total capital adequacy ratio]. If the capital adequacy ratio fulfills the corresponding requirements, and corporate governance and the elimination of bad assets meet the corresponding requirements, after an acceptance check and confirmation, the central bank can convert notes into cash. Rural credit cooperatives that receive converted cash can expand their financial services and increase loan services. Because the rural loan interest rate has been enlarged to flow within [0.9, 2.0] of the standard interest rate, it has more room for gain.

There are further levels and requirements above the three levels. After determining a basic and healthy development direction, it must also improve in the following years (of course, we have not fully disclosed the future plan and incentive mechanisms) so that rural credit cooperatives can reach the equivalent capital adequacy ratio, capability of risk resistance, and bad asset rate that is required in ordinary financial institutions.

Because of constraints of personnel quality and environment, fundamental rural financial organizations cannot reach the same level as municipal financial institutions in terms of corporate governance and management but, in general, the above reform actions can guide rural credit cooperatives in the right direction. Therefore, the policy is designed with the hope of establishing a successive, excellent, and large-scale positive incentive mechanism and then supervising and urging rural credit cooperatives to develop in the right direction.

### Prevent from going downhill and keep away ethical risk

Given the relatively low personnel quality in rural credit cooperatives and the relatively high market risk, rural administrative intervention may still exist even after reform. The general rural credit environment may not be good, and various problems may occur in the near future. The central government assumed the historical burden and advanced rural credit cooperative reform. But if rural credit cooperatives go downhill again, or if their fraudulent operation leads to a credit cooperative crisis, their seeking of support from the government after operation failure will result in huge ethical risk and reverse selection. Thus, the policy design should consider the situation with regard to going downhill and ethical risk.

To a large extent, prevention from going downhill depends on supervision. When we passed through the previous levels of incentive mechanisms, the government helped to relieve the corresponding historical burdens and substantiate contributed capital so that rural credit cooperatives possessed sufficient counter-risk capabilities. In addition, we should establish a policy by which we can prevent rural credit cooperatives from going downhill from any of the levels. The critical policy is prompt correction action (PCA). Specifically, when the capital adequacy ratio in a financial institution is declining, the administration department should immediately adopt actions to confine its business development and bonus distribution. This makes rural credit cooperatives aware of the strong effect of "*Jin Gu Zhou;*"[2] if the capital adequacy ratio declines further, the administration department should ask for a purchase or merger and, finally, the administration department should close the problematic organization before the net worth becomes negative. The application of PCA is slightly different in various countries. We must also seek and establish a set of similar actions to prevent institutions from going downhill. One main reference is the Federal Deposit Insurance Company Improvement Act (FDICIA) 1991 from the American Federal Deposit Insurance Company. The details are: the capital adequacy ratio in a depository intermediary should generally reach 10 percent; a warning will be issued when the capital adequacy ratio falls to 8 percent and, when it falls to 6 percent, corresponding confined actions such as limitations on the opening of new business and absorption of batch deposits will be adopted. When it falls to 4 percent, the depository intermediary will ask to be purchased and merged. When it falls to 2 percent, the depository intermediary will go bankrupt. That is, the problematic organization will be closed before depositors lose money.

We should design and adopt such action and employ the tighter and tighter principle of "*Jin Gu Zhou*" to prevent this problem from worsening. As for the PCA practiced in rural credit cooperatives in our country, three aspects need to be addressed. First, rural credit cooperatives are dispersed and fundamental; thus, a seamless administration system is needed. Second, associated with China's specific situation, a prompt and effective retreat system should also be established. Taking rural credit cooperatives as an example, when their net value declines close to zero, we should order rural credit cooperatives to close business and retreat because more problems will be discovered when dealing with liquidation, which will make equity become negative, thus infringing on depositors' interests. The key point in establishing a retreat system is to protect medium and small depositors and provide them with compensation. So we need to set up deposit insurance provisions immediately. As to closing problematic organizations, the key is firm action. Because closing one or two credit cooperatives will probably affect local agriculture in the short term, strong appeals will occur. If we ignore this, ethical risk and reverse selection will consequently emerge. Third, along with the closure of poorly performing financial institutions, we should allow new financial institutions to be established, financial organizational licenses to be issued, and creative financial organizations to provide financial services to the rural area. In our country, there is only one rural credit cooperative in a village. If it is closed, no financial service will be available in this village. Of course, the examination criteria should not have any bias. With respect to this problem, the Ministry of

Agriculture continues to explore community banks and new types of rural finance forms. During the previous liquidation period for financial institutions, the issuing of new licenses was not advocated. However, we must clearly recognize that, when reform enters a new phase, we should consider allowing and encouraging new organizations to substitute for the problematic organizations; otherwise, no action will be taken about the problematic organizations and new organizations will not be allowed to operate. Thus, new ethical risk and reverse selection will be generated. Of course, risk exists as to whether a new organization will perform well, which is determined by the organization itself as well as the continuous administration.

## Steer capital flow and reinforce services for the rural sector

First, we require postal savings to maintain the same levels as rural credit cooperatives with respect to pricing policy, and we prevent a continuous unequal policy, which results in a competitive difference between them. In order to maintain the relationship between postal savings and rural credit cooperatives, approved by the State Council, the People's Bank of China has reduced the transfer and deposit interest rate of postal savings since 1 August 2003, and allows postal savings to increase deposits and self-management. This allows the gradual elimination of old transfer postal savings within five years. The first step is to reduce the current interest rate to the reserve rate level within five years; next, to enlarge the postal saving organization's self-management of old and transfer savings capital year after year and, finally, gradually to extend the scope of self-managed postal savings capital. The administration department gradually establishes the normal allowance system for comprehensive postal services.

Second, we refer to and study the implementation experience of the American Community Reinvestment Act (CRA) and encourage our deposit financial institutions to take certain feedback responsibilities and develop community financial services. In October 1977, the Community Reinvestment Act of CRA997, passed by the American Congress, explicitly regulated federal banks and depository intermediaries who participate in insurance to make them accountable for supporting credit and service convenience to the communities in which their absorbing and depository business is located. In order to encourage financial institutions to implement this regulation actively, the CRA adopted two primary measures. First, administration institutions must publicize on a regular basis the records in which each financial institution has satisfied the credit demands and supplies of the communities. Second, when administration institutions assess various financial institutions' applications for federal concessions, deposit insurance from deposit or insurance companies, headquarters movement or establishment and subdivision movement, and the purchase of other organizations, they must consider how well such institutions implement the regulation before deciding to approve or not. Under the promotion of the CRA, the framework of cooperation was established in financial institutions and depository intermediaries related to the CRA and in some communities where they operate. Some financial institutions, especially those who pay attention to their reputation and plan to purchase other organizations, implement the CRA actively. Many banks and depository intermediaries set up new locations to provide more services and strengthen credibility and other bank business services. They adopt more flexible credit guarantee standards and expand loans to residents with low and medium income. Through the CRA, community banks reinvest deposit funds, which are absorbed from their community to the local market with which they are relatively familiar. The CRA plays an active role in the prosperity of some communities whose economies are not developed and in the relief funds from non-developed communities to developed communities. Although we need statutory and specific preparation for technology provision if similar services are to develop in our country, we can explore this with further discussion and studies on this topic and then head in this direction.

Third, we need to exert the functionality of the capital price mechanism. The key point is to expand the floating range of loan rates, gradually opening loan rates at county and below county level. Based on the practical investigation, the floating range of loans at our rural credit cooperatives in 2003 has enlarged to [0.9, 2.0]. In the future, we should ensure that the loan rates of rural financial institutions can reflect loan risk levels and maintain their persistence. At the same time, we have guaranteed that the interest differences of a financial institution can be used to offset costs and risks. Generally speaking, we should prevent the excessive competition resulting from raising deposit rates. Interest rates are not only a means of capital guidance but also a means of business guidance. This aspect is evident in this rural credit cooperative reform. The higher rate in rural credit cooperatives than in other financial institutions is one of the stimuli to attract relevant capital to enter rural credit cooperatives. If financial institutions want to provide services, their finance can be maintained with subsistence levels. Without financial support, they must follow commercial rules. The fundamental commercial rule is that financial institutions operating currencies should be entitled to price the financial products. So should rural credit cooperatives. Rural financial institutions cannot develop without rate marketization.

On account of space restrictions, I will not elaborate on aspects of rural policy finance, rural insurance, and the development of order agriculture (order agriculture can integrate well agricultural insurance, future agricultural products, and agricultural loans to reduce risks), but these are important aspects of rural financial reform.

## Timely establishment of a deposit insurance mechanism

According to PCA, after this round of reform, rural credit cooperatives should be made to close when they are found to be going downhill and their equity is approaching zero. Therefore, theoretically, closing bad institutions will not influence rural depositors' capital conversion. However, the practical operation is not simple. Based on the closing situation of many Chinese financial institutions, conversion problems can occur and damage depositors' interests. The relative dispersion of rural credit cooperatives provides more difficulties for administration and more suspicion about their authenticity. Hence, in the process of fulfilling PCA, when entering into the closure phase, the results provided by practical auditors might already have been zero. Compensation for personal deposits has become a significant issue. Therefore, we should recognize the urgency of establishing a deposit insurance mechanism. Former large financial institutions in China were state owned. Medium-sized financial institutions are mainly joint-stock systems dominated by the government. Although rural credit cooperatives are cooperative systems, the government undertakes an implicit warranty. In this rural credit co-operative reform, there is a strong trend toward diversity and privatization development. During this round of reform, after the government has helped to eliminate the historical burden, rural credit cooperatives primarily depend on private capital. Investment may come from local private companies, villagers, and credit co-operative personnel. Even though there are a variety of sources, they are basically private. At the end of 2006, with the fulfillment of the commitments on entering the World Trade Organization (WTO), China's financial markets were opened to the world. Its ownership will become more diverse. Under such circumstances, it is unsuitable for the state to undertake an implicit warranty any longer.

## Corporation governance in the reform of the rural credit community

The reform of the rural credit community in terms of investment increment and expansion of shareholders in eight provinces proceeds smoothly, in general. In provinces such as Jilin, villagers, staff of the rural credit community, and private shareholders show enthusiasm. The amount achieved doubled the quota expected in this capital increment and share expansion. The situation is not as good in other provinces as in Jilin; however, they are learning from each other. People may suspect some behaviors during capital increment and share expansion, such as some local governments showing leadership, some town and village admin-istrators taking an initiative to buy shares, and under their impact, villagers also buying shares enthusiastically, and staff in credit communities also purchasing shares. In some places, private enterprises have a large amount of private capital. In some poor areas, however, it is hard to find a new shareholder who is willing to invest large amounts of money. In principle, we hope to have some big share-holders who are capable of using their expertise in corporation governance. All in all, these issues make us question the future corporation governance of the rural credit community.

The Organization for Economic Cooperation and Development (OECD) of-ficially stated five principles regarding corporation governance in 1999, and pro-duced a revised edition of these principles in 2004. There is a statement on stake-holders in both editions. Regarding the stakeholder, there exists the employee stock ownership plan in the US. Other countries also emphasize stakeholders. In our country, basic units are not well educated and the management level is not high either. If the shareholders are made up of community representatives, community members, credit community staff, even the sum of the three accounts totaling 50 percent in some places, it is not necessarily good.

Our suspicion and criticism of interested stakeholders holding stocks stem from some scandals caused by the compensation that employees could purchase equivalent shares before market exchange in the 1980s to early 1990s: "As soon as face by the snake is nipped, ten years fear the grass rope." Since the fifteenth session of the Chinese People's Representative Congress (Fourth Meeting), in which the term "corporate governance" was applied, during the past five or six years of the promulgation of the notion of corporate governance and the improvement in corporate level, we have begun to stress the OECD corporate governance principle regarding shareholder titles, identical treatment for shareholders, information disclosure availability and transparency, and the responsibilities of the board of directors. It still circumvents the issues with respect to interested stakeholders' rights, their functions, and how to protect them based on some policies. The rural credit cooperative reform that started in the summer of 2003 did not propose any conclusion of these issues. However, in rural credit cooperatives, the organizations possess strong community characteristics, and we cannot exclude the possibility of exploration of stakeholders' function and new types of corporate governance.

The reforms in the rural credit community, which began in the summer of 2003, have not resulted in any conclusion; however, the possibility of investigating the functionality of stakeholders, and the structural model of a new corporation governance in this highly community-based organization is not excluded.

In fact, as far as corporation governance is concerned, the rural credit community ought to differ from urban financial organizations and from private enterprises as well. To a large extent, the rural credit community is similar to a shareholding system, but it is like the community cooperative system on the surface. It is actually a hybrid of a shareholding system and a community cooperative system. There exist some criticisms of it, but personally I think we need to observe it patiently and not rush to draw conclusions.

### Notes

1 The Basel Committee consists of representatives from central banks and regulatory authorities of the G10 countries, plus others, especially Luxembourg and Spain. The Basel Accord was issued in 1988 and sets out the basics, such as credit risk. This was updated in 1996 to cover market risk and to clarify and extend the first Accord.
2 "*Jin Gu Zhou*" is the incantation of the Golden Hoop, which is used by the Monk in the novel *Pilgrimage to the West* to keep the Monkey King under control – inhibition (*A Chinese–English Dictionary*, The Commercial Press, 1981).

# 3 Is public listing a way out for China's state-owned enterprises?

*Xiaozu Wang, Lixin Colin Xu, and Tian Zhu*

## Introduction

Until recently, China avoided privatizing state-owned enterprises (SOEs) and instead sought to reform them through piecemeal measures, such as by increasing managers' decision-making autonomy, introducing financial incentives, and bringing in performance contracts between the government and SOEs (Naughton, 1995; Shirley and Xu, 2001). These reform measures were accompanied by improved productivity of SOEs during the 1980s (Groves *et al.*, 1994; Jefferson *et al.*, 1996; Zhuang and Xu, 1996; Li, 1997). However, the performance of Chinese state industry has since steadily deteriorated (Lardy, 1998). Faced with mounting losses in the state sector, in the early 1990s, the Chinese government began to shift the focus of SOE reform to privatization of small SOEs and the corporatization of larger ones (Cao *et al.*, 1999; Lin and Zhu, 2001).

The corporatization strategy aims to turn SOEs from public sole proprietorships controlled by industry-specific government agencies at various administrative levels into shareholding companies that are, at least in theory, independent in decision-making and diverse in ownership (Lin and Zhu, 2001). Public listing of SOEs on the domestic stock exchanges is a key measure of corporatization. Indeed, the vast majority of China's publicly listed companies are formerly state-owned or state-controlled firms, mostly the larger and better performing ones.[1] Given the importance of public listing as a means of reforming large SOEs in China, it is surprising that there are virtually no systematic studies on the effects of public listing in the country.[2] In this chapter, we attempt to fill this void.

Recent years have seen two strands of surging empirical literature on the impact of public listing or initial public offering (IPO) on company performance (Roell, 1996; Megginson and Netter, 2001). The first strand of literature focuses on developed countries, particularly the United States, and finds that public listing of privately held companies tends to worsen company performance. Ritter (1991) finds that IPO firms underperform a set of comparable firms matched by size and industry. Loughran and Ritter (1995) find that both IPOs and seasoned equity offerings significantly underperform relative to non-issuing firms for five years after the offering date. Degeorge and Zeckhauser (1993), Jain and Kini (1994), and Mikkelson *et al.* (1997) find that the performance of IPO firms – measured by return on assets (ROA) or return on sales (ROS) – declines in the first few years following the offering but does not decline further afterwards.

The above findings raise the question of why IPOs might worsen performance. One explanation is the agency cost. According to the agency theory set out by Jensen and Meckling (1976), public listing may heighten the conflicts of interest between managers and shareholders by increasing ownership dispersion, and the resulting higher agency costs lead to reduced performance. An empirical implication of the theory is that post-IPO performance should be positively correlated with managerial ownership. This hypothesis is partially supported by Jain and Kini (1994) and Holthausen and Larcker (1996), who find a positive relationship between performance and ownership stakes retained by pre-offering shareholders or insiders around IPOs.[3]

Another explanation for the performance decline after listing is that the pre-listing performance may be exaggerated. For example, offering firms may window dress their accounting figures before going public. They may also time the offerings to coincide with periods of unusually good performance or favorable market valuations. Consequently, the overstated pre-IPO performance would result in a superficial decline in post-IPO performance (Laughran and Ritter, 1995; Pagano *et al.*, 1998).

The second strand of literature on public listing deals with share issue privatization, which uses public listing to divest the government's ownership in SOEs.[4] Share issue privatization has been one of the major forms of privatizing SOEs around the world since the 1980s. In summarizing the long-run performance of share issue privatization, Megginson and Netter (2001) state that, "the average long-term, market-adjusted return earned by international investors in share issue privatizations is economically and significantly positive."

While public listings in developed countries either turn a privately held company into a more widely held public company or transform an SOE into a privately owned public company, public listings in China are largely used to *corporatize* SOEs. China's share issue corporatization aims to transform an SOE into a modern form of corporation that features both significant state and significant non-state institutional shareholders in addition to small individual shareholders. If public listings of private firms worsen company performance in developed capitalist economies and share issue privatization of SOEs improves company performance, it is an intriguing question as to whether public listing would improve or worsen company performance in the intermediate case of share issue corporatization.

SOEs' low efficiencies are often attributed to a lack of managerial autonomy, soft budget constraints, and the agency-incentive problem (Groves *et al.*, 1994; □ian, 1996; □ian and Roland, 1996). The central goal of corporatization, including public listing, is to establish a "modern enterprise system" in China featuring corporate governance structures that separate the government from enterprises. The separation is deemed necessary both for enterprises to achieve full autonomy in structural and operational decisions and for the government to limit its liabilities to the enterprises, hence hardening the budget constraints. It is also hoped that corporatization will improve managerial incentives by installing a more clearly defined structure of rights and responsibilities and by introducing shareholders with incentives and abilities to monitor the managers. Another objective is to raise capital for SOEs and reduce their high debt-to-asset ratios by increasing direct finance through selling equity ownership stakes to the public as well as employees.

If the above objectives have, at least in part, been achieved, we would expect that post-listing performance should exceed the pre-listing level and that debt-to-asset ratios should decline, whereas capital expenditure should grow at a faster rate after listing. Given China's weak accounting and disclosure system, it would not be surprising if most of the firms' pre-listing performance is overstated. In that case, we might expect post-listing performance to be lower than the pre-listing level.[5] However, if public listing helps in establishing better corporate governance, improving managerial incentives, and loosening firms' financial constraints, then company performance after the IPO year should improve over time and be better than that in the IPO year.

In this chaper, we use a panel of pre- and post-listing data from all publicly listed companies in China to investigate the actual effects of public listing against its intended effects. We find that, overall, public listing as a means of reforming SOEs has not worked wonders. Company performance from the first post-listing year onward is sharply lower than the levels in both the pre-listing years and the IPO years. Moreover, the effects of public listing on performance are not significantly affected by the percentage of state shares or of the total shares held by top shareholders, but are positively correlated with a more balanced ownership structure among these shareholders. While the debt level is initially reduced after listing, it converges to the pre-listing level over time. Moreover, rather than increasing capital expansion, public listing actually reduces it.

In the following section, we provide some background information on public listings and the development of the stock market in China. The next section describes the data, defines the variables to be used in the regression analysis, and presents some summary statistics. The main findings are then reported and the last section concludes.

## Public listings in China

China's stock markets opened in 1990 with the establishment of the Shanghai Stock Exchange (SHSE) when eight firms first went public. In the following year, Shenzhen Stock Exchange (SZSE) was also established. The following decade witnessed phenomenal growth in the stock market. By the end of 2000, the SHSE composite index grew to 2,073 from 100 on its base day of 19 December 1990, and the SZSE composite index grew to 635 from 100 on its base day of 3 April 1991.

Table 3.1 outlines the development of China's stock market. At the end of 2000, 1,088 firms were listed on the two exchanges, with a total market capitalization close to 5 trillion yuan (about US$0.6 trillion[6]) or 54 percent of China's

Table 3.1 The development of China's stock market

| Year | 1990 | 1991 | 1992 | 1993 | 1994 | 1995 | 1996 | 1997 | 1998 | 1999 | 2000 |
|---|---|---|---|---|---|---|---|---|---|---|---|
| Total number of listed firms | 10 | 14 | 53 | 183 | 291 | 323 | 530 | 745 | 851 | 949 | 1,088 |
| Capital raised[a] (billion yuan) | 4.59 | 0.5 | 9.4 | 31.407 | 13.827 | 11.854 | 34.144 | 93.397 | 79.504 | 88.297 | 142.829 |
| Market capitalization[b] (billion yuan) | N/A | N/A | 104.813 | 353.101 | 369.061 | 347.428 | 984.238 | 1,752.924 | 1,950.564 | 2,647.117 | 4,809.094 |
| Market capitalization/GDP (%) | N/A | N/A | 3.93 | 10.2 | 7.89 | 5.94 | 14.5 | 23.44 | 24.9 | 32.32 | 54.03 |
| Number of investors[c] (million) | N/A | N/A | 2.1665 | 7.7766 | 10.5898 | 12.4247 | 23.0723 | 33.3333 | 39.107 | 44.8197 | 58.0113 |
| Total book value of assets (billion yuan) | N/A | N/A | 48.1 | 182.1 | 330.9 | 429.5 | 635.2 | 966.058 | 1,240.752 | 1,610.736 | 1,796.027 |
| State shares (as a % of total shares) | N/A | N/A | 41.38 | 49.06 | 43.31 | 38.74 | 35.42 | 31.52 | 34.25 | 36.11 | 38.90 |
| Legal person shares (as a % of total shares) | N/A | N/A | 27.86 | 23.07 | 23.51 | 24.99 | 28.38 | 32.74 | 30.39 | 27.73 | 24.45 |

Source: China Securities Regulatory Commission (1999) *China Securities and Futures Statistical*, Beijing: China Finance and Economic Publishing House, and CSRC's official website: http://www.csrc.gov.cn/CSRCSite/deptlistcom/stadata/stadata.htm. Some of the statistics were not kept by the CSRC until 1992 (N/A).

Notes

a   By the end of 2000, the Chinese market had total market capitalization of US$580.942 billion, which was only slightly lower than US$616.34 billion (HK$4,795.150 billion) of the main board of Hong Kong Stock Exchange.

b   Including both initial public offer (IPO) and seasoned offerings of A and B shares.

c   Including institutional and individual accounts.

gross domestic product (GDP). The stock market has also become an increasingly important means of raising capital for China's SOEs, resulting in more than 480 billion yuan of new equity issuance in 2000 alone.

China's publicly listed companies are allowed to issue four types of shares. The predominant type is A shares; these are listed in China, denominated in renminbi (RMB), and restricted to domestic investors. B shares are also listed in China and denominated in RMB and, until June 2001, their purchase was restricted to foreign investors using foreign currency. The two other types of shares are H shares and N shares, which are issued in Hong Kong and the United States, respectively, by A-share or B-share issuing firms. While most companies only issue A shares, the majority of B-share issuing companies also issue A shares. By the end of 2000, among the 114 B-share issuing firms only 28 issued B shares exclusively; the rest also issued A shares. All the 19 H-share firms also issued A shares.

The shares of listed companies are classified into five categories: state owned, legal person (institution) owned, employee owned, individual owned, and foreign owned. The first two categories of shares cannot be traded on the stock exchanges, and their transfer requires special approval from the China Securities Regulatory Commission (CSRC). IPO firms are required by law to hold at least 35 percent of the total shares issued, and 25 percent of the total shares must be individual or foreign owned. Large shareholders are usually state or legal persons. The distinction between state and legal person shareholders is in many cases superficial. State shares are held by government bodies, such as state asset management agencies, or institutions authorized to hold shares on behalf of the state, such as a wholly state-owned investment company. Legal person shares are shares held by any entity or institution with a legal person status, including an SOE or a company controlled by an SOE. We do not have precise information about the identity of legal person shareholders, but it is safe to say that state ownership, directly or indirectly, accounts for a significant portion of all the legal person shares. Employee-owned shares are issued to employees of the issuing firm and are allowed in trading only three years after the IPO if the firm can get the CSRC's approval.

In China, the question of whether a company can make an IPO is determined largely by an administrative process rather than the market process seen in developed economies. When an SOE wants to go public, it must seek permission from the local government and/or its affiliated central government ministries, which receive an IPO quota from the CSRC.[7] Under this quota system, how many and which firms go public in each year depends not only on the quality of the firm and the macroeconomic conditions, but also the availability and distribution of the quota. All firms in our sample became listed under the quota system.

## Data, variables, and summary statistics

The data for this study is a panel of financial and ownership data from all the companies listed on the SHSE or SZSE from 1990 to June 2000. There are 1,057 firms in our initial data set. Missing values or invalid data entries reduce our sample to 992 firms. A majority of the firms deleted were listed before 1994 and lack pre-listing data. The data were purchased from a major financial information service company in China.

A novel feature of our data set is that it contains pre-listing information. The current law requires IPO firms to provide three years of audited accounting data prior to listing. However, since the CSRC was established in 1992, two years after the first stock exchange was established, and major disclosure rules were only issued in 1993 and not immediately strictly enforced, the disclosure standard was not consistent during the first half of the 1990s. As a result, firms listed in or before 1994 have incomplete pre-listing as well as some post-listing data. Nonetheless, the majority of firms in our data set have complete pre-listing financial data, which allows us to compare their pre- and post-listing performance.

Another feature of the data set is that it is free of survival bias that may cause problems in studying listing effects on company performance. No firm in our data set ceased operations or was de-listed after going public. Although China's bankruptcy law was passed in 1986, listed companies can usually count on the government or state-owned banks to bail them out of financial difficulties and hence avoid bankruptcy. Also, no publicly listed firms returned to private ownership in our sample period. Only in 2001 did we observe the first incidence of de-listing.

In our regression analysis, we follow the existing literature in choosing our dependent and explanatory variables. This allows us to highlight the similarities as well as the differences in the effects of public listing in China in comparison with countries that have been examined previously in the literature. Definitions of the dependent and explanatory variables to be used in our regression analysis are listed in Table 3.2.

We report summary statistics in Table 3.3 for both the full sample and a sub-sample of balanced panels. The full sample is unbalanced, including all observations that are used in at least one of the subsequent regressions. For each variable, the balanced panel consists of firms that have valid observations for the variable from one year before IPO ($t = -1$) to four years after IPO ($t = 4$). The IPO year is denoted by $t = 0$. The balanced panel is constructed only for the period from year $-1$ to year 4 because a more stringent requirement, say from $-1$ to 6, would result in too small a sample: only 291 firms were listed in China by the end of 1994, and the rest had less than six years of post-listing history by the end of our sample period. As it is useful to know what went on for years 5 and 6, we also report the summary statistics for these two years for firms included in our balanced sample when the data are available for those periods. The interpretation for the last two years requires extra caution because of the changes in the composition of the firms.

To minimize the possibility of a small number of outliers driving the results, we follow other authors in the literature to Winsorize the data. Specifically, we reset the value of a variable that is in the tail one percentile of the full sample to that of the first percentile and the 99th percentile respectively. The summary statistics of the full sample are listed in column 3 of Table 3.3. The average size of the firm, measured by either book value of assets (denoted as *asset*) or sales (*sales*), is quite

*Table 3.2* Definition of variables

| Variable name | Definition |
|---|---|
| asset | Book value of asset |
| OI | Operating income before depreciation, amortization, and extraordinary items |
| debt | Ratio of total debt to debt plus total shareholders' equity. Calculated as (short-term debt + long-term debt)/(short-term debt + long-term debt + shareholders' equity) |
| ROA | Return on assets: operating income (OI) of year $t$ divided by book value of assets at the end of year $t-1$ |
| ROS | Return on sales, calculated as the ratio of OI to sales |
| ln_sales | Natural log of sales, used to measure firm size and as a proxy of market power |
| capex | Capital expenditure, scaled by net fixed assets |
| salegrow | Growth rate of sales. Calculated as $(sales_t sales_{t-1})/sales_{t-1}$ |
| tax_oi | Ratio of paid tax to OI |
| state_shares | Percentage of state-owned shares |
| A5 | Shares held by top the five shareholders divided by the total number of shares |
| Herfindahl_top5 | Herfindahl index of ownership concentration among the top five shareholders. Calculated as $\sum S_i^2$, where $S_i$ is the ratio of shares held by the $i$th shareholder to the total shares held by all of the top five shareholders |

large, with mean value of assets of 1.2 billion yuan and average sales of 701 million yuan. The average debt-to-asset ratio (*debt*) is 0.30. The average return on assets (*ROA*) is 10.9 percent. Firms generally experience sales growth (*salegrow*) during the sample period with the average annual growth rate of 20 percent. But the cross-sectional and time series variations in sales growth are quite high, with a standard deviation of over 61 percent.

Ownership is highly concentrated: the top five shareholders hold close to 60 percent of the total shares (*A5*). Furthermore, ownership concentration among the top five shareholders is also very high – the Herfindahl concentration index of shareholding among the top five shareholders (*Herfindahl_top5*) is 0.648. (If the shares were distributed equally among them, the Herfindahl index would be 0.2.)

Summary statistics for the balanced subsample depict the changes over time. Overall, firms experience performance deterioration after public listing. The average return on assets (*ROA*) drops steadily, from 19.6 percent in the year immediately prior to IPO to 2.7 percent in the sixth year after IPO. The average return on sales (ROS) also decreases from 16.6 percent one year before listing to 0.2 percent in the sixth year after listing. It is worth noting that the decline in both operating performance measures does not level off, as is found in the literature on listing for firms in western countries. The average operating income (*OI*) also deteriorates, despite the growth in both firm assets and sales during

Table 3.3 Summary statistics[a]

| | | Full sample[b] | Balanced panel[c] | | | | | | | |
| | | | t=-1 | t=0 (IPO) | t=1 | t=2 | t=3 | t=4 | t=5 | t=6 |
|---|---|---|---|---|---|---|---|---|---|---|
| asset (million yuan) | Mean | 1,183.997 | 1,230.728 | 530.864 | 843.479 | 1,034.541 | 1,198.152 | 1,326.709 | 1,466.001 | 1,752.552 |
| | SD | 3,108.648 | 3,221.904 | 1,027.012 | 1,595.529 | 1,700.946 | 1,823.214 | 1,961.404 | 2,081.066 | 2,443.456 |
| | Obs | 6,904 | 7,296 | 456 | 456 | 456 | 456 | 456 | 456 | 254 |
| sales (million yuan) | Mean | 700.926 | 705.034 | 511.371 | 600.480 | 644.255 | 643.119 | 708.525 | 770.268 | 857.417 |
| | SD | 1,367.097 | 1365.408 | 850.413 | 1,063.418 | 1,100.858 | 1,141.417 | 1,312.600 | 1,359.032 | 1,428.980 |
| | Obs | 6,964 | 7,353 | 443 | 443 | 443 | 443 | 443 | 443 | 243 |
| OI (million yuan) | Mean | 87.956 | 88.002 | 65.567 | 80.045 | 71.247 | 62.170 | 67.156 | 73.480 | 58.091 |
| | SD | 211.756 | 219.527 | 167.615 | 201.406 | 141.338 | 175.038 | 234.006 | 193.743 | 159.165 |
| | Obs | 6,239 | 6,575 | 285 | 285 | 285 | 285 | 285 | 285 | 105 |
| ROA | Mean | 0.109 | 0.196 | 0.154 | 0.097 | 0.074 | 0.06 | 0.044 | 0.028 | 0.027 |
| | SD | 0.111 | 0.147 | 0.118 | 0.094 | 0.094 | 0.087 | 0.08 | 0.06 | 0.055 |
| | Obs | 5,483 | 115 | 115 | 115 | 115 | 115 | 115 | 59 | 57 |
| ROS | Mean | 0.135 | 0.166 | 0.162 | 0.137 | 0.078 | 0.044 | 0.053 | -0.003 | 0.002 |
| | SD | 0.179 | 0.132 | 0.108 | 0.148 | 0.211 | 0.239 | 0.239 | 0.252 | 0.246 |
| | Obs | 6,239 | 285 | 285 | 285 | 285 | 285 | 285 | 105 | 94 |
| debt | Mean | 0.304 | 0.328 | 0.264 | 0.28 | 0.293 | 0.305 | 0.319 | 0.343 | 0.361 |
| | SD | 0.196 | 0.202 | 0.178 | 0.18 | 0.185 | 0.188 | 0.196 | 0.203 | 0.216 |
| | Obs | 6,827 | 430 | 430 | 430 | 430 | 430 | 430 | 230 | 217 |

| | | | | | | | | | |
|---|---|---|---|---|---|---|---|---|---|
| *capex* | Mean | 0.268 | 0.743 | 0.577 | 0.431 | 0.282 | 0.16 | 0.13 | 0.025 | 0.038 |
| | SD | 0.630 | 1.025 | 0.856 | 0.731 | 0.652 | 0.598 | 0.518 | 0.399 | 0.324 |
| | Obs | 5,766 | 136 | 136 | 136 | 136 | 136 | 136 | 75 | 71 |
| *salegrow* | Mean | 0.198 | 0.287 | 0.478 | 0.222 | 0.105 | 0.238 | 0.134 | 0.124 | 0.165 |
| | SD | 0.613 | 0.859 | 1.147 | 0.812 | 0.554 | 0.752 | 0.599 | 0.652 | 0.597 |
| | Obs | 6,114 | 250 | 250 | 250 | 250 | 250 | 250 | 185 | 181 |
| *tax_oi* | Mean | 0.133 | 0.144 | 0.151 | 0.142 | 0.123 | 0.126 | 0.092 | 0.088 | 0.108 |
| | SD | 0.173 | 0.14 | 0.163 | 0.198 | 0.232 | 0.216 | 0.186 | 0.238 | 0.258 |
| | Obs | 6,239 | 285 | 285 | 285 | 285 | 285 | 285 | 105 | 94 |
| *A5* | Mean | 0.598 | 0.662 | 0.586 | 0.581 | 0.574 | 0.577 | 0.558 | 0.577 | 0.558 |
| | SD | 0.154 | 0.230 | 0.157 | 0.151 | 0.142 | 0.136 | 0.139 | 0.143 | 0.132 |
| | Obs | 4,831 | 199 | 199 | 199 | 199 | 199 | 199 | 71 | 63 |
| *Herfindahl_top5* | Mean | 0.648 | 0.622 | 0.640 | 0.622 | 0.617 | 0.618 | 0.604 | 0.610 | 0.602 |
| | SD | 0.242 | 0.247 | 0.235 | 0.238 | 0.229 | 0.227 | 0.230 | 0.230 | 0.232 |
| | Obs | 4,941 | 230 | 230 | 230 | 230 | 230 | 230 | 87 | 96 |

Notes

a   The values of *ROA, ROS, debt, capex, salegrow, tax_oi, A5,* and *Herfindahl_top5* are expressed as fractions, while *asset, sales,* and *OI* are in million yuan. The values for *sales* are adjusted by the gross domestic product (GDP) deflator (1995 = 100). Summary statistics are based on Winsorized data. Winsorization is done by resetting a value belo□

b   An observation is included in full sam□ are added over time, and a firm may re-enter the panel after disappearance.

c   A firm is included in the balanced pane□ public offer (IPO) (*t* = −1) to four years afterwards (*t* = 4). (The IPO year is marked by *t* = 0.) In other words, the panel from *t* = −1 to *t* = 4 is balanced. To give a more complete picture, we also present summary statistics for a subsample of firms in the balanced panel in years *t* = 5 and *t* = 6.

SD, standard deviation: Obs, number of observations.

the post-IPO period. Leverage (*debt*) is generally lower after listing, consistent with the findings in the literature. Capital expenditure (*capex*) drops steadily in post-IPO years. Interestingly, listed firms initially pay more taxes as a percentage of their operating income after the IPO; however, very soon they pay *lower* taxes than before listing. This is in contrast to what is commonly found in the literature on western firms where a cost of listing is the potentially higher tax burden associated with heightened scrutiny for listed firms.

As many factors, such as macroeconomic factors during this particular sample period, could play a role in these changes in firms' performance, in the next section, we examine whether performance decline and the changes in other measures remain intact once additional factors are controlled for.

## Regression analysis

### *Ex post effects of listing*

We now examine how public listings affect a variety of outcome measures of interest. We use ROA as the overall performance measure. Because IPO firms often experience rapid expansion in their asset base, which alone can be responsible for the drop in ROA, we also examine ROS, another conventional measure of operating performance, to check the robustness of what we may find about the changes in ROA. To fully understand the impact of public listing in China and to compare it with some earlier findings in the literature, we include other measures of the outcomes of public listing in our investigation: sales growth, investment rate, financial leverage, and tax burden. The basic regression used to measure the effects of going public is the following:

$$y_{it} = \alpha_0 + \beta_i + \alpha_t + \sum_{t=0}^{6} \gamma_t PL_{it} + \varepsilon_{it}$$

(3.1)

Here, we have included fixed effects and year effects. $PL_{it}$ is the dummy variable, which is 1 when firm $i$ is $t$ years after going public and zero otherwise. The use of fixed effects implies that we use the pre-listing outcome as the benchmark to measure the effects of listing. As the firms went public in distinct years, controlling for year dummies ($\alpha_t$) would isolate the macro effects on the dependent variables, capturing effects such as the credit cycle and macro boom and bust. Note that we allow the listing effects to differ by the number of years after listing, a flexible functional form to capture the total effects of listing. Because our benchmark is the pre-listing values of the independent variables, the sample used for the regression consists only of listed firms with data for both year −1 and year 0. If a firm also has data for year −2, then both year −2 and −1 data are used in the regression, and the benchmark is the average of the values for the two pre-listing years.

Our identifying assumption is that differences between pre- and post-listing performance capture the listing effects. In contrast, most of the authors on the effects of listing use the matching approach to identify the listing effects. That is, they find a matched sample for their sample of listed firms and then compute the listing effects as the before-and-after difference for the listed sample minus the before-and-after difference for the matched sample. Matching is usually done through the closest match based on size–industry category (e.g., Pagano *et al.*, 1996, 1998). Matching, however, poses serious requirements for data (Heckman *et al.*, 1997, 1998). The researcher needs to have access to another, much larger data set in which important characteristics of the sample firm – most often performance, size, and industry – are close to the listing firms. Poor matching often results in mis-specified test statistics and biased estimates.

As we do not have access to a large sample of firms that satisfy the strict matching requirements, we cannot use the common method of matching. Moreover, it is difficult, if not impossible, to find reasonable matches for our sample: these are overwhelmingly large firms, and there is currently no Chinese data set that surveys the large firms – state or non-state – between 1990 and 2000 and that contains the necessary financial information. Without matching, however, we need to qualify our results on the listing effects: they should be understood as the effects of listing on the "listed" sample, not as the effects of random assignment of listing on *any* firm.

The regression results are reported in Table 3.4. (Table 3.5 reports the number of observations for each year for each dependent variable. Depending on the specification, the number of firms included in the regressions ranges from 605 to 961.) Public listing is associated with a significant drop in operating performance measured by ROA (columns 2). The zero, first, second, third, fourth, and fifth/sixth post-listing year effects on ROA are –1.5, –5.7, –4.9, –5.2, –3.8, and –3.1 percentage points respectively.[8] In other words, the overall operating performance of listed firms in China is significantly lower than pre-listing levels for many years after listing.

The decline in performance, however, cannot simply be attributed to the sharp increase in assets. As total assets normally increase significantly after IPOs, it is possible that operating income scaled by assets potentially has a downward bias. However, operating income scaled by sales (i.e., ROS) also shows a similar decline after listing. Column 3 of Table 3.4 shows that the listing effects on ROS from the listing year to the fifth/sixth year are 1.4, 0.0, –2.0, –4.6, –3.6, and –6.4 respectively. Note that the negative effects of listing on ROA and ROS are very precisely estimated. The decline in ROS after listing is not due to an increase in the scale of production. Column 4 of Table 3.4 shows that the growth rate of sales (*salegrow*) does not significantly change as a result of listing, except for years 4–6, when sales growth drops roughly 8 percentage points (with *t*-statistics about 1.55).

Furthermore, the decline in operating performance as a result of listing cannot be fully explained by the possibility of pre-listing performance being overstated. If this were the case, and if the listing had achieved its intended goals to some degree, then we would not be able to explain why the performance one year after

Table 3.4 Effects of public listing: part I

| | ROA | ROS | salegrow | capex | debt | tax_oi |
|---|---|---|---|---|---|---|
| | (1) | (2) | (3) | (4) | (5) | (6) |
| t = 0 | -0.015 | 0.014 | 0.019 | 0.103 | -0.110 | 0.017 |
| | (3.44)*** | (2.38)** | (0.68) | (2.93)*** | (20.06)*** | (2.40)** |
| t = 1 | -0.057 | 0.000 | -0.006 | -0.021 | -0.094 | 0.009 |
| | (10.04)*** | (0.03) | (0.20) | (0.44) | (14.96)*** | (0.98) |
| t = 2 | -0.049 | -0.020 | -0.030 | -0.135 | -0.074 | -0.014 |
| | (6.97)*** | (2.41)** | (0.84) | (2.19)** | (10.33)*** | (1.40) |
| t = 3 | -0.052 | -0.046 | -0.023 | -0.221 | -0.060 | -0.025 |
| | (6.04)*** | (4.67)*** | (0.58) | (2.89)*** | (7.48)*** | (2.13)** |
| t = 4 | -0.038 | -0.036 | -0.083 | -0.240 | -0.038 | -0.028 |
| | (3.39)*** | (3.00)*** | (1.57) | (2.46)** | (3.88)*** | (1.95)* |
| t = 5 or 6 | -0.031 | -0.064 | -0.085 | -0.359 | -0.015 | -0.024 |
| | (2.36)** | (4.52)*** | (1.54) | (3.08)*** | (1.41) | (1.36) |
| Constant | 0.341 | 0.285 | 0.348 | 0.902 | 0.371 | 0.127 |
| | (22.04)*** | (5.42)*** | (6.08)*** | (5.96)*** | (8.40)*** | (1.97)** |
| Observations | 3,317 | 5,096 | 4,800 | 3,572 | 6,545 | 5,096 |
| Number of firms | 605 | 792 | 766 | 654 | 961 | 792 |
| R-squared | 0.44 | 0.13 | 0.03 | 0.10 | 0.13 | 0.03 |

Notes
*, **, and *** represent statistical significance at the 10%, 5%, and 1% levels.
The coefficients for year dummies are not reported.
$t = 5$ or 6 is the listing age dummy for firms in the fifth or sixth year after the initial public offer (IPO).

*Table 3.5* Number of firms in each "listing age" cohort used in regressions

|  | ROA | ROS | salegrow | capex | debt | tax_oi |
|---|---|---|---|---|---|---|
| $t = -2$ | 514 | 535 | 702 | 538 | 662 | 535 |
| $t = -1$ | 605 | 792 | 766 | 654 | 961 | 792 |
| $t = 0$ | 605 | 792 | 766 | 654 | 961 | 792 |
| $t = 1$ | 501 | 681 | 665 | 553 | 857 | 681 |
| $t = 2$ | 422 | 604 | 566 | 454 | 756 | 604 |
| $t = 3$ | 317 | 499 | 461 | 347 | 647 | 499 |
| $t = 4$ | 126 | 304 | 250 | 136 | 430 | 304 |
| $t = 5$ or 6 | 133 | 229 | 366 | 146 | 447 | 229 |
| Total | 3,317 | 5,096 | 4,800 | 3,572 | 6,545 | 5,096 |

Note
The sample is selected in such a way that a firm must have valid observations in both the initial
public offer (IPO) year and the year before.

the IPO is so much lower than during the IPO year, nor why the performance does not significantly improve over time during the post-listing years.

One of the most cited reasons for going public is that it loosens the financial constraints faced by firms (Roell, 1996; Pagano *et al.*, 1998). If so, the post-listing growth in capital expansion should speed up. Listing does not appear to play such a role in China (Column 5, Table 3.4, *capex*). The share of capital expenditure in net fixed assets increases only during the listing year, then decreases from year 2 until year 6 after listing at an accelerating pace. Thus, the expansion in production capacity happens at most only in the first post-listing year and quickly slows down over time. Not surprisingly, listing leads to a reduction in the debt-to-asset ratio (Column 5, Table 3.4, *debt*), especially initially. With the lapse of time, however, the leverage ratio converges to the pre-listing level, as demonstrated by the statistically insignificant coefficient for the dummy of years 5–6.

A posited hypothesis in the literature is that, because of more stringent financial disclosure requirements, going public might lead to higher tax payments (Pagano *et al.*, 1998). We find the opposite in the case of Chinese firms. Column 6 of Table 3.4 (*tax_oi*) shows that, while the ratio of tax to operating income initially increases by 1.7 percentage points, it is actually *lower* than the pre-listing level in post-listing years 2–6 (with some coefficients being statistically insignificant). Thus, there does not appear to be an increased scrutiny in collecting taxes after public listing.

It remains possible that other time-varying variables correlated with the listing variables explain the variations in our dependent variables. To check this, we control for some variables that are the "usual suspects" in explaining the outcome regardless of whether a firm is listed or not (as in Pagano *et al.*, 1998). To this end, we add in the right-hand side of Eq. (1) *log (lagged sales)* to capture size effects, i.e., larger firms may exert more market power and therefore generate more

Table 3.6 Effects of public listing: part II

| | ROA | ROS | salegrow | capex | debt | tax_oi |
|---|---|---|---|---|---|---|
| | (1) | (2) | (3) | (4) | (5) | (6) |
| t = 0 | -0.017 | 0.006 | 0.044 | 0.128 | -0.110 | 0.016 |
| | (3.97)*** | (1.05) | (1.81)* | (3.60)*** | (17.06)*** | (2.00)** |
| t = 1 | -0.058 | -0.004 | 0.035 | 0.010 | -0.090 | 0.008 |
| | (10.36)*** | (0.50) | (1.22) | (0.20) | (11.91)*** | (0.85) |
| t = 2 | -0.051 | -0.019 | 0.045 | -0.088 | -0.074 | -0.012 |
| | (7.28)*** | (2.18)** | (1.33) | (1.41) | (8.36)*** | (1.10) |
| t = 3 | -0.055 | -0.041 | 0.058 | -0.155 | -0.058 | -0.024 |
| | (6.50)*** | (4.03)*** | (1.50) | (2.00)** | (5.68)*** | (1.81)* |
| t = 4 | -0.042 | -0.022 | -0.005 | -0.150 | -0.023 | -0.022 |
| | (3.78)*** | (1.78)* | (0.09) | (1.52) | (1.75)* | (1.35) |

| | (1) | (2) | (3) | (4) | (5) | (6) |
|---|---|---|---|---|---|---|
| $t = 5$ or $6$ | -0.034 | -0.035 | -0.092 | -0.295 | -0.011 | -0.019 |
| | (2.60)*** | (2.36)** | (1.69)* | (2.49)** | (0.75) | (0.97) |
| $\ln\_sales_{t-1}$ | 0.003 | 0.049 | -0.562 | -0.098 | 0.004 | 0.022 |
| | (1.05) | (11.21)*** | (32.49)*** | (4.18)*** | (0.89) | (3.84)*** |
| $\ln\_debt_{t-1}$ | 0.002 | -0.000 | -0.000 | -0.008 | | -0.001 |
| | (4.60)*** | (0.22) | (0.13) | (2.81)*** | | (1.64) |
| Constant | 0.338 | -0.645 | 11.212 | 3.103 | 0.254 | -0.231 |
| | (5.25)*** | (7.27)*** | (31.94)*** | (6.44)*** | (3.05)*** | (2.00)** |
| Observations | 3,282 | 4,307 | 4,235 | 3,511 | 4,380 | 4,307 |
| Number of firms | 604 | 790 | 734 | 648 | 734 | 790 |
| R-squared | 0.44 | 0.17 | 0.26 | 0.11 | 0.16 | 0.04 |

Notes

*, **, and *** represent statistical significance at the 10%, 5%, and 1% levels.

The coefficients for year dummies are not reported.

$t = 5$ or $6$ is the listing age dummy for firms in the fifth or sixth year after the initial public offer (IPO).

profits, and *log* (*lagged leverage ratio*) to control for financial structure and its informational contents. The results are reported in Table 3.6.[9]

Most of the qualitative findings in Table 3.4 remain intact. There is one minor change. The initial positive and statistically significant effects of listing on ROS become insignificant in the listing year (i.e., year 0). In the meantime, lagged sales (*ln sales$_{t-1}$*) have a positive and significant role in post-listing ROS, which suggests that increased market power gives rise to higher profit margins.

### Ownership structure and listing effects on performance

Public listing changes the ownership structure of a company. When used to transform an SOE, public listing in China is intended to introduce non-state shareholders with better abilities and incentives to monitor and exercise effective control over the management. As managerial ownership is negligible for the vast majority of Chinese firms, a very dispersed ownership structure with numerous small shareholders clearly cannot achieve such a goal. Thus, for most listed firms in China, the majority of shares are held by the state and/or a number of legal persons. In what follows, we examine the impact of the ownership structure on the listing effects. In particular, we examine two aspects of ownership effects: whether the listing effects differ by direct state ownership, and how ownership concentration by top shareholders and the balance of power among them affect the listing effects.

The issue of whether state ownership affects listing effects is a natural question in the context of Chinese listed firms. The most important owners of Chinese listed firms tend to be either the state or legal persons, with smaller shares going to foreign and individual owners. While many of the legal person shares are often owned by state-owned or state-controlled enterprises/institutions, it is still important to find out whether the listing effects differ by the presence of direct state involvement. To examine the potential differences between listed firms with and without direct state ownership, we decomposed the sample into two groups, depending on whether there was any direct state ownership in the year of listing. We have 389 firms with state ownership in year 0, and 193 firms without any state ownership. State ownership for the rest of the firms cannot be identified because of missing values of state shares.[10] Among firms with direct state ownership, the state on average owns about 40 percent of the total shares. Table 3.7 presents the regression results.

The differences in performance between firms with and without direct state ownership appear to be quite small. The coefficients associated with various post-listing years for both sets of firms are almost identical for the *ROA* regressions (see columns 3 and 4). This finding is consistent with our earlier remark that the distinction between state and legal person shareholders is in many cases superficial, and our conjecture that state ownership, directly or indirectly, accounts for a significant portion of all the legal person shares.

When *ROS* is the dependent variable, however, there are some differences. For companies with direct state ownership, there is a monotone decline in *ROS*. For companies without direct state ownership, however, there is a monotone decline only until year 3, when the reversal begins. Combined with the statistically insignificant decline in ROA for firms without direct state ownership in the fifth/sixth year, this seems to suggest that these firms may experience a shorter and less severe post-listing decline in performance than firms with direct state ownership.

We now turn to the issue of how listing effects hinge on the extent of state ownership and on the firm's ownership concentration structure.[11] Following Demsetz and Lehn (1985), we construct two measures of ownership concentration: (1) the percentage of shares held by the top five shareholders (*A5*); and (2) the Herfindahl concentration index of ownership among the top five shareholders (*Herfindahl_top5*). It should be noted that the way we construct the Herfindahl index is slightly different from other authors. Demsetz and Lehn (1985), for example, use the Herfindahl index to capture the concentration of ownership among *all* shareholders. Under our construction, the Herfindahl index measures the concentration of control power among the top five shareholders. A high Herfindahl index implies that control power is likely to be in the hands of the largest shareholder, while a small Herfindahl index means that ownership is more evenly distributed, and there is a balance of control power among the large shareholders.

The regression we run is:

$$y_{it} = \alpha_0 + \alpha_i + \gamma X_{it} + \beta_1 A5_{it} + \beta_2 Herfindahl\_top5_{it} + \beta_3 state\_shares$$
$$+ \beta_4 list_{it}(1 + \beta_5 A5_{it} + \beta_6 Herfindahl\_top5_{it} + \beta_7 state\_shares) + \varepsilon_{it} \qquad (3.2)$$

Here *list* is a listing dummy, and *X* represents other control variables that we mentioned earlier. We could use a formulation similar to Equation 3.1 and allow ownership variables to interact with a dummy for each of the post-listing years, but that would lead to too many interaction terms and, potentially, collinearity and identification problems. Therefore, we adopt the parsimonious specification of one listing dummy, and allow the listing dummy to interact with the ownership variables. The total effects of listing on the dependent variable are then:

$$\beta_4 + \beta_4\beta_5 A5_{it} + \beta_4\beta_6 Herfindahl\_top5_{it} + \beta_4\beta_7 state\_shares$$

Table 3.8 reports the regression results. The extent of state ownership only has a marginal negative impact on the effects of listing on ROA: the coefficient of the interaction term between listing and state ownership (*list\*state shares*) is negative but statistically insignificant.[12] Moreover, the total effects of state shares on the ROA of listed firms are immaterial. In other words, *ceteris paribus*, the performance of listed firms is not affected by the extent of state ownership. These results are in line with the findings reported in Table 3.7 that firms without state ownership and those with state ownership all experience a similar pattern of performance deterioration.

Ownership concentration has only marginal direct impacts on performance: the direct effects of both *A5* and *Herfindahl_top5* are statistically insignificant. Moreover, the listing effects do not hinge on ownership concentration measured

Table 3.7 Listing effects on performance: firms with or without state ownership

| | ROA | | | ROS | | |
|---|---|---|---|---|---|---|
| | Full sample | With state ownership | Without state ownership | Full sample | With state ownership | Without state ownership |
| | (1) | (2) | (3) | (4) | (5) | (6) |
| $t = 0$ | -0.017 | -0.014 | -0.014 | 0.006 | -0.009 | -0.025 |
| | (3.97)*** | (2.42)** | (1.57) | (1.05) | (1.05) | (2.00)** |
| $t = 1$ | -0.058 | -0.051 | -0.065 | -0.004 | -0.023 | -0.067 |
| | (10.36)*** | (6.29)*** | (5.36)*** | (0.50) | (1.96)* | (4.00)*** |
| $t = 2$ | -0.051 | -0.047 | -0.049 | -0.019 | -0.043 | -0.081 |
| | (7.28)*** | (4.57)*** | (3.07)*** | (2.18)** | (2.95)*** | (3.70)*** |
| $t = 3$ | -0.055 | -0.050 | -0.051 | -0.041 | -0.067 | -0.100 |
| | (6.50)*** | (3.85)*** | (2.57)** | (4.03)*** | (3.66)*** | (3.63)*** |
| $t = 4$ | -0.042 | -0.038 | -0.040 | -0.022 | -0.105 | -0.076 |
| | (3.78)*** | (2.29)** | (1.59) | (1.78)* | (4.45)*** | (2.15)** |

| $t = 5$ or 6 | -0.034 | -0.032 | -0.016 | -0.035 | -0.110 | -0.058 |
|---|---|---|---|---|---|---|
| | (2.60)*** | (1.60) | (0.51) | (2.36)** | (3.84)*** | (1.36) |
| $\ln\_sales_{t-1}$ | 0.003 | 0.006 | -0.013 | 0.049 | 0.039 | 0.016 |
| | (1.05) | (1.42) | (2.36)** | (11.21)*** | (6.55)*** | (2.02)** |
| $\ln\_debt_{t-1}$ | 0.002 | 0.002 | 0.001 | -0.000 | 0.001 | -0.001 |
| | (4.60)*** | (4.05)*** | (2.23)** | (0.22) | (0.76) | (0.89) |
| Constant | 0.338 | 0.279 | 0.598 | -0.645 | -0.472 | -0.061 |
| | (5.25)*** | (3.22)*** | (5.42)*** | (7.27)*** | (3.84)*** | (0.40) |
| Observations | 3,282 | 2,072 | 1,052 | 4,307 | 2,072 | 1,052 |
| Number of firms | 604 | 389 | 193 | 790 | 389 | 193 |
| R-squared | 0.44 | 0.45 | 0.47 | 0.17 | 0.20 | 0.13 |

Notes

*, **, and *** represent statistical significance at the 10%, 5%, and 1% levels.

A firm is identified as having direct state ownership if a positive amount of state-owned shares is observed in the initial public offer (IPO) year. If a firm reports a missing value of state ownership that is not clearly identifiable, it is deleted from the "with state ownership" and "without state ownership" subsamples. Therefore, the total number of firms with and without state ownership is smaller than the number of firms in the full sample.

*Table 3.8* Ownership structure and listing effects on performance

| | (1) ROA | (2) ROS |
|---|---|---|
| list | 0.029 | −0.012 |
| | (0.98) | (0.21) |
| A5 | 0.025 | 0.000 |
| | (0.75) | (0.00) |
| list * A5 | −0.004 | −0.002 |
| | (0.10) | (0.03) |
| Herfindal_top5 | −0.040 | 0.074 |
| | (0.97) | (0.97) |
| list * Herfindahl_top5 | −0.071 | −0.055 |
| | (2.48)** | (1.03) |
| state_shares | 0.033 | −0.053 |
| | (1.56) | (1.34) |
| list * state_shares | −0.032 | 0.078 |
| | (1.31) | (1.72)* |
| $ln\_sales_{t-1}$ | −0.017 | 0.041 |
| | (2.91)*** | (3.90)*** |
| $ln\_debt_{t-1}$ | 0.002 | 0.001 |
| | (3.00)*** | (0.71) |
| Constant | 0.754 | −0.595 |
| | (5.22)*** | (2.24)** |
| Observations | 873 | 873 |
| Number of firms | 163 | 163 |
| R-squared | 0.39 | 0.13 |

Notes
*, **, and *** represent statistical significance at the 10%, 5%, and 1% levels.
The coefficients for year dummies are not reported.

by *A5* – as demonstrated by the insignificant coefficients on the interaction term of *list* and *A5*. However, the balance of power among the largest shareholders does matter. The interaction term of *list* and *Herfindahl_top5* is negative and significant in the *ROA* equation. Thus, an ownership structure that features more balance of power among top owners appears to be more conducive to positive listing effects on operating performance. Our results are consistent with the notion that checks and balances among large shareholders may reduce the likelihood of a dominant shareholder maximizing his or her own private interest at the expense of other shareholders. The test of the role of checks and balances in corporate governance and its effect on company performance is, to our collective knowledge, the first in the literature.[13]

## Conclusions

Using a comprehensive panel data set of financial and ownership information on China's publicly listed firms between 1990 and 2000, we explore the effectiveness of public listing as a means of reforming SOEs in China. Overall, our findings suggest that public listing in China has not achieved its intended goals. Specifically, we find that public listing is associated with a sharp deterioration in performance for up to six years after the year of listing, and it is true for firms with or without direct state ownership. The effects of listing on performance are not significantly affected by the percentage of shares held by the state or by large shareholders.

These findings suggest that firms without formal state ownership do not behave so much differently from firms with state ownership in their quest for profits, and that ownership concentration by large shareholders is ineffective in improving performance when they are likely to be the state agencies or SOE-like institutions. As long as there is a significant presence of direct or indirect state ownership in listed firms, small variations in the percentage of state shares do not matter much to performance. The findings also suggest that China's stock market and legal systems are not sufficiently functional for the listed firms to establish effective corporate governance that protects the interest of small public shareholders.

Our finding that a more balanced ownership structure among top shareholders improves the listing effects on performance suggests that, when these very large shareholders themselves are not profit oriented, introducing checks and balances to prevent misbehavior by dominant shareholders may be important in designing a corporate governance framework in China.

After comparing the positive effects of share issue privatization, as found in the literature, with the poor effects of share issue corporatization, as experienced by Chinese firms, one may be tempted to conclude that share issue corporatization does not work as a way to reform SOEs. However, given the short history of China's stock market, we do not want to make too strong a claim about the success (or failure) of public listing solely based on our findings. It is possible that public listing may eventually become useful in transforming SOEs and improving their performance as the stock market, legal systems, and other market institutions develop over time, and as more private entrepreneurs accumulate sufficient wealth to acquire more stakes and become the large shareholders of listed firms. It would be very interesting to see whether corporatization in general, and public listing in particular, is a viable alternative to privatization in the long run.

## Acknowledgments

Tian Zhu gratefully acknowledges financial support from the Hong Kong Research Grants Council (grant no. HKUST6146/03H) and from CEIBS.

**Notes**

1 Our data set, to be described later, does not contain information about the ownership types of the share-issuing firms. Based on our interviews with officials of the China Securities Regulatory Commission (1999), about 75 percent of listed companies are formerly state-owned. Another 10 percent are formerly shareholding companies that mostly had significant shares held by SOEs. Only less than 10 percent of listed companies are formerly privately owned firms or foreign-invested firms, which in most cases had SOEs as their joint venture partners.

2 Xu and Wang (1999) study the impact of ownership concentration and the share of state ownership on the performance of listed companies in China, but their study does not deal with the issue of whether or not public listing itself improves company performance. Chen *et al.* (2000) use a sample of about 330 IPOs in China between 1992 and 1995 to compare the differences in performance between A shares and B shares, which are issued to domestic and foreign investors respectively. However, they also do not address the issue of how public listing affects company performance.

3 However, Mikkelson *et al.* (1997) find the relationship between a direct measure of managerial ownership stakes and post-listing performance to be statistically insignificant.

4 For an excellent survey of the literature on share issue privatization, see Megginson and Netter (2001) and the literature cited therein.

5 On the other hand, listed companies also exaggerate reported earnings (Burgstahler and Dichev, 1997). Earnings management is a more serious problem in China than in developed countries. It offsets at least some, if not all, of the exaggeration of the pre-listing performance.

6 The exchange rate was roughly US\$1 = 8.2 yuan.

7 There are no explicit rules governing quota allocations. Information on how much quota is issued to which agencies is hard to obtain. But based on our interviews with investment bankers in China, we find that a quota may even be allocated to non-economic organizations such as the National Union of Women and the Communist Youth League. In 2000, the government decided to abandon the quota system and let the market determine which firms can go public. The first non-quota IPO appeared in 2001.

8 We bundle the fifth and sixth years together because there are relatively too few observations for each year.

9 We have also tried adding more variables such as the share of intangibles in total assets and investment rate (both lagged by one period) as additional explanatory variables, and we obtained qualitatively similar results. However, in doing so, we lost a significant number of observations.

10 Note, however, that there may still be indirect state ownership as some legal person shares might be indirectly owned by the state.

11 Note that our focus here is on how ownership structure affects the effects of public listing on company performance rather than on how it affects company performance itself as in, for example, Claessens and Djankov (1999), who study the effects of ownership concentration on corporate performance in the context of voucher privatization in the Czech Republic.

12 However, state ownership has a positive and statistically significant listing effect on ROS. In other words, a firm's profit margins improve more after listing when it has a higher percentage of state shares. Given the negative effect of listing on ROA, the positive effect on ROS seems to suggest that the increase in total assets as a result of public listing generates a smaller increase in sales in firms with more state shares.

13 Our result is related to the work of Claessens *et al.* (2000), who find widespread presence of opportunities for expropriation in East Asian corporations. It is also related to recent findings by Cull *et al.* (2001), who provide evidence consistent with the

hypothesis that dominant owners and/or managers may "strip resources from a firm they own in part and transfer them to a firm they own in whole or to their personal accounts" (p. 29).

# References

Burgstahler, D. and I. Dichev (1997) "Earnings Management to Avoid Earnings Decreases and Losses," *Journal of Accounting and Economics*, 24: 99–126.

Cao, Y., Y. ☐ian, and B.R. Weingast (1999) "From Federalism, Chinese Style to Privatization, Chinese Style," *Economics of Transition*, 7: 103–31.

Chen, G., M. Firth, and J.-B. Kim (2000) "The Post-issue Market Performance of Initial Public Offerings in China's New Stock Markets," *Review of Quantitative Finance and Accounting*, 14: 319–39.

China Securities Regulatory Commission (1999) *China Securities and Futures Statistics*, Beijing: China Finance and Economic Publishing House.

Claessens, S. and S. Djankov (1999) "Ownership Concentration and Corporate Performance in the Czech Republic," *Journal of Comparative Economics*, 27: 498–513.

Claessens, S., S. Djankov, and L.H.P. Lang (2000) "The Separation of Ownership and Control in East Asian Corporations," *Journal of Financial Economics*, 58: 81–112.

Cull, R., J. Matesova, and M. Shirley (2001) "Ownership Structure and the Temptation to Loot: Evidence from Privatized Firms in the Czech Republic," *World Bank Policy Research Working Papers* 2568, World Bank.

Degeorge, F. and R. Zeckhauser (1993) "The Reverse LBO Decision and Firm Performance: Theory and Evidence," *Journal of Finance*, 48: 1323–48.

Demsetz, H. and K. Lehn (1985) "The Structure of Corporate Ownership: Causes and Consequences," *Journal of Political Economy*, 93: 1155–77.

Groves, T., Y. Hong, J. McMillan, and B. Naughton (1994) "Autonomy and Incentives in Chinese State Enterprises," *Quarterly Journal of Economics*, 109: 183–209.

Heckman, J., H. Ichimura, and P. Todd (1997) "Matching as an Econometric Evaluation Estimator: Evidence from Evaluating a Job Training Programme," *Review of Economic Studies*, 64: 605–54.

Heckman, J., H. Ichimura, and P. Todd (1998) "Matching as an Econometric Evaluation Estimator," *Review of Economic Studies*, 65: 261–94.

Holthausen, R.W. and D.F. Larcker (1996) "The Financial Performance of Reverse Leveraged Buyouts," *Journal of Financial Economics*, 42: 293–332.

Jain, B.A. and O. Kini (1994) "The Post-issue Operating Performance of IPO Firms," *Journal of Finance*, 49: 1699–726.

Jefferson, G.H., T.G. Rawski, and Y. Zheng (1996) "Chinese Industrial Productivity: Trends, Measurement Issues, and Recent Developments," *Journal of Comparative Economics*, 23: 146–80.

Jensen, M.C. and W.H. Meckling (1976) "Theory of the Firm: Managerial Behavior, Agency Costs and Ownership Structure," *Journal of Financial Economics*, 3: 305–60.

Lardy, N.R. (1998) *China's Unfinished Economic Revolution*, Washington, DC: Brookings Institution.

Li, W. (1997) "The Impact of Economic Reform on the Performance of Chinese State Enterprises, 1980–1989," *Journal of Political Economy*, 105: 1080–106.

Lin, Y. and T. Zhu (2001) "Ownership Restructuring in Chinese State Industry: An Analysis of Evidence on Initial Organizational Changes," *China Quarterly*, 166: 305–41.

Loughran, T. and J.R. Ritter (1995) "The New Issue Puzzle," *Journal of Finance*, 50: 23–51.

Megginson, W.L. and J.M. Netter (2001) "From State to Market: A Survey of Empirical Studies on Privatization," *Journal of Economic Literature*, 39: 321–89.

Mikkelson, W.H., M.M. Partch, and K. Shah (1997) "Ownership and Operating Performance of Companies That Go Public," *Journal of Financial Economics*, 44: 281–307.

Naughton, B. (1995) *Growing Out of the Plan: Chinese Economic Reform, 1978–1993*, New York: Cambridge University Press.

Pagano, M., F. Panetta, and L. Zingales (1996) "The Stock Market as a Source of Capital: Some Lessons from Initial Public Offering in Italy," *European Economic Review*, 40: 1057–69.

Pagano, M., F. Panetta, and L. Zingales (1998) "Why Do Companies Go Public? An Empirical Analysis," *Journal of Finance*, 53: 27–64.

□ian, Y. (1996) "Enterprise Reform in China: Agency Problems and Political Control," *Economics of Transition*, 4: 422–47.

□ian, Y. and G. Roland (1996) "The Soft Budget Constraint in China," *Japan and the World Economy*, 8: 207–23.

Ritter, J. (1991) "The Long-run Performance of Initial Public Offering," *Journal of Finance*, 46: 3–27.

Roell, A. (1996) "The Decision to Go Public: An Overview," *European Economic Review*, 40: 1071–81.

Shirley, M. and L.C. Xu (2001) "The Empirical Effects of Performance Contracts," *Journal of Law, Economics, and Organization*, 17: 168–200.

Xu, X. and Y. Wang (1999) "Ownership Structure and Corporate Governance in Chinese Stock Companies," *China Economic Review*, 10: 75–98.

Zhuang, J. and C. Xu (1996) "Profit-sharing and Financial Performance in the Chinese State Enterprises: Evidence from Panel Data," *Economics of Planning*, 29: 205–22.

# 4 Financing of private enterprises and deepening financial reform

*Yingfeng Xu*

## Introduction

After more than two decades of economic reform, China has been turned from a planned economy into a market economy. Non-state enterprises (NSEs) have become the main contributor to economic growth. The future vitality of the Chinese economy continues to lie in further expansion of NSEs and shrinking of state-owned enterprises (SOEs). However, NSEs still face many obstacles and handicaps in their expansion. In particular, there is a widely shared perception that NSEs have been constrained in their external finance because state banks have been preoccupied with supporting SOEs. Hence, it is necessary to carry out further financial reforms with a view to redirecting funds from SOEs to NSEs. Proposals range from curtailing loans to SOEs to setting up private banks.

The object of the present chapter is to critically assess this common perception. Specifically, I intend to make the following arguments. First, the distinction between SOEs and NSEs is fast losing significance. What influences the lending decisions of banks most is the size of enterprises rather than the type of ownership of enterprises. Although many NSEs do experience severe difficulty in securing external finance, it is largely because they are small and medium-sized enterprises (SMEs). Large enterprises are more favored than SMEs in bank lending, regardless of ownership. Second, the remedy for the external finance problems of NSEs is not a curtailment of lending to SOEs and an expansion of private banks. The real remedy is a faster expansion in the supply of risk-taking equity capital relative to risk-averse bank lending. A real remedy to the current financing difficulties requires further financial reforms, product innovations and institutional changes, and deregulations that would improve the matching between the demand for and supply of funds in terms of their risk characteristics.

The following section reviews the expansion of NSEs and observes that most NSEs are SMEs. The next section discusses the apparent bias in bank lending against SMEs, and the last section discusses the external finance problems encountered by NSEs in detail and their proposed remedies.

## A changing landscape of enterprises

### *Expansion of NSEs*

In China, a meaningful way to classify enterprises in terms of ownership is not SOEs versus private enterprises. It should be SOEs versus non-state enterprises (NSEs). In turn, NSEs are an evolving concept. In the 1980s, collective enterprises, especially rural township and village enterprises (TVEs), were the main NSEs. The distinction between SOEs and NSEs is really that the former was still significantly involved in the planning track, while the latter operated exclusively in the market track of the dual-track system. Strictly in terms of ownership, TVEs can be further divided into collective enterprises and private enterprises. However, such an ownership distinction is not necessary with regard to the behavior of TVEs. What distinguishes them as a group is that they operate entirely in the market track. Later on, foreign investment came to China in increasing quantities so that foreign-invested enterprises (FIEs) became another major component of NSEs. Many FIEs were joint ventures with SOEs so that they retained a significant element of state ownership. Again, what makes FIEs into NSEs is not strictly the legal definition of ownership, but rather the fact that FIEs operate mostly in the market track. In the 1990s, the reform of SOEs reached new heights. The government was ready to redefine the strategic role of the state sector in the economy. SOEs were to be withdrawn from most competitive segments of the economy. The main thrust of the SOE reform is to restructure them in accordance with the new company law. This drive is often referred to as corporatization conversion. Small and medium-sized SOEs are to be restructured as limited liability companies and large SOEs as joint-stock companies, many of which have been listed on the two stock exchanges of Shanghai and Shenzhen. At the same time, collective enterprises are restructured as cooperative shareholding companies or sold to individual investors as private enterprises. The strategic goal of this corporatization conversion is to grasp the large and release the small. The shares of large enterprises remain to be owned by the state for the moment. At the same time, a majority of SMEs have been turned into NSEs. Between 1995 and 2003, 85 percent of state-owned SMEs completed ownership conversion. The number of state-owned SMEs was reduced from 245,000 to 147,000. Even with large enterprises, a controlling state share may be regarded as transitional. There is a practical constraint in transferring the shares of large enterprises to the private sector quickly. There are simply not many wealthy individual investors out there in China who would be capable of taking over the existing state-held shares. It is inevitable that the government has to play the role of a caretaker for many large enterprises for a while. In sum, the enterprise landscape has changed dramatically, compared with that in 1978 when economic reform started. At that time, state ownership and central planning prevailed in production, whereas now NSEs and market exchanges are the predominant view in industry and commerce.

## Employment

How large is the non-state sector in the Chinese economy now? Some guess-work is needed, for reliable comprehensive data on the non-state sector are not available. Perhaps, a best overall indication of the size of NSEs comes from em-ployment data. Table 4.1 presents a picture of the evolving composition of em-ployment in terms of ownership. It is derived from Table 5.1 of *The Statistical Yearbook of China 2002.*

Let us examine the remaining state sector in terms of employment first. In 1998–2001, employment in SOEs declined at an average annual rate of 5.5 per-cent. It fell from 90.6 million in 1998 to 76.4 million in 2001. This is a net reduc-tion of about 15 million. Its share in total employment fell from 12.8 percent in 1998 to 10.5 percent in 2001. A more meaningful alternative relative measure is its share in urban employment. This fell from 41.9 percent in 1998 to 31.9 percent in 2001. That is a dramatic reduction of 10 percentage points in only three years. What the data reflect is the impact of the corporatization conversion and the mas-sive layoffs in SOEs that were carried out in those years. Upon completion of corporate restructuring, many former SOEs are now reclassified as limited liabil-ity companies, joint-stock companies, and cooperative shareholding companies. Therefore, an important new aspect of the Chinese economy is that SOEs, as a dominant business organization, are withering away. The remaining SOEs cover mainly large state-owned and state-controlled enterprises, the public sector (gov-ernment agencies and non-profit organizations), and those state owned SMEs still in the pipeline to be corporatized, taken over, merged, or liquidated. Conversely, NSEs have become the dominant business organization in all the competitive sec-tors of the economy.

Is the state sector, at 31.9 percent of urban employment, still too large? For a proper perspective, it is useful compare it with Canada, a good representative of developed economies. In Canada, a roughly comparable measure of the public sector employment share is 26.6 percent in 2002 (government, 5 percent; other services, 4.5 percent; education, 6.6 percent; health, 10.4 percent). A big difference between China and Canada is that finance, insurance, and real estate are largely private in Canada (5.8 percent) whereas they are public in China (1.85 percent of urban employment). By this rough comparison, the size of the public sector in China seems to be approaching a reasonable level. While there remains consider-able room to convert some large SOEs and financial institutions into joint-stock companies, further reductions in the employment of SOEs may well be offset by expansion in the rest of the public sector, especially in health and education.

In examining the rest of urban employment, it is useful to divide listed enterprise categories into two main groups. What I call NSEs_I include urban collective-owned units, cooperative units, joint ownership units, limited liability companies, and joint-stock companies. Basically, they used to be state or collectively owned, but they have become NSEs through the recent corporatization conversion. In relative terms, this group is also shrinking. Its share of urban employment fell

*Table 4.1* Composition of employment by ownership

| Description | 1998 (million) | % of total employment | 1999 (million) | % of total employment | 2000 (million) | % of total employment | 2001 (million) | % of total employment | 1998–2001 Average growth (%) |
|---|---|---|---|---|---|---|---|---|---|
| Labor force | 720.87 | 102.1 | 727.91 | 102.0 | 739.92 | 102.6 | 744.32 | 101.9 | 1.1 |
| Employment | 706.37 | 100.0 | 713.94 | 100.0 | 720.85 | 100.0 | 730.25 | 100.0 | 1.1 |
| Urban employment | 216.16 | 30.6 | 224.12 | 31.4 | 231.51 | 32.1 | 239.40 | 32.8 | 3.5 |
| State-owned units | 90.58 | 12.8 | 85.72 | 12.0 | 81.02 | 11.2 | 76.40 | 10.5 | −5.5 |
| NSEs_I | 30.41 | 4.3 | 29.25 | 4.1 | 28.40 | 3.9 | 28.13 | 3.9 | −2.6 |
| Urban collectively owned units | 19.63 | 2.8 | 17.12 | 2.4 | 14.99 | 2.1 | 12.91 | 1.8 | −13.0 |
| Cooperative units | 1.36 | 0.2 | 1.44 | 0.2 | 1.55 | 0.2 | 1.53 | 0.2 | 4.0 |
| Joint ownership units | 0.48 | 0.1 | 0.46 | 0.1 | 0.42 | 0.1 | 0.45 | 0.1 | −2.1 |
| Limited liability companies | 4.84 | 0.7 | 6.03 | 0.8 | 6.87 | 1.0 | 8.41 | 1.2 | 20.2 |
| Shareholding companies | 4.10 | 0.6 | 4.20 | 0.6 | 4.57 | 0.6 | 4.83 | 0.7 | 5.6 |

| | | | | | | | | | |
|---|---|---|---|---|---|---|---|---|---|
| NSEs_II | 38.19 | 5.4 | 40.79 | 5.7 | 40.46 | 5.6 | 43.29 | 5.9 | 4.3 |
| Private enterprises | 9.73 | 1.4 | 10.53 | 1.5 | 12.68 | 1.8 | 15.27 | 2.1 | 16.2 |
| Overseas Chinese-invested enterprises | 2.94 | 0.4 | 3.06 | 0.4 | 3.10 | 0.4 | 3.26 | 0.4 | 3.5 |
| Foreign-invested enterprises | 2.93 | 0.4 | 3.06 | 0.4 | 3.32 | 0.5 | 3.45 | 0.5 | 5.6 |
| Self-employed individuals | 22.59 | 3.2 | 24.14 | 3.4 | 21.36 | 3.0 | 21.31 | 2.9 | -1.9 |
| Other urban employment | 56.98 | 8.1 | 68.36 | 9.6 | 81.63 | 11.3 | 91.58 | 12.5 | 17.1 |
| Rural employment | 490.21 | 69.4 | 489.82 | 68.6 | 489.34 | 67.9 | 490.85 | 67.2 | 0.0 |
| NSEs_III | 171.29 | 24.2 | 175.00 | 24.5 | 168.93 | 23.4 | 169.02 | 23.1 | -0.4 |
| Township and village enterprises | 125.37 | 17.7 | 127.04 | 17.8 | 128.20 | 17.8 | 130.86 | 17.9 | 1.4 |
| Private enterprises | 7.37 | 1.0 | 9.69 | 1.4 | 11.39 | 1.6 | 11.87 | 1.6 | 17.2 |
| Self-employed individuals | 38.55 | 5.5 | 38.27 | 5.4 | 29.34 | 4.1 | 26.29 | 3.6 | -12.0 |
| Others/farmers | 318.92 | 45.1 | 314.82 | 44.1 | 320.41 | 44.4 | 321.83 | 44.1 | 0.3 |

Source: *The Statistical Yearbook of China 2002*, Table 5.1.

from 14.1 percent in 1998 to 13.1 percent in 2001, with an average annual rate of decrease of –2.6 percent.

The other group, which I call NSEs_II, includes overseas Chinese-invested enterprises, FIEs, private enterprises, and self-employed individuals. These enterprises are usually regarded as proper NSEs. This group's share of urban employment rose gradually from 17.7 percent in 1998 to 18.2 percent in 2001, with an average annual growth rate of 4.3 percent in 1998–2001. In particular, it appears that many self-employed individuals have developed into private enterprises. Accordingly, from 1998 to 2001, the share of the self-employed fell from 10.5 percent to 8.9 percent, while the share of private enterprises rose from 4.5 percent to 6.4 percent.

Table 4.1 also reveals the gross inadequacy of published employment statistics. There is a very large residual urban employment, computed as what is left out in Table 5.1 of *The Statistical Yearbook of China 2002*. In 1998, that residual urban employment was 57 million, and its share of urban employment was 26.4 percent. In 2001, the same figures were 92 million and 38.3 percent respectively. Most of the residual urban employment is provided by SMEs.

Beside urban NSEs, rural non-agricultural enterprises are another main component of NSEs. I call the sum of TVEs, private enterprises, and self-employed the NSEs_III group. Rural non-agricultural employment remained sizeable. In 2001, it amounted to 169 million, falling slightly from 171 million in 1998, reflecting the limited potential for further expansion of TVEs.

In sum, a new landscape of enterprises is emerging. The traditional state sector has been shrinking. What the state owns and controls nowadays are mostly large enterprises. Even for those enterprises, the relationship between government and enterprise management has changed significantly. In place of the traditional planning agency, state asset management companies now supervise enterprise management as a major shareholder.

### Industrial production

Another way to assess the size of NSEs is to examine the output data. China does not publish data on the composition of aggregate output by ownership. However, useful data are available for the composition of industrial output by ownership. Table 13.1 of *The Statistical Yearbook of China 2002* provides detailed information about the composition of industrial enterprises and production. The following relevant facts can be observed.

First, remaining SOEs accounted for only 20.2 percent of enterprises and 18.1 percent of industrial output in 2001. The SOE share of industrial production was on a steady declining trend. In 1996, the corresponding SOE share of industrial production was 28.5 percent. Clearly, the bulk of industrial production is now produced by NSEs. It is also important to observe that the output share of remaining SOEs is smaller than their number share. This implies that the remaining SOEs are largely SMEs. Most of the large SOEs have already been converted into modern corporations. It can be expected that those remaining small and medium-sized SOEs are to be converted, acquired, merged, or liquidated. In short, SOEs are withering away in industrial production.

Second, it can observed that, by international standards, industrial production in China is more fragmented than concentrated. In 2001, the share of joint-stock companies (mostly large enterprises) was 3.3 percent in number and 13.3 percent in output. The share of superlarge and large enterprises was 5 percent in number and 47 percent in output. Compared with such large domestic enterprises, FIEs are somewhat smaller. The share of FIE (multinationals) was 7.7 percent in number and 16.1 percent in output. Therefore, there remains a long way for China to go in consolidation and rationalization.

Finally, limited liability companies and joint-stock companies accounted for 14.4 percent of industrial enterprises and 29.3 percent of industrial output together. They are the large enterprises among NSEs. In contrast, other NSEs are much smaller. In 2001, cooperative shareholding companies accounted for 6.3 percent of industrial enterprises and 3.1 percent of industrial output. The remaining collective enterprises accounted for 18.1 percent of industrial enterprises and 10.5 percent of industrial output. By implication, a quarter of collective enterprises had been converted into cooperative shareholding companies and private companies. Private enterprises accounted for 21.1 percent of industrial enterprises but only 9.2 percent of industrial production. In comparison, most of them were small businesses, although some of them have grown to be very large. Overseas Chinese-invested enterprises accounted for 10.7 percent of enterprises and 12.4 percent of output. Their scale of production is slightly above the national average. In comparison, FIEs are larger. They accounted for 7.7 percent of enterprises but 16.1 percent of output. In sum, most NSEs are SMEs. Large NSEs are either modern companies restructured out of former SOEs or FIEs.

### Fixed investment

While NSEs have expanded tremendously either from their own growth or from conversion from former SOEs and collective enterprises, a quite different picture is seen in fixed investment. There is a common perception that NSEs underinvest as a result of the constraint of external finance. Is that true? This is a tricky question.

In 2003, fixed investment by SOEs was 3,974.8 billion yuan, about 72 percent of total fixed investment. SOEs' share of fixed investment is much larger than their share of production and employment. Does that necessarily imply that NSEs have been so constrained that they could not invest as much as it would be optimal for them to invest? A proper assessment also needs to take account of two other relevant facts of the Chinese economy. One fact is that a big chunk of fixed investment has been infrastructure: communication and transport network, dams and irrigation networks, utilities, and transit. At present, infrastructure investment has largely been the responsibility of the government. The private sector is not yet ready to take a major part in infrastructure investment. The state's involvement in infrastructure investment accounts for a big part of the fixed investment by SOEs.

The other relevant fact is that data classification in production and fixed investment may not be consistent with each other. Many large enterprises have gone through the corporatization conversion, but the state continues to be the controlling shareholder. In production data, they may be classified as limited liability companies or joint-stock companies but, in investment data, they continue to be treated as part of the state sector. This is because the bulk of their fixed investment must be approved by the state and incorporated into the national fixed investment plan. Furthermore, such large enterprises tend to be in capital-intensive industries. That is another important reason why the SOEs' share in fixed investment is much larger than their share in production and employment.

Therefore, it is not valid to infer from a simple comparison of production and fixed investment data that NSEs were constrained in their fixed investment because of their difficulty with external finance. To corroborate the above argument, we observe that, in 1985–88, TVEs expanded dramatically, despite the fact that they did not have privileged access to bank loans and had to rely mainly on their own savings and retained earnings to fund their expansion. In contrast, their access to bank funds improved considerably in the 1990s, but their fixed investment and production actually slowed down. What explains such a contrast in performance between the two periods? It is the evolving market environment. In the 1980s, shortages prevailed for most goods, and the market economy was a virgin land. In that environment, operational flexibility conferred a distinct advantage to NSEs, especially TVEs. However, in the 1990s, markets for most products matured so that enterprises had to compete in price, production scale, and quality. In that new environment, the disadvantages of the small production scale and weak technological capabilities of most SMEs, especially TVEs, became serious constraining handicaps.

To recapitulate the above discussion, we have argued the following. First, NSEs are now the predominant player in production and commerce. Traditional SOEs have been withering away. Now they account for only 20 percent of industrial production and 31 percent of urban employment. Second, NSEs consist of four elements: private enterprises and individuals, collective enterprises, FIEs, and former SOEs that have completed the corporatization conversion. The first two elements are mostly SMEs, while the last two elements can be very large. Third, size is the most important factor that accounts for the differences among enterprises in terms of fixed investment. By and large, most NSEs are SMEs, while most SOEs are large enterprises. SMEs generally operate in competitive labor-intensive industries, have limited access to long-term loans from the banking system, and cannot tap the resources of the capital market. In contrast, large enterprises, most of which are state owned or state controlled, operate in capital-intensive industries, and their fixed investment is funded by long-term bank loans and securities issued in the capital market. Fourth, the state remains a dominant player in guiding and coordinating fixed investment, especially fixed investment in infrastructure. The fixed investment plan is closely integrated with the fixed asset lending of the banking system. However, the role of banks has been evolving steadily from a mere plan executioner in the past to an independent financier at present. Banks now can decide by themselves which projects in the state fixed investment plan are to be funded. Finally, it is important to be aware of two fundamental structural adjustments necessary for economic growth in discussing the role of SMEs. The first structural adjustment is urbanization. People will migrate from rural villages to towns and cities, perhaps at an accelerating pace. Most new employment will be generated in urban areas, especially in urban service sectors. SMEs will be the dominant players in job creation. The second structural adjustment is that, in manufacturing, consolidation and rationalization will be a fundamental driving force to generate productivity growth through enlarging production scale, improving quality, reducing costs, and reaping benefits from innovations and technological upgrading. In relative terms, the role of SMEs will decline.

## The access of NSEs to external finance

Now we turn to analyze the pattern of credit flows and the structure of the current financial system. To what extent has the current financial system constrained the expansion of NSEs?

### *Credit flows*

The Chinese financial system is largely a bank-based system. Substantial progress has been made to modernize it from a mono-bank since economic reform began in 1978. The M2–GDP[1] ratio rose dramatically from 0.25 in 1978 to 1.65 in 2001. At this level, the size of the banking sector is already very large according to international standards. The potential for further banking enlargement in terms of credit flows and bank branches may already have reached a saturation limit. This is a relevant fact in discussing the options for reforming and upgrading the present financial system.

Bank loans are the main source of external finance. In 2001, 1,294.36 billion yuan (with an annual growth rate of 13 percent) was raised in loans, against 125.23 billion yuan of funds raised in stocks (–40.5 percent growth because of a much smaller amount of foreign issues) (both domestic and foreign issues), and 374.92 billion yuan in government bonds (net issues, treasury bonds, and policy financial bonds (*The Statistical Yearbook of China 2002*: Table 19.2). Gross corporate bond issuance was tiny. Gross issues were merely 14.7 billion yuan. Therefore, the financial sector has largely remained bank based. Despite the tremendous expansion achieved in the 1990s, the Chinese capital market is still small. Among loans, short-term loans accounted for 60 percent, while medium- and long-term loans for 35 percent. Most of the medium- and long-term loans were extended to SOEs and government infrastructure projects that were coordinated by government planning agencies.

While it is not straightforward to assess how efficient credit allocation has been, we can say, at least, that the adjustment in lending is in the right direction.

Categories of loans that experience fast expansion are construction loans (with a growth rate of 29.8 percent) and loans to individuals and private businesses (with a growth rate of 40.2 percent). In other words, increasingly, a fast expanding business for banks is mortgage loans and emergent consumer credit, especially finance for car purchases. This is the right direction for adjusting credit allocation.

It is not clear how much bank credit is extended to NSEs or SMEs. There are no published statistics on credit allocation by ownership that are comparable to those statistics on production and employment. The People's Bank of China (PBOC) claims that now more than 50 percent of bank loans are extended to NSEs. Nevertheless, it is probably true that the share of SOEs in credit allocation is greater than their share in production and employment, reflecting their larger share in fixed investment. This is mainly due to two factors. First, SOEs play a more important role in fixed investment, as discussed above. Second, banks are more inclined to lend to large enterprises. To the extent that many large enterprises are owned and controlled by the state, it would necessarily imply a larger loan share for SOEs. Furthermore, large enterprises generally operate in capital-intensive industries so that they tend to be heavy users of bank loans.

However, there are numerous informal or unsanctioned channels through which NSEs may obtain external finance directly or indirectly from state banks. NSEs often get substantial trade credit or loans from their partners in the state sector. While some loans may be classified as lending to SOEs, they may, in fact, be loans to NSEs. For example, individuals with good (political) connections could easily secure loans from state banks either explicitly or anonymously. In a way, much of the non-performing loans and financial frauds are in effect an implicit or illicit way for some people to lay hands on funds from state banks.

How important are the indirect channels through which NSEs may access external finance? They can be very important, according to OECD's study, *China in the World Economy*, 2002 (Table 7.4, p. 242). As proportions of short-term loans from all financial institutions, lending to TVEs was 6.7 percent in 1997 and 6.6 percent in 1999, lending to private enterprises and individuals was only 0.5 percent in 1997 and 0.6 percent in 1999, lending to FIEs was 2.5 percent in 1997 and 3.2 percent in 1999. In particular, about two-thirds of the lending to TVEs came from rural credit cooperatives. So it appears that the bank loan share of NSEs was much smaller than their share in production.

However, quoting the internal surveys of the PBOC, the OECD study reports that the share of direct and indirect outstanding loans to NSEs was 38.9 percent in 1997 and 47.7 percent in 1999. The figure is proportional to the relative importance in a local economy. It was much higher in coastal provinces than in inland provinces. For example, in 2000, the share of loans to NSEs was 65 percent in Jiangsu province, 49.8 percent in Shandong province, 74.2 percent in Zhejiang province, 37.8 percent in Heilongjiang province, 37.6 percent in Hubei province, 47 percent in Sichuan province, 42.1 percent in Shanxi province, and 22.8 percent in Xinjiang province.

### Capital structure of industrial enterprises

If we focus narrowly on industrial enterprises, we can get some useful comparative information about their capital structure. Table 4.2 presents the capital structure information, derived from Table 13.5 of *The Statistical Yearbook of China 2002*. It is important to observe the following features.

First, SOEs and state-controlled enterprises (they may appear as NSEs in other contexts) are larger and more capital intensive than the national averages. Their total assets-to-gross output ratio was 2.1 against the national average of 1.4, and their ratio of fixed assets to total assets was 0.44 against the national average of 0.41. They had the best access to long-term bank loans. Their ratio of long-term liabilities to total assets was 0.21 against the national average of 0.17. In terms of external funds, this group of enterprises perhaps has the best access. Interestingly, their ratio of equity to total assets was similar to the national average of 0.41.

Second, shareholding companies, among NSEs, are a bit less capital intensive. Their ratio of total assets to gross output was 1.5, at about the national average level. However, their ratio of fixed assets to total assets was 0.44, the same as that of state-owned and state-controlled enterprises. As they are less capital intensive, they make a bit less use of long-term debt. Their ratio of long-term liabilities to

*Table 4.2* Capital structure by ownership and size

| | Total assets/ gross output | Fixed assets/total assets | Short-term liabilities/ total assets | Long-term liabilities/ total assets | Equity/ total assets |
|---|---|---|---|---|---|
| National total | 1.42 | 0.41 | 0.41 | 0.17 | 0.41 |
| By ownership | | | | | |
| State-owned and state-holding enterprises | 2.07 | 0.44 | 0.38 | 0.21 | 0.41 |
| Collectively owned enterprises | 0.80 | 0.33 | 0.53 | 0.10 | 0.36 |
| Shareholding limited corporations | 1.47 | 0.44 | 0.33 | 0.15 | 0.50 |
| Foreign-invested enterprises | 1.02 | 0.39 | 0.43 | 0.10 | 0.46 |
| Overseas Chinese-invested enterprises | 1.07 | 0.39 | 0.45 | 0.10 | 0.44 |
| By size | | | | | |
| Large enterprises | 1.77 | 0.43 | 0.36 | 0.19 | 0.44 |
| Medium-sized enterprises | 1.44 | 0.39 | 0.48 | 0.17 | 0.35 |
| Small enterprises | 1.00 | 0.37 | 0.49 | 0.12 | 0.38 |

Source: *The Statistical Yearbook of China*, 2002, Table 13.5.

total assets was 0.15, close to the national average of 0.17. They appear to have more equity, so they depend less on short-term debt. Their ratio of short-term liabilities to total assets was 0.33, the lowest among all the enterprise groups.

Third, FIEs are less capital intensive than shareholding enterprises. Their ratio of total assets to gross output was 1.0 for FIEs and 1.1 for overseas Chinese-invested enterprises. Accordingly, their ratio of fixed assets to total assets was 0.39, lower than that of shareholding enterprises. Thus, they make less use of long-term debt. Their ratio of long-term liabilities to total assets was only 0.10. But they appear to be comfortably capitalized with equity. Their ratio of equity to total assets was 0.46 for FIEs and 0.44 for overseas Chinese-invested enterprises.

Finally, collective enterprises are the least capital intensive of all. Their ratio of total assets to gross output was 0.8, and their ratio of fixed assets to total assets was 0.33; both are the lowest among all enterprises. Accordingly, they have the least access to long-term debt. Their ratio of long-term liabilities to total assets was 0.102, the lowest. Also significant is the fact that they are inadequately capitalized. Their ratio of equity to total assets was only 0.36, the lowest among all enterprise groups. Inevitably, they have to rely mainly on short-term debt. Their ratio of short-term liabilities to total assets was 0.53, the highest among all enterprise groups.

To recapitulate the above analysis, the structure of external finance has more to do with the size of an enterprise than with ownership. Generally speaking, large enterprises are capital intensive, and they tend to have better access to long-term external funds. In contrast, small enterprises are mostly labor intensive, tend to be undercapitalized with equity, and have more difficulty in accessing long-term external funds. There is no generalized external finance problem of NSEs. The real problem is the external finance difficulty experienced by SMEs. To the extent that many large enterprises are state owned or state controlled and most SMEs are NSEs, there exists an appearance that the financial system is biased in favor of SOEs and against NSEs.

## Current issues and remedies

Having reviewed the role of NSEs in the Chinese economy, we proceed to analyze the issues of their alleged difficulty in securing external finance and explore remedial options. As argued above, the financing problem of NSEs is really that of SMEs. Large enterprises, many of which are indeed state owned or state controlled, generally do not experience the same kind of financing difficulty as small and medium-sized NSEs. They can get not only enough bank loans, but also some of them can raise funds in the equity market. It is also important to be aware that the financing difficulty of SMEs is a generic one, not confined to China.

Two common remedies have been proposed and widely discussed for some time. One is that state banks need to curtail their lending to SOEs so that more funds can be released to fund SMEs. This remedy is premised on the belief that lending to SOEs crowds out lending to SMEs. In fact, state banks have been instructed in recent years to beef up their lending to SMEs. This proposal seeks to alleviate the NSEs' financing difficulty within the existing financial framework. The other remedy is more radical. It advocates the creation of private banks, especially small and medium-sized private banks. This remedy is premised on the belief that state banks cannot be reformed fundamentally to improve lending to "private enterprises." Only private banks can solve that problem. While looking plausible, neither remedy addresses the root cause of the financing difficulty for SMEs. Accordingly, they are not real solutions.

### Curtail lending to SOEs

With regard to the first remedy, lending to SMEs is not really constrained by lending to SOEs. In recent years, Chinese banks have been awash with excess funds for which they do not secure profitable uses. Using the data from the Asian Development Bank's *Key Indicators 2004*, the ratio of domestic credit to the private sector to M2 declined steadily from 0.857 in 1998 to 0.724 in 2001, although it recovered significantly to 0.773 in 2002 and 0.781 in 2003. In the three years 1999–2001, the growth rate of loans to the private sector (11.6 percent in 1999, 11.4 percent in 2000, and 2.9 percent in 2001) was persistently below that of M2 (14.7 percent in 1999, 12.3 percent in 2000, and 17.6 percent in 2001). The banking sector has had plentiful liquidity. In other words, lending to SOEs does not crowd out lending to SMEs. Hence, cutting back the lending to SOEs may not improve the access of SMEs to bank loans when the real obstacles lie elsewhere.

So what are the real obstacles for SMEs to access adequate external finance? As a matter of fact, SMEs are themselves to blame to a large extent. Lack of equity capital, collaterals, absence of good credit history, and opaque accounting make SMEs a high-risk group for banks. Fundamentally, the scale of lending to SMEs is constrained by the asymmetric information problem inherent in credit transactions. It is useful to observe that SMEs' financing difficulty due to asymmetric information is a worldwide problem. Compared with large companies, especially public companies whose shares are traded on stock exchanges, SMEs find it more difficult to access external finance. The main difference between SMEs and large companies lies in the extent of the asymmetric information problem. Large companies are more transparent with regard to their financial situation, have a long and established history of good credit, and possess more collateral securities.

A piece of corroborative evidence for such a view is that the external finance problem worsened considerably for SMEs in the second half of the 1990s when formerly state-owned SMEs were being privatized. Privatization implies that the previous implicit government support was effectively withdrawn. At the same time, the banking reform deepened, and banks were urged to improve risk management in their lending. As a result, banks tightened their lending criteria so as to contain and reduce their non-performing loans. It has been widely reported that, in 1998–2000, the expansionary monetary policy to stimulate aggregate demand was ineffective, largely because the new injection of reserve money was not turned into new lending when banks became more cautious and conservative. Consequently, a huge pool of liquidity was being built up in the banking sector.

In a market economy, a proper balance is needed between bank loans and other forms of finance, especially risk-taking equity capital. There is no simple rule to determine the optimal balance, which may vary with the level of economic sophistication and the type of financial system. Bank loans alone cannot provide the sole source of external finance for SMEs. This has never been the case in the rest of the world. Therefore, it is critical not to focus only on bank lending when we address the financing problem of SMEs.

Given the liquid nature of bank deposits, bank loans must be safe and secure. Therefore, the primary use of bank loans is to fund working capital needs, secured with accounts receivable, inventory, or other collaterals, and cushioned by the equity capital of borrowers. In other words, the amount of (working capital) loans that SMEs can access is a function of the kind of sale orders and accounts receivable and the kind of collaterals and equity cushion that they can put up. Bank lending is only one side of the problem. Equally important is the other side on the part of SMEs.

In general, it is fair to presume that, right now in China, a profitable SME with a competitive market position does not generally experience significant external finance problems, at least in so far as working capital needs are concerned, whether it is a private enterprise, a FIE, a limited liability company, or a cooperative shareholding company. Such enterprises are attractive to banks because they have predictable sale orders and accounts receivable. With solid and stable profits, they would have sizeable equity to ensure the safety of bank loans. In fact, such profitable enterprises are fiercely competed for by Chinese banks.

In contrast, SMEs that experience difficulties in accessing bank loans tend to be in a shaky competitive position in their respective markets. Typically, they do not have a market niche so that their products or services enjoy steady and growing market demand. Further, they do not possess adequate collaterals and deep equity. In short, they are a high-risk group from the perspective of banks. And it is prudent of banks to take a conservative lending approach towards them, especially in the context of a huge stock of existing, extensive, non-performing loans in the banking sector. Therefore, in this case, the constraining factors for weak SMEs to access bank loans are their own risk characteristics, not the crowding out of funds due to excessive lending to SOEs on the part of banks. In fact, it has been state policy for some time to support SMEs. State banks have been urged to increase lending to SMEs. According to the PBOC's *Monetary Report 2002*, by September 2002, the lending to SMEs of the four state banks reached 3,700 billion yuan, 53 percent of their total lending. Why are banks still reluctant in expanding lending to SMEs, despite all the government policy guidance and incentives to promote lending to SMEs? The simple truth is that such lending is not profitable. Therefore, the real remedies for the external finance problem of SMEs must tackle the obstacles at the root.

However, it may be argued that, given the same financial and credit characteristics, a state-owned SME is more likely to secure bank lending. So there may exist an ownership bias against NSEs in bank lending. While it sounds reasonable, this argument misses the crucial point. The existence of such an ownership actually further proves the significance of the risk characteristics of an enterprise as an effective constraint on external finance. Why may a state-owned SME be more likely to secure a bank loan? This is because it often has some kind of implicit government backing or guarantee, offsetting the weak risk characteristics of that SOE. Therefore, banks may find it more attractive to lend to those SMEs with implicit government backing or guarantees. However, it is wrong to argue that the government should provide similar backing to SMEs in other types of ownership.

As far as the implicit government backing to financially weak state-owned SMEs is concerned, it is important to place it in a proper historical context. In most cases, such bank lending is mainly motivated by social concerns to limit the scale of massive layoffs and closures in the state sector. Much progress has been made in the past six years in hardening the budget constraints for SOEs and commercializing state banks. The drive of grasping the large and releasing the small has turned many SOEs into NSEs through corporatization, acquisitions and mergers, asset sales, and liquidation. At the same time, existing banks have been pushed to operate on more of a commercial basis by reducing policy lending and directed credit. It is fair to say that the soft budget cushion that used to be enjoyed by many SOEs in the past is being hardened.

Furthermore, it may not be in the national interest to discontinue soft lending to unprofitable SOEs immediately and completely. Two relevant points need to be borne in mind. One is that soft lending to unprofitable SOEs is a transitional phenomenon and, over time, the severity of the problem is diminishing steadily. The other point is that, in the present context of weak aggregate demand and excessive liquidity in the banking sector, some soft lending to SOEs in financial difficulty should be regarded as a transfer payment to prop up demand and maintain social cohesion. Therefore, as long as the shrinking of SOEs is proceeding at a pace constrained by the degree of social tolerance for closing down unprofitable SOEs and laying off workers, soft lending may be unavoidable.

### *Private banks*

Recently, the case for private banks has received great interest. There are two principal arguments for private banks. One is related to China's accession to the WTO. It is rightly argued that what is open to foreign banks should also be open to domestic private ownership. The other is that only private banks would correct the lending bias against NSEs.

In the long run, there is no question that there will be more private banks in China, just as there will be more competition from foreign banks. China has committed itself to opening up the banking sector to more foreign competition. More domestic competition is also natural. However, setting up more small private banks may not be an appropriate quick fix for the immediate problem of improving external finance for SMEs. Banking is a skill-intensive business that requires an extensive accumulation of experience and human capital. Economies of scale and scope matter a lot. The entry of foreign banks may bring in new financial products and services and open the eyes of domestic banks to advanced banking and risk management skills. However, new domestic private banks cannot be expected to yield the same kind of benefits.

While promoting more private ownership in the banking sector is a desirable long-term goal, it is risky to loosen up regulatory thresholds so as to speed up the emergence of many private banks at present. Internationally, there has been extensive experience showing that hasty financial liberalization that allows many new inexperienced banks to emerge suddenly in a short period of time often results in frauds, excessive risk taking, and destructive competition. Eventually, an initial banking boom often fizzles out into a costly financial crisis. There were numerous such occurrences in the financial liberalization experience in the early 1980s in Latin America (Diaz-Alejandro, 1985). Caprio and Klingebiel (1996) found in their cross-country study that many banking crises have been preceded by financial liberalization that resulted in a sudden entry of new banks.

Furthermore, the existing banking branch network in China is already quite saturated. Beside the four large state-owned banks, there are a significant number of other national and regional banks. There is a significant risk that opening more private banks and setting up more bank branches may lead to excessive self-destructive price competition, potentially triggering a banking crisis. In the early 1990s, China had a bad experience with the sudden emergence and expansion of rural cooperative funds, most of which became insolvent soon afterwards. Therefore, the policy priority should not be to rush in more new domestic private banks. Instead, it should accelerate the commercialization pace of the existing state banks. Enhancing corporate governance through selling part of the shares of regional banks and credit cooperatives to private investors may be a more appropriate policy option.

Part of the advocacy for private banks also comes from some private companies in China. They have shown a keen interest in setting up their own banks as a way for them to access more funds from the public. This raises another important banking issue. That is whether universal banking in which banks are owned or controlled by some exclusive non-financial businesses is appropriate in China. In terms of market structure, the Chinese banking sector is similar to the Canadian banking sector, in that both are highly oligopolistic and concentrated. With such a market structure, control of banks by some exclusive non-financial interests may not be in the public interest. Therefore, a longstanding regulatory issue in Canada has always been to ensure diverse ownership of domestic banks. No single investor can own more than 10 percent of the shares of one of the six big chartered banks. Similar regulation may also be advisable in China when more private banks emerge in the future.

### Loan guarantees

If the above two proposed remedies cannot effectively resolve the external finance problem for SMEs, what are the remedies that can work? As the external finance for NSEs is in effect constrained by the risk characteristics of NSEs and the asymmetric information, the search for remedies should start from there. One remedy to offset a lack of collaterals is for a public agency or a private company to provide loan guarantees to banks in exchange for a fee charged to borrowers. Government-sponsored loan guarantee agencies have already been widely set up in China since 1999. This is a widely adopted approach in the rest of the world.

What is the rationale for government-sponsored loan guarantee agencies or programs? Loan guarantees substitute collateral securities that SMEs often lack in securing loans from banks. The use of collaterals and guarantees is one effective way in which lenders attempt to overcome the asymmetric information problem. However, do government-sponsored loan guarantee agencies have a comparative advantage in resolving the asymmetric information of SMEs and pricing loan guarantees at least on a cost-recovery basis? Obviously they do not. It really would be a miracle if government bureaucracies could be superior to market agents in this situation. Then, what is the justification for government-sponsored loan guarantee agencies? In China, as well as in the rest of the world, loan guaranteeing unavoidably requires public subsidies. Government-sponsored loan guarantee agencies are rarely viable on a commercial basis.

Can public subsidies in the form of loan guaranteeing be a real solution to the external finance problem of SMEs? If it can, all SMEs should really be owned by the state. This is absurd, of course. Public subsides through loan guaranteeing do not solve the asymmetric information problem. They are only justifiable if they are used to achieve certain social objectives. For example, China faces enormous pressures of unemployment. SMEs would be the main source to create jobs for new school graduates, laid-off workers from SOEs, and rural migrant workers. Therefore, certain public loan guaranteeing aimed at employment creation in target areas can be justified.

### *More flexible interest rate regulation*

What can be done on the part of banks to improve the access of SMEs to external finance? Banks are now under pressure to operate commercially and improve profitability. Lending to SMEs is a conventional area of business for commercial banks. As long as loans are priced appropriately, it should be profitable for commercial banks to serve SMEs. There may be a natural division of labor between local banks and large national banks. Local banks may be more inclined to serve local SMEs, while national banks may be keener to chase after large enterprises. As mentioned above, an important reason for the difficulty of SMEs in getting loans is that banks do not find it profitable. By its nature, lending to SMEs involves high costs of information collection and high credit risks. In short, lending to SMEs involves high-risk premiums. However, current interest rate regulations often constrain banks to charge adequate risk premiums to cover their full costs. As a result, banks are discouraged from lending to SMEs. Ironically, some of the current interest rate regulations are motivated to make loans more affordable through price ceilings. However, the effect is the opposite. The supply of funds to SMEs is actually reduced, exacerbating the external finance difficulty of SMEs.

To improve SMEs' access to bank loans, what is needed is to relax current interest rate regulations so that banks can charge a risk premium that is consistent with the risk profile of their borrowers. In developed market economies, the interest rate charged by credit card companies can be more 10 percent higher than the prime rate. Why are credit card interest rates so high? It is mainly because there is a high rate of defaults among credit card holders. The same principle should apply to lending to SMEs. Currently, the PBOC regulates both deposit rates and loan rates to forestall price competition among banks, which is perceived to be self-destructive for state banks that are already financially weak. While the prudential concern for interest rate regulation is understandable, rigid regulation of interest rates constrains market competition and discourages commercial banks from serving SMEs. Therefore, it is important to accelerate the pace of planned interest rate liberalization. It is already planned that liberalization of loan rates would precede that of deposit rates. This is the right order of liberalization.

### *Proper pricing and transfer of credit risk*

It may well be true that more discretion on the part of banks in pricing risk premiums would not help much in improving SMEs' access to bank loans. This is because state banks are still very bureaucratic and may not be the most effective and efficient collector and analyzer of the credit information of SMEs. Therefore, the risk premiums charged on a full cost-recovery basis may be so high that many SMEs are deterred from borrowing.

However, there may exist another group of agents who can perform that function more effectively and efficiently. This may include individuals, companies, local governments, and insurance companies. Assessing the credit risk of SMEs usually requires proximity to borrowers and private information. If some entities other than banks can do a better job of risk assessment, there is a market for market-based loan guaranteeing and insurance. Lending to SMEs can be decomposed into risk-free lending by banks and risk assumption by loan-guaranteeing individuals and companies. In effect, a specialized private loan-guaranteeing company behaves very much like an insurance company. This market segment borders on finance and real business. It can be open to companies of all types of ownership, private or public, domestic or foreign. As is well known, a financial system performs three basic functions: provision of money with stable value, intermediation of funds between borrowers and lenders, risk pricing and transferring. In China, the third function of risk pricing and transferring is very much underdeveloped. Therefore, an important measure to improve SMEs' access to credit is to strengthen the function of risk pricing and transferring through institutional innovations and liberalization.

As an application of the general principle of insurance, loan guarantee fees (risk premiums) should be related to the risk characteristics of SMEs. Those SMEs with strong management, predictable sales revenue, quality accounting records, and collaterals should pay low guarantee fees/risk premiums. In this way, proper pricing of the credit risk of SMEs can serve as a strong incentive for SMEs to make serious efforts to improve their credit risk profile through disclosure and transparency, a key element of corporate governance. Accordingly, more accurate pricing of risk premiums can alleviate the asymmetric information of SMEs. As a result, the access of SMEs to credit can be improved substantially.

### Investment funds and the supply of equity capital

As mentioned above, an important factor for the high-risk profile of many SMEs is that they do not have adequate equity capital. For them, the problem is not so much an inadequate supply of bank loans than a shortage of equity capital. More supply of banking lending is only part of the solution. Injection of more equity capital would help much more. Equity capital is not only a major source of funding, but also determines how much a SME can access to bank loans.

When a SME is private in the sense that its shares are not publicly traded, it is under no obligation to be transparent to external creditors and investors. By their nature, the asymmetric information problem of such SMEs is more serious. Therefore, equity capital supplied by insiders is naturally an important source of funding, especially for long-term expansion. In most market economies, SMEs are run and funded by well-off or wealthy individuals, and their expansion is funded with retained earnings. In a 1999 World Bank survey of 600 Chinese private enterprises, Gregory and Tenev (2001) found that private enterprises relied mainly on self-financing and were constrained in their access to external loans and equity. From the perspective of banks, lending to individual consumers with a stable income and marketable collaterals (apartments and automobiles) may actually be less risky than lending to SMEs with no marketable collaterals. Therefore, it is natural that SMEs rely mainly on self-finance. In the context of the Chinese economy, a transitional situation emerges in which many SMEs are undercapitalized with insiders' equity. This problem is particularly acute now as a result of the *de facto* privatization of most state-owned or collective SMEs in recent years. And this may be a more critical factor that constrains their access to external funding.

Undercapitalization of many SMEs is not due to a lack of domestic saving. In fact, the banking sector is awash with personal deposits. The national savings rate is well above the world average. Hence, this is where the real inadequacy of the present Chinese financial system lies. It is underdeveloped and insufficiently diversified so that, on the one hand, there are too many risk-avoiding bank deposits, while there is not enough risk-taking equity capital. What is needed are institutional innovations and regulatory reforms that would correct such an imbalance and mismatch between demand and supply in terms of the risk characteristics of funds. This is the missing link in the present financial system.

What is not so obvious is the form of such a missing link. What is needed here is some kind of collective investment schemes (CISs) that pool funds from risk-taking investors through either public offerings or private placements and invest them in SMEs through equity or convertible bonds or other vehicles in exchange for managerial control or involvement. Such CISs are positioned on the borderline between financial intermediaries and non-financial companies. Accordingly, it is not clear how they should be regulated. Unlike regulated mutual funds, they are not bound to invest only in marketable securities in financial markets. In fact, they serve as the counterpart of mutual funds by investing in private SMEs. The actual institutional forms they take can be flexible. In the present context of China, several institutions such as holding companies and trust and investment companies (TICs) perform part of such a function. To a certain extent, the new state asset management agency performs a similar function for SOEs. Perhaps, a holding company is closest to the concept of such a CIS. The operation of such a CIS will end up as a holding company for a kind of conglomerate of mixed businesses. The constituent parts of such a conglomerate can be related or unrelated.

In terms of the regulatory framework, there is not much problem on the side of non-financial business. Such CISs can be structured as shareholding companies and limited partnerships. What is problematic is on the financial side. The present financial regulatory framework imposes strict restrictions on which institutions can raise funds from the public. Partly because of the less successful and pleasant experience with TICs in the 1980s and rural cooperative funds in the early 1990s, China's current financial regulatory framework stifles the emergence of non-bank financial institutions that operate at the far end of high-risk/high-returns intermediation. What is needed on the side of financial regulation is to loosen up the restrictions on which kind of entities can raise speculative funds from risk-taking investors. In principle, it is desirable to push some funds out of the banking system to become equity capital.

### High-tech start-ups and venture capital

A particular example of such CISs is venture capital that nurtures high-tech start-ups, a special subset of SMEs. High-tech start-ups have the potential for exceptional growth if the products and services under development turn out to be successful. But, in the initial phase, there are no revenues and profits. Hence, they are not the ideal clients for bank loans, because they have no accounts receivable, inventory, collaterals, and equity. That is where venture capital fits in and is the right kind of intermediary. It provides funds in the form of equity. In exchange for their investment, they usually control or are deeply involved with the management of such high-tech start-ups. The mission of venture capital is to bring a high-tech start-up company to the stage of an IPO when the company has successfully commercialized new products and services. At that stage, venture capital can recover its investment with a handsome reward and pass the company to the capital market and banks for external finance. In the context of the Chinese economy, many venture capital funds have been set up. Many of them are invested by the government. In the future, what is needed is funds with private capital.

## Management buyouts

Management leveraged buy-outs (MBOs) are another case that may involves such CISs. In privatizing sizeable SOEs, one method that has been considered and used is MBOs. In this case, top managers would like to take over the control of a SOE. However, in many cases, managers may not have adequate funds of their own. They need access to external finance. Again, in this case, MBOs are risky undertakings, so they are not an appropriate use of bank loans. In fact, it is prohibited under current financial regulations in China. In America, MBOs were in fashion in the late 1980s, fueled by large issues of junk bonds. The use of junk bonds is another case of high-risk/high-returns financial intermediation outside the banking channels. In America, the bond market is developed enough to serve as a deep source of funds. In China, the corporate bond market is still in the infant stage. The use of junk bonds through public offerings is not yet feasible. Yet, privately placed convertible bonds purchased by the CISs as described above may be a feasible arrangement in China today. In fact, many foreign strategic investors have come to China with a view to purchase those SOEs on offer in collaboration with insider managers. Such a vehicle of equity investment should be available to domestic investors as well.

## Consolidation and rationalization

So far, we have been discussing various remedies to improve the external finance of SMEs. It is also important to observe that not all SMEs should be helped. In many sectors, there is excessive fragmentation and duplication. Therefore, a fundamental structural adjustment that China needs to undertake is consolidation and rationalization. This process is now being facilitated and accelerated by the recent construction of highway networks and a gradual reduction in regional trade barriers. Spatially, the Chinese economy is becoming more integrated.

Consolidation and rationalization have two important implications for the financial sector. One implication is that the financial sector needs to facilitate mergers and acquisitions (MAs) with financial innovations. So far, consolidation into large enterprise groups has been largely marriages arranged by the government. Such government-arranged marriages are necessary as a transitional measure because, in the past, most large enterprises involved in acquisitions and mergers were state owned and/or still in the corporatization process. However, such forced marriages will not work in the long run. What is needed urgently is a market-based process of consolidation and restructuring. On the part of financial institutions, a merchant banking sector specialized in MAs is still a very underdeveloped area in China. The underdevelopment of merchant banking is largely due to the regulatory restrictions, on the one hand, and the lack of suitable candidates for MAs, on the other hand. But now the situation has changed dramatically. The corporatization process has been largely completed, especially for most SMEs. Traditional SOEs have been withering away. NSEs have become the main players in industry and commerce. With accession to the WTO, foreign investment can come in not only as greenfield investment, but also through MAs. The stage for a boom in MAs has been set. The only thing needed is a takeoff in merchant banking and MA activities.

By their nature, MA activities are a high-risk venture. Bank loans may not be the most appropriate source of funding. Therefore, risk-taking investors need to play an active role. Further financial innovations and regulatory modernization are required to channel alternative sources of funds into MAs either from the organized capital market or through private placements. Again, the CISs described above may serve as a useful vehicle for pooling the funds from risk-taking investors.

The other implication for the financial sector is not to prop up many weak SMEs in manufacturing with more funding. Consolidation requires not only the formation of large enterprises through acquisitions and mergers, but also the weeding out of many unviable SMEs. Both are part and parcel of the same process.

## Conclusion

The enterprise landscape in China has changed fundamentally. NSEs have become the predominant players in production and commerce. Traditional SOEs are withering away. What is perceived to be the external finance problem is mainly a problem for SMEs. What is perceived as a bias in the lending of state banks is largely a natural bias for large capital-intensive enterprises. Curtailing lending to SOEs really does help to solve SMEs' problem. But a mushrooming of many private banks does not provide an effective immediate fix. To improve the access to external finance for SMEs, efforts must be made simultaneously on the part of the financial sector as well as on the part of SMEs. The financial institutions need to improve corporate governance, possibly through divesting some of their shares to foreign and private investors. Also important is more flexibility for these institutions to set lending rates according to the risk premium of their clients. More importantly, vehicles must be found through innovation and deregulation to enhance the supply of risk-taking equity capital to SMEs. On the part of SMEs, one way to improve their access to external finance is consolidation, especially in manufacturing. By getting larger through growth, merger, or being acquired, they can attain better access not only to bank loans, but also possibly to the capital market. To facilitate market-based consolidation, it is urgent to encourage the development of merchant banking and open up various avenues of risk-taking funds.

### Note

1   M2 – the sum of currency and bank deposits, approximately.

### References

Asian Development Bank (2005) *Key Indicators 2004: Population and Human Resource Trends and Challenges*, Asian Development Bank.

Caprio, G. and D. Klingebiel (1996) "Bank Insolvency: Cross-Country Experiences," *World Bank Working Paper* 1620, World Bank.

Diaz-Alejandro, C. (1985) "Good-Bye Financial Repression, Hello Financial Crash," *Journal of Development Economics*, 19: 1–24.

Gregory, N. and S. Tenev (2001) "The Financing of Private Enterprise in China," *Finance and Development*, 38: 14–17.

National Bureau of Statistics of China (various issues) *The Statistical Yearbook of China*, National Bureau of Statistics of China.

OECD (2002) *China in the World Economy: The Domestic Policy Challenges*, OECD.

The People's Bank of China (2003) *Monetary Policy Report, 2002*, The People's Bank of China.

# 5 Commercial bank regulation and supervision

## US experiences and implications for China

*Jing Lu*

## Introduction

China's banking industry is facing even more prominent challenges. The largely state-monopolized banks are severely handicapped with non-performing loans. The existing large volume of non-performing loans already presents a daunting task for banks to remain solvent, let alone to have room for further changes and development. Also, China's growing market economy increasingly demands more effective and efficient financial services. The degree of financial development signifies the sophistication of a market economy. China's backwardness in its banking operations will likely hinder the further development of its market economy, if not destabilize the financial and economic systems. In addition, China's membership of the World Trade Organization (WTO) entails opening up its financial sector to foreign competition. In the face of fierce competition from global financial conglomerates, China's situation will likely place it in a vulnerable position. The gain from manufacturing industry is likely to be compromised by its ill-functioning financial industry.

Along with the general consensus that eminent reformation of China's banking industry is inevitable, an important logistic question is how to incorporate bank regulation and supervision as an integral package into China's banking reforms. This chapter presents two major discussions based on the author's several years of hands-on experience in the US Federal Reserve System and at a global banking organization. The first part lays the foundation for bank regulation and supervision as they are currently carried out in the US by the Federal Reserve System (FRS). It should be noted, while the banking industry encompasses a number of areas and sectors, this chapter focuses more exclusively on commercial banks, as they are the focal point of the FRS' regulation and supervision, and they are most relevant to the current banking system in China. This section also provides discussions on banks' self-regulation and corporate governance, as they are an indispensable part of banks' management and have been particularly emphasized recently by the regulators. The second part discusses a number of implications from the US experience for China's banking reforms. The US currently possesses the most advanced and sophisticated banking system with a rich history of checks and balances. China can inevitably draw many lessons from this wealth of knowledge to provide benchmarks and shortcuts for its future endeavors.

Specifically, this chapter is organized as follows. The first section of the first part defines a commercial bank in relation to other banking and financial institutions. It is important to distinguish the function and boundary of each institution, even though the distinction has become blurred in recent decades. Only after making such a distinction will we be able to narrow our discussions to what FRS' regulation and supervision are about in the subsequent sections. The second section presents the regulatory structure of a typical commercial bank. A commercial bank in the US is usually subject to examination by a number of regulators with different mandates and priorities. The third and fourth sections provide a more detailed account of bank regulation and supervision, respectively, as they are currently practiced in the FRS. A list of regulations and policy and procedures is presented in these two sections. The fifth section describes the importance of a bank's internal control and corporate governance in the prudent management of a bank, without which government regulation and supervision will not come to fruition.

The first section of the second part describes the urgency of China's banking reforms in light of domestic pressure and international competition based on economic theory and evidence. The second section calls for stringent and comprehensive bank regulation and supervision as the financial sector possesses a unique characteristic of self-fulfilling prophecy in which confidence plays a critical role. On the other hand, as discussed in the third section, regulators need to be flexible and forward looking to design a system that can accommodate the dynamics of the highly innovative financial market. The fourth section cautions that there needs to be close coordination among regulators as the distinction between product and institution lines will become blurred. Regulators need to present a consistent and non-overlapping approach in supervising banks and other institutions. The fifth section emphasizes the importance of staff training and retention, as they are the backbone for carrying out the logistic functions. The last section of this part re-emphasizes the importance of the self-regulation of a bank, above and beyond government regulation and supervision.

## Commercial bank regulation and supervision in the US

### *Commercial banks and other financial institutions*

A commercial bank is traditionally defined as a financial institution that accepts deposits, makes business loans, and offers related services, also called a depository institution. The core of commercial banking is to intermediate the business of borrowing and lending money. The borrowers are mostly businesses, individuals, and governmental units with a variety of needs for funding. The lenders or depositors are businesses and individuals with savings or excess cash to invest.

Depository institutions are important in the economy, holding a large share of the nation's money stock in the form of various types of deposits, and providing for the transfer of those funds to effect the payments that keep the economy functioning. They also lend these funds directly to consumers and businesses for a full range of purposes and lend them indirectly by investing in securities. They play a key role in the transmission of monetary policy to the financial markets, to borrowers and depositors and, ultimately, to the real economy. For many decades, commercial banks were unique in conducting all types of banking.

Over the past quarter of a century, banking in the US has changed dramatically. With banking deregulation under the pressure of competition, broader access to the money and capital markets, and the advancement of information and technology, the banking landscape in the US has been irrevocably reshaped. Other depository institutions have been established to compete with the services traditionally provided by commercial banks. These so-called thrifts, comprising savings banks, savings and loan associations, provide individuals with selected banking services, such as savings accounts, mortgage loans, and even checkable deposits. As a result, commercial banks have dropped considerably in their share of the deposit-taking and lending businesses. However, they are still the dominant force behind the bulk of the myriad commercial transactions.

More dramatic changes in the financial sector lie in the erosion of traditional banking services by non-depository institutions. From the liability side of a bank, for example, savings deposits have historically been the exclusive purview of depository institutions. However, a money market mutual fund can provide equivalent liquidity, easy access, and a more competitive rate, which serves as an appealing alternative to a savings account. Also, a security broker's cash management account is functionally identical to a checking account, providing check-writing and other related services. From the asset side of a bank, corporate, state, and government borrowers can now find substitutes for bank loans by borrowing from the commercial paper and bond market through an investment bank. Also, with the development of derivative products such as options, futures, and swaps, the line between banks and insurance companies is blurred. Many insurance companies are using, say, the tool of options to provide insurance/hedge to their customers.

The effects of increased competition with banks for deposits and loans are apparent. Measured in relative terms, the commercial banking industry's balance sheet has shrunk dramatically since the mid-1970s. Commercial banking deposits as a share of all household assets have fallen to the lowest level. Bank credit as a share of domestic non-financial debt has also declined sharply. These balance sheet trends have led some observers to pronounce the "decline" of banking.[1]

Commercial banks have expanded the scope of their services in the past several decades. They have increasingly overlapped with other financial industries, such as the securities and insurance businesses, in the services they offer. For example, in recent years, banking organizations have established and marketed mutual funds, packaged their loans and sold them as securities, entered the bond guarantee issuance and securities brokerage businesses, and begun to underwrite and trade corporate debt through their non-bank affiliates. All these activities can be manifested by the fact that non-interest income has become increasingly important in contributing to a bank's revenue versus the traditional interest income, which is derived from the interest spread of loans and deposits. Specifically, the non-interest income includes investment banking services (advisory, brokerage, and underwriting), revenues from venture capital investments, servicing fees [data processing, automated teller machine (ATM) usage fees, etc.], income from asset securitization activities, insurance commissions and fees, and proceeds from sales of loans, other real estate, and other assets. Commercial banks have also ventured into non-traditional areas of investment banking, insurance, and asset securitization. Consolidation of banks and other types of financial institutions is one of the most notable features of the international financial landscape over the past decade and is likely to persist.

As a result of such a market trend of consolidation among financial institutions and of the concern for competitiveness of the US corporations, the Federal Reserve System approved the 1998 merger of Citigroup. Citigroup is a conglomerate financial institution combining three giants in their respective industries: a commercial bank (Citibank), an investment bank (Salomon Smith Barney), and an insurance company (Travelers Group). The creation of Citigroup is an important landmark in the US banking industry, signaling a breakdown of the Glass–Steagall Act. The Glass–Steagall Act, passed during the great depression era of the 1930s, forced the separation of commercial banks from investment banks. This act dominated US finance for half a century. In 1999, the Glass–Steagall Act was abolished and replaced by the Gramm–Leach–Bliley Act, which permits the integration of financial services under one conglomerate company, a so-called financial holding company. The Gramm–Leach–Bliley Act represents an important landmark in US financial history. It reversed the arbitrariness of the separation of commercial banking from investment banking, and acknowledged the efficiency and synergy gained by offering financial services under one roof. The Gramm–Leach–Bliley Act is arguably the most significant banking legislation to emerge from the last quarter of the twentieth century.

### Regulatory structure of commercial banks

A commercial bank in the US can be either federally/nationally chartered or state chartered. In the former case, it is called a national bank; in the latter, it is called a state chartered bank. All national banks are chartered by the federal government through the Office of the Comptroller of the Currency (OCC)[2] in the Department of the Treasury. They are required to obtain membership of the Federal Reserve System (FRS).[3] State chartered banks are chartered through each different state. While they have the option of becoming a member of the FRS, most large banks opt for this membership for the convenience and services provided by the FRS.

All nationally chartered banks, such as Citibank and Bank of China's US branches, are under the supervision and regulation of the OCC. In the case of state chartered banks who are members of the FRS, such as JP Morgan Chase and Bank of New York, the FRS and the respective State Banking Department[4] have the responsibility to examine banks on an alternating yearly basis. State chartered banks without FRS membership are examined alternately by the State Banking Department and the Federal Deposit Insurance Corporation (FDIC).[5]

A bank is also a public company whose stocks are exchange traded, and is under the supervision of the Securities and Exchange Commission (SEC),[6] whose priority is to ensure the transparency of information and truthfulness of financial statements.

If a commercial bank has international presence, its foreign branches and offices are also subject to examination by foreign regulators, such as the Financial Services Authority in the UK, the Financial Services Agency of Japan, the Monetary Authority of Singapore, etc.

For the rest of this chapter, discussions will be centered on the practices of bank regulation and supervision by the FRS, as the Federal Reserve has been given most mandates in the stabilization of the US financial system and is most familiar to the author. Nevertheless, as bank supervisors increasingly exercise coordinated supervision, issue common regulations and laws, and leverage off each other's experiences, the differences among them are blurred. For example, all regulators emphasize the safety and soundness of a bank's operations using a risk-focused approach; FRS and the State Banking Department iterate their examination on a yearly basis and coordinate their findings and follow-ups.

In general, bank regulation and supervision are distinct but complementary activities. Bank regulation entails making and issuing specific regulations and guidelines governing the structure and conduct of banking, under the authority of legislation. Bank supervision involves monitoring, inspecting, and examining banking organizations to assess their condition and compliance with relevant laws and regulations.

The establishment of financial holding companies, such as Citigroup, which encompasses commercial banks, investment banks, and insurance services, has presented new challenges to the regulatory structure. Which government agency is responsible for the regulation and supervision of such a conglomerate is one of those challenges. A legislative statute has been established under the Gramm–Leach–Bliley Act stating that such a have-all financial holding company requires a coordinated effort among regulators. Specifically, the FRS is assigned to be an umbrella supervisor for the financial holding company, playing a coordinating role between functional regulators. Functional regulators are responsible for their respective industries. For example, in the case of Citigroup, OCC is responsible for the Citibank, SEC is responsible for Salomon Smith Barney, and the state insurance regulator is responsible for the Travelers entity. It has been emphasized repeatedly that supervision and regulation should be comprehensive yet non-overlapping, so as to have nothing fall through the cracks while reducing regulatory burdens on institutions.

An interesting case study to note is the roller coaster of the thrift industry in the 1970s and 1980s. As mentioned in the previous section, thrifts are deposit-taking, commercial bank-like savings and loan associations. They were initially established to complement the services provided by commercial banks. While commercial banks made loans to businesses, thrifts found a niche with small savers and consumers. While commercial banks favored short-term business loans, thrifts lent to small consumers who wanted long-term real estate loans. Thrifts flourished as a result of deregulation (in particular, Regulation □), which allowed them to compete with commercial banks for deposits by offering higher interest rates on deposits. Over time, the power of the thrift institutions expanded to overlap those of commercial banks. However, the sharply rising interest rates in the 1970s and 1980s forced them to pay high interest rates on short-term liabilities that were unfortunately balanced by low-interest rate, long-term earning assets. To compensate for this shortfall in interest spread, many thrifts gambled on high-risk assets such as high yields, further compounding their problems. Resulting from the savings and loan crisis, more than 40 percent of thrifts went bankrupt, and the Office of Thrift Supervision (OTS)[7] was created to regulate and supervise this loosely controlled industry. More recently, financial institutions have gone through a wave of merger and acquisition as a result of further deregulation. Many thrift institutions, particularly those with financial difficulties, have either merged or been bought out. This contraction of the thrift industry has left commercial banks the predominant depository institution.

### Bank regulation by the federal reserve system

The FRS as a whole is responsible for establishing standards to ensure the safe and sound operation of financial institutions. The regional Federal Reserve Banks are responsible for enforcing these regulations, rules, policy guidelines, and supervisory interpretations at the institutions they supervise. The FRS also enforces various laws and regulations related to fair and equitable treatment in financial transactions, to margin requirements in securities and futures markets, and to record keeping and reporting by depository institutions. Table 5.1 gives a brief description of each of the FRS regulations.

Apart from the aforementioned regulations, there are also Supervision and Regulation Letters, commonly known as SR Letters, that address significant policy and procedural matters related to the FRS' supervisory responsibilities. Issued by the Board of Governors' Division of Banking Supervision and Regulation, SR Letters are an important means of disseminating information to banking supervision staff at the Board and the Reserve Banks and, in some instances, to supervised banking organizations. For example, the important Basel Capital Accord for banks' capital adequacy requirements was issued through SR Letters.

SR Letters are classified into the following eight main functional areas: Applications (APP); Enforcement (ENF); General (GEN); National Information Center (NIC); Specialized Banking Activities (SPE); Surveillance (SRV); Financial Institution Supervision (SUP); Training (TRN).

Other policies and procedures related to FRS' supervisory responsibilities are also disseminated through the following manuals, which are available from the FRS website. They include:

*Table 5.1* Regulation codes

| Regulation code | Title |
| --- | --- |
| A | Extensions of credit by Federal Reserve Banks |
| B | Equal credit opportunity |
| C | Home mortgage disclosure |
| D | Reserve requirements of depository institutions |
| E | Electronic fund transfers |
| F | Limitations on interbank liabilities |
| G | Disclosure and reporting of Community Reinvestment ACT (CRA)-related agreements |
| H | Membership of state banking institutions in the Federal Reserve System |
| I | Issue and cancellation of Federal Reserve Bank capital stock |
| J | Collection of checks and other items by Federal Reserve Banks and funds transfers through Fedwire |
| K | International banking operations |
| L | Management official interlocks |
| M | Consumer leasing |
| N | Relations with foreign banks and bankers |
| O | Loans to executive officers, directors, and principal shareholders of member banks |
| P | Privacy of consumer financial information |
| Q | Prohibition against payment of interest on demand deposits |
| S | Reimbursement to financial institutions for providing financial records; record-keeping requirements for certain financial records |
| T | Credit by brokers and dealers |
| U | Credit by banks or persons other than brokers or dealers for the purpose of purchasing or carrying margin stocks |
| V | Fair credit reporting (proposed) |
| W | Transactions between banks and their affiliates |
| Y | Bank holding companies and change in bank control |
| Z | Truth in lending |
| AA | Unfair or deceptive acts or practices |
| BB | Community reinvestment |
| CC | Availability of funds and collection of checks |
| DD | Truth in savings |
| EE | Netting eligibility for financial institutions |
|  | Miscellaneous interpretations |

- Bank Holding Company Supervision Manual;
- Bank Secrecy Act Manual;
- Commercial Bank Examination Manual;
- Examination Manual for US Branches and Agencies of Foreign Banking Organizations;
- FFIEC Information Systems Handbook;
- Guidelines and Instructions for Examination of Edge Corporations;
- Manual on Procedures for Processing Applications and Notifications for Bank Holding Companies and State Member Banks;
- Trading and Capital Markets Activities Manual;
- Transfer Agent Examination Manual;
- Trust Examination Manual.

These manuals contain important policies and procedures for the regulators and the banks. Take the Commercial Bank Examination Manual as an example, it presents examination objectives and procedures that FRS examiners follow in evaluating the safety and soundness of state member banks. It is intended as guidance to Federal Reserve supervisory personnel in planning and conducting bank examinations. On the other hand, banking institutions can use it to plan for FRS examinations and to reasonably anticipate upcoming procedures. The manual should not, however, be considered as a legal reference to the regulations of the Federal Reserve Board and federal banking laws.

### Bank supervision by the Federal Reserve System

*Objectives*

There are four major objectives of the supervisory process:

1  Provides flexible and responsive supervision. Supervision is considered to be a dynamic and forward-looking process. It should respond to technological advances and product innovations.
2  Fosters consistency, coordination, and communication among the appropriate supervisors. Supervision should be seamless and non-overlapping so as to reduce regulatory burden and duplication. It should use resources already available such as internal and external risk assessment and monitoring systems.
3  Promotes safety and soundness of financial institutions. Supervision includes evaluation of risk management systems, financial condition, and compliance with laws and regulations.
4  Provides a comprehensive assessment of the institution. It should integrate specialty areas, such as information technology (IT), trust, capital markets, and consumer compliance, into a comprehensive assessment of the institution.

*Risk-based approach*

Historically, bank examiners relied significantly on a transaction testing approach and verified the transaction's adherence to internal policies, procedures, and control. Typically, they selected a sample of representative transactions, largely loans, and assessed whether they satisfied the requirements of safe and sound operation surrounding the transactions.

In a highly dynamic banking market, however, transaction testing by itself is not sufficient for ensuring continued safety and soundness. Evolving financial instruments and markets have enabled banking organizations to rapidly reposition their portfolio risk exposures. Therefore, periodic assessment cannot keep pace with the fast paced changes occurring in financial risk profiles.

Today, bank supervisors adopt a risk-focused approach in examining banks. They base their analysis more on risky areas and the strength of controls surrounding the risks, rather than on the strength of the balance sheet. When the risks are low, no transaction testing will be necessary. Types of risks that supervisors focus on include credit, market, liquidity, operational, legal, and reputational. This change in approach reflects the responsiveness of bank regulators toward changing business imperatives and dynamics.

*Off-site supervision and on-site examination*

Supervision practices consist of off-site supervision and on-site examination. Off-site supervision pertains to periodic review of financial and other information about banks. Information includes reports of recent examinations and inspections, information published in the financial press, and, most important, the standard financial regulatory reports filed by institutions. All the information prepares supervisors for their on-site examination.

During on-site examination, examiners evaluate the soundness of the institution's assets and the effectiveness of internal operations, policies, and management, analyze key financial factors such as capital, earnings, liquidity, and sensitivity to interest rate risk, assess the institution's exposure to off-balance-sheet risks, check for compliance with banking laws and regulations, and determine the institution's overall soundness and solvency.

*Process and products*

The examination process is categorized into the six steps, and the resulting paperwork shown in Table 5.2.

*Rating of a bank – CAMELS*

During an on-site bank examination, supervisors gather private institutional information, such as details on problem loans or losses in trading. This information is used to evaluate a bank's financial condition and control, and to monitor its

*Table 5.2* Steps in the bank examination process

| Steps | Products |
| --- | --- |
| Understanding the institution | Institutional overview – describe organization structure, business strategies, financial condition, internal and external audit reports, etc. |
| Assessing the institution's risk | Risk matrix and risk assessment – highlight strengths and weaknesses of the institution in managing and controlling risks and the focus of supervisory concerns. Risks are classified as high, medium, or low in each risk area |
| Planning and scheduling supervisory activities | Supervisory plan and examination program – prioritize supervisory resources to higher risk areas, coordinate examinations of different disciplines and with other regulators, provide general logistic information and a comprehensive list of examination activities, etc. |
| Defining examination activities | Scope memorandum and entry letter – scope memo documents specific objectives of the projected examinations, activities and risks to be reviewed, and procedures that are to be followed, etc. Entry letter is presented to the institution stating the examination objective and procedures, and usually includes a list of information requests |
| Performing examination procedures | Functional examination modules – list steps taken to determine whether the institution's management understands and adequately controls the levels and types of risks that are assumed |
| Reporting the findings | Examination reports – a comprehensive summary report is issued to the institution that supports the organization's assigned ratings and encompasses the results of the entire supervisory cycle |

compliance with laws and regulatory policies. A key product of such an examination is a supervisory rating of the bank's overall condition, commonly referred to as a CAMELS rating.

This rating system was created in 1979 by regulatory agencies, and is used by the three federal banking supervisors (FRS, FDIC, and OCC) and other financial supervisory agencies to provide a convenient summary of bank conditions during an examination.

The acronym "CAMEL" refers to the five components of a bank's condition that are assessed: capital adequacy, asset quality, management, earnings, and liquidity. A sixth component, a bank's sensitivity to market risk, was added in 1997 to reflect the increasing importance of market risk for an institution. Thus, the acronym was changed to CAMELS. Ratings are assigned for each component in addition to the overall rating of a bank's financial condition. The ratings are assigned on a scale from 1 to 5. Banks with ratings of 1 or 2 are considered to present few, if any, supervisory concerns. Banks with ratings of 3, 4, or 5 present moderate to extreme degrees of supervisory concern.[8]

*Supervisory actions*

In the course of ongoing supervision, the FRS may determine that a bank has problems that affect the institution's safety and soundness, or it is not in compliance with laws and regulations. In these circumstances, the FRS may place the organization under a supervisory action to ensure that it undertakes measures to correct the deficiencies or weaknesses. The degree of risk to the institution, or the extent of non-compliance with laws and regulations, will, among other factors, dictate the scope of the supervisory action.

Generally, these findings are first communicated during the examination process through meetings and correspondence with management and directors of the organization. Bank management typically addresses the deficiencies, and no further action is needed. However, in some situations, the FRS may need to take an informal supervisory action, by requesting that an institution adopt a broad resolution or agree to the provisions of a "memorandum of understanding" to address the problem.

If necessary, the FRS may take formal enforcement actions to compel the management and directors of a troubled banking organization to address the organization's problems. In these instances, the FRS may enter into a written agreement with the institution, or may issue a cease and desist order against the institution or individual associated with the institution, including an officer or director. The FRS may also assess a fine and/or remove an officer or director from office and permanently bar him or her from the banking industry.[9]

### Corporate governance

There has recently been a great deal of attention paid to the importance of corporate governance. Supervisory experience underscores the necessity of having the appropriate levels of accountability and checks and balances within each bank. Sound corporate governance enhances supervisors' capability and provides supervisors with an extra degree of confidence. Corporate governance can also contribute to a collaborative working relationship between bank management and bank supervisors. Put another way, regulatory supervision will not function as well if sound corporate governance is not in place. Consequently, regulatory supervisors have a strong interest in ensuring that there is effective corporate governance in every banking organization.

Corporate governance is divided into internal control and market discipline. For the former, there are four important forms of internal oversight that should be included in the organizational structure of any bank to ensure appropriate checks and balances. They should be viewed as critical elements of any internal control process.

First, there should be oversight by the board of directors or supervisory board. Board members should be qualified for their positions, have a clear understanding of their role in corporate governance, and not be subject to undue influence from management or outside concerns. The board, along with senior managers, should establish strategic objectives and a set of corporate values that are communicated through the banking organization.

Second, there should be oversight by senior managers not involved in the day-to-day running of various business areas. Senior managers should set strategies for the banks' operations and establish accountability for executing these strategies. There should be transparency of information related to existing conditions.

Third, there should be clear lines of responsibility and accountability throughout the organization. There should also be processes in place to ensure the fulfillment of those roles and responsibilities.

Last, but not the least, institutions should establish independent risk management and audit functions. They provide another independent set of judgments on the risks taken by business lines and the effectiveness of control surrounding the risks.

For external control mechanisms, regulators have put strong emphasis on information disclosure and transparency. Information is crucial to market participants such as external audits, credit-rating agencies, stock exchanges, investors, and many others to make well-informed judgments, and discipline the institution when necessary. As institutions have grown in size and scope, innovative financing techniques have made it more difficult for outside investors to understand a particular firm's risk profile and the performance of its business lines. To reduce this opaqueness, it is necessary that sufficient, timely, accurate, and relevant information be available to market participants for them to evaluate a firm's risk profile and adjust the availability and pricing of funds to promote a more efficient allocation of financial resources. The Financial Accounting Standards Board and the bank supervisory agencies have enhanced disclosure and financial reporting requirements to make bank risks more transparent. Adequate disclosure and accounting are fundamental to bringing about effective market discipline.

## Implications of China's banking reforms

### Necessity and urgency of banking reform

There used to be a fallacy in China, as well as among western economists, that the manufacturing (including agriculture) industry was the most important sector in the economy. Manufacturing produced concrete tangible goods for consumption and increasing well-being. Meanwhile, the service industry, such as retail/wholesale and finance, was regarded as of a lower order. It merely maneuvered products from one end to the other. Sometimes, it might even wreak havoc on the economy, like the speculative financial sector, disrupting the manufacturing cycle.

Over the decades, as markets have matured and economic thinking has been developed, this fallacy has been abandoned. Accepted and supported are the theory[10] and evidence that the service industry is an indispensable and integral part of a market economy. Moreover, as markets deepen, this sector will play an increasingly important role.

A market economy, by name, is a market-centered infrastructure that promotes labor specialization, increases productivity, and thus creates more wealth. It differs fundamentally from a self-sufficient society; it does not produce its own consumption; rather, it produces for the consumption of other people. This creates a gap between production and consumption, and a central problem of how to match production with consumption. Supposedly, a market economy closes this gap through various markets, as its name suggests; however, it does not perform this job automatically. It requires multiple market makers to play a role matching, screening, price setting, information filtering, quality guaranteeing, etc. In other words, market makers, also called intermediaries, bring consumers and producers together, making demand and supply intersect. They are critical in sustaining the market economy. Even though they do not add concrete value to the products, without them, a market economy will cease to function and fail to exist.

As the market deepens and expands further with more sophisticated labor specialization and product differentiation, there will be a stronger demand for intermediaries to link the ever more specialized and fragmented markets. It is only natural to witness the increasing importance of the service sector. This increasing importance is also manifested by the fact that the service industry, compared with manufacturing industry, has contributed to an increasingly larger share of gross national product (GNP) and employed an increasingly larger portion of the labor force in developed countries. No wonder some developed countries are debating over becoming service-oriented economies.

The financial sector is but one of the intermediaries in the economy to facilitate funding transactions, channeling funds from suppliers who have an excess of capital to consumers who are in need of capital. An efficient and effective financial sector helps potential borrowers and lenders to find the most advantageous terms. It brings cheaper funding to corporations and households, providing various feasible alternatives to corporations and investors. It reduces financial transaction costs and enables a market economy to run more efficiently. The flip side of the same argument contends that, if financial intermediaries operate in a less efficient and effective manner, they will hamper the development or advancement of the market economy, creating dead-weight loss to other sectors. It is likely that the hard-won gain from other sectors will easily be sacrificed by the poorly operating financial sector.

The current situation in China's financial sector is less than optimistic. The largely state-monopolized banks are severely handicapped with non-performing loans. The non-performing loans account for nearly 30–40 percent of banks' assets. This existing large volume of non-performing loans, regardless of its origin in state-run enterprises, policy loans, or even fraud, places banks in a vulnerable position. It is a daunting task for the banks to balance their balance sheets and remain solvent, let alone transform themselves into market-driven enterprises to catch up with the increasingly market-oriented economy.

Furthermore, in the face of domestic and international pressure to open up the financial market, China's banks are likely to suffer further dire consequences of losing funds and customers while being trapped by bad loans. In the end, when customers start to lose their confidence in China's banking system, fear for the safety of their deposits, and withdraw their funds in hordes, a series of bank runs will likely occur, and financial crisis will soon follow.

In summary, China should not be complacent about its current success in a labor-intensive manufacturing sector. To successfully remodel itself into a market economy and catch up with leading economies, it has to carry out a lot of ingenious hard work and create comparable market institutions. Among all its other endeavors, the reformation and transformation of the banking sector is imperative.

### Stringent and comprehensive bank regulation and supervision

The banking industry in the US is one of the most heavily regulated industries; among all banks, commercial banks endure the toughest restrictions. Banks commonly complain that they are over-regulated and underloved. On the other hand, however, commercial banks are also greatly protected by the government. There is a high entrance barrier for outsiders attempting to penetrate the US market.[11] Once having become an insider, commercial banks enjoy certain privileges such as the FRS' clearing and payment services. Commercial banks also benefit from the FDIC's deposit insurance safety net.

All these stringent requirements or barriers do not come indefinitely or automatically. They have been accumulated over a century's worth of trial and error, theory and practice. The numerous bank runs, the great depression, the self-fulfilling prophecy, and principal–agent problems all contribute to the current status.

The finance industry is the sector where invisible-hand efficiency market theory often fails to hold. The unique characteristic of financial markets is that they operate efficiently only to the extent that market participants have confidence in their ability to perform the roles they were designed for. The failure of one institution to honor its commitments leads to a general loss of confidence as individuals fear commitments made by similar institutions may also be dishonored. This loss of confidence exacerbates the failure of other similar institutions, leading to a series of bank runs. In economic theory, this is called a self-fulfilling prophecy.

Bank failure results in not only the loss of public confidence in the banking system or a greater risk of financial collapse, it could also provoke an economic downturn by restricting the supply of money and credit, and distorting economic perspective. Examples of such abound. Given such unique characteristics of the financial market where confidence plays an important role, regulators need to exert a strong influence in this market, acting as "lender of last resort" and standing ready to step in to restore market confidence.[12]

China's banking reforms should equally follow this principle, ensuring that the finance sector is a strength rather than a weakness of the economy. The strong regulation and supervision should be established to ensure that the banking sector operates in a safe and sound manner, and particularly to provide public confidence in the health and effectiveness of the banking sector. Also, the executive order from the government should gradually subside to the order of rules and laws. The principle of government intervention should be to prevent market failure in a stressful scenario, rather than to replace market function and fine-tuning under normal circumstances. Also, membership of the WTO and the Bank for International Settlements (BIS) should facilitate China's transition to keep pace with international standards. China faces challenges and pressures to modernize its bank regulation and supervision. This is one step toward reforming its domestic banking sector and regulating foreign banks in China.

China's banking reform can learn the importance of stringent bank regulation and supervision from the debacle of the savings and loan crisis in the 1980s in the US, as described previously. Savings and loan associations, also called thrifts, are depository institutions, functioning similarly to commercial banks. As a result of government deregulation of the banking sector, thrifts thrived and, in one instance, threatened the supremacy of commercial banks. Because of the nature of the thrifts in taking short-term deposits and offering long-term mortgage loans, during the interest rate hikes of the 1970s and 1980s, thrifts had severe financial crunches. In the face of such financial difficulties, some gambled in the junk-bond market, also euphemistically called the high-yield market, in an attempt to strike it rich, only to fail more miserably. As a result of this episode of reckless risk-taking without sufficient prudence and government regulation and supervision, 40 percent of thrifts failed and eventually went bankrupt. FDIC and, ultimately, taxpayers paid dearly for this downfall. Subsequently, the OTS was established in 1989 as a primary regulator for the largely neglected thrifts, supervising thrifts along the same lines as the OCC with national commercial banks and the FRS with state chartered commercial banks.

In summary, while it is well recognized that China's banking system falls behind international standards for a market economy, so that reformation is imperative, in terms of strategic considerations in the process of transformation, China should implement stringent and comprehensive bank regulation and supervision. China should reap the benefits of international experiences while avoiding the mishaps suffered by other countries.

### *Dynamics and flexibility of regulation and supervision*

The financial world is dynamic and innovative, aided by advancements in communications and technology. The regulation and supervision system should also be born out of the need to be forward looking and to design a system to be responsive to technological advances and product innovations. The job of bank supervisors is not to hinder the responsible pursuit of new opportunities and profits, not to eliminate risk, and perhaps not even to lower risk-taking activities. Rather, the objective of a supervisor is to assist in the banks' management of risk and to ensure that their controls evolve with their businesses.

The history of the FRS reveals how it has responded to new problems and changing conditions by significantly modifying its primary goals and techniques to achieve them. A few examples follow.

*Basel Capital Accord II*

The Basel Capital Accord I, when implemented in 1988, was considered to be pioneering and innovative. It designed a rule-based criterion to assign minimum capital requirements to banks to support their risk-taking activities. Over the years, however, Basel I has fallen behind industry developments in which some large, complex, internationally active banking organizations have started to use sophisticated portfolio techniques to measure risk. These more advanced and rigorous risk management techniques are useful for credit decision-making, and are also central to the development of new instruments for hedging, pricing, and mitigating credit risk.

To respond to industry advancement, the BIS committee is now actively working on Basel II in an attempt to accommodate the needs of these large institutions and to encourage their advancement in portfolio credit risk management.[13]

*Risk-focused approach versus transaction testing approach*

As described previously, bank examiners used to depend upon the transaction testing approach to verify an institution's safety and soundness. In a highly dynamic banking market, however, transaction testing by itself is not adequate. Financial instruments have evolved, and banking organizations can rapidly reposition their portfolio risk exposures. For example, security instruments are fairly liquid, unlike loan portfolios, which can sit on the books for years. More importantly, it is the risk of most concern to regulators, rather than the products. If the risks are low, no transaction testing will be necessary. Since the 1990s, the focus has been shifted to risk-based methodology.

*Market risk and credit risk*

Credit risk used to be a major risk factor that could drive a bank into insolvency. A bad loan to a corporation could be a significant loss on a bank's balance sheet. Over the years, banks tended to mitigate credit risk by diversifying their portfolio and installing a rigorous control process. In recent years, market risk has taken a prominent role. A few incidents have indicated that market risk alone could be quite costly, sometimes fatal, to a bank. Barings' collapse is one example; Sumitomo's copper scandal is another.[14] A rogue trader could have the means to increase a bank's risk profile significantly in a very short time. To emphasize the importance of market risk and the surrounding controls, the CAMEL rating system of the Federal Reserve has been changed to CAMELS with S added to signify sensitivity to market risk. Some Federal Reserve district banks even organized market risk teams to focus on market risk areas in a bank such as foreign exchange, interest rate, equity, and commodity.

Inevitably, China's banking sector will evolve rapidly, especially in light of the WTO-related participation of global institutions in China's market. Regulators in China are facing the daunting challenges of not only transforming domestic banks, but also regulating and supervising international banks. While China's regulators should tightly control and monitor the banking sector, they should also demonstrate foresight and flexibility in this changing environment. Ingenuity in regulation and supervision should encompass the fact that new financial products are to be developed to evade government regulation, many barriers to international capital mobility will be removed, and the global financial markets will become more fluid and liquid.

### Coordination among regulators

China now practices both the segregation of financial business for financial institutions and the segregation of supervision by the supervisory authorities. Specifically, banks in China cannot engage in insurance or securities business. The securities and insurance institutions cannot be involved in each other or in the banking business. The three industries, banking, securities, and insurance, are regulated by the Commission of Banking Regulation, the Commission of Securities Regulation, and the Commission of Insurance Regulation respectively. It has not been long since this system was put into practice, and its long-term efficiency is unknown.

This rudimentary regulatory structure is a first step toward systematic financial regulation and supervision. It demonstrates the dedication of the government to the modernization of this area. On a positive note, this regulatory structure has so far avoided the multilayered and often cumbersome regulatory structure in the US. A commercial bank in the US can potentially choose between three regulatory agencies, the FRS, the OCC, and the State Banking Department, each of which has the same mandate and uses a similar approach in examining the safety and soundness of a bank. The US structure requires tremendous coordination among regulators and is susceptible to bureaucracy, inefficiency, and regulatory burden on institutions. Learning from the awkwardness of the US structure, the UK has created a one-regulator system since 2000, Financial Services Authority, in an attempt to reduce the coordination problem. China's current regulatory structure has a clear distinction between institution lines and regulatory responsibilities. It should continue to present a unified, efficient, and consistent approach, maximizing the effectiveness of regulation and supervision while minimizing regulatory burden on institutions.

More challenges lie ahead as a result of the fiercely dynamic and innovative financial world. New products and strategies are constantly emerging to either gain competitive edge or achieve regulation. It is reasonably expected that the segregation of financial institutions will take place more in name than in reality. Products can offer both a security function and an insurance/hedging nature, and thus can literally be used by all three sectors. The line between all three sectors could be blurred, which presents a challenge to the regulators as to how to coordinate their regulation and supervision functions. A coordination failure could bring about unintended results, such as regulatory arbitrage, account arbitrage, or business arbitrage. The creation of Citigroup in the US, a conglomerate of commercial banking, investment banking, and insurance, is an indication that not only can product lines be blurred, but institutions can merge to offer all financial services on one spot. As a result of such a reality, the US has created umbrella supervision, with the FRS as the lead supervisor coordinating other functional supervisors.

Therefore, bank supervision and regulation should be seamless and non-overlapping so as to reduce regulatory burden and duplication. A well-designed policy may not work down the road. A separation of business into commercial banks, insurance, and securities may be blurred due to innovation of instruments. It is important that communication be well established between regulators. There is a fine line between regulation and over-regulation. On one hand, there needs to be regulation but, on the other hand, there is a risk of over-regulation. Over-regulation not only inhibits competition and innovation, but can also cause the very instability that it seeks to avoid. In the face of blurred product lines and institutions, there is a strong requirement for regulators to coordinate and cooperate, to provide comprehensive yet non-burdensome supervision.

### Staff training and retention

When it comes to the actual practice of bank supervision, a logistical concern is the skills and experience of staff members who carry out examinations and investigations. More effective regulation and supervision would require a capable body of examiners to be able to understand the businesses, identify the risks, keep abreast of market developments, and successfully execute the examination programs. Thus, a challenge facing many regulators systematically recruiting and training examiners is not only to bring them up to the speed of banking operations, but also to familiarize them with government rules and laws and the examination approach.

The FRS has a rigorous training program for new-hire bank examiners, so-called assistant examiners. It involves a three-level approach that starts when the assistant examiner is hired and continues until he or she is commissioned. This program usually lasts about two to three years, and is intertwined with the examiner's on-the-job experience. It takes about two months each year to complete the training, some of which is paid training, maybe at another location in a different state, and some of which is personal time.

Level One stresses the core knowledge needed by every examiner regardless of the area of specialization. It provides a foundation of core knowledge of the regulatory and banking business. At this level, an examiner receives training on: (1) regulatory responsibilities; (2) financial analysis; (3) the business of banking; (4) identifying and assessing risks associated with the business of banking, and understanding basic integrated supervision concepts; and (5) interpersonal communication.

Level Two emphasizes an assistant examiner's specialty area. The training program includes four areas of specialization: safety and soundness, consumer affairs, information technology, and trust. In safety and soundness, for example, courses include operations and analysis school, report writing, conducting meetings with management, loan analysis school, and a number of self-study programs on regulations (such as Regulation Y and O, B, change in control), business concepts (such as information technology, mortgage securities, asset/liability management), and/or other technical information (such as how to read information contained in various reports).

Level Three focuses on understanding a bank's daily operations from the perspective of bank management. This level emphasizes operating a financial institution and managing the risks, rather than examining and regulating a financial institution. The assistant examiner also continues to develop the necessary skills for evaluating risk management examination processes and identifying supervisory issues prevalent in other specialty areas under an integrated approach. Courses include management skills, bank management, examination management, and other self-study materials.

Aside from this systematic training across the FRS, there are other training seminars and conferences organized by each district reserve bank. For example, in the New York Federation, because of the sophistication of the instruments and advanced technical tools used on Wall Street, examiners often need to go through training in exotic products and quantitative analysis. It is important that examiners do not fall behind the industry in their ability to identify problems before they become critical.

Another challenge facing regulators is retaining experienced examiners in the public regulatory sector. After going through the rigorous training program, examining a number of banks and gaining a valuable cross-institution perspective of banking operations, examiners usually become a hot property in the market for their experience. Further compounding the retention problem is the fact that the private sector is able to offer a higher salary and often better benefits. This makes it difficult for the regulators to retain talent and keep up with industry development. To respond to such a challenge, some district reserve banks have the discretion to adjust salary based on needs rather than on grade-level confinement. They may also have more liberty in hiring directly from the industry rather than from colleges.

### Corporate governance and self-regulation

Great emphasis has been laid recently on the importance of banks' corporate governance, including internal control and market discipline. Without sound corporate governance, regulatory supervision will not function as well, and supervisory actions will not be followed. Regulators have a strong interest in ensuring a proper internal check and balance is in place, and that management is capable of identifying weaknesses before they develop into systemic problems. In addition, market forces are a source of discipline. Market participants have a strong incentive to monitor and control the risks they assume because they bear the bottom-line consequences of their risk-taking decisions.

China's regulators should equally raise awareness of the value of good corporate governance. They should strive for effective implementation and enforcement of corporate governance laws and regulations. Banks should establish similar forms of internal oversight in the organizational structure, as described in the first part of this chapter. These forms of oversight should be viewed as critical components of the internal control of the corporate governance process. When examiners look into the operations of a bank, one critical aspect to check is the effectiveness of these components. With assurance of internal control, regulators can gain confidence in a bank's safety and soundness.

In a similar vein, critical components for external monitoring are information transparency and disclosures. They are central to well-informed investment decisions and market discipline. The adoption of international accounting, audit, and financial disclosure standards and practices will facilitate transparency, as well as comparability, of information across different institutions. Such features, in turn, strengthen market discipline as a means of improving corporate governance practice. To this end, regulators can identify a wide range of policy actions to realize the enormous potential of self-regulation and mobilize civil society in the enforcement process.

## Conclusion

International experience shows that an efficient and effective financial system promotes the sound operation of a market economy, whereas an ill-functioning financial apparatus not only threatens the collapse of its own but also endangers the normal functioning of other sectors. China's impoverished banking system has increasingly become a drag to its market economy. In the face of such domestic pressure and also international competition, urgent measures need to be taken to transform and modernize China's banking sector before it wreaks havoc on the whole economy.

This chapter discusses some ideas and thoughts on bank regulation and supervision, which should serve as an integral part of China's banking reform. In summary, bank regulation and supervision should be rigorous and comprehensive, and yet still be flexible and accommodating toward industry development. The success of bank regulation and supervision depends on coordination and cooperation among regulators, between regulators and banks, the quality of regulatory staff, and the self-regulation of the banking industry.

### Notes

1 For a more detailed account and statistics, refer to *US Monetary Policy and Financial Markets*, 1998, published by the Federal Reserve Bank of New York. The whole book can be downloaded from the website: http://www.ny.frb.org/pihome/addpub/monpol.

2 The OCC was established in 1863 by the National Currency Act as a bureau of the US Department of the Treasury. The OCC charters, regulates, and supervises all national banks. It also supervises the federal branches and agencies of foreign banks. Headquartered in Washington, DC, the OCC has six district offices plus an office in London to supervise the international activities of national banks.

3 The FRS, also known as the Fed, is the central bank of the United States. It was created by the Federal Reserve Act in 1913. The FRS is composed of a central, governmental

agency – the Board of Governors – in Washington, DC, and 12 regional Federal Reserve Banks located in major cities throughout the nation. Its mandate, apart from promoting the stability of the financial system, including bank regulation and supervision, includes conducting national monetary policy by influencing money and credit conditions in the economy, providing banking services to depository institutions and to the federal government, and ensuring that consumers receive adequate information and fair treatment in their interactions with the banking system.

4   Each State Banking Department has a mandate under the laws of its respective state. In general, it is the primary regulator for state-licensed and state chartered financial entities, including domestic banks, foreign agencies, branches and representative offices, savings institutions, and trust companies, mortgage bankers and brokers, and other financial institutions operating in the state.

5   The FDIC was created in 1933 as a result of the Banking Act of that year to provide insurance to deposits and promote safe and sound banking practices. Its mission is to maintain the stability of and public confidence in the nation's financial system. The FDIC, in conjunction with other federal and state regulatory agencies, examines financial institutions to ensure that they are conducting business in compliance with consumer protection rules and in a way that minimizes risk to their customers and to the deposit insurance funds.

6   The SEC was established in 1934 following the passage of the Securities Act of 1933 and the Securities Exchange Act of 1934. The primary mission of the SEC is to protect investors and maintain the integrity of the securities markets. The SEC requires public companies to disclose meaningful financial and other information to the public, which provides a common pool of knowledge for all investors to use to judge for themselves if a company's securities are a good investment. Headquartered in Washington, DC, the SEC has 11 regional and district offices throughout the country.

7   The OTS was established as a bureau of the US Department of the Treasury in 1989 as a result of the thrift crisis in the 1980s. Its mission is to effectively and efficiently supervise thrift institutions to maintain their safety and soundness.

8   All examination materials are highly confidential, including the CAMELS. A bank's CAMELS rating is known directly only by the bank's senior management and the appropriate supervisory staff. CAMELS ratings are never released by supervisory agencies, even on a lagged basis. While examination results are confidential, the public may infer such supervisory information on bank conditions based on subsequent bank actions or specific disclosures. Overall, the private supervisory information gathered during a bank examination is not disclosed to the public by supervisors, although studies show that it does filter into the financial markets.

9   There are a number of well-known cases in which the Federal Reserve and other regulatory agencies exercised formal enforcement actions. One case is the Salomon Brothers' Treasury auction scandal of 1991. A head trader submitted fraudulent bids for the US Treasury, in an attempt to garner a larger portion of the auction and ultimately dominate the market. After this scandal was discovered, the trader was fired, and his superiors at Salomon, all the way up the chain to Chief Executive Officer and Chairman, were forced to resign in disgrace. Salomon agreed to pay a penalty of US$290 million. It barely survived its primary dealership status in the US Treasury market.

Another case closer to China is the US$20 million penalty imposed by the OCC on the Bank of China's New York branch. The Bank of China has three branches in the US, two in New York and one in Los Angeles. OCC is the regulator for these US branches. The penalty was geared toward one of the New York branches, which was allegedly showing preferential treatment to certain customers, resulting in significant losses. The US$20 million fine was split equally between the OCC and the People's Bank of China, the regulator for the parent Bank of China.

10   The pioneer in this theory is Professor Ronald Coase, 1991 Nobel Laureate in Eco-

nomics. He discovered and clarified the significance of transaction costs for the institutional structure and functioning of the economy. Another pioneer in this field is Professor Douglas North, who was awarded the Nobel Prize in Economics in 1993 for his research in economic history which integrated economics, sociology, statistics, and history to explain economic and institutional change and the role that institutions play in economic growth. Both Professor Coase and Professor North are instrumental in "the new institutional economics."

11  Regulation H stipulates numerous qualitative and quantitative requirements for setting up banking offices and branches. Many Chinese banks, such as the Construction Bank, have tried to obtain a license to operate in the US, but have not succeeded so far. Also, it is easier to set up a limited-scope office than a full-blown branch. A full-scale branch can take deposits from the general public, which would act more like a commercial bank than otherwise.

12  There are numerous instances that demonstrate the FRS' readiness to intervene in the market for the purpose of restoring confidence and preventing market failure. In the summer of 1998, the stock market was crashing following the Asian currency crisis and the Russian treasury debt default. On one day (31 August 1998), the Dow Jones Industrial Average plunged 512 points, wiping out a year's worth of gains. World markets panicked. Immediately, the Federal Reserve Board announced that it would stand ready to provide liquidity services to any banks in need of such help. Also in 1998, the effort to bail out Long Term Capital Management was out of concern that, should it fail, its liquidation of billions worth of assets would likely create a downward spiral to the financial world, making the already depressed market even more gloomy.

13  The Bank for International Settlements (BIS) is an international organization that fosters international monetary and financial cooperation and serves as a bank for central banks. The third consultative paper of Basel II can be downloaded from the BIS website: http://www.bis.org. Currently, the Basel Committee aims to complete the New Capital Accord by the fourth quarter of 2003, with implementation to take effect in member countries by year-end 2006.

14  Barings, a 200-year-old British merchant bank, was brought down in 1995 by a rogue trader, Nick Leeson, who was trading unauthorized futures and options in Singapore. He had accumulated such a scale of loss that it exceeded the capital availability of Barings, which ultimately had to be bought out.

    The copper trading operation of Sumitomo Corporation, a non-financial company, had an accumulated loss of about US$2.6 billion in 1996 attributed to its head trader, Yasuo Hamanaka, for a period of more than ten years. He forged key documents that allowed him to conduct allegedly unauthorized trading in New York and London and corner the world copper market. Sumitomo did not fail as a result of this scandal thanks to its huge capital base, but its chairman and other senior managers resigned; Mr. Hamanaka was sentenced to eight years in jail.

# Part II

# Private enterprises, efficiency, and economic growth

# 6 Private enterprise development and the profitability of China's regional state-owned enterprises

*Shuanglin Lin and Wei Rowe*

## Introduction

After completing socialist economic reforms in 1957, China established numerous state-owned enterprises (SOEs). However, the inefficiency of the SOEs and other economic failures forced China to implement market-oriented economic reforms in 1978. Instead of privatizing SOEs instantaneously, as Russia did in the early 1990s, China has taken various measures to boost the profits of SOEs. Nevertheless, China's SOEs' profitability has declined significantly over the years. For example, return on total assets was 16.1 percent in 1978 and down to 3.3 percent in 2001. Specifically, regional SOEs' financial situations are worse than centrally controlled SOEs. For instance, in 2000, centrally controlled SOEs' total profits were 223.4 billion yuan, while regional SOEs' total profits were only 60 billion yuan, although regional SOEs' investment was higher than centrally controlled SOEs' investment.[1] In addition, SOEs' profitability is substantially different across various regions. Statistics show that, in 2001, the profit margin on net assets was 6.6 percent in Guangdong and −8.3 percent in Heilongjiang.[2]

Why is the profitability of SOEs lower in some regions than in others? Which policies, if any, can be implemented to improve regional SOEs' profitability?[3] Low profitability of SOEs has been well documented in the literature, and has been a major concern of economists and policy-makers as it is closely related to the state-owned banks' bad loan problems and, eventually, the government fiscal debt.[4] The central government, as well as regional governments, has searched for ways to enhance SOEs' profitability. However, a consensus on the determinants of SOEs' profitability has not been reached, and effective policy suggestions are still needed. This chapter intends to identify the determinants of the profitability of China's regional SOEs using data from 31 Chinese provinces.

Prior contributions on the determinants of profitability of China's SOEs have concentrated on two important issues; however, no consensus has been reached. The first issue is how does the development of non-state enterprises affect SOEs' profitability? Naughton (1992, 1995) and Jefferson and Rawski (1994) argued that the competition between the state and the non-state enterprises, as well as among the state enterprises, reduces the monopoly power of state enterprises and, therefore, the profits of SOEs. Jefferson and Rawski (1994: 60) mentioned that ". . . our calculation shows that profitability with the state industry is lowest in provinces where the output of non-state industry has grown most rapidly." Raiser (1997), using five-year data from 1982, 1985, and 1990–92, also argued that growing competition from non-state enterprises is the cause of the decline in the profitability of SOEs. Using sectorial data from 1993 to 1997, Guo (2004) recently showed that SOEs in industries with larger output shares of non-state enterprises had lower profitability. Nevertheless, using data from 300 large and medium-sized SOEs for the period 1984–88, Fan and Woo (1996) showed that the decline in SOEs' profitability is related to labor remuneration, instead of competition. Also, Holz (2002a) showed that competition and labor remuneration hypotheses are not mutually exclusive. The issue raised above has important policy implications. If private and other enterprises constitute a threat to SOEs' profitability, the government may not enthusiastically promote private and other enterprise development.

The second issue is how does the debt ratio (i.e., debt/asset ratio, liability/asset ratio) affect SOEs' profitability? Wu (1997) argued that the decline in profitability was caused by an increase in the debt ratio (i.e., debt/asset ratio, liability/asset ratio) of the SOEs. The liability/asset ratio had increased from 18.7 percent in 1980 to 67.9 percent in 1994 and to 65.0 percent in 2001.[5] It was argued that high debt incurs high interest payments and lower profits for the SOEs. This hypothesis is based on the assumption that the cost of external borrowing is higher than the cost of using the firms' own assets.[6] However, Holz (2002b) showed that a high liability/asset ratio tends to imply a high level of profitability based on the data for 37 industrial sectors from 1993 to 1997. It was argued that borrowing SOEs are subject to banks' supervision, and this external supervision may force the SOEs to improve productivity.[7]

All of the above contributions are based on either industry-level or enterprise-level data. This chapter will utilize regional data from 31 Chinese provinces to test some new hypotheses, as well as re-examining some of the existing hypotheses discussed aforesaid. The cross-regional analyses using regional data allow us to see how the economic factors in a province affect the profitability of SOEs in a province, and to provide policy suggestions useful to a province. Also, a regional analysis may reveal some insights that industry-level analyses could not. For example, within the machinery industry, the entry of new private enterprises may constitute competition with the existing SOEs and, therefore, may reduce the profitability of the SOEs; however, if new private enterprises are established in the restaurant industry or other service industries, the SOEs in the machinery industry may be better off as these private enterprises may absorb redundant workers from the SOEs.[8] Of course, one may also argue that the development of non-state enterprises may spill over benefits (management, technologies, etc.) to SOEs and enhance the profitability of the SOEs in the same industry. The hypotheses to be tested are as follows. First, we will examine the relationship between the development of non-state enterprises and the profitability of the SOEs by testing the hypothesis that SOEs in provinces with a large percentage of investment from non-state enterprises have higher profitability than those in provinces with a smaller percentage of non-state investment. Second, we will re-examine the relationship between the debt ratio and SOEs' profitability. Debt financing is important for Chinese enterprises because the undeveloped Chinese stock market makes equity financing difficult. As mentioned earlier, two conflicting conclusions exist in the literature. The issue will be re-examined using the most recent regional data and with various measures of indebtedness.

In addition, we will examine two new factors in the determination of SOEs' profitability. One is how openness to trade affects the profitability of SOEs. The other is how local government size affects SOEs' profitability. Openness increases competition because domestic customers can buy from abroad, which may hurt SOEs' profitability. Meanwhile, openness forces firms to improve production technology in order to compete effectively, and enables firms to explore the international market for higher prices. The importance of openness has been increasingly emphasized in the literature on economic development. It would be useful to examine how openness and the profitability of China's SOEs are related. We will use both export and import shares of gross domestic product (GDP) to test the hypothesis that openness enhances the profitability of SOEs. Government size is usually measured by the share of government spending in GDP (see Landau, 1983; Barro, 1991). It has been shown that large government size is detrimental to economic growth. A larger government size may lead to tighter government control and added competition between government and enterprises for resources and, therefore, hurt SOEs' profitability.[9] The hypothesis that government size is negatively related to the profitability of SOEs will be tested. This is the first attempt in the literature to relate government size to SOEs' profitability. If the data support this hypothesis, then more efforts should be made to reduce the size of local governments.

Five alternative measures of profitability will be utilized, including the rate of return on assets, the rate of return on equity, profit margin on net assets, profit earnings multiples, and profit margin on sales. The data on profitability are from various volumes of *The Finance Yearbook of China*, the official publication of China's Ministry of Finance. This unique data set has not been used by any previous studies. Other data items in this study are obtained from various volumes of *The Statistical Yearbook of China*. Our final data set includes regional data for 31 Chinese provinces (regions) for the period 1997 to 2001.[10] There exists doubt over the Chinese official data. However, Chow (1993: 810) argued that Chinese statistics, by and large, were internally consistent and accurate enough for empirical study.[11] Our study will shed new light on the debate over the determinants of the profitability of China's SOEs based on the best available regional data. This study will also provide useful policy implications for Chinese regional and central governments, as well as for other transitional and developing economies with a large number of SOEs.

The following section will discuss China's SOEs from a historical perspective, the decline in the profitability of SOEs, and the profitability of regional SOEs across provinces. Then the regression model is presented along with a discussion of the data used in the analysis. The next section presents the regression results, followed by conclusions.

## China's SOEs, reforms, and profitability

### *Evolution of China's SOEs*

The Chinese government has been heavily involved in productive activities for nearly one and half centuries. Modern enterprises in China emerged in the 1860s. These industries were all run by the government of the ☐ing Dynasty and engaged exclusively in military hardware production, such as guns and ships. Coal and steel production also emerged to meet the needs of military production. In the 1870s, three different types of ownership of enterprises emerged, namely "state ownership (*guan ban*)," "state and private co-ownership (*guan shang he ban*)," and "private ownership with government monitoring (*guan du shang ban*)." In the 1880s, state-owned telecommunication enterprises were established and, in the 1890s, state-owned textile enterprises appeared in China. Along with state-invested enterprises, private enterprises emerged in industries such as textile, paper-making and printing, flour-milling, mining, and ship-repairing.

SOEs expanded during a series of wars before the communists took power in 1949.[12] For example, in the modern manufacturing and mining industries, the capital share of state enterprises in total capital stock was 10 percent in 1935; it increased to 50.5 percent in 1944, and reached 70–80 percent in 1947. The coal output share of state enterprises was 12.4 percent in 1944 and 38.8 percent in 1947. The steel output share of state enterprises was 77.9 percent in 1944 and more than 90 percent in 1947. The spinning output share of state enterprises was 47.1 percent in 1944 and 39 percent in 1947. In addition, oil, iron, and non-ferrous metal industries were monopolized by the government.[13]

In 1949, the People's Republic of China (PRC) was founded. The new government seized all large enterprises and turned them into SOEs. The initial government policy toward the medium and small private enterprises was gradually to turn them into state or collective enterprises through purchasing. The process was called "the socialist reform." The initial plan was to complete the reform by 1967. However, as the economy recovered and became stronger, the government lost its patience. Using administrative power, the government completed the "socialist reform" by the end of 1957. Since then, for more than 20 years, private enterprises have been illegal in China. When the government was less hostile, there were street vendors, occasionally selling farm products (e.g., eggs and fruits), or craftsmen (i.e., repairing shoes). When various political movements started, such as the Socialist Education and the Cultural Revolution, these kinds of business activities were criticized as "the tail of capitalism" and were harshly suppressed.

Following socialist economic principles, SOEs aimed at output maximization, i.e., producing the maximum output to satisfy the needs of the people. SOEs carried out government planning, submitting all profits to the government and having all expenses covered by the government. SOEs relied on political propaganda and ranking promotion, instead of explicit material rewards, to motivate workers and managers. Incentive problems, or the principal and agent problem, appeared as early as the 1950s. Prominent economists such as Sun Yefang argued that the government should require SOEs to make profits and use some of these profits to reward workers (see Sun and Fung, 1982).[14] However, he was strongly criticized for departing from socialist principles.

The Chinese planning system before reform might have been the most rigid one, compared with systems in other centrally planned economies. In fact, Eastern European countries and the former Soviet Union started economic reform in the 1950s after the death of Stalin. They raised agricultural product prices to stimulate agriculture, and introduced material incentives to motivate workers in the SOEs. These reforms had been strongly criticized as "revisionism" by the Chinese authorities until the Chinese government started its own reforms.

### SOEs reforms

In 1978, China started market-oriented economic reforms. The essence of the reforms has been to decentralize the economy (i.e., shift allocation decisions toward the enterprises) and allow SOEs to provide the material incentives to workers to improve productivity. In 1979, the government allowed the state enterprises to keep part of their profit in order to expand production and to issue bonuses and rewards to workers.[15] This policy greatly stimulated the workers' incentive to work and therefore increased output significantly.

In 1983, a reform commonly called substituting taxes for profit ("*li gai shui*") began. SOEs were required to pay taxes, instead of profits, to the government. This reform was completed in 1984. In December 1986, the contract responsibility system (CRS) was introduced. Under the CRS, enterprises were contracted to pay income tax and adjustment tax on a specific level of profit. If they did not achieve that level of profit, they were supposed to make up the rest of the taxes from their own resources. If they exceeded the contract level of profit, they paid taxes at a lower rate on their additional profits. The CRS provided strong incentives for state enterprises to make profits, but it still could not boost profitability to the pre-reform level.

In 1989, SOEs no longer had the privilege of using the before tax profits to repay debt resulting from investment. To increase the firms' ability to repay their debts, the government lowered the income tax rate for small firms. The tax rate for large and medium enterprises was still 55 percent but, for small enterprises, the tax rate was set uniformly at 35 percent. In 1994, a new tax system – the tax sharing system – was established. Several significant changes in the tax system took place including: a reduction in the types of tax from 37 to 23; unification of the income tax rate for all enterprises to 33 percent (foreign enterprises and joint ventures preserved their preferential tax rates); division of taxes into three categories, namely national taxes, which were paid to the central government, joint taxes, which were shared by the central and regional governments, and regional taxes, which were paid to regional governments.

Along with tax reforms, the government also implemented price and loan policy reforms. To encourage SOEs to produce more output, the government allowed SOEs to sell the extra products at a higher price after they fulfilled the production quota set by the government. This dual price system provided incentives for the SOEs to produce more output and partially released the burden of shortages caused by strict planning. However, the policy also opened the door for intense corruption. Since 1983, the government has no longer provided funds to SOEs for investment, and SOEs must borrow from the banks to finance their investment and must repay the loans and interest. This reform is called loan for grant.

Ownership reforms began in the early 1990s. The government started experimenting with shareholding ownership ("*gu fen zhi*") reforms in the early 1990s. The government hoped that, by giving workers and managers some share of the enterprises, they would have more incentive to work and care more about the SOEs' long-term profits. There are three types of shareholders: government (or state), legal persons (other enterprises, banks, and non-bank financial institutions), and individuals (employees of the enterprises and other individuals if the stock was traded in the market). The government has adopted preferential policies to encourage the SOEs to become shareholding companies.[16] For example, before 1994's tax reform, the government shareholding enterprises were subject to low income tax. Also, the government gave the shareholding enterprises more freedom in making managerial, production, and marketing decisions.

In 1992, Deng Xiaoping visited the southern special economic zones and called for the widening and deepening of economic reforms. In 1993, the government declared its intention to establish a socialist market economy. Facing competition from private enterprises and other non-state enterprises, many SOEs had been losing money for many years. In 1994, the government passed the Corporation Law. This law provided a legal framework for SOE reforms. Since then, government policy has been "holding on to the big SOEs and letting go of the small ones." The government began to corporatize large SOEs and privatize some loss-making SOEs. Many small SOEs at the city and county level have been privatized. The number of SOEs fell by 40 percent in the period 1996–2001 (see Garnaut *et al.*, 2003). However, the government still controls the large and profitable SOEs.

Why has the government been reluctant to privatize large SOEs? We believe that there are four main reasons. First, SOEs are mainly in heavy industries, which are considered to be important for the national economy and the people's livelihood ("*guoji minsheng*"). With SOEs, the government can have more control over the economy. Second, SOEs have employed large numbers of workers and assumed many social responsibilities that must otherwise be performed by the government. The employment share of SOEs was 65.27 percent in 1997 and remained at 53.90 percent in 2001. A sudden large-scale privatization of SOEs will cause a large decrease in the output, employment, and growth rate of the economy. That was exactly what happened in the East European countries and the former Soviet Union. Third, SOEs are currently the most important source of government revenues. Government revenue from SOEs accounted for 87 percent of total revenue in 1978 and 71 percent of total revenue in 1995.[17] Fourth, the government believes that production efficiency can be achieved without changing the ownership of the large SOEs.[18]

Instead of privatizing SOEs as quickly as Russia did, the Chinese government kept all SOEs at the beginning of the reform period as state owned and allowed private enterprises to grow. With many SOEs being unprivatized, China successfully maintained a steady growth rate in output.[19] However, output growth and profit growth are not the same. SOEs' profits have declined significantly since economic reforms began in the late 1970s.

### SOEs' profitability

Profitability can be measured by several variables, return on assets, return on equity, and profit margin on net assets, etc. The detailed definitions of these measures and other variables are given in Table 6.1. Table 6.2 shows the main financial indicators of industrial SOEs from 1997 to 2001. During this period, the number of SOEs decreased from 26,200 to 17,400. The percentage of profit-making SOEs increased from 34 percent to 49 percent. Total profits (profits of profit-making enterprises minus losses of loss-making enterprises) were 79.1 billion yuan in 1997, 114.6 billion yuan in 1999, and 281.1 billion yuan in 2001. The rate of return on assets was 2.3 percent in 1997 and increased to 3.3 percent in 2001; profit margin on net assets increased from 1.7 percent in 1997 to 4.6 percent in 2001; and the profit margin on sales increased from 1.2 percent in 1997 to 3.7 percent in 2001. From Table 6.2, we can see that Chinese SOEs' profitability has improved in recent years. In 2002, the total profit of SOEs reached 250 billion yuan, a record high.[20]

Table 6.3 shows the average profitability of regional SOEs in 31 Chinese provinces from 1997 to 2001, measured by the return on total assets, return on equity, profit margin on net assets, profit-earning multiples, and profit margin on sales. Large differences exist in profitability among regions. For example, the profit margin on net assets was 5.4 percent, 5.0 percent, and 4.8 percent in Shanghai, Guangdong, and Zhejiang, respectively, whereas it was –10.0 percent, –9.6 percent, –8.7 percent, and –5.7 percent in Jilin, Gansu, Heilongjiang, and Xinjiang respectively. Why is the profitability of SOEs so different among provinces? What policies can be implemented to improve the profitability of regional SOEs?[21] The following sections explain the reasons for the differences in profitability among provinces.

### Hypotheses, data, and definitions of variables

The objective of this chapter is to empirically investigate the determinants of SOEs' profitability, which can be measured in various ways. The basic empirical framework involves the following cross-sectional specification:

*Table 6.1* Definitions of variables

| Variable name | Definition |
|---|---|
| *roa* | Return on assets, equal to $\{\sum[(total\ profits + interest\ expenditures)/average\ total\ assets)]_i\}/5$, where $i = 1997, 1998, 1999, 2000$, and $2001$ |
| *roe* | Return on equity, equal to $[\sum(roa \times em)_i]/5 = \{\sum[roa * (total\ assets/equity)]_i\}/5$, where $i = 1997, 1998, 1999, 2000$, and $2001$ |
| *pmna* | Profit margin on net assets, equal to $[\sum(total\ profits/net\ assets)_i]/5$, where $i = 1997, 1998, 1999, 2000$, and $2001$ |
| *pem* | Profit-earning multiple, equal to $\{\sum[(total\ profits + interest\ expenditures)/interest\ expenditures)]_i\}/5$, where $i = 1997, 1998, 1999, 2000$, and $2001$; among which: *interest expenditures = (long-term borrowing + short-term borrowing)* $\square$ *average lending rate for one year* |
| *pmsale* | Profit margin on sales, equal to $[\sum(total\ profits/total\ sales)_i]/5$, where $i = 1997, 1998, 1999, 2000$, and $2001$ |
| *export* | Export/GDP ratio, which is equal to $(\sum exports_i/GDP_i)/5$, where $i = 1997, 1998, 1999, 2000$, and $2001$ |
| *import* | Import/GDP ratio, which is equal to $(\sum imports_i/GDP_i)/5$, where $i = 1997, 1998, 1999, 2000$, and $2001$ |
| *nonstate* | Investment share of non-state enterprises, which is equal to $[\sum(total\ investment\ of\ non\text{-}state\ enterprises/total\ investment\ nationwide)_i]/5$, where $i = 1997, 1998, 1999, 2000$, and $2001$ |
| *govern* | Government expenditure share in GDP, equal to $[\sum(total\ government\ expenditures/total\ GDP)_i]/5$, where $i = 1997, 1998, 1999, 2000$, and $2001$ |
| *alratio* | Liability/asset ratio, equal to $[\sum(total\ liabilities/total\ assets)_i]/5$, where $i = 1997, 1998, 1999, 2000$, and $2001$. Total liabilities include the minority shareholders' equity, and total assets exclude the value of land |
| *unhealthy* | Unhealthy asset/equity ratio, equal to $[\sum(unhealthy\ assets/equity)_i]/5$, where $i = 1997, 1998, 1999, 2000$, and $2001$ |
| *eastcoast* | Provinces located in the eastern and coastal region, including 11 provinces on the east and south coasts: Tianjing, Hebei, Liaoning, Shanghai, Jiangsu, Zhejiang, Fujian, Shandong, Guangdong, Guangxi, and Hainan |

Sources: China's Bureau of Statistics (various issues) *The Statistical Yearbook of China*, Beijing: Publishing House of China's Bureau of Statistics; and China's Ministry of Finance (various issues) *The Finance Yearbook of China*, Beijing: Publishing House of Financial Journals.

*Table 6.2* Main financial indicators of state-owned enterprises (units: 100 million yuan unless specified)

| | 1997 | 1998 | 1999 | 2000 | 2001 |
|---|---|---|---|---|---|
| Consolidated number of enterprises (10,000 units) | 26.2 | 23.8 | 21.7 | 19.1 | 17.4 |
| Total assets | 124,975.2 | 134,779.9 | 145,288.1 | 160,068.0 | 179,244.9 |
| Total net assets | 46,164.6 | 50,370.7 | 53,813.2 | 57,975.6 | 61,436.2 |
| Sales revenue | 68,132.0 | 64,685.1 | 69,136.6 | 75,081.9 | 76,355.5 |
| Total profit | 791.2 | 213.7 | 1,145.8 | 2,833.8 | 2,811.2 |
| Total profit of profit-making enterprises | – | 3,280.2 | 3,290.7 | 4,679.8 | 4,804.7 |
| Total losses of loss-making enterprises | – | –3,066.5 | –2,144.9 | –1,846 | –1,993.6 |
| Profit-making enterprises (%) | 34.1 | 31.3 | 46.5 | 49.3 | 48.8 |
| Assets/liabilities ratio (%) | 67.1 | 65.5 | 65.4 | 66.0 | 65.0 |
| Return on total assets (%) | 2.3 | 2.1 | 2.7 | 3.3 | 3.3 |
| Profit margin on net assets (%) | 1.7 | 0.4 | 2.1 | 4.9 | 4.6 |
| Profit margin on sales (%) | 1.2 | 0.3 | 1.7 | 3.8 | 3.7 |
| Profit-earning multiple | 1.2 | 1.1 | 1.4 | 1.9 | 1.9 |
| Ratio of unhealthy assets to equity (%) | 22.6 | 24.8 | 27.5 | 31.4 | 31.2 |
| Total state-owned assets | 44,340.2 | 48,051.6 | 53,306.0 | 57,554.4 | 59,827.2 |

Source: China's Ministry of Finance (2002) *The Finance Yearbook of China*, Beijing: Publishing House of Financial Journals.

*Table 6.3* Profit and loss of state-owned enterprises across regions during 1997–2001 (%)

| Provinces | Return on total assets (roa) | Return on equity (roe) | Profit margin on net assets (pmna) | Profit-earning multiple (pem) | Profit margin on sales (pmsale) |
|---|---|---|---|---|---|
| Beijing | 2.3 | 6.2 | 3.0 | 162.0 | 2.9 |
| Tianjin | 1.4 | 4.4 | 0.5 | 106.0 | 0.4 |
| Hebei | 1.7 | 6.3 | −0.3 | 98.0 | −0.3 |
| Shanxi | 1.2 | 3.9 | −1.0 | 82.0 | −1.0 |
| Inner Mongolia | 1.8 | 6.3 | −0.6 | 98.0 | −0.5 |
| Liaoning | 0.9 | 3.4 | −2.5 | 74.0 | −2.0 |
| Jilin | 0.4 | 2.6 | −10.0 | 50.0 | −5.8 |
| Heilongjiang | 1.6 | 10.6 | −8.7 | 60.0 | −4.9 |
| Shanghai | 3.0 | 9.6 | 5.4 | 210.0 | 4.3 |
| Jiangsu | 1.6 | 5.4 | 0.3 | 104.0 | 0.1 |
| Zhejiang | 3.3 | 8.9 | 4.8 | 208.0 | 3.0 |
| Anhui | 1.4 | 5.6 | −1.4 | 86.0 | −0.9 |
| Fujian | 2.2 | 6.3 | 2.0 | 136.0 | 1.5 |
| Jiangxi | 1.2 | 5.4 | −4.0 | 72.0 | −2.2 |
| Shandong | 2.1 | 7.3 | 1.4 | 122.0 | 0.8 |
| Henan | 1.7 | 7.2 | −1.8 | 88.0 | −1.0 |
| Hubei | 1.0 | 4.2 | −3.1 | 72.0 | −2.0 |
| Hunan | 0.5 | 0.7 | −4.7 | 58.7 | −2.9 |
| Guangdong | 3.1 | 10.3 | 5.0 | 182.0 | 3.5 |
| Guangxi | 0.9 | 2.6 | −2.9 | 62.0 | −2.3 |
| Hainan | 0.7 | 2.6 | −2.4 | 74.0 | −2.9 |
| Sichuan | 1.2 | 4.6 | −2.0 | 78.0 | −1.6 |
| Guizhou | 1.9 | 6.3 | −0.5 | 92.0 | 0.1 |
| Yunnan | −0.7 | −1.5 | −3.6 | -32.0 | −7.2 |
| Xizang | 1.1 | 5.0 | −4.4 | 62.0 | −2.8 |
| Shaanxi | 0.8 | 2.9 | −3.5 | 58.0 | −3.2 |
| Gansu | 0.3 | 0.8 | −9.6 | 38.0 | −6.3 |
| Qinghai | 1.6 | 6.3 | −2.8 | 74.0 | −1.7 |
| Ningxia | 0.9 | 2.4 | −5.0 | 54.0 | −3.1 |
| Xinjiang | 0.9 | 3.5 | −5.7 | 54.0 | −3.3 |
| Chonging | 1.9 | 6.3 | −0.1 | 100.0 | 0.0 |

Source: China's Ministry of Finance (1998–2002) *The Finance Yearbook of China*, Beijing: Publishing House of Financial Journals.

$$\pi = \alpha + \beta X + u \tag{6.1}$$

where $\pi$ is the profitability of SOEs, $X$ is a vector of explanatory variables, $\alpha$ is the constant, $\beta$ is a coefficient vector conformable to $X$, and $u$ is a stochastic error term. Five alternative measures of profitability are used, namely return on assets (*roa*), return on equity (*roe*), profit margin on net assets (*pmna*), profit earnings multiples (*pem*), and profit margin on sales (*pmale*). Each ratio measures SOEs' profitability from different angles. Of the five profitability measures, return on assets (*roa*) and return on equity (*roe*) are the two most common measures of business success for a public company in a market economy. Return on assets (*roa*) measures how efficiently a company uses its assets to generate returns. Return on equity (*roe*) measures returns relative to investment in a company. Profit earnings multiples (*pem*) provide insight into a company's return relative to its borrowing cost. Profit margin on net assets (*pmna*) indicates the level of profit from each dollar of net assets, and profit margin on sales (*pmale*) indicates the level of profit from each dollar of sales. Applying different measures of profitability allows us to examine the various aspects of SOEs' profitability determination and provides us with a check of the robustness of our results.

Factors that could affect the profitability of SOEs in each province include the following. First, non-state enterprise development (*nonstate*). The biggest problem of SOEs is in the redundant workers they employed. The government has been reluctant to encourage SOEs to lay off redundant workers for fear of an increase in unemployment and social instability. The development of non-state enterprises can absorb redundant workers from the SOEs, reduce the SOEs' wage bills, and increase SOEs' profits. Non-state enterprises may also spill over positive externalities to the SOEs, such as managerial skills, modern business cultures, and modern technologies, enabling the SOEs to produce more efficiently and earn more profits. Also, the development of non-state enterprises boosts competition, which forces SOEs to improve technology and management and, thus, enhances the SOEs' profitability. Thus, the development of non-state enterprises should help the SOEs to improve their profitability. The development of non-state enterprises can also be measured by the output share of non-SOEs in total output. However, only the non-SOEs' share in industrial output is available, and the total output share of non-SOEs is not available.

Second, unhealthy assets of SOEs over equity (*unhealthy*). Over the years, the Chinese SOEs have been burdened by unhealthy assets, which bring little or no return to the firms. Unhealthy assets include unproductive equipment, machinery, and buildings, as well as bad loans to other state enterprises. In China, many SOEs are on a production chain, i.e., one uses the others' output as input. Many SOEs could not get payment from selling their products to other SOEs that had bad loans. The unhealthy assets negatively affect a firm's productivity, paint a depressing future for the firm, and dampen the firm's incentives to invest. Thus, unhealthy assets should negatively affect the SOEs' profitability.

Third, liability/asset ratio (*alratio*). Based on the Modigliani–Miller (M&M) theorem (see Modigliani and Miller, 1958), the financial methods of a firm do not matter to a firm's performance, and debt and equity financing of investment should be irrelevant. The M&M theorem is based on some restrictive assumptions, such as complete ownership of physical capital by corporations, frictionless capital markets, free access to debt and equity markets by corporations, etc.[22] The effect of the indebtedness of Chinese SOEs on the profitability of the SOEs is still controversial. Wu (1997) argued that, in China, high debt incurs high interest payments and lower profits for the SOEs, based on the assumption that the interest rate is higher on external borrowing than the rate of return on the firms' own assets. However, Holz (2002b) found evidence that the liability/asset ratio is insignificantly related to the profitability of SOEs. The issue will be re-examined using a new set of data.

Fourth, openness to international trade. On one hand, openness increases competition because domestic customers can buy from abroad, which may hurt SOEs' profitability. On the other hand, openness will enable the firms to: (1) explore the international market, overcome the domestic demand constraint, and sell products at higher prices; (2) adopt new production technologies and new management styles in order to compete effectively in the international market; and (3) engage in product innovation. All these will improve the firms' profitability. Openness has been measured by export share or import share in output (see, for example, Romer, 1989).[23] As imports are likely to reduce the profitability of SOEs, we will use the import share of GDP (*import*) in addition to the export share in GDP (*export*) to measure the openness of a province. Our hypothesis is that openness enhances the profitability of SOEs in a province.

Fifth, government size (*govern*). Government size is usually measured by the share of government spending in GDP (see, for example, Landau, 1983; Barro, 1991). If the government spends on property rights protection, contract enforcement, and infrastructure provisions, then firms' profitability may be enhanced. If the government spends on unproductive activities, a large government size may decrease the firms' profitability. The local government in China is formed to carry out the political agendas and economic plans of the central government. The size of local government has been extremely large. Local government spends a large amount on the wages of their employees and administrative expenditures. Larger government size may lead to tighter government control and additional competition between government and enterprises for resources, and can, therefore, reduce SOEs' profitability.

Finally, east coast dummy variable (*eastcoast*). Substantial differences exist across regions in the abundance of human and fiscal resources, business/commerce history, and government policies. Therefore, enterprises on the east coast might have advantages and perform better than enterprises in other locations. We include an east coast dummy variable to test this hypothesis.

As mentioned earlier, our data are mainly from various issues of *The Statistical Yearbook of China*, published by China's Bureau of Statistics, and various issues of *The Finance Yearbook of China*, published by China's Ministry of Finance. The definitions of variables are consistent with those given by the Chinese government in official statistics. Table 6.4 shows summary statistics of the major variables. The

*Table 6.4* Descriptive statistics (%)

| Variable | n | Minimum | Maximum | Mean | SD |
|---|---|---|---|---|---|
| roa | 31 | −0.7 | 3.3 | 1.4 | 0.9 |
| roe | 31 | −1.5 | 10.6 | 5.0 | 2.8 |
| pmna | 31 | −10.0 | 5.4 | −1.9 | 3.8 |
| pem | 31 | −32.0 | 210.0 | 89.8 | 49.6 |
| pmsale | 31 | −7.2 | 4.3 | −1.3 | 2.8 |
| export | 31 | 2.6 | 79.7 | 13.1 | 16.0 |
| import | 31 | 2.1 | 64.4 | 11.9 | 15.8 |
| nonstate | 31 | 5.8 | 63.6 | 43.6 | 12.6 |
| govern | 31 | 6.4 | 55.0 | 13.8 | 8.9 |
| alratio | 31 | 56.2 | 87.9 | 74.8 | 6.6 |
| unhealthy | 31 | 15.0 | 157.4 | 55.7 | 31.8 |

Notes
*roa*, return on assets; *roe*, return on equity; *pmna*, profit margin on net assets; *pem*, profit-earning multiple; *pmsale*, profit margin on sales; *export*, export/GDP ratio; *import*, import/GDP ratio; *nonstate*, investment share of non-state enterprises; *govern*, government expenditure share of GDP; *alratio*, liability/asset ratio; *unhealthy*, unhealthy asset/equity ratio.

mean returns on assets (*roa*) in all 31 provinces was 1.4 percent, with −0.7 percent (Tibet) and 3.3 percent (Zhejiang) as the minimum and maximum respectively. The mean return on equity (*roe*) was 5.0 percent, with −1.5 percent (Tibet) and 10.6 percent (Heilongjiang) as the minimum and maximum respectively. The mean profit margin on net assets (*pmna*) was −1.9 percent, with 5.4 percent (Shanghai) being the maximum and −10.0 percent (Jilin) being the minimum. The other two provinces with the lowest profit margins on net assets from 1997 to 2001 were □inghai (−9.6 percent) and Jilin (−8.7 percent). The mean profit earnings multiple (*pem*) was 89.8 percent, with the highest being 210 percent and the lowest being 32 percent. The mean profit margin on sales (*pmsale*) was −0.013 percent, with 0.072 percent and 0.043 percent being the minimum and maximum. The mean export share in GDP (*export*) was 13.1 percent, with 2.6 percent (Henan) and 79.7 percent (Guangdong) being the minimum and maximum respectively. The mean import share in GDP (*import*) was 11.9 percent, with 2.1 percent (Anhui) and 64.4 percent (Zhejiang) being the minimum and maximum respectively. The mean investment share of non-state enterprises (*nonstate*) was 43.6 percent, with 5.8 percent (Tibet) and 63.6 percent (Guangdong) being the minimum and maximum respectively. The mean liability/asset ratio (*alratio*) was 74.8 percent, with 56.2 percent (Tibet) and 87.9 percent (Jilin) being the minimum and maximum respectively. Also, the *alratio* for Heilongjiang was 86.7 percent, the highest after to Jilin. The mean unhealthy assets (unhealthy assets/equity) (*unhealthy*)

*Table 6.5* Pearson correlations

|  | roa | roe | pmna | pem | pmsale | export |
|---|---|---|---|---|---|---|
| roa | 1 | 0.901 | 0.794 | 0.948 | 0.916 | 0.608 |
| roe | 0.901 | 1 | 0.560 | 0.766 | 0.712 | 0.488 |
| pmna | 0.794 | 0.560 | 1 | 0.836 | 0.933 | 0.650 |
| pem | 0.948 | 0.766 | 0.836 | 1 | 0.941 | 0.691 |
| pmsale | 0.916 | 0.712 | 0.933 | 0.941 | 1 | 0.653 |
| export | 0.608 | 0.488 | 0.650 | 0.691 | 0.653 | 1 |
| import | 0.545 | 0.412 | 0.631 | 0.669 | 0.645 | 0.925 |
| nonstate | 0.621 | 0.482 | 0.525 | 0.672 | 0.652 | 0.436 |
| govern | −0.525 | −0.499 | −0.232 | −0.523 | −0.486 | −0.172 |
| alratio | −0.312 | −0.063 | −0.721 | −0.369 | −0.479 | −0.389 |
| unhealthy | −0.504 | −0.234 | −0.867 | −0.527 | −0.694 | −0.396 |
| eastcoast | 0.440 | 0.288 | 0.573 | 0.537 | 0.519 | 0.599 |

Notes

*roa*, return on assets; *roe*, return on equity; *pmna*, profit margin on net assets; *pem*, profit-earning multiple; *pmsale*, profit margin on sales; *export*, export/GDP ratio; *import*, import/GDP ratio;

was 55.7 percent, with 15 percent (Zhejiang) and 157.4 percent (Jilin) being the minimum and maximum respectively.

Table 6.5 shows the correlation coefficients of the independent variables. It can be seen that different measures of the indebtedness of enterprises, liability/asset ratio (*alratio*) and the rate of unhealthy assets (*unhealthy*), are strongly correlated, with a correlation coefficient of 0.875. The export share in GDP (*export*) and the import share in GDP (*import*) are strongly correlated, with a correlation coefficient 0.925. In addition, the investment share of non-state enterprises (*nonstate*) and government size (*govern*) are also highly correlated, with a correlation coefficient −0.799. To avoid the problem of multicollinearity, the strongly correlated variables will not be used in the same regression equation. As a result, there are 13 regressions for each of the five profitability measures (see Tables 6.6–6.10).

## Regression results

A number of interesting results are found from the regression analysis. Tables 6.6–6.10 show the regression results of profitability measured by return on equity, return on assets, profit margin on net assets, profit margin on sales, and profit earnings multiples, on openness, non-state enterprise development, government size, indebtedness, and the east coast dummy variable.

No matter which measure of profitability is used, export share in GDP is always positively related to the profitability of SOEs, as shown in Tables 6.6–6.10. That is, SOEs' profitability in provinces with larger shares of exports in GDP is

| import | nonstate | govern | alratio | unhealthy | eastcoast |
|--------|----------|--------|---------|-----------|-----------|
| 0.545  | 0.621    | −0.525 | −0.312  | −0.504    | 0.440     |
| 0.412  | 0.482    | −0.499 | −0.063  | −0.234    | 0.288     |
| 0.631  | 0.525    | −0.232 | −0.721  | −0.867    | 0.573     |
| 0.669  | 0.672    | −0.523 | −0.369  | −0.527    | 0.537     |
| 0.645  | 0.652    | −0.486 | −0.479  | −0.694    | 0.519     |
| 0.925  | 0.436    | −0.172 | −0.389  | −0.396    | 0.599     |
| 1      | 0.345    | −0.105 | −0.417  | −0.400    | 0.495     |
| 0.345  | 1        | −0.799 | −0.059  | −0.226    | 0.668     |
| −0.105 | −0.799   | 1      | −0.384  | −0.090    | −0.352    |
| −0.417 | −0.059   | −0.384 | 1       | 0.875     | −0.364    |
| −0.400 | −0.226   | −0.090 | 0.875   | 1         | −0.439    |
| 0.495  | 0.668    | −0.352 | −0.364  | −0.439    | 1         |

*nonstate*, investment share of non-state enterprises; *govern*, government expenditure share of GDP; *alratio*, liability/asset ratio; *unhealthy*, unhealthy asset/equity ratio; *eastcoast*, east coast provinces.

higher than that in provinces with smaller shares of exports in GDP. One may argue that exports enable domestic firms to sell their products in the world market and will obviously enhance their profitability. However, when the import share in GDP is used to measure openness, we obtain the same result, i.e., the import share in GDP is also positively related to the profitability of SOEs. As discussed before, imports may have two opposite effects on SOEs' profitability. On one hand, foreign goods and services compete with the products of SOEs for market share, which tends to lower the profitability of SOEs. On the other hand, imports of goods and services amount to pressure on SOEs to improve their management and production technology, which may increase the profitability of SOEs. It seems that the positive effects of imports on SOEs' profitability dominate the negative effects of imports.

The development of non-state enterprises (including individual household businesses, collective enterprises, and foreign enterprises) is significantly positively related to the SOEs' profitability in all regressions in Tables 6.6–6.10. That is, SOEs in provinces with more investment in non-state enterprises have higher profitability than those in provinces with less investment in non-state enterprises. Thus, the development of non-state enterprises improves the profitability of SOEs. The non-state enterprises compete with state enterprises in resource and product markets, tending to reduce the profitability of SOEs. They also absorb redundant workers from SOEs, spill over benefits to SOEs, such as efficient management skills, a hard-working ethic, and efficient production technologies, and put pressure on SOEs to improve their efficiency. Our results show that non-state

*Table 6.6* Determinants of profitability, returns on equity

|  | *reg 1* | *reg 2* | *reg 3* | *reg 4* | *reg 5* | *reg 6* |
|---|---|---|---|---|---|---|
| *constant* | 0.045 | −0.001 | −0.013 | 0.004 | −0.002 | −0.014 |
|  | (7.378)* | (−0.061) | (−0.223) | (−0.211) | (−0.088) | (−0.233) |
| *export* |  | 0.081 | 0.083 | 0.077 |  |  |
|  |  | (2.434)** | (2.383)** | (2.262)** |  |  |
| *import* |  |  |  |  | 0.061 | 0.063 |
|  |  |  |  |  | (1.905)□ | (1.847)□ |
| *nonstate* |  | 0.109 | 0.105 | 0.111 | 0.113 | 0.110 |
|  |  | (2.396)** | (2.175)** | (2.403)** | (2.415)** | (2.212)** |
| *govern* |  |  |  |  |  |  |
| *alratio* |  |  | 0.017 |  |  | 0.017 |
|  |  |  | (0.221) |  |  | (0.217) |
| *unhealthy* |  |  |  | −0.009 |  |  |
|  |  |  |  | (−0.584) |  |  |
| *eastcoast* | 0.016 | −0.017 | −0.017 | −0.021 | −0.013 | −0.012 |
|  | (−1.620) | (−1.381) | (−1.221) | (−1.476) | (−0.986) | (−0.842) |
| Adjusted $R^2$ | 0.051 | 0.302 | 0.278 | 0.286 | 0.250 | 0.222 |
| *n* | 31 | 31 | 31 | 31 | 31 | 31 |

Notes
*roe*, return on equity; *export*, export/GDP ratio; *import*, import/GDP ratio; *nonstate*, investment share of non-state enterprises; *govern*, government expenditure share of GDP; *alratio*, liability/asset ratio; *unhealthy*, unhealthy asset/equity ratio; *eastcoast*, east coast provinces.

enterprises do more good than harm to SOEs' profitability. Based on data from industries, Naughton (1992, 1995) and Jefferson and Rawski (1994) found that competition between the non-state and state enterprises as well as among the state enterprises reduces the monopoly power of state enterprises and, therefore, reduces the profits of SOEs. Our analysis of 31 provinces for the period 1997–2001 clearly shows that the expansion of non-state enterprises enhances the profitability of SOEs. This robust result has useful policy implications, i.e., a policy to promote private enterprises can improve SOEs' profitability.

Government size (i.e., the ratio of government spending to GDP) is negatively related to profitability measured by return on equity (*roe*), return on assets (*roa*), and profit earnings multiples (*pem*), with a level of significance at 1 percent for all regressions (see Tables 6.6, 6.7, 6.9, and 6.10). This indicates that SOEs in the provinces with a larger government size have lower profitability. Government size is negatively related to profit margin on net assets (*pmna*) of SOEs in regressions

| reg 7 | reg 8 | reg 9 | reg 10 | reg 11 | reg 12 | reg 13 |
|---|---|---|---|---|---|---|
| 0.004 | 0.063 | 0.139 | 0.079 | 0.065 | 0.142 | 0.082 |
| (–0.170) | (6.772)* | (1.96)□ | (5.128)* | (6.688)* | (1.885)□ | (4.986)* |
|  | 0.090 | 0.082 | 0.083 |  |  |  |
|  | (2.885)* | (2.538)** | (2.644)** |  |  |  |
| 0.056 |  |  |  | 0.070 | 0.060 | 0.062 |
| (–1.693) |  |  |  | (2.303)** | (1.890)□ | (2.000)□ |
| 0.116 |  |  |  |  |  |  |
| (2.431)** |  |  |  |  |  |  |
|  | –0.149 | –0.187 | –0.168 | –0.152 | –0.190 | –0.170 |
|  | (–3.09)* | (–3.133)* | (–3.363)* | (–3.004)* | (–3.036)* | (–3.251)* |
|  |  | –0.090 |  |  | –0.092 |  |
|  |  | (–1.076) |  |  | (–1.032) |  |
| –0.009 |  |  | –0.019 |  |  | –0.019 |
| (–0.564) |  |  | (–1.284) |  |  | (–1.221) |
| –0.015 | –0.011 | –0.016 | –0.016 | –0.005 | –0.010 | –0.010 |
| (–1.099) | (–1.011) | (–1.364) | (–1.410) | (–0.443) | (–0.853) | (–0.878) |
| 0.230 | 0.375 | 0.378 | 0.389 | 0.316 | 0.318 | 0.328 |
| 31 | 31 | 31 | 31 | 31 | 31 | 31 |

\*   Significance level of 1% for a two-tailed test.
†   Significance level of 5% for a two-tailed test.
□   Significance level of 10% for a two-tailed test.
*t*-values are in parentheses.

9, 10, 12, and 13 in Table 6.8. The significance level is 1 percent. However, in regressions 8 and 11 in Table 6.8, the signs of the coefficients are still negative, but the *t*-values become insignificant. From the Pearson correlations given in Table 6.5, we find that the correlation coefficient between profit margin on net assets (*pmna*) and government size (*govern*) is only –0.232. Thus, regional government size and profit margin on net assets may not be closely related based on the data in our sample.

The relationship between SOEs' liability/asset ratio and the profitability of SOEs depends on the measurement of profitability. When profitability is measured by the profit margin on net assets (*pmna*), profit earnings multiples (*pem*), and profit margin on sales (*pmsale*), the liability/asset ratios of SOEs negatively affect their profitability, and the coefficients are highly significant (see Tables 6.8, 6.9, and 6.10). That is to say, SOEs with higher liability/asset ratios were less profitable than SOEs with lower liability/asset ratios. However, when return on

*Table 6.7* Determinants of profitability, returns on assets

|  | reg 1 | reg 2 | reg 3 | reg 4 | reg 5 | reg 6 |
|---|---|---|---|---|---|---|
| constant | 0.011 | −0.004 | 0.016 | 0.001 | −0.005 | 0.015 |
|  | (6.526)* | (−0.968) | (−1.153) | (−0.232) | (−1.001) | (−1.023) |
| export |  | 0.027 | 0.024 | 0.023 |  |  |
|  |  | (3.131)* | (2.736)** | (2.923)* |  |  |
| import |  |  |  |  | 0.023 | 0.019 |
|  |  |  |  |  | (2.760)** | (2.234)** |
| nonstate |  | 0.038 | 0.043 | 0.041 | 0.039 | 0.044 |
|  |  | (3.210)* | (3.580)* | (3.858)* | (3.240)* | (3.567)* |
| govern |  |  |  |  |  |  |
| alratio |  |  | −0.290 |  |  | −0.028 |
|  |  |  | (−1.548) |  |  | (−1.418) |
| unhealthy |  |  |  | −0.010 |  |  |
|  |  |  |  | (−2.774)** |  |  |
| eastcoast | 0.008 | −0.004 | −0.006 | −0.007 | −0.003 | −0.004 |
|  | (2.636)** | (−1.207) | (−1.657) | (−2.093)** | (−0.811) | (−1.247) |
| Adjusted $R^2$ | 0.166 | 0.500 | 0.526 | 0.600 | 0.468 | 0.488 |
| n | 31 | 31 | 31 | 31 | 31 | 31 |

Notes
  *roa*, return on assets; *export*, export/GDP ratio; *import*, import/GDP ratio; *nonstate*, investment
  share of non-state enterprises; *govern*, government expenditure share of GDP; *alratio*, liability/
  asset ratio; *unhealthy*, unhealthy asset/equity ratio; *eastcoast*, east coast provinces.

equity (*roe*) is used as a measure of profitability of China's SOEs, the relationship
between profitability and liability/asset ratios becomes insignificant (see Table
6.6). As discussed in the previous section, *roe* may not be an appropriate measure
of the profitability of SOEs in China. This is because many SOEs have not issued
any stock, and a higher *roe* in a province (such as Heilongjiang) may not necessarily represent higher profitability. Nevertheless, when return on assets (*roa*) is used
as a measure of profitability, the relationship with the coefficient of liability/asset
ratios is negative, but only at the 80 percent level of statistical significance (see
Table 6.7).

The ratio of unhealthy assets to equity (*unhealthy*) is also negatively related
to the profitability of SOEs, as shown in Tables 6.7–6.10. That is to say, SOEs
with a higher ratio of unhealthy assets to equity had low profitability. However,
when return on equity (*roe*) is used as an indicator of the SOEs' profitability,
the relationship between profitability and unhealthy assets becomes insignificant,

| reg 7 | reg 8 | reg 9 | reg 10 | reg 11 | reg 12 | reg 13 |
| --- | --- | --- | --- | --- | --- | --- |
| 0.001 | 0.016 | 0.740 | 0.027 | 0.017 | 0.075 | 0.028 |
| (−0.149) | (6.443)* | (4.635)* | (7.913)* | (6.432)* | (4.312)* | (7.498)* |
| | 0.030 | 0.023 | 0.025 | | | |
| | (3.504)* | (3.197)* | (3.57)* | | | |
| 0.018 | | | | 0.026 | 0.018 | 0.02 |
| (2.336)** | | | | (3.093)* | (2.458)** | (2.837)* |
| 0.042 | | | | | | |
| (3.825)* | | | | | | |
| | −0.043 | −0.072 | −0.055 | −0.044 | −0.073 | −0.056 |
| | (−3.246)* | (−5.313)* | (−4.973)* | (−3.216)* | (−5.039)* | (−4.723)* |
| | | −0.069 | | | −0.069 | |
| | | (−3.644)* | | | (−3.366)* | |
| −0.010 | | | −0.013 | | | −0.013 |
| (−2.590)** | | | (−3.921)* | | | (−3.613)* |
| −0.005 | −0.001 | −0.005 | −0.005 | 0.001 | −0.003 | −0.003 |
| (−1.637) | (−0.329) | (−1.842)□ | (−1.762)□ | (0.254) | (−1.215) | (−1.090) |
| 0.561 | 0.503 | 0.658 | 0.676 | 0.466 | 0.614 | 0.631 |
| 31 | 31 | 31 | 31 | 31 | 31 | 31 |

\* Significance level of 1% for a two-tailed test.
† Significance level of 5% for a two-tailed test.
□ Significance level of 10% for a two-tailed test.
*t*-values are in parentheses.

although the sign of the coefficient remains negative (see Table 6.6). Our cross-sectional analysis is unable to statistically identify the causal relationship between profitability and unhealthy assets, as well as other variables. Nevertheless, our results do show an associative link between profitability and these variables.

The east coast dummy variable is significant and with a positive sign if it is used in the regression of profitability alone. However, after we include variables such as openness, investment share of non-state enterprises, and SOE indebtedness, the east coast dummy variable becomes insignificant. That implies that the variables we include in the regressions are sufficient to explain the differences between the east coast provinces and the rest of the provinces.

*Table 6.8* Determinants of profitability, profit margin on net assets

|  | reg 1 | reg 2 | reg 3 | reg 4 | reg 5 | reg 6 |
|---|---|---|---|---|---|---|
| *constant* | −0.035 | −0.068 | 0.192 | −0.018 | −0.070 | 0.186 |
|  | (−4.848)* | (−3.098)* | (4.419)* | (−1.836)□ | (−3.242)* | (4.134)* |
| *export* |  | 0.112 | 0.069 | 0.074 |  |  |
|  |  | (2.751)† | (2.561)† | (4.491)* |  |  |
| *import* |  |  |  |  | 0.111 | 0.063 |
|  |  |  |  |  | (2.972)* | (2.422)† |
| *nonstate* |  | 0.070 | 0.137 | 0.099 | 0.075 | 0.140 |
|  |  | (1.249) | (3.655)* | (4.463)* | (1.377) | (3.707)* |
| *govern* |  |  |  |  |  |  |
| *alratio* |  |  | −0.369 |  |  | −0.362 |
|  |  |  | (−6.299)* |  |  | (−5.994)* |
| *unhealthy* |  |  |  | −0.089 |  |  |
|  |  |  |  | (−12.083)* |  |  |
| *eastcoast* | 0.045 | 0.011 | −0.010 | −0.012 | 0.014 | −0.007 |
|  | (3.760)* | (0.686) | (−0.927) | (−1.812)□ | (0.944) | (−0.627) |
| Adjusted $R^2$ | 0.305 | 0.449 | 0.773 | 0.913 | 0.468 | 0.768 |
| *n* | 31 | 31 | 31 | 31 | 31 | 31 |

Notes
*pmna*, profit margin on net assets; *export*, export/GDP ratio; *import*, import/GDP ratio; *nonstate*,
investment share of non-state enterprises; *govern*, government expenditure share of GDP; *alratio*,
liability/asset ratio; *unhealthy*, unhealthy asset/equity ratio; *eastcoast*, east coast provinces.

## Conclusions

The profitability of China's SOEs has been a debated issue among economists
worldwide and a central concern of policy-makers in China. Using data from
31 Chinese provinces from 1997 to 2001, this chapter has identified major determinants of profitability for China's SOEs across regions. Our new findings
are as follows. Investment share of non-state enterprises is positively related to
the profitability of SOEs, i.e., SOEs' profitability is higher in provinces with a
larger investment share of non-state enterprises than in provinces with a smaller
investment share of non-state enterprises. The result holds regardless of which
profitability measure is used. This result is contrary to the popular view that the
development of non-state enterprises is the reason for the decline in the profitability of China's SOEs. Openness, measured by either export share in GDP or
import share in GDP, is positively related to SOEs' profitability, i.e., SOEs' profitability is higher in provinces with a higher export share or import share in GDP.

| reg 7 | reg 8 | reg 9 | reg 10 | reg 11 | reg 12 | reg 13 |
|---|---|---|---|---|---|---|
| −0.02 | −0.038 | 0.385 | 0.042 | −0.037 | 0.381 | 0.042 |
| (−1.996)□ | (−3.053)* | (8.062)* | (5.236)* | (−3.011)* | (7.646)* | (5.060)* |
|  | 0.116 | 0.068 | 0.08 |  |  |  |
|  | (2.776)† | (3.122)* | (4.849)* |  |  |  |
| 0.067 |  |  |  | 0.113 | −0.059 | 0.072 |
| (4.260)* |  |  |  | (2.947)* | (2.801)* | (4.514)* |
| 0.104 |  |  |  |  |  |  |
| (4.559)* |  |  |  |  |  |  |
|  | −0.024 | −0.238 | −0.117 | −0.031 | −0.238 | −0.119 |
|  | (−0.375) | (−5.893)* | (−4.49)* | (−0.488) | (−5.74)* | (−4.442)* |
|  |  | −0.504 |  |  | −0.497 |  |
|  |  | (−8.935)* |  |  | (−8.453)* |  |
| −0.088 |  |  | −0.096 |  |  | −0.094 |
| (−11.510)* |  |  | (−12.422)* |  |  | (−11.759)* |
| −0.009 | 0.021 | −0.008 | −0.005 | 0.025 | −0.004 | −0.001 |
| (−1.318) | (1.440) | (−1.022) | (−0.894) | (1.877)□ | (−0.523) | (−0.185) |
| 0.909 | 0.420 | 0.852 | 0.913 | 0.436 | 0.844 | 0.907 |
| 31 | 31 | 31 | 31 | 31 | 31 | 31 |

\* Significance level of 1% for a two-tailed test.
† Significance level of 5% for a two-tailed test.
□ Significance level of 10% for a two-tailed test.
*t*-values are in parentheses.

The result indicates that openness to international competition may increase the profitability of China's SOEs. Consistent with Wu (1997), we find that the debt ratio significantly affects profitability, and SOEs' profitability is lower in provinces with higher liability/asset ratios. Unhealthy assets over equity are negatively related to profitability. SOEs in provinces with higher unhealthy assets have lower profitability than SOEs in provinces with lower unhealthy assets. The findings seem to suggest that the cost of SOE's high debt interest payments offsets the benefit of banks' external supervision toward borrowing SOEs and reduces SOE's profitability. Government size is negatively related to the profitability of SOEs. SOEs in provinces with a higher ratio of government spending in GDP have lower profitability. SOEs in east coast provinces are more profitable than SOEs in the middle and western part of China. However, when major explanatory variables are included in our regression analyses, the east cost dummy variable becomes insignificant. The results from this study shed new light on the literature regarding the determinants of SOEs' profitability in China. Our study suggests that, to

*Table 6.9* Determinants of profitability, profit-earnings multiples

|  | reg 1 | reg 2 | reg 3 | reg 4 | reg 5 | reg 6 |
|---|---|---|---|---|---|---|
| constant | 0.703 | −0.183 | 1.081 | 0.110 | −0.212 | 0.893 |
|  | (7.399)* | (−0.779) | −1.558 | −0.479 | (−0.924) | −1.268 |
| export |  | 1.693 | 1.492 | 1.480 |  |  |
|  |  | (3.868)* | (3.465)* | (3.758)* |  |  |
| Import |  |  |  |  | 1.638 | 1.431 |
|  |  |  |  |  | (4.125)* | (3.534)* |
| nonstate |  | 2.086 | 2.399 | 2.247 | 2.173 | 2.451 |
|  |  | (3.484)* | (4.026)* | (4.219)* | (3.722)* | (4.152)* |
| govern |  |  |  |  |  |  |
| alratio |  |  | −1.789 |  |  | −1.565 |
|  |  |  | (−1.914)☐ |  |  | (−1.654) |
| unhealthy |  |  |  | −0.516 |  |  |
|  |  |  |  | (−2.913)* |  |  |
| eastcoast | 0.548 | −0.146 | −0.249 | −0.280 | −0.091 | −0.183 |
|  | (3.431)* | (−0.839) | (−1.429) | (−1.748)☐ | (−0.561) | (−1.092) |
| Adjusted $R^2$ | 0.264 | 0.618 | 0.653 | 0.702 | 0.636 | 0.658 |
| n | 31 | 31 | 31 | 31 | 31 | 31 |

Notes
*pem*, profit-earning multiple; *export*, export/GDP ratio; *import*, import/GDP ratio; *nonstate*, investment share of non-state enterprises; *govern*, government expenditure share of GDP; *alratio*, liability/asset ratio; *unhealthy*, unhealthy asset/equity ratio; *eastcoast*, east coast provinces.

improve the profitability of China's regional SOEs, Chinese provinces should en-courage investment in non-state enterprises, promote international trade, reduce SOEs' debt ratios and unhealthy assets, and reduce local government size.

## Notes

1 China's Ministry of Finance, *The Finance Yearbook of China, 2003.*
2 China's Ministry of Finance, *The Finance Yearbook of China, 2002.*
3 Improving profitability does not imply that SOEs should not be privatized. In fact, in industrialized countries, governments often privatize profitable enterprises.
4 For example, Zhang *et al.* (2002) found that, from 1996 to 1998, the growth rate in the profitability of SOEs lagged behind that of firms in other ownership structures.
5 China's Ministry of Finance, *The Finance Yearbook of China*, various issues.
6 Unlike many developed countries, such as the US, there is no tax shelter for using bank loans in China.

| reg 7 | reg 8 | reg 9 | reg 10 | reg 11 | reg 12 | reg 13 |
|---|---|---|---|---|---|---|
| 0.061 | 0.956 | 4.276 | 1.524 | 0.977 | 4.120 | 1.517 |
| −0.266 | (7.245)* | (5.457)* | (8.632)* | (7.62)* | (5.136)* | (8.589)* |
| | 1.861 | 1.484 | 1.603 | | | |
| | (4.195)* | (4.151)* | (4.442)* | | | |
| 1.402 | | | | 1.794 | 1.389 | 1.512 |
| (3.809)* | | | | (4.436)* | (4.065)* | (4.463)* |
| 2.327 | | | | | | |
| (4.402)* | | | | | | |
| | −2.274 | −3.953 | −2.932 | −2.381 | −3.942 | −2.987 |
| | (−3.325)* | (−5.962)* | (−5.131)* | (−3.554)* | (−5.894)* | (−5.237)* |
| | | −3.956 | | | −3.746 | |
| | | (−4.274)* | | | (−3.951)* | |
| −0.482 | | | −0.678 | | | −0.646 |
| (−2.703)† | | | (−4.017)* | | | (−3.798)* |
| −0.218 | 0.035 | −0.193 | −0.151 | 0.105 | −0.114 | −0.073 |
| (−1.415) | (0.226) | (−1.471) | (−1.151) | (0.751) | (−0.904) | (−0.593) |
| 0.705 | 0.607 | 0.760 | 0.748 | 0.624 | 0.789 | 0.749 |
| 31 | 31 | 31 | 31 | 31 | 31 | 31 |

\*   Significance level of 1% for a two-tailed test.
†   Significance level of 5% for a two-tailed test.
☐   Significance level of 10% for a two-tailed test.
*t*-values are in parentheses.

7  Other studies focused on change in the accounting system for the change in SOEs' profitability. Some argued that most state enterprises under-report profits because reported profits belong to the state, whereas hidden profits accrue to management (Rawski, 1994; Zhang, 1999), while others showed that many SOEs under-reported their losses (Di, 1992). Under-reporting both profits and losses could be true in China. If losses are too large, the leaders of the SOEs might have to be removed from their posts. If profits are high, the SOEs must pay more taxes. The tax reforms have converted profits into taxes and reduced after-tax profits (Zhang, 1999).

8  Overemployment is a characteristic of China's SOEs and a difficult problem to solve (Yin, 2001).

9  Unlike some western countries, the Chinese government at various levels mainly employs well-educated persons for administrative positions.

10  Some data items were not available in *The Finance Yearbook of China* until 1997, such as various measurements of profitability, unhealthy assets to equity ratio, etc. Also, Chongqing was independent from Sichuan province and became a municipality directly under central government control in 1997.

*Table 6.10* Determinants of profitability, profit margin on sales (pmsale)

|  | reg 1 | reg 2 | reg 3 | reg 4 | reg 5 | reg 6 |
|---|---|---|---|---|---|---|
| constant | −0.024 | −0.072 | 0.046 | −0.044 | −0.073 | 0.037 |
|  | (−4.425)* | (−5.087)* | −1.224 | (−4.482)* | (−5.400)* | −0.978 |
| export |  | 0.087 | 0.067 | 0.066 |  |  |
|  |  | (3.308)* | (2.897)* | (3.878)* |  |  |
| import |  |  |  |  | 0.088 | 0.067 |
|  |  |  |  |  | (3.739)* | (3.122)* |
| nonstate |  | 0.114 | 0.144 | 0.130 | 0.118 | 0.146 |
|  |  | (3.163)* | (4.499)* | (5.669)* | (3.417)* | (4.643)* |
| govern |  |  |  |  |  |  |
| alratio |  |  | −0.167 |  |  | −0.156 |
|  |  |  | (−3.313)* |  |  | (−3.097)* |
| unhealthy |  |  |  | −0.049 |  |  |
|  |  |  |  | (−6.393)* |  |  |
| eastcoast | 0.029 | −0.007 | −0.017 | −0.020 | −0.005 | −0.014 |
|  | (3.271)* | (−0.700) | (−1.802)□ | (−2.896)* | (−0.528) | (−1.593) |
| Adjusted $R^2$ | 0.244 | 0.555 | 0.675 | 0.820 | 0.588 | 0.688 |
| n | 31 | 31 | 31 | 31 | 31 | 31 |

Notes
*pmsale*, profit margin on sales; *export*, export/GDP ratio; *import*, import/GDP ratio; *nonstate*, investment share of non-state enterprises; *govern*, government expenditure share of GDP; *alratio*, liability/asset ratio; *unhealthy*, unhealthy asset/equity ratio; *eastcoast*, east coast provinces.

11   We have contacted the publishers many times to clarify the data we use.
12   In the first part of the twentieth century, China experienced three major civil wars, the war against the northern warlords (1926–27), the first war between Communists and Nationalists (1927–36), the second war between Communists and Nationalists (1947–49), and a war against Japanese invaders (1937–45).
13   Editorial Group, Department of Political Economy, People's University, Modern Chinese Economic History, Volume 2, 1981, p. 158.
14   Sun argued that enterprises are like a cow and profits are like the nose of the cow. If you hold the nose of the cow, it will follow you and function well.
15   What China did to its SOEs in the 1980s was similar to what the Soviet Union did to its SOEs after the death of Stalin.
16   Shareholding companies ("*gufenzhi qiye*") are companies that issue shares to the workers and other investors. However, the government usually holds the vast majority of shares in these companies. The shares may not be traded on the stock market. For SOEs' trade stocks in the stock market, the government usually controls most of the shares. If the government starts to sell its shares, the stock price will plunge. That is the problem of China's stock market.

| reg 7 | reg 8 | reg 9 | reg 10 | reg 11 | reg 12 | reg 13 |
|---|---|---|---|---|---|---|
| −0.047 | −0.011 | 0.244 | 0.038 | −0.010 | 0.236 | 0.038 |
| (−4.788)* | (−1.362) | (6.58)* | (5.672)* | (−1.299) | (6.314)* | (5.755)* |
|  | 0.096 | 0.067 | 0.073 |  |  |  |
|  | (3.527)* | (3.951)* | (5.355)* |  |  |  |
| 0.065 |  |  |  | 0.096 | 0.064 | 0.071 |
| (4.161)* |  |  |  | (3.925)* | (4.037)* | (5.677)* |
| 0.133 |  |  |  |  |  |  |
| (5.963)* |  |  |  |  |  |  |
|  | −0.115 | −0.244 | −0.172 | −0.121 | −0.243 | −0.175 |
|  | (−2.754)† | (−7.786)* | (−7.921)* | (−2.998)* | (−7.818)* | (−8.294)* |
|  |  | −0.304 |  |  | −0.293 |  |
|  |  | (−6.937)* |  |  | (−6.638)* |  |
| −0.047 |  |  | −0.059 |  |  | −0.057 |
| (−6.272)* |  |  | (−9.122)* |  |  | (−9.064)* |
| −0.017 | 0.003 | −0.014 | −0.013 | 0.006 | −0.011 | −0.01 |
| (−2.688)† | (0.335) | (−2.308)† | (−2.583)† | (0.730) | (−1.869)□ | (−2.092)† |
| 0.830 | 0.524 | 0.827 | 0.882 | 0.558 | 0.830 | 0.890 |
| 31 | 31 | 31 | 31 | 31 | 31 | 31 |

\*   Significance level of 1% for a two-tailed test.
†   Significance level of 5% for a two-tailed test.
□   Significance level of 10% for a two-tailed test.
*t*-values are in parentheses.

17  See China's Bureau of Statistics, *The Statistical Yearbook of China*, 1998, p. 272.
18  This is also the view of some prominent economists including Stiglitz (1994), who believes that, if public enterprise managers enjoy enough independence in their business decisions, they behave rationally (equalize marginal revenue to marginal cost), that is the efficiency of the free market system can be reproduced without private property.
19  The problem with the gradualist approach is corruption and related income inequality. With the gradualist approach, the enterprise is privatized implicitly. Those who have powers gradually steal the state assets.
20  See   http://news.chinatimes.com/chinatimes/0,3546,110505+112002122100070,00. htm. 20 December 2002.
21  Improving profitability does not imply that SOEs should not be privatized. In fact, in industrialized countries, governments often privatize profitable enterprises.
22  For a detailed discussion, see Megginson (1997: 316).
23  Export and import shares depend greatly on the size of a country (Edwards, 1993). A small country may have a larger share of exports and imports in GDP, while a large country may have a relatively smaller ratio of international trade in output even

though it might be free trade oriented. The current study is a cross-province study and, within one country, the problem mentioned by Edwards might be less severe.

# References

Barro, R. (1991) "Economic Growth in a Cross Section of Countries," *Quarterly Journal of Economics*, 106: 407–43.

China's Bureau of Statistics (various issues) *The Statistical Yearbook of China*, Beijing: Publishing House of China's Bureau of Statistics.

China's Ministry of Finance (various issues) *The Finance Yearbook of China*, Beijing: Publishing House of Financial Journals.

Chow, G.C. (1993) "Capital Formation and Economic Growth in China," *Quarterly Journal of Economics*, 108: 809–42.

Di, N. (1992) "Guoying gongye qiye qiankui jingren," *Jingji Yanjiu Can Kao*, 22: 2–8.

Editorial Group (1981) "Modern Chinese Economic History," 2, Department of Political Economy, People's University.

Edwards, S. (1993) "Openness, Trade Liberalization, and Growth in Developing Countries," *Journal of Economic Literature*, 31: 1358–93.

Fan, G. and W.T. Woo (1996) "State Enterprise Reform as a Source of Macroeconomic Instability: The Case of China," *Asian Economic Journal*, 10: 207–24.

Garnaut, R., S. Ligang, T. Stoyan and Y. Yang (2003) *A Study of Firm Restructuring in China*, Washington, DC: The World Bank.

Guo, B. (2004) "Contribution of China's SOEs in Industrial Sectors: 1993–1997," China Social Sciences.

Holz, C. (2002a) "The Impact of Competition and Labor Remuneration on Profitability in China's Industrial State-owned Enterprises," *Journal of Contemporary China*, 11: 515–38.

—— (2002b) "Impact of the Liability–Asset Ratio on Profitability in China's Industrial State-owned Enterprises," *China Economic Review*, 13: 1–26.

Jefferson, G. and T. Rawski (1994) "Enterprises Reform in Chinese Industry," *Journal of Economic Perspectives*, 8: 47–70.

Landau, D. (1983) "Government Expenditure and Economic Growth: a Cross-Country Study," *Southern Economic Journal*, 49: 783–92.

Megginson, W. (1997) *Corporate Finance Theory*, Reading, MA: Addison-Wesley Educational Publishing.

Modigliani, F. and M. Miller (1958) "The Cost of Capital, Corporation Finance, and the Theory of Investment," *American Economic Review*, 48: 261–97.

Naughton, B. (1992) "Implications of the State Monopoly over Industry and its Relaxation," *Modern China*, 18: 14–41.

—— (1995) *Growing Out of the Plan: Chinese Economic Reforms 1978–1993*, Cambridge: Cambridge University Press.

Raiser, M. (1997) "Evaluating Chinese Industrial Reforms: SOEs between Output Growth and Profit Decline," *Asian Economic Journal*, 11: 299–323.

Rawski, T. (1994) "Chinese Industrial Reform: Accomplishments, Prospects, and Implications," *American Economic Review*, 84: 271–75.

Romer, P.M. (1989) "What Determines the Rate of Growth and Technological Change?," *Working Paper no. 279*, Washington, DC: World Bank.

Stiglitz, J. (1994) *Whither Socialism?* Cambridge, MA: The MIT Press.

Sun, Y. and K.K. Fung (1982) *Social Needs Versus Economic Efficiency in China: Sun Yefang's Critique of Socialist Economics*, New York: M.E. Sharpe.

Wu, X. (1997) *Research Reports on Debt Restructuring of China's State Sector (zhongguo guoyou jinji zaiwu chongzu yanjiu baogao)*, Beijing: China Financial Press.

Yin, X. (2001) "A Dynamic Analysis of Overstaff in China's State-owned Enterprises," *Journal of Development Economics*, 66: 87–99.

Zhang, A., Y. Zhang and R. Zhao (2002) "Profitability and Productivity of Chinese Industrial Firms: Measurement and Ownership Implications," *China Economic Review*, 13: 65–88.

Zhang, W. (1999) "China's SOE Reform: A Corporate Governance Perspective," manuscripts, Guanghua School of Management, Peking University.

# 7 A panel data sensitivity analysis of regional growth in China

*Kerk L. Phillips and Baizhu Chen*

## Introduction

One of the phenomena that confront economists interested in East Asia in general, and China in particular, is the episodes of very rapid growth that have occurred and are occurring here.[1] From an empirical and theoretical standpoint, this phenomenon cries out to be understood, especially as it contrasts so sharply with the experience in other parts of the world. From a welfare perspective, as well, the issue looms very large indeed. When one begins to grasp the potential size of the Chinese economy if it were more fully developed and the numbers of people that would be affected, it is difficult to think of other areas of economics where a clearer understanding yields greater potential benefits.

One potential way to gain a better understanding of the growth process in China is to look at differences in growth across regions or provinces in China. In the past two decades of double digit annual growth for China, the bulk of the growth has occurred in the coastal provinces of Jiangsu, Zhejiang, Fujian, and Guangdong. Growth in other parts of China has been respectable, but nowhere near as strong. The discrepancies in growth rates in different provinces have resulted in enlarged per capita income across regions, which may undermine the social instability of the country. Why are the regional differences in growth rates so large? What are the major factors that drive faster growth in coastal regions and what are the factors that inhibit economic growth in other regions? Answers to these questions are not only important to the policy-makers in China to understand the mechanisms of economic growth, but can also contribute to a vast literature of economic growth in understanding the factors of long-run growth.

In conjunction with the impressive growth rate in China, there has been a rising interest in understanding the nature of Chinese economic growth. Chow (1993) was probably the first to try to decompose the factors of Chinese growth. He concluded that capital formation, but not technological progress, played a principle role in China's economic growth from 1952 to 1980. Borensztein and Ostry (1996) also tried to perform growth accounting for the Chinese data and found that productivity was the driving force behind economic growth after the Chinese economic reforms in 1978. Chen and Fleisher (1996) compared the total factor productivity of China's coastal and non-coastal provinces. They found that investment in higher education and direct foreign investment helped to explain the productivity gap and the long-term growth of these provinces. In a cross-province study based on the post-reform data, Chen and Feng (2000) found that the factors contributing to the difference in growth rates included human capital, the degree of openness, the share of state-owned enterprises, and the fertility rate. Bao *et al.* (2002), on the other hand, found that geographic location is the dominant explanation for the divergent provincial economic growth rates in China. These studies all suggest that there are many variables that could potentially be important for explaining long-run economic growth in China.

One problem associated with the empirical growth literature is its *ad hoc* nature of including explanatory variables. Numerous empirical studies since the seminal work of Barro (1991) have identified a substantial number of variables that can explain long-run economic growth. Often, many of these variables become no longer significant once some other variables are included in the regression equations. In fact, Levine and Renelt (1992) conclude that very few or no variables are able to robustly explain the long-run growth rate, after applying Leamer's (1985) extreme-bounds test. This result has seriously challenged the empirical growth literature. On the other hand, Sala-i-Martin (1997) argues that the methodology employed by Levine and Renelt (1992) is too restrictive for any variables to pass the test. He has thus redesigned the test to look at the entire distribution of the coefficient estimators to calculate the confidence levels. The Chinese growth literature is also subject to similar criticisms of the *ad hoc* nature of the regression functions. Many variables that are found to be important growth-driving factors in some empirical studies are no longer important in regression equations in other studies. To confidently identify the factors that drive economic growth in China and thus provide solid policy guidance, it is necessary to apply a similar test to that of Sala-i-Martin (1997) to the Chinese data. This is what this chapter intends to do.

The following section describes the data set. Then, the methodology for carrying out the test is illustrated, and the test results are provided, followed by the conclusions.

## Data set

Our data set consists of various data taken from Chinese statistical publications that are compiled at the provincial level every year. Our sample runs from 1978 to 1999 and includes 30 provinces, autonomous regions, and independently administered cities. The city of Chongqing was made independent from Sichuan province in 1996. We aggregate these two regions for 1996–99, making it consistent with earlier observations.

We are able to gather a reasonably complete set of data for the variables listed in Table 7.1. We have double checked this data for accuracy and, in cases where there are obvious, yet uncorrectable, errors, we have omitted the observations. With data for 21 years and 30 provinces, we potentially have 630 observations, although we often have less than that in practice.

*Table 7.1* Adjusted data used in regressions, 30 provinces, 1978–97

| Variable | Description | Units |
|---|---|---|
| RGDPPC | Real GDP per capita | 10,000 1995 RMB |
| GRGDPPC | Annual growth of real GDP per capita | Percentage |
| TFP | Total factor productivity | Number |
| GTFP | Growth of TFP | Percentage |
| RINVPC | Real investment per capita | 1995 RMB |
| RFINVPC | Real fixed investment per capita | 1995 RMB |
| SOEEMPP | SOE staff and workers as a percentage of total employment | Percentage |
| SOEPRODP | SOE industrial output as a percentage of total industrial output | Percentage |
| SOECONP | Value of SOE construction as a percentage of total construction value | Percentage |
| SOERETP | SOE retail sales as a percentage of total retail sales | Percentage |
| SOEINVP | SOE investment as a percentage of total fixed capital investment | Percentage |
| GPOP | Annual growth in population | Percentage |
| MPOPP | Percentage of population that is male | Percentage |
| AGPOPP | Percentage of population classified as "agricultural" | Percentage |
| GOVTGDPP | Government consumption as a percentage of GDP | Percentage |
| IISGDPP | Change in inventories as a percentage of GDP | Percentage |
| NEXGDPP | Net exports as a percentage of GDP | Percentage |
| CAPINVP | Percentage of fixed capital investment classified as "constuction of fixed capital" | Percentage |
| INNINVP | Percentage of fixed capital investment classified as "innovation capital" | Percentage |
| RFCAUPC | Real value of "foreign capital actually utilized" per capita | RMB |
| RFLONPC | Real value of foreign loans | RMB |
| RFDIPC | Real value of foreign direct investment | RMB |
| LGRGOVP | Local government revenue as a percentage of government consumption | Percentage |
| LGEGOVP | Local government expenses as a percentage of government consumption | Percentage |
| LTAXLGRP | Local government tax revenue as a percentage of local government revenue | Percentage |
| LGCCLGEP | Local government capital consumption as a percentage of local government expenditure | Percentage |
| LGINLGEP | Local government innovation investment as a percentage of local government expenditure | Percentage |

| Variable | Description | Units |
|----------|-------------|-------|
| LGAGLGEP | Local government agricultural supports as a percentage of local government expenditure | Percentage |
| LGOTLGEP | Local government other expenses as a percentage of local government expenditure | Percentage |
| LGADLGEP | Local government administrative expenses as a percentage of local government expenditure | Percentage |
| DEPGDPP | National bank deposits as a percentage of GDP | Percentage |
| EDEPGDPP | Enterprise bank deposits as a percentage of GDP | Percentage |
| PSEPC | Primary school students enrolled as a percentage of population | Percentage |
| SSEPC | Secondary school students enrolled as a percentage of population | Percentage |
| RSEPC | Regular secondary school students enrolled as a percentage of population | Percentage |
| HEEPC | Higher education students enrolled as a percentage of population | Percentage |
| PSTPC | Primary school teachers as a percentage of population | Percentage |
| SSTPC | Secondary school teachers as a percentage of population | Percentage |
| RSTPC | Regular secondary school teachers as a percentage of population | Percentage |
| HETPC | Higher education teachers as a percentage of population | Percentage |
| HINSPC | Health institutions per capita | Number |
| HOSPPC | Hospitals per capita | Number |
| HIBEDPC | Health institution beds per capita | Number |
| HOBEDPC | Hospital beds per capita | Number |
| MEDPC | Medical technians per capita | Number |
| DOCPC | Doctors per capita | Number |
| RRDDEN | Kilometers of railroad per square kilometer of area | Number |
| HWYDEN | Kilometers of highway per square kilometer of area | Number |
| TELPC | Telephones per capita | Number |
| RSOEIO | Real SOE industrial output | 10,000 1995 RMB |
| GRSOEIO | Growth of real SOE industrial output | Percentage |
| MIGRATE | Implied population migrating into a province | 10,000 persons |
| MRATE | Implied population migrating into a province | Per 1,000 |

Note
GDP, gross domestic product; RMB, renminbi; SOE, state-owned enterprise.

Our major sources of data are all ultimately traceable to the National Bureau of Statistics, although they have come to us by a variety of methods. Some are from yearbooks published in China. Others come from Hsueh *et al.* (1993), an excellent source of provincial data up to 1989. Additional sources include the English/Chinese language *China Statistical Yearbook* in various printed and CD-ROM editions. Finally, the CD-ROM on *Fifty Years of Chinese Statistical Data* was also a useful source.

We gathered data on as many series as we could find that could arguably be important for economic growth and development. There are, of course, literally thousands of kinds of data that fit this criterion. However, the need for consistently reported data from all or most provinces for the bulk of the sample period turns out to be a great winnower of data. We end up with the series reported in Table 7.1.

These variables can be broadly classified into nine categories:

1  Investment and types of investment: real investment per capita, real fixed investment per capita, and percentage of fixed capital investment classified as "construction of fixed capital." As a large component of investment is made by state-owned enterprises (SOEs) and government, to capture this important feature of the Chinese economy, we also include SOE investment as a percentage of total fixed capital investment, and both local government capital consumption and innovation investment as a percentage of local government expenditures.

2  SOE variables: SOE staff and workers as a percentage of total employment, SOE industrial output as a percentage of total industrial output, the value of SOE construction as a percentage of total construction values, real SOE industrial output, growth of real SOE industrial output, etc.

3  Population and demographic variables: annual growth in population and percentage of the population that is male, implied population migrating into a province, and implied population rate migrating into a province per 1,000 population.

4  Openness: net exports as a percentage of gross domestic product (GDP), real value of foreign capital actually utilized per capita, real value of foreign loans, and real value of foreign direct investment.

5  Financial market development: national bank deposits as a percentage of GDP and enterprise bank deposits as a percentage of GDP.

6  Education and human capital: primary school students enrolled as a percentage of the population, secondary school students enrolled as a percentage of the population, secondary school teachers as a percentage of the population, health institutions per capita, hospital beds per capita, etc.

7  Infrastructure: railroad per square kilometer of area, highway per square kilometer of area, and telephones per capita.

8  Urbanization: percentage of the population classified as "agricultural."

9  Government consumption: government consumption as a percentage of GDP, local government revenue as a percentage of government consumption, etc.

## Methodology

In the past two decades, there has been a blossoming of research in economics concentrating on economic growth. Much of this work has been empirical in nature, and the bulk of it has used data from cross-country regression analysis. Advances in statistical analysis and increases in available computing power have made it possible to move away from cross-sectional studies that use long-run (30-year averages) growth across a sample of several dozen countries. Instead, focus has begun to shift to panel regressions that utilize data from several countries observed at several points in time.

Levine and Renelt (1992) showed that very few things can be said to robustly explain growth. Using a cross-section of 119 countries, they find that initial GDP per capita, investment as a percentage of GDP, and secondary school enrollment rates are the only robustly significant variables in their data set. Other variables can be shown to be sometimes significant and other times insignificant, depending on exactly what set of explanatory factors is used.

Sala-i-Martin (1997) shows that, when a less restrictive (but arguably more reasonable) criterion is used, many of these variables can be said to have robust effects on growth. Many of these variables are national in nature, however. That is, their effects impact roughly equally on all regions within a country. Examples are variability of inflation rates, degree of property rights enforcement, financial market efficiency, etc. One of the challenges that this chapter faces is finding which things can explain differences within a country.

For this chapter, we employ our panel of data from Chinese provinces and estimate regressions with $g_{it}$ as the dependent variable and $y_{it-1}$ and $x_{it-1}$ as regressors. $g_{it}$ is the per capita growth rate in province $i$ over time period $t$, $y_{it-1}$ is the lagged value of the regressor in which we are interested, and $x_{it-1}$ is a set drawn from a pool of other lagged regressors listed in Table 7.2. We choose all possible permutations of three regressors in $x_{it-1}$. Unlike Levine and Renelt (1992) and Sala-i-Martin (1997), we do not a priori assign any of our variables to a list of permanent regressors, which are always included. To control for panel data fixed effects, we do include a set of province and year dummies in every regression, however. The form for the regression is:

$$g_{it} = F_{it}'\beta_F + y_{it-1}\beta_y + x_{it-1}'\beta_x + \varepsilon_{it} \tag{7.1}$$

where $g_{it}$ is the dependent variable, $F_{it}$ is a vector of province and time period dummy variables and the lagged value of real GDP per capita,[2] $y_{it}$ is a scalar, $x_{it}$ is a $3 \times 1$ vector, and $\beta_F$, $\beta_y$ and $\beta_x$ are the corresponding coefficient vectors.

We have a serious problem with missing observations in our data set. In order to compare the results of thousands of regression permutations, it is essential that we use the same sample set for all of them. However, if we restrict ourselves to observations where data are available for all regressors, we lose almost two-thirds of our data (242 available observations out of 630). This method ignores

*Table 7.2* Percentage of regressions where variable is significantly different from zero

| Variable | Non-missing observations | | | Dummies for missing observations | | |
|---|---|---|---|---|---|---|
| | *90%* | *95%* | *99%* | *90%* | *95%* | *99%* |
| RINVPC | 1.07 | 0.12 | 0.00 | 16.43 | 6.06 | 2.49 |
| RFINVPC | 3.72 | 1.36 | 0.03 | 18.07 | 5.64 | 0.91 |
| SOEEMPP | 36.32 | 17.50 | 1.17 | 68.44 | 40.85 | 7.81 |
| SOEPRODP | **94.87** | 71.35 | 12.39 | 4.96 | 0.45 | 0.00 |
| SOECONP | 0.54 | 0.01 | 0.00 | 0.00 | 0.00 | 0.00 |
| SOERETP | 17.02 | 5.56 | 0.67 | 0.00 | 0.00 | 0.00 |
| SOEINVP | 28.43 | 14.00 | 0.93 | 0.00 | 0.00 | 0.00 |
| GPOP | 0.00 | 0.00 | 0.00 | 2.04 | 0.50 | 0.02 |
| MPOPP | 0.05 | 0.00 | 0.00 | 2.34 | 0.45 | 0.00 |
| AGPOPP | 0.16 | 0.01 | 0.00 | 0.78 | 0.19 | 0.01 |
| GOVTGDPP | 3.67 | 0.06 | 0.00 | 6.74 | 6.24 | 5.74 |
| IISGDPP | 0.00 | 0.00 | 0.00 | 0.01 | 0.00 | 0.00 |
| NEXGDPP | 20.96 | 4.05 | 0.01 | **100.00** | **99.99** | **99.17** |
| CAPINVP | 8.85 | 3.35 | 0.01 | 0.00 | 0.00 | 0.00 |
| INNINVP | **100.00** | **100.00** | **100.00** | 99.24 | 78.12 | 0.08 |
| RFCAUPC | 49.97 | 20.39 | 0.49 | 1.28 | 0.01 | 0.00 |
| RFLONPC | 64.70 | 48.80 | 11.72 | 1.21 | 0.38 | 0.00 |
| RFDIPC | 7.35 | 0.31 | 0.00 | 2.46 | 0.18 | 0.00 |
| LGRGOVP | **98.94** | **97.81** | **90.74** | **93.95** | **93.58** | 85.87 |
| LGEGOVP | 0.06 | 0.01 | 0.00 | **99.15** | 88.99 | 24.86 |
| LTAXLGRP | 18.37 | 5.69 | 0.09 | 0.00 | 0.00 | 0.00 |
| LGCCLGEP | 0.00 | 0.00 | 0.00 | 0.01 | 0.00 | 0.00 |
| LGINLGEP | 3.65 | 1.35 | 0.01 | 0.00 | 0.00 | 0.00 |
| LGAGLGEP | 0.21 | 0.00 | 0.00 | 0.09 | 0.00 | 0.00 |
| LGOTLGEP | 0.01 | 0.00 | 0.00 | 28.72 | 12.26 | 1.37 |
| LGADLGEP | 0.00 | 0.00 | 0.00 | 0.20 | 0.02 | 0.00 |
| DEPGDPP | **97.13** | **92.43** | 62.11 | **98.88** | **95.25** | 88.92 |
| EDEPGDPP | 87.91 | 71.96 | 13.62 | **93.01** | 88.92 | 72.20 |
| PSEPC | **90.69** | 75.48 | 15.14 | 32.43 | 7.51 | 0.15 |
| SSEPC | 10.92 | 6.05 | 0.17 | 19.59 | 13.30 | 2.02 |
| RSEPC | 2.42 | 0.54 | 0.02 | 4.85 | 1.35 | 0.03 |
| HEEPC | 12.64 | 5.19 | 0.06 | 10.88 | 7.00 | 0.47 |
| PSTPC | 0.79 | 0.29 | 0.00 | 0.00 | 0.00 | 0.00 |
| SSTPC | 31.75 | 20.09 | 5.89 | 9.63 | 6.49 | 1.14 |

| Variable | Non-missing observations | | | Dummies for missing observations | | |
|---|---|---|---|---|---|---|
| | *90%* | *95%* | *99%* | *90%* | *95%* | *99%* |
| RSTPC | 22.27 | 10.86 | 0.42 | 6.23 | 2.13 | 0.08 |
| HETPC | **100.00** | **99.98** | **94.39** | 65.19 | 41.62 | 14.75 |
| HINSPC | 14.47 | 7.29 | 0.35 | **91.69** | 43.11 | 5.02 |
| HOSPPC | 1.31 | 0.32 | 0.00 | **94.46** | 71.69 | 1.42 |
| HIBEDPC | 28.35 | 10.55 | 1.00 | 0.25 | 0.08 | 0.00 |
| HOBEDPC | 3.38 | 1.01 | 0.27 | 2.73 | 0.30 | 0.01 |
| MEDPC | 17.54 | 9.12 | 1.42 | 8.56 | 2.87 | 0.17 |
| DOCPC | 2.00 | 0.97 | 0.07 | 6.21 | 2.60 | 0.05 |
| RRDDEN | 65.56 | 33.68 | 18.46 | 49.43 | 31.22 | 18.66 |
| HWYDEN | 0.84 | 0.24 | 0.00 | 0.00 | 0.00 | 0.00 |
| TELPC | 79.70 | 63.07 | 19.48 | **94.35** | **90.22** | 86.64 |
| RSOEIO | 28.37 | 14.66 | 5.81 | 0.68 | 0.06 | 0.00 |
| GRSOEIO | 11.03 | 1.98 | 0.01 | 33.21 | 9.97 | 0.03 |
| MIGRATE | **93.75** | **93.75** | **93.72** | **93.75** | **93.75** | **93.75** |
| MRATE | **93.92** | **93.75** | **93.55** | **93.75** | **93.75** | **93.75** |

Notes
Numbers in bold refer to more than 90% of times rejecting the null hypothesis of insignificance of
the variable in the growth regressions.
For meaning of variable abbreviations, see Table 7.1.

useful information from non-missing regressors. Therefore, we estimate using
this sample, but we also use a second method.

For every regressor, we create a dummy variable set to 1 if the regressor is
missing and 0 otherwise. We set missing values to 0 and estimate including both
the regressor and the dummy variable. The form of the estimated equation in this
case is:

$$g_{it} = F_{it}\beta_F + y_{it-1}(1 - d_{it-1}^y)\beta_y + d_{it-1}^y\beta_{dy} + x_{it-1}(I - d_{it-1}^x)\beta_x + d_{it-1}^x\beta_{dy} + \varepsilon_{it}$$
(7.2)

where $d_{it-1}^y$ is a scalar and $d_{it-1}^x$ is a diagonal $2 \times 2$ matrix of missing/non-missing
dummy variables for $y_{it-1}$ and $x_{it-1}$.

This method includes effects conditional on regressors being missing as well
as their effects when observable. It allows us to include the full sample of 630
observations. We focus our attention on the $\beta_y$ coefficient, particularly its robustness and significance.

## Results of estimation

We estimate Equations 7.1 and 7.2 for each of the 49 regressors in Table 7.2 using ordinary least squares (OLS). Each regression includes all permutations of three of the remaining 48 regressors for a total of 211,876 regressions or 4324 per regressor[3] in which we are interested. To examine significance and robustness, we adopt three different approaches following Sala-i-Martin (1997).[4]

First, we test the significance of $\beta_y$ for each regression. We do this with a simple $t$-test. We then tally the number of times we reject the null hypothesis that $\beta_y$ is zero. These results for both regressions, Equation 7.1 and Equation 7.2, are shown in Table 7.2. We show the percentage of rejections for one-tailed tests at 90 percent, 95 percent and 99 percent confidence levels. Table 7.2 is one step away from the restrictive extreme-bounds test by looking at the entire distribution of the estimator of $\beta_y$.[5] The results in Table 7.2, however, do not provide us with definite answers as to which variables are robust. All they tell us is which variables are more likely to be significant in growth regressions. For example, we can reject 100 percent at even the 99 percent level of significance that IN-NINVP (percentage of fixed capital investment classified as "innovation capital") is not robust, for the regression (Equation 7.1) with non-missing observations. Compared with other variables, INNINVP is more likely to be significant in a growth regression. Similarly, comparing LGRGOVP (local government revenue as a percentage of government consumption) with LGCCLGEP (local government capital consumption as a percentage of local government expenditures) in the non-missing observation regression, there is a bigger chance that LGRGOVP is robust than LGCCLGEP. We also note that the results can change when we use regression (Equation 7.2) with dummies for missing observations instead of (Equation 7.1) with non-missing observations. For example, at the 99 percent level of significance, there is only 0.08 percent of times that we can reject that INNINVP is not robust.

Second, we calculated the weighted average of the coefficient estimates, $\beta_y$, and the weighted average of the variances,[6] for all the regressions corresponding to the regressor $y$. The $t$-statistics can then be calculated based on the weighted average of the coefficient estimates and variances.[7] The corresponding significance from two-tailed tests is reported in Table 7.3.

The first is LGRGOVP, local government revenue as a percentage of total government consumption. This coefficient is robustly negative, using both non-missing observations and dummies for missing observations. It is a measure of the relative size of local government, but it also includes a ratio of revenue to expenses. As other measures of government size, such as local government expenditures as a percentage of total government consumption, are not robustly significant, we interpret this result as coming from the ratio of revenue to expenses. The results indicate that provinces that collect more revenue, but spend less, will have lower growth rates. This is consistent with Keynesian notions of fiscal stimulus, but it is also consistent with inefficiencies induced by taxation.

A second pair of robust variables is DEPGDPP and EDEPGDPP. These are

*Table 7.3* Simple averages

| Variable | Non-missing observations | | | Dummies for missing observations | | |
|---|---|---|---|---|---|---|
| | Coefficient | t-statistics | Significance | Coefficient | t-statistics | Significance |
| RINVPC | −3.4E−07 | −0.335 | − | 7.94E−07 | 1.066 | − |
| RFINVPC | −1.6E−07 | −0.175 | − | 6.45E−07 | 0.879 | − |
| SOEEMPP | −0.25659 | −1.353 | − | −0.22583 | −1.882 | * |
| SOEPRODP | −0.10894 | −2.186 | ** | −0.04121 | −1.058 | − |
| SOECONP | 0.02689 | 0.817 | − | 0.00178 | 0.069 | − |
| SOERETP | 0.11645 | 1.336 | − | −0.00537 | −0.181 | − |
| SOEINVP | 0.08497 | 1.407 | − | 0.00218 | 0.069 | − |
| GPOP | −0.01894 | −0.036 | − | 0.03866 | 0.700 | − |
| MPOPP | 0.09273 | 0.085 | − | −0.3592 | −0.559 | − |
| AGPOPP | −0.03332 | −0.254 | − | 0.05548 | 0.552 | − |
| GOVTGDPP | 0.25014 | 1.206 | − | 0.12219 | 1.063 | − |
| IISGDPP | 0.00868 | 0.071 | − | −0.01807 | −0.242 | − |
| NEXGDPP | −0.055 | −1.088 | − | −0.15062 | −4.145 | *** |
| CAPINVP | −0.04366 | −0.655 | − | −0.02276 | −0.676 | − |
| INNINVP | 0.3901 | 4.415 | *** | 0.13157 | 2.093 | ** |
| RFCAUPC | 2.3E−05 | 1.457 | − | 6.12E−06 | 0.401 | − |
| RFLONPC | 4.18E−05 | 1.622 | * | −3.9E−06 | −0.122 | − |
| RFDIPC | 1.75E−05 | 0.871 | − | 1.1E−05 | 0.600 | − |
| LGRGOVP | −0.01504 | −3.186 | *** | −0.00722 | −2.996 | *** |
| LGEGOVP | −0.00267 | −0.212 | − | 0.01679 | 2.455 | ** |
| LTAXLGRP | 0.03829 | 1.260 | − | 0.01581 | 0.714 | − |
| LGCCLGEP | 0.03853 | 0.256 | − | 0.00507 | 0.071 | − |
| LGINLGEP | −0.01994 | −0.186 | − | 0.00982 | 0.133 | − |
| LGAGLGEP | −0.1371 | −0.686 | − | 0.07422 | 0.737 | − |
| LGOTLGEP | 0.03513 | 0.252 | − | 0.13093 | 1.512 | − |
| LGADLGEP | 0.01527 | 0.104 | − | 0.01739 | 0.175 | − |
| DEPGDPP | 0.09354 | 2.761 | *** | 0.07625 | 3.201 | *** |
| EDEPGDPP | 0.11105 | 2.036 | ** | 0.10949 | 2.609 | *** |
| PSEPC | 0.65408 | 2.194 | ** | 0.33948 | 1.523 | − |
| SSEPC | 0.6418 | 0.764 | − | 0.47974 | 1.348 | − |
| RSEPC | −0.31337 | −0.351 | − | 0.11095 | 0.314 | − |
| HEEPC | −10.2829 | −0.918 | − | 3.15955 | 0.696 | − |
| PSTPC | −0.00051 | −0.388 | − | 0.000625 | 0.671 | − |
| SSTPC | −0.00197 | −1.119 | − | −0.00081 | −0.992 | − |
| RSTPC | −0.00174 | −0.916 | − | 0.000306 | 0.340 | − |

*Table 7.3* continued

| Variable | Non-missing observations | | | Dummies for missing observations | | |
|---|---|---|---|---|---|---|
| | Coefficient | t-statistics | Significance | Coefficient | t-statistics | Significance |
| HETPC | −0.02316 | −3.366 | *** | −0.00647 | −1.937 | * |
| HINSPC | −0.00906 | −1.253 | – | 0.01283 | 1.968 | ** |
| HOSPPC | 0.0162 | 0.768 | – | 0.03995 | 2.084 | ** |
| HIBEDPC | −32.8089 | −1.436 | – | 4.3872 | 0.398 | – |
| HOBEDPC | −15.2398 | −0.759 | – | 11.89772 | 0.976 | – |
| MEDPC | 17.08841 | 0.913 | – | 10.57837 | 0.858 | – |
| DOCPC | 4.96143 | 0.184 | – | 7.63932 | 0.465 | – |
| RRDDEN | −1.58807 | −2.094 | ** | −1.23205 | −1.923 | * |
| HWYDEN | −0.01687 | −0.157 | – | −0.02207 | −0.296 | – |
| TELPC | 3.63E–05 | 1.986 | ** | 4.85E–05 | 3.046 | *** |
| RSOEIO | 2.09E–05 | 1.416 | – | 5.0E–06 | 0.416 | – |
| GRSOEIO | 0.02775 | 0.973 | – | 0.04984 | 1.556 | – |
| MIGRATE | −0.00025 | −3.043 | *** | −0.00033 | −4.382 | *** |
| MRATE | −0.00096 | −3.615 | *** | −0.00117 | −3.704 | *** |

Notes
\*    90% confidence.
\*\*   95% confidence.
\*\*\* 99% confidence.
For meaning of variable abbreviations, see Table 7.1.

bank deposits to GDP and a subset of bank deposits, "enterprise" bank deposits, to GDP ratios. These variables can be interpreted as measures of the depth of the financial market. They are both significantly positive. This indicates that having a greater amount of savings deposits within the province itself is positively correlated with growth. One interpretation could be that savings are used to finance investment, and there are barriers between provinces of some sort that make local savings an important source of these funds. This view is bolstered by the fact that the investment to GDP ratio is also robustly significant, albeit at lower confidence levels. Another possibility is that the result is due to the presence of large numbers of entrepreneurs.

A third set of robustly negative variables is MIGRATE and MRATE, which are measures of net migration into a province. These measures were calculated by taking the difference from year to year in the reported population statistics along with reported birth and death rates, and then solving for the number of migrants necessary to make the figures match exactly. This is a very rough measure of migration and subject to all sorts of measurement errors, and it probably understates the actual amount of migration. If birth rates are under-reported, but population numbers are accurate, the migration measures will reflect these unreported births. In reality, population figures are probably not accurate, particularly for provinces and municipalities with large urban populations and the accompanying large numbers of illegal migrants from the countryside. It is likely, therefore, that this statistic proxies for population growth in some way, although it should be noted that population growth is included as a regressor and is never significant.

A fourth robust variable is INNINVP. This is the percentage of fixed capital investment classified as "innovation capital." This variable is significantly positive in both regressions. Given that all the other investment variables are not significant, this suggests the importance of innovation and implies that provinces that devote a larger amount of investment capital for innovation are likely to experience higher growth.

We also find that both SOEPRODP and SOEEMPP are negative in the regressions. SOEPRODP is the SOE industrial output as a percentage of total industrial output. SOEEMPP is the SOE staff and workers as a percentage of total employment. Both variables measure the importance of the state sector in each province. We find that SOEPRODP is significantly negative in the regressions with non-missing observations, although not in Eq. (2). Similarly, we only find SOEEMPP to be significantly negative in regression with dummies for missing observations, but not in Eq. (1). However, both are negative in the growth equation. They are consistent with the findings of Chen and Feng (2000).

Of our infrastructure variables, TELPC, the number of telephones per capita, is robustly positive. However, RRDDEN, the kilometers of railroad per square kilometer of area in a province, is robustly negative, and this is quite puzzling to us. For all these variables, there is also a difficulty in establishing causality. The regression lags all regressors one year, but this may not be sufficient to make them truly exogenous.

In addition to these variables, there are others that are robust at lower levels of confidence, or appear to be robust by some measures and in one sample size, but not in others. Some of the variables have the signs, which are counterintuitive and are opposite to what a standard growth theory predicts. For example, higher education students enrolled as a percentage of the population is negatively correlated with growth. We find that the primary school enrollment per capita is positively correlated with economic growth. The variable PSEPC is significant in Eq. (1) at the 95 percent level of significance, but not in Eq. (2). We also find, against our intuition, that the number of higher education teachers per capita is negatively correlated. Finally, using the full sample only, net exports as a percentage of GDP are negatively correlated with growth.[8]

In Table 7.4, we rerun the regressions of Table 7.3 using the weighted least squares method to control for the heteroskedasticity. The weights are proportional to the likelihood value for each regression calculated in Table 7.3. Table 7.4 replicates Table 7.3 using this weighting scheme.

## Conclusions

In this chapter, we asked the question: "what factors are likely to be robustly correlated with economic growth in China?" To answer this question, we applied the

Table 7.4 Weighted averages

| Variable | Non-missing observations | | | Dummies for missing observations | | |
|---|---|---|---|---|---|---|
| | Coefficient | t-statistics | Significance | Coefficient | t-statistics | Significance |
| RINVPC | –4.1E–07 | –0.419 | | 6.07E–07 | 0.822 | |
| RFINVPC | –2.73E–07 | –0.292 | | 4.24E–07 | 0.576 | |
| SOEEMPP | –0.22543 | –1.159 | | –0.23294 | –1.939 | * |
| SOEPRODP | –0.11589 | –2.283 | ** | –0.03868 | –0.995 | |
| SOECONP | 0.02494 | 0.771 | | 0.000775 | 0.030 | |
| SOERETP | 0.10815 | 1.254 | | –0.00382 | –0.130 | |
| SOEINVP | 0.08261 | 1.399 | | 0.00163 | 0.052 | |
| GPOP | –0.0479 | –0.092 | | 0.03962 | 0.712 | |
| MPOPP | 0.02589 | 0.023 | | –0.36463 | –0.563 | |
| AGPOPP | –0.03215 | –0.249 | | 0.06129 | 0.613 | |
| GOVTGDPP | 0.22234 | 1.109 | | 0.13572 | 1.151 | |
| IISGDPP | 0.00448 | 0.037 | | –0.02163 | –0.289 | |
| NEXGDPP | –0.04856 | –0.971 | | –0.15148 | –4.207 | *** |
| CAPINVP | –0.03917 | –0.592 | | –0.02163 | –0.649 | |
| INNINVP | 0.39493 | 4.509 | *** | 0.12847 | 2.051 | ** |
| RFCAUPC | 2.16E–05 | 1.422 | | 3.68E–06 | 0.244 | |
| RFLONPC | 4.01E–05 | 1.579 | * | –1.26E–05 | –0.392 | |
| RFDIPC | 1.69E–05 | 0.862 | | 9.19E–06 | 0.508 | |
| LGRGOVP | –0.01465 | –3.199 | *** | –0.00726 | –2.988 | *** |
| LGEGOVP | –0.00137 | –0.110 | | 0.01768 | 2.570 | ** |
| LTAXLGRP | 0.03697 | 1.232 | | 0.01483 | 0.675 | |
| LGCCLGEP | 0.03404 | 0.232 | | 0.00711 | 0.100 | |
| LGINLGEP | –0.00568 | –0.053 | | 0.0143 | 0.194 | |
| LGAGLGEP | –0.14136 | –0.716 | | 0.06245 | 0.619 | |
| LGOTLGEP | 0.01419 | 0.103 | | 0.13677 | 1.587 | |
| LGADLGEP | 0.00818 | 0.056 | | 0.02843 | 0.287 | |
| DEPGDPP | 0.10507 | 3.274 | *** | 0.07834 | 3.356 | *** |
| EDEPGDPP | 0.12733 | 2.420 | ** | 0.11122 | 2.765 | *** |
| PSEPC | 0.6416 | 2.178 | ** | 0.33244 | 1.493 | |
| SSEPC | 0.76687 | 0.922 | | 0.50277 | 1.445 | |
| RSEPC | –0.23767 | –0.267 | | 0.18837 | 0.553 | |
| HEEPC | –12.1405 | –1.072 | | 1.81355 | 0.399 | |
| PSTPC | –0.000613 | –0.472 | | 0.00057 | 0.620 | |
| SSTPC | –0.00155 | –0.896 | | –0.00067 | –0.832 | |
| RSTPC | –0.00129 | –0.697 | | 0.000516 | 0.592 | |

| Variable | Non-missing observations | | | Dummies for missing observations | | |
|---|---|---|---|---|---|---|
| | Coefficient | t-statistics | Significance | Coefficient | t-statistics | Significance |
| HETPC | −0.02402 | −3.548 | *** | −0.0073 | −2.192 | ** |
| HINSPC | −0.0087 | −1.224 | | 0.01313 | 2.036 | ** |
| HOSPPC | 0.01774 | 0.849 | | 0.04027 | 2.135 | ** |
| HIBEDPC | −31.09315 | −1.386 | | 3.77846 | 0.346 | |
| HOBEDPC | −15.31964 | −0.773 | | 11.02071 | 0.916 | |
| MEDPC | 22.56012 | 1.191 | | 10.58929 | 0.865 | |
| DOCPC | 7.43062 | 0.279 | | 7.05764 | 0.433 | |
| RRDDEN | −2.07077 | −3.009 | *** | −1.49846 | −2.473 | *** |
| HWYDEN | −0.02299 | −0.215 | | −0.02301 | −0.310 | |
| TELPC | 4.93E–05 | 2.648 | *** | 5.05E–05 | 3.205 | *** |
| RSOEIO | 2.23E–05 | 1.517 | | 5.70E–06 | 0.475 | |
| GRSOEIO | 0.02646 | 0.929 | | 0.05009 | 1.573 | |
| MIGRATE | −0.000251 | −3.193 | *** | −0.00033 | −4.575 | *** |
| MRATE | −0.001 | −3.779 | *** | −0.0012 | −3.907 | *** |

Notes
\*    90% confidence.
\*\*   95% confidence.
\*\*\* 99% confidence.
The meaning of the variable abbreviations is given in Table 7.1.

method used by Sala-i-Martin (1997) to a panel of data that covers 30 provinces, autonomous regions, and direct administered cities of China, from 1978 to 1999. We ran 211,876 regressions with a total of 49 variables being considered, probably the maximum number of variables that we can find for this time period.

We find that quite a few variables are robustly correlated with provincial growth. Among these variables, we specifically find that provinces with more innovation capital and bank deposits tend to grow faster. We also find that provinces with more government revenues but less spending tend to grow more slowly. Out of the 49 variables, other factors that negatively correlated with growth rates also include implied population (both numbers and ratio) migrating into a province, SOE industrial output as a percentage of total industrial output, and SOE staff and workers as a percentage of total employment. Primary school students enrolled as a percentage of the population and telephones per capital are found to be positively correlated with growth.

We have also left some unanswered questions for future research. Our study found that infrastructure investment, as measured by kilometers of railroad per square kilometer of area, is negatively correlated with provincial GDP growth. This is contrary to what most growth theories suggest. Similarly, endogenous growth literature predicts that human capital and openness should both enhance economic growth. However, both human capital, if measured by high education teachers per capita, and openness, if measured by net exports relative to GDP, are negatively correlated with growth in our studies.

## Acknowledgments

We thank Gene Chang, Gan Li, and David Li for helpful comments.

## Notes

1  Young (2000), on the other hand, argued that China's aggregate growth rates were in fact overstated because of a systematic understatement of inflation.
2  The growth literature robustly found a convergence effect by which the economy with lower income tends to grow faster, other things being equal. The lagged value of real GDP per capita is included in each regression to control for convergence effects.
3  Each of the 49 variables serves as a regressor in which we are interested. Three of the remaining 48 variables are included with permutations. Thus, the total number of regressions is $48 \times 47 \times 46 \times 45/(4 \times 3 \times 2 \times 1) = 211,876$.
4  We have also used the extreme-bounds test proposed by Leamer (1985) and used by Levine and Renelt (1992); only INNINVP is robustly significant.
5  In an extreme-bounds test, one calculates the lower extreme bound as the lowest value of $\beta_{yj} - \omega_{yj}$, and the upper extreme bound as the largest value of $\beta_{yj} + \omega_{yj}$, for all the possible regressions. The extreme-bounds test for variable $y$ says that, if the lower extreme bound is negative and the upper extreme bound is positive, then variable $y$ is not robust. This implies that, as long as there is one regression for which the sign of the coefficient changes or is not significant, then the variable is not robustly influential.
6  The weighted average of the point estimates, $\beta_{yj}, j = 1, 2, \ldots 4324$, is calculated as

$$\hat{\beta}_y = \sum_{j=1}^{4234} \omega_{yj} \hat{\beta}_{yj}$$

where the weights are proportional to the likelihoods

$$\omega_{yj} = \frac{L_{yj}}{\sum_{j=1}^{4234} L_{yj}}$$

and $L_{yj}$ is the computed likelihood ratio of the regression. Similarly, the estimated variance is calculated using the weights, $\omega_{yj}$.
7  The way we calculate the variances and standard deviations is exactly the same as that of Sala-i-Martin (1997).
8  Sala-i-Martin (1997) also finds that primary exports have a negative coefficient in his regression equations. No explanation is provided in his paper.

## References

Bao, S., G. Hsin Chand, J.D. Sachs, and Wing Thye Woo (2002) "Geographic Factors and China's Regional Development Under Market Reforms, 1978–98," *China Economic Review*, 13: 89–111.

Barro, R.J. (2001) "Human Capital and Growth," *American Economic Review*, 91(2): 12–17.

Borensztein, E. and J.D. Ostry (1996) "Accounting for China's Growth Performance," *American Economic Review*, 86: 224–8.

Chen, B. and Y. Feng (2000) "Determinants of Economic Growth in China: Private Enterprises, Education, and Openness," *China Economic Review*, 11: 1–15.

Chow, G. (1993) "Capital Formation and Economic Growth in China," *Quarterly Journal of Economics*, 108: 809–42.

Hsueh, Tien-tung and Li □iang (1993) *China's Provincial Statistics: 1949–1989*, Boulder, CO: Westview Press, p. 1999.

Leamer, E.E. (1985) "Sensitivity Analyses Would Help," *American Economic Review*, 75: 308–13.

Levine, R. and D. Renelt (1992) "A Sensitivity Analysis of Cross-Country Growth Regressions," *American Economic Review*, 82: 942–63.

National Bureau of Statistics, People's Republic of China (various editions and CD-ROMs) *China Statistical Yearbook*, Beijing: China Statistics Press, Xinhua Publishers [Zhongguo tong ji chu ban she].

Sala-i-Martin, X. (1997) "I Just Ran Two Million Regressions," *American Economic Review*, 87: 178–83.

Young, A. (2000) "Gold into Base Metals: Productivity Growth in the People's Republic of China during the Reform Period," National Bureau of Economic Research (NBER), Working Papers 7856, August.

# 8 Private, state-owned, and foreign-invested enterprises

## An analysis of investment sources on growth in China

*Yi Feng and Yi Sun*

Resource allocation in enterprises with different ownership types has different effects on economic growth. China has substantial state production; its resource reallocation during the process of economic reform influences economic growth. This chapter investigates China's cross-province data after the middle of the 1990s. We find that the share of investment in collective and individual enterprises is positively related to the growth rate of per capita industry output, while the share of state-owned enterprises (SOEs) is negatively related to the growth rate. In our test, foreign investment does not make a significant impact on economic growth.

## Introduction

Since the launching of economic reforms in 1978, the Chinese economy has grown at a record-setting rate of about 10 percent annually. Many factors have played important roles, including rural reforms that made the household the unit of agricultural production, the opening of the market to international trade and foreign investment, and various price and enterprise reforms, which introduced material incentives to SOE management. These are discussed in the existing literature and are deemed to be important factors in China's early rapid growth. After Deng Xiaoping's speeches during his visit to South China in 1992, Chinese reforms gathered momentum, releasing the constraints on the private economy at various levels. Since then, a flourishing non-state sector has become the most dynamic force in the Chinese economy. Economic growth can be generated through different policy tools including private investment, SOE reforms, and foreign investment. This chapter evaluates the effects of these factors on China's economic growth by examining the impacts of resource allocation on types of enterprise ownership and the growth rate of per capita industrial output, using the data from about 30 Chinese provinces starting in the mid-1990s.

The following section reviews the literature; the next section explains the data, defines the variables, and discusses the methodology used in the test; then, the empirical results on the relationship between resource allocations and the rate of economic growth are presented, followed by the conclusions.

## Literature review

In the last two decades, views concerning the role of the state in the economy have changed substantially in former centrally planned economies. Policy-makers in developing countries are relying more on the private sector and foreign investment in promoting economic growth. The relationship between investment in enterprises of different ownerships and the rate of growth has been the subject of considerable research in recent years. A particular issue of interest is whether domestic private investment has a larger effect on the rate of growth than that of public sector and foreign investment.

The common core of growth theories focuses on the formation of capital taking either a physical or a human form (Solow, 1956; Lucas, 1988; Romer, 1986). Private investment, in multiple studies, has demonstrated positive effects on economic growth in China (Chen and Feng, 2000; Lin, 2000), consistent with the findings of the relationship between private investment and economic growth in cross-country settings (Barro, 1991; Levine and Renelt, 1992; Feng, 2003).

While the effect of private investment on growth is positive, the effect of public investment on growth tends to be ambiguous. Public sector investment can reduce private investment when it utilizes scarce physical and financial resources that would otherwise be available to the private sector, or if it produces marketable output that competes with private output. Furthermore, the financing of public sector investment – whether through taxes, issuance of debt, or seigniorage – will lower the resources available to the private sector and thus depress private investment activity (Khan and Reinhart, 1990).

In addition, scholars contend that public ownership is less efficient in production. Friedman and Friedman (1980) maintain that, when a country's physical resources are government owned, individuals have no direct interest in maintaining and improving the quality of the resources. Therefore, incentives for investment will be dampened as a result of lack or absence of private property rights. Therefore, policies aimed at decreasing public expenditure and promoting private investment will be successful in raising the long-run growth rate. Using some endogenous development models, Romer (1989), Jones and Manuelli (1990), King and Rebelo (1990), and Rebelo (1991) also demonstrate that economic growth will be slowed under the circumstances of overspending in the public sector through increased taxes.

In contrast, recent empirical and theoretical literature emphasizes the positive effect of public investment on growth rate through its complementary effects on private investment. The literature shows that certain public expenditures, notably infrastructure, education, and defense, are important conditions for economic growth. The private sectors cannot effectively produce these pubic goods because of the collective action problems. Therefore, public investment may indirectly contribute to growth. For example, improving infrastructure will not lead directly to growth, but can indirectly induce private investments by the private sector, thus promoting long-run growth. Likewise, public investment improves human resources such as education and health, which in turn enhance growth. Thus, public investment may act as a complement to private investment, thereby increasing economic growth (Kelly, 1997; Lopcu and Oguz, 2001).

The effect of public investment on private investment is ambiguous. Public investment could either increase or decrease private investment, and then affect economic growth. Some empirical studies indicate that public investment will crowd out other investment resulting in less growth (Khan and Reinhart, 1990; Chen and Feng, 2000; Lin, 2000). In contrast, other studies indicate no statistically significant difference between the impact of public and private investment and, in some cases, public expenditure can even be positively related to growth rate (Nazmi and Ramirez, 1997).

In this chapter, we study a particular kind of "public investment." Our focus here is the investment of SOEs in fixed capital, which is different from government investment in defense, education, or infrastructure. These are typically public goods provided by the government. The accumulation of fixed capital by SOEs generates benefits mostly to SOEs themselves, which lack efficiency in an emerging market such as China, and therefore leads to an increase in investment cost.

In developing countries, foreign capital is another important source of investment. Except for the direct impact on investment increases, foreign direct investment inflows in developing countries tend to crowd in other investment and are associated with an overall increase in total investment (Feng and Zhang, 2000). In addition to providing finance, foreign direct investment helps to promote growth in developing economies by facilitating technology transfer, increasing labor force skills, improving management, promoting competition, and increasing exports. The spillover effects translate into greater productivity growth in the whole economy (World Bank, 1999). Borensztein *et al.* (1998) found a one percentage point rise in the ratio of foreign direct investment to gross domestic product (GDP) increases the rate of per capita growth of the host country by 0.8 percent. Tso (1998) identifies the share of foreign firms' output in China's GDP as growing from 0.6 percent in 1980 to more than 16 percent in 1994. According to Sun (1998), foreign direct investment accounts for 17 percent of China's GDP growth from 1983 to 1995.

However, developing countries do not always benefit from foreign direct investment, and the positive impact of foreign direct investment on economic growth depends on the quality of the policy environment in the recipient country. Several studies of the impact of foreign direct investment in some 30 countries, covering 183 projects over more than 15 years, found that a number of projects (25 percent or more, depending on the study and methodology) had a negative effect on the economic welfare of the recipient country (Moran, 1998). Overwhelmingly, the reason for this result is the lack of competitiveness of input and output markets, often influenced by the regulations in the recipient countries. If international firms are protected from competition and are able to generate and appropriate oligopoly rents from barriers to entry, firms may misallocate resources and potentially leave the recipient country worse off than if it had not received investments (World Bank, 1999).

To explore the differentiated effects on growth of investment of different kinds of ownerships, we employ the method used by Lin (2000) to examine their impacts on output growth in China. Lin (2000) studied data from 30 Chinese provinces for the period 1983–96. He investigated the differences between public and private investment in their contributions to aggregate output growth. The basic empirical framework in his article takes the following cross-sectional specification:

$$y / y = \alpha + \beta X + \varepsilon$$

where $y / y$ is the growth rate of per capita GDP, and $X$ is a vector of explanatory variables, including share of investment, initial per capita output level, growth of population, illiteracy rate, etc. He found that the share of private investment is positively related to the growth rate of GDP in 1983–96, and the share of state-owned investment has a negative relationship. This implies that the provinces that invest more in private enterprises will grow faster than the provinces that invest more in state enterprises.

As we have mentioned above, the Chinese economy has achieved another rapid growth period after a temporary setback in 1989–92. The economic environment has changed a great deal during this period. The investment climate saw an appreciable improvement in the private sector after the mid-1990s. During this period, foreign investment experienced a volatile fluctuation during the Asian financial crisis. Few empirical works have studied the sources of Chinese development in this period. With updated data and detailed categories on investment, we are able to compare the contributions of different kinds of investment and investigate the effects of resource allocation on Chinese growth.

## The model and the data

Based on the previous discussion and findings, we adopt the following basic multivariate statistical model:

$$g_i = \beta_0 + \beta_1 Ishare_i + \beta_2 Inioutput_i + \beta_3 Nedu_i + \beta_4 Region_i + \beta_5 Year_i + \varepsilon$$

where $i$ denotes provinces, $g$ denotes the growth rate in real provincial industrial output value per capita, *Inioutput* is the initial level of industrial output, *Nedu* refers to illiteracy rate, *Ishare* stands for the share of *investment in fixed assets* for enterprises of different ownership, including SOEs, collective enterprises, foreign-funded enterprises, individual enterprises, and others.

Our data are from *The Statistical Yearbooks of China* published by the National Bureau of Statistics of China. We collected the data on gross industrial output values in two periods, 1992–97 and 1998–2002. Years are divided into two periods because China's Statistics Bureau has changed the way it measures gross industrial output since 1998. After 1998, the available data for gross industrial output are only for all state-owned and those non-state-owned industrial enterprises whose annual sales are above 5 million yuan. The non-state-owned industrial enterprises with annual sales income below 5 million yuan were no longer reported.

In the study, the ex-factory price indices of industrial products[1] are used to convert nominal gross industrial output into real terms, and the provincial population is used to calculate the per capita industrial output for each province. In our model, the initial level and growth rate of real per capita output are all calculated as a logarithm, and the annual growth rate is then calculated as follows:

$$g_{year\ i} = \ln(real\ per\ capita\ output_{year\ i})-\ln(real\ per\ capita\ output_{year\ i-1})$$

$$g_{yeari,j} = [\ln(real\ per\ capita\ output_{year\ j})-\ln(real\ per\ capita\ output_{year\ i})] \div (j-i)$$

As for the independent variables, our basic model includes the share of investment for enterprises as well as other variables commonly used in estimating growth. In our tables, SOE, Collective, Foreign, and Individual refer to the share of investment in fixed assets of the SOEs, collective enterprises, foreign-funded enterprises, and private enterprises respectively. All investment shares are presented as a percentage of the total provincial investment in fixed assets.

As mentioned, public investment can have both negative and positive effects on economic growth. However, in most Chinese provinces, the investment share of state enterprises is much more than is needed to provide public goods or complementary products for other ownerships. It is reasonable to expect that the crowding-out effect of state-owned investment will dominate its complementary effects, and the investment share of SOEs will be negatively related to the growth rate of the economy. Correspondingly, the shares of private and foreign investment are expected to be positively related to growth for the reasons discussed earlier.

Chinese collective enterprises encompass urban and rural collectively owned enterprises. The latter are famously known as the township and village enterprises (TVEs), which fueled rapid industrial growth in rural China and absorbed millions of surplus farm workers. Collective companies are affiliated to a district government, or a township government and villages, but are not directly under central government planning control. In the data, collective companies are classified outside the state sector, and yet cannot be considered part of the private sector in the strict sense of the word. To complicate things further, many essentially "private" firms have embraced collective ownership. They made themselves "collectives" by sharing ownership with local governments in order to obtain the security and privileges that those governments extend to collective firms. Recently, as the climate for private enterprise has improved, many of these pseudo-collectives have increasingly sought to take off their "red hats." Therefore, the effect of investment by collective firms has not yet been determined.

In our model, we include the initial level of industrial output as an important determinant of growth, drawing heavily on major findings in the study of economic growth. The neoclassical model of growth argues that the growth rate tends to be negatively related to the level of per capita output, owing to diminishing returns to capital (Solow, 1956); numerous empirical findings support this argument (e.g., Barro, 1991; Feng, 2003). The implication of these theoretical and empirical results is that, given similar preferences and technologies, poor counties tend to grow faster than rich countries, converging toward the same level of income. Therefore, we expect that the initial output level will impose a negative effect on growth.

In this study, we use the previous year's real per capita output as our indicator of initial levels in the panel data analysis. The real per capita output in 1992 and 1998 is used as an initial-level indicator for the long-term effect analysis during the periods 1993–97 and 1999–2002 respectively.

Human capital plays a critical role in endogenous growth models. These conclude that knowledge-driven growth can lead to a constant, or even increasing, rate of return. In Romer (1990), for instance, human capital is the major factor that influences the development and implementation of advanced technologies. Countries with a larger human capital stock are likely to grow faster. Empirical evidence has revealed a positive relationship between education and growth. Barro (1991) uses the elementary school enrollment rate as a proxy for the stock of human capital. Similarly, we use the illiteracy rates in 1990 and 1996 as the indicators of initial human capital accumulation for our two periods. We expect illiteracy rates to have a negative effect on growth.

Previous literature (e.g., Chen and Feng, 2000; Lin, 2000) found variances in growth rates between the east coast and the west inner provinces of China, resulting from differences in natural resources, international trade, policy environment, and historical factors. To control for such effects, provinces are divided into three regional groups, the east, the middle, and the west, and we include two dummy variables in our model: *Dum_mid* and *Dum_west*. Furthermore, it is reasonable to control the time effect in our panel data analysis. This study includes four time dummies in the first period (1993–97) and three time dummies in the second period (1999–2002).

Growth of labor has an important effect in the classical growth model. Labor is not included in our model because the mobility of labor within a country is much greater than across countries. Because China is a labor-abundant country, we assume that production function is not constrained by labor. Labor movement across provinces makes it difficult to find a suitable proxy for this factor. We used population growth as a proxy in our model; the result did not yield any theoretic or empirical explanatory power. Our model does not include labor or population growth. Table 8.1 presents a summary of the variables in the model.

## Empirical results

This section reports statistical results estimating cross-province growth rates in China. We conduct regression analyses separately for both periods, using OLS estimation. For each kind of ownership, we first regress only on shares of investment, initial illiteracy rates, and initial output levels. Then we control for the

*Table 8.1* Statistical summary

| Variables | Observations | Mean | SD | Minimum | Maximum |
|---|---|---|---|---|---|
| 1993–97 | | | | | |
| Output growth (ln) | 30 | 0.090 | 0.047 | −0.014 | 0.172 |
| Nedu 1990 (%) | 30 | 24.086 | 11.728 | 11.03 | 67.58 |
| Output92 per capita | 30 | 0.7687 | 0.886 | −1.882 | 2.768 |
| Ishare (state owned) | 30 | 62.106 | 14.443 | 32.326 | 94.514 |
| Ishare (collective) | 30 | 11.943 | 8.246 | 0.999 | 32.750 |
| Ishare (foreign) | 30 | 8.009 | 6.443 | 0.022 | 21.841 |
| Ishare (individuals) | 30 | 13.236 | 6.964 | 1.748 | 26.317 |
| Ishare (others) | 30 | 4.705 | 3.062 | 1.932 | 17.826 |
| 1999–2002 | | | | | |
| Output growth (ln) | 31 | 0.102 | 0.035 | 0.033 | 0.190 |
| Nedu 1996 (%) | 31 | 19.481 | 10.840 | 7.33 | 61.13 |
| Output98 per capita | 31 | 1.440 | 0.878 | −0.633 | 3.631 |
| Ishare (state owned) | 31 | 54.096 | 11.837 | 35.91 | 93.3 |
| Ishare (collective) | 31 | 10.981 | 6.817 | 0.70 | 28.89 |
| Ishare (foreign) | 31 | 6.789 | 6.208 | 0.39 | 22.90 |
| Ishare (individuals) | 31 | 14.859 | 6.182 | 2.83 | 27.65 |
| Ishare (others) | 31 | 13.275 | 5.303 | 2.78 | 24.87 |

Notes
Nedu, illiteracy rate; Ishare, the share of investment in fixed assets for enterprises of different ownership, including state-owned enterprises, collective enterprises, foreign-funded enterprises, individual enterprises, and others.
SD, standard deviation.

regions and years to see whether the effect of time and region will change our results.

Table 8.2 represents the regressions based on the data from 1993–97. Equations 8.1, 8.2, and 8.3 are regressed on the share of investment by the SOEs. As expected, all the equations have shown a significant negative relationship between the share of investment by SOEs and the provincial growth rate. Equations 8.4, 8.5, and 8.6 are regressed on the share of investment by the collective enterprises. These equations have shown a strong positive relationship between the investment share by collective firms and the annual output growth rate. All coefficients are highly significant with *t*-values above 3. Equations 8.7, 8.8, and 8.9 test the effect of investment of foreign funds on growth. The results illustrate negative effects on growth output, especially when controlling for the regional effect. This is a surprising finding, as foreign direct investment is considered to be the major engine for the dramatic growth of China. One possible explanation for this contradictory finding may be the overinflows of foreign investment in those years. Foreign direct investment has largely flowed into the east coast of

China. Diminishing marginal productivity has rendered it unwise for provinces to depend on foreign direct investment rather than other sources of investment that may bring higher marginal returns. Equations 8.10, 8.11, and 8.12 investigate the relationship between economic growth and the share of investment by individual enterprises. The results reveal that investment from individual enterprises has strong positive effects on growth.

Table 8.3 represents the regressions based on the 1999–2002 data. Compared with those in 1993–97, Table 8.3 has provided similar results on the coefficients of share of investment. In Equations 8.1, 8.2, and 8.3, investment by SOEs is significantly and negatively related to the growth rate, whereas in Equations 8.4, 8.5, 8.6, 8.10, 8.11, and 8.12, investment originating in collective or individual enterprises is positively associated with growth rate. The data do not give us significant negative results, as for the former period, which may imply that the efficiency of foreign investment has improved after the 1997 Asian financial crisis.

With respect to the control variables in Table 8.2, the illiteracy rate and the initial level of output have both displayed a negative linkage to growth rate. These results are consistent with our expectations. Growth rates have a tendency to converge across provinces, and the level of human capital stock has a positive effect on growth, although the coefficient for the latter is not as significant as that for the former. In Table 8.3, the illiteracy rate and initial output levels have a positive effect on growth. Most of the $t$-values for the coefficients of illiteracy rate are positive and greater than 90 percent significance levels, which imply that the growth in this period cannot be explained by the accumulation of human capital.

The dummy variables for different regions demonstrate differences in growth rates between the east and the west of China. For both periods, western provinces grew much slowly than the east coast provinces, with over 6 percent lag in growth rates during 1993–97 and a 3 percent lag during 1998–2002. This problem seems to be mitigated somewhat during 1999–2002. Part of the reason is that the Chinese government started to pay serious attention to inequality and formulated policies to benefit favorable western provinces in order to attract investment to the region.

One potential objection to the use of panel data analysis is that the effect of investment should be studied in the long run, using the aggregate data over a number of years instead of based on annual data. The logic for this lies in the fact that the effect of investment may only be reflected in the growth rate of lagged years. The following analysis adopts an aggregate framework to study the "long-run" growth.

In the following analysis, we average the values of the relevant variables in each period to measure the long-run tendency. For the dependent variables, we use $g_{92,97}$ and $g_{98,02}$ as the long-term growth rate for the two periods. For the independent variables, the real industrial output per capita in 1992 and 1998 is used as the proxy of initial levels for the two periods. Illiteracy rates in 1990 and 1996 are used as indicators for the human capital level. The variable *Ishare* has become the average of shares of investment for each period.

Table 8.4 presents the results regarding the long-run effects on growth. The

*Table 8.2* Regressions on industrial output growth rates in China (1993–97)

| | (1) | (2) | (3) | (4) | (5) | (6) |
|---|---|---|---|---|---|---|
| Intercept | 0. 2361 | 0.2300 | 0.2949 | 0.1358 | 0.1645 | 0.1556 |
| | (3.85***) | (3.50***) | (5.17***) | (3.56***) | (3.27***) | (4.30***) |
| Nedu 1990 | −0.0011 | −0.0003 | −0.0003 | −0.0020 | −0.0014 | −0.0014 |
| | (−0.85) | (−0.27) | (−0.34) | (−1.80**) | (−1.14) | (−1.35*) |
| Initial output | −0.0301 | −0.0411 | −0.0231 | −0.0467 | −0.0592 | −0.0348 |
| | (−1.96**) | (−2.23**) | (−1.67**) | (−2.85***) | (−3.07***) | (−2.23**) |
| SOE | −0.0015 | −0.0011 | −0.0019 | | | |
| | (−2.32***) | (−1.62*) | (−3.21***) | | | |
| Collective | | | | 0.0041 | 0.0036 | 0.0034 |
| | | | | (3.51***) | (3.07***) | (3.16***) |
| Dum_mid | | −0.0091 | | | −0.0135 | |
| | | (−0.35) | | | (−0.55) | |
| Dum_west | | −0.0645 | | | −0.0654 | |
| | | (−2.04***) | | | (−2.19***) | |
| Dum_94 | | | −0.0234 | | | −0.0088 |
| | | | (−0.99) | | | (−0.37) |
| Dum_95 | | | −0.1192 | | | −0.0968 |
| | | | (−4.99) | | | (−4.01***) |
| Dum_96 | | | −0.11038 | | | −0.0858 |
| | | | (−4.57) | | | (−3.54***) |
| Dum_97 | | | −0.0290 | | | −0.0005 |
| | | | (−1.20) | | | (−0.02) |
| *R*-squared | 0.0439 | 0.0830 | 0.2614 | 0.0857 | 0.1237 | 0.2600 |
| Root MSE | 0.1021 | 0.1007 | 0.0910 | 0.0999 | 0.0985 | 0.0911 |

Notes
Observations: 150 = 5 years * 30 provinces.
Numbers in parentheses are *t*-statistics for the coefficients.
MSE, ??; SOE, state-owned enterprise.

share of investment for each kind of ownership assumes the same signs as before, and their levels of significance remain about the same. For the periods 1992–97 and 1998–2002, state-owned investments have a strong negative relationship to growth, and collective and individual investments have a significant positive effect on growth. For example, in 1992–97, a 10 percent decrease in investment share by SOEs will have the effect of a 2 percent increase in the annual growth rate of aggregate output. A 10 percent increase in collective or individual investment share will have the effect of a more than 3 percent increase. In 1998–2002, a 10 percent decrease in state-owned investment share will have the effect of about a 2 percent

| (7) | (8) | (9) | (10) | (11) | (12) |
|---|---|---|---|---|---|
| 0.1324 | 0.2445 | 0.1527 | 0.0862 | 0.1399 | 0.1000 |
| (3.27***) | (3.84***) | (4.02***) | (1.89**) | (2.65***) | (2.40***) |
| −0.0009 | −0.0009 | −0.0003 | −0.0005 | −0.0002 | 0.0002 |
| (−0.82) | (−0.78) | (−0.29) | (−0.47) | (−0.131) | (0.21) |
| −0.0123 | −0.0415 | −0.0076 | −0.0109 | −0.0370 | 0.0017 |
| (−0.80) | (−2.28***) | (−0.54) | (−0.75) | (−2.04***) | (0.13) |
| −0.0010 | −0.0039 | 0.0002 | | | |
| (−0.70) | (−2.13**) | (0.13) | | | |
| | | | 0.0021 | 0.0024 | 0.0029 |
| | | | (1.73**) | (1.93**) | (2.69***) |
| | −0.0586 | | | −0.0345 | |
| | (−1.85**) | | | (−1.29*) | |
| | −0.1232 | | | −0.0905 | |
| | (−3.41***) | | | (−2.97***) | |
| | | −0.0184 | | | −0.0218 |
| | | (−0.75) | | | (−0.91) |
| | | −0.1112 | | | −0.1192 |
| | | (−4.46***) | | | (−4.92***) |
| | | −0.0997 | | | −0.1088 |
| | | (−3.98***) | | | (−4.48***) |
| | | −0.0171 | | | −0.0268 |
| | | (−0.69) | | | (−1.10) |
| 0.0119 | 0.0949 | 0.2079 | 0.0285 | 0.0900 | 0.2462 |
| 0.1038 | 0.1001 | 0.0943 | 0.1030 | 0.1004 | 0.0920 |

\*    Significant at the 0.10 level, one-tailed.
\*\*   Significant at the 0.05 level, one-tailed.
\*\*\* Significant at the 0.01 level, one-tailed.

increase in growth, and a 10 percent increase in collective and private investment will also cause a 2 percent increase in growth. Foreign investment does not show any significant effect on growth for both periods. Among the dummy variables, western provinces grew much slowly than the eastern provinces, with a 4 percent gap in their annual growth rates. The initial output level and illiteracy rates do not seem to have a significant influence on growth for either period. The effects of human capital and convergence in incomes are not supported in our test. All these results are generally consistent with the panel data analysis.

*Table 8.3* Regressions on industrial output growth rates in China (1999–2002)

|  | (1) | (2) | (3) | (4) | (5) | (6) |
|---|---|---|---|---|---|---|
| Intercept | 0.1810 | 0.1730 | 0.1840 | 0.0436 | 0.0692 | 0.0915 |
|  | (5.03***) | (4.19***) | (5.22***) | (2.03***) | (1.90***) | (4.15***) |
| Nedu 1996 | 0.0019 | 0.0023 | 0.0015 | 0.0008 | 0.0009 | 0.0005 |
|  | (3.03***) | (3.12***) | (2.34***) | (1.26) | (1.34*) | (0.97) |
| Initial level | 0.0070 | 0.0070 | 0.0077 | 0.0141 | 0.0066 | 0.0079 |
|  | (0.92) | (0.66) | (1.04) | (1.81**) | (0.58) | (1.09) |
| SOE | −0.0024 | −0.0024 | −0.0018 |  |  |  |
|  | (−4.25***) | (−3.97***) | (−3.03***) |  |  |  |
| Collective |  |  |  | 0.0020 | 0.0017 | 0.0025 |
|  |  |  |  | (2.32***) | (1.93**) | (3.12***) |
| Dum_mid |  | 0.0069 |  |  | −0.0117 |  |
|  |  | (0.37) |  |  | (−0.62) |  |
| Dum_west |  | −0.0130 |  |  | −0.0287 |  |
|  |  | (−0.65) |  |  | (−1.41*) |  |
| Dum_99 |  |  | −0.0451 |  |  | −0.0657 |
|  |  |  | (−3.10***) |  |  | (−4.80***) |
| Dum_00 |  |  | −0.0361 |  |  | −0.0492 |
|  |  |  | (−2.60***) |  |  | (−3.62***) |
| Dum_01 |  |  | −0.0339 |  |  | −0.0416 |
|  |  |  | (−2.49***) |  |  | (−3.08***) |
| *R*-squared | 0.1879 | 0.2014 | 0.2597 | 0.1057 | 0.1226 | 0.2631 |
| Root MSE | 0.0550 | 0.0550 | 0.0532 | 0.0577 | 0.0576 | 0.0530 |

Notes
Observations: 124 = 4 years * 31 provinces.
Numbers in parentheses are *t*-statistics for the coefficients.
* Significant at the 0.10 level, one-tailed.

## Summary and policy implications

While a host of articles have investigated the sources of Chinese economic de-velopment, few empirical tests been conducted to study the effects of re-source allocation on China's growth rates after the mid-1990s. The objective of this chapter is to use updated data on the Chinese provinces to test the effects of investments by different ownerships and compare their contributions to the an-nual growth rate.

The principal conclusion of this study was that resource allocation appears to have significant effects on Chinese provincial economic growth for the period

| (7) | (8) | (9) | (10) | (11) | (12) |
|---|---|---|---|---|---|
| 0.0549 | 0.0821 | 0.1046 | −0.0282 | 0.0007 | 0.0358 |
| (2.55***) | (2.08***) | (4.58***) | (−0.72) | (0.01) | (0.89) |
| 0.0007 | 0.0010 | 0.0006 | 0.0018 | 0.0019 | 0.0014 |
| (1.26) | (1.47*) | (0.97) | (2.47***) | (2.49***) | (1.96**) |
| 0.0177 | 0.0110 | 0.0094 | 0.0348 | 0.0249 | 0.0276 |
| (1.86**) | (0.96) | (1.04) | (3.83***) | (1.98***) | (3.14***) |
| 0.0007 | −0.0001 | 0.0015 | | | |
| (0.58) | (−0.04) | (1.32) | | | |
| | | | 0.0027 | 0.0025 | 0.0020 |
| | | | (2.46***) | (2.32***) | (1.94**) |
| | −0.0133 | | | −0.0109 | |
| | (−0.61) | | | (−0.59) | |
| | −0.0364 | | | −0.0322 | |
| | (−1.59*) | | | (−1.62*) | |
| | | −0.0635 | | | −0.0563 |
| | | (−4.47***) | | | (−4.00***) |
| | | −0.0471 | | | −0.0423 |
| | | (−3.35***) | | | (−3.03***) |
| | | −0.0403 | | | −0.0382 |
| | | (−2.89***) | | | (−2.76***) |
| 0.0681 | 0.0950 | 0.2134 | 0.1105 | 0.1345 | 0.2265 |
| 0.0589 | 0.5854 | 0.0548 | 0.0576 | 0.0572 | 0.0544 |

** Significant at the 0.05 level, one-tailed.
*** Significant at the 0.01 level, one-tailed.
MSE, ??; SOE, state-owned enterprise.

1993–2002. Provinces investing more in private and collective enterprises grew faster, and provinces depending more on public investment grew more slowly. We also find that the share of foreign-funded investment did not show significant influences on the growth rate, despite improving efficiency. From these facts, we find the answer to our initial question: during the period 1993–2002, the private and collective enterprises contributed most to the rapid growth of the Chinese economy. Policy reforms aimed at releasing constraints on the private sector are the major factor accounting for continuous growth in these years. Our study also found that western provinces grew much more slowly than the provinces on the east coast. The economic gap between the east and the west enlarged during this period, although the gap in the growth rates narrowed. Finally, we did not find strong or significant evidence on convergence in income and the effect of human capital on aggregate growth for the period 1993–2002.

The major policy implications are straightforward. The government should aim at decreasing its unnecessary investments in SOEs and creating conditions that make investment in private and collective enterprises an attractive option. SOEs compete with the private sector for scarce resources such as banking loans. The resources channeled into SOEs have higher opportunity costs, as they could have generated a higher rate of return in the private sector.

The government can also reduce the presence of SOEs by auctioning their entities or parts to private agents, of whom domestic agents tend to have better performance than their international counterparts. Keeping everything else constant, the investment of Chinese private enterprises has performed better than foreign direct investment.

## Acknowledgments

We acknowledge the useful comments from Ronald Edwards and participants at the 2004 International Symposium on Private Enterprises and China's Economic Development in Beijing. All errors are our responsibility.

## Note

1 Provincial data are from *China Statistics Yearbook* (2003).

## References

Barro, R. (1991) "Economic Growth in a Cross Section of Countries," *Quarterly Journal of Economics*, May: 407–43.

Borensztein, E., J. de Gregorio and J.-W. Lee (1998) "How Does Foreign Direct Investment Affect Economic Growth?," *Journal of International Economics*, 45: 115–35.

Chen, B. and Y. Feng (2000) "Determinants of Economic Growth in China: Private Enterprise, Education and Openness," *China Economic Review*, 11: 1–15.

Feng, Y. (2003) *Democracy, Governance and Economic Performance: Theory and Evidence*, Cambridge, MA: The MIT Press.

Feng, Y. and H. Zhang (2000) "Provincial Distribution of Direct Foreign Investment in China 1992–1996: A Pooled Time-Series Empirical Study," in: Chen, B., J.K. Dietrich and Y. Feng (eds), *Financial Market Reform in China: Progress, Prospects and Problems*, Boulder, CO: Westview, pp. 401–24.

Friedman, M. and R. Friedman (1980) *Free to Choose*, New York: Harcourt Brace and Jovanovich.

Jones, L. and R. Manuelli (1990) "A Convex Model of Equilibrium Growth: Theory and Policy Implications," *Journal of Political Economy*, October: 1008–38.

Kelly, T. (1997) "Public Investment and Growth: Testing the Non-Linearity Hypothesis," *International Review of Applied Economics*, 11: 249–62.

Khan, M.S. and C.M. Reinhart (1990) "Private Investment and Economic Growth in Developing Countries," *World Development*, 18: 19–27.

King, R. and S. Rebelo (1990) "Public Policy and Economic Growth: Developing Neoclassical Implications," *Journal of Political Economy*, October: 126–51.

Levine, R. and D. Renelt (1992) "A Sensitivity Analysis of Cross-Country Growth Regressions," *American Economic Review*, 82: 942–63.

Lin, S. (2000) "Resource Allocation and Economic Growth in China," *Economic Inquiry*, 38: 515–26.

Lopcu, K. and O. Oguz (2001) "Public and Private Investment and Growth: A Panel Approach," International Conference in Economics, Ankara.

Lucas, R.E. (1988) "On the Mechanics of Economic Development," *Journal of Monetary Economics*, 22: 3–42.

Moran, T. (1998) *Foreign Direct Investment and Development: The New Policy Agenda for Developing Countries and Economies in Transition*, Washington, DC: Institute for International Economics.

Nazmi, N. and M.D. Ramirez (1997) "Public and Private Investment and Economic Growth in Mexico," *Contemporary Economic Policy*, 15: 65–75.

Rebelo, S. (1991) "Long-Run Policy Analysis and Long-Run Growth," *Journal of Political Economy*, June: 500–21.

Romer, P.M. (1986) "Increasing Returns and Long-Run Growth," *Journal of Political Economy*, 94: 1002–37.

Romer, P. (1989) "Capital Accumulation in the Theory of Long-Run Growth," in: Barro, R. (ed.), *Modern Business Cycle Theory*, Cambridge, MA: Harvard University Press.

Romer, P. (1990) "Capital, Labor and Productivity," *Brookings Papers on Economic Activity: Microeconomics*, 1990: 337–67.

Solow, R.M. (1956) "A Contribution to the Theory of Economic Growth," *Quarterly Journal of Economics*, 34: 65–94.

Sun, H. (1998) *Macroeconomic Impact of Direct Foreign Investment in China: 1979–1996*, Oxford: Blackwell Publishers.

Tso, A.Y. (1998) "Foreign Direct Investment and China's Economic Development," *Issues and Studies: Journal of Chinese Studies and International Affairs*, 34: 1–34.

World Bank (1999) *Global Development Finance – Analysis and Summary Tables*, Washington, DC: The World Bank.

**Part III**

# Openness, legal protection, and private enterprises

# 9 Trade, foreign direct investment, and productivity of China's private enterprises

*Bin Xu*

## Introduction

Despite its murky classification in China's statistics, private enterprise has indubitably entered the center stage of the Chinese economy in the twenty-first century. According to a recent report by the Asian Development Bank (ADP) (2003: 2), "private activity already comprises the predominant share of the PRC economy, with that share lying somewhere between one-half and two-thirds (in total gross industrial output) depending on how narrowly one defines the term 'private'." The lower bound of one-half comes from a narrow definition of private sector as privately owned firms ("*siying qiye*") and individually owned businesses ("*getihu*"), while the upper bound of two-thirds comes from a broad definition of the private sector as non-state-owned firms. In an earlier study by the International Finance Corporation (IFC) (2000: 16), China's private sector ("*siying qiye*" and "*getihu*") was estimated to account for about 33 percent of gross domestic product (GDP) in 1998.

The rapid growth of private enterprises from next to nothing in 1985 to over half of China's gross industrial output or a third of China's GDP in the late twentieth century has had a profound impact on the Chinese economy, as documented by the ADB and IFC reports. It is well known that China's policy environment has been heavily biased in favor of state-owned enterprises (SOEs) and also provides favorable treatment to foreign enterprises. In contrast, China's private sector has been at a severe disadvantage, particularly in access to capital, skilled labor, infrastructure, and markets. According to the International Finance Corporation (2000), in the period from 1991 to 1997, the share of private sector investment in the national total was in the range of 15–27 percent, significantly lower than its share in national output. In a recently published book, Huang (2003) argued that China's becoming a leading recipient of foreign direct investment is largely a result of the weak policy environment for Chinese domestic private firms compared with that for foreign firms.

Because of the increasing role of private enterprise in the Chinese economy, it becomes important to assess its impact quantitatively. In particular, one would like to know what has contributed to its fast growth, despite facing severe constraints in resource access and policy support. Moreover, private firms in China face restraints on direct access to foreign trade. For example, private firms were not allowed to export directly prior to 1998 when foreign firms and many state-owned firms had this right. It is interesting to investigate what role exporting plays in the fast growth of private firms in China. As China proceeds further in privatization and openness, a sound understanding of the above issues regarding private enterprise is useful for policy-makers to formulate future development strategies for the Chinese economy.

In this chapter, we examine the productivity growth of private firms in China based on a survey of 1,500 Chinese firms conducted by the World Bank in 2001. Using these data, we construct a sample of private firms. For comparison, we construct a sample of public firms (government owned and collectively owned) and a sample of foreign firms. We will discuss the samples in the following section. As a starting point for our statistical analysis, we estimate production functions for the three ownership groups and present the results in the next section. Our goal is to identify and estimate the key determinants of productivity growth in private firms. For this purpose, we will examine the characteristics of private firms and carry out a regression analysis in the following section. The regression results allow us to estimate total factor productivity (TFP); the TFP analysis is then presented followed by a summary of the main results and the conclusions drawn.

## Sample

Our study uses data from a survey of 1,500 Chinese firms conducted by the World Bank in 2001.[1] The survey contains two sets of questions about each firm's ownership. First, a firm reports its legal status in ten categories and may report multiple categories. Second, a firm provides information on ownership shares by private ownership (domestic and foreign) and public ownership (state, local, and collective).

Our goal is to investigate the productivity of China's private firms. The difficulty in defining "private firm" in China's statistics is well known.[2] We adopt the following classification. If a firm reports its legal status as "subsidiary/division of a multinational firm" or "joint venture of a multinational firm," or if a firm reports foreign ownership exceeding 50 percent, we classify it as a *foreign firm*. If a firm reports its legal status as "state-owned company" or "cooperative/collective," or if a firm reports public ownership (including cooperative/collective) exceeding 50 percent, we classify it as a *public firm*. We classify any firm that is neither a foreign firm nor a public firm as a *private firm*. Thus, our group of private firms includes firms that have minority foreign ownership or minority public ownership but do not have a legal status as a foreign firm, state-owned firm, or cooperative/collective firm.

Table 9.1 reports the summary information in our sample. Based on the above classification, 450 firms in the survey are private firms, which account for 30 percent of the total. Some 562 firms are public firms, accounting for 37 percent, and

*Table 9.1* Sample summary

|  | *Full sample* | *Private firms* | *Public firms* | *Foreign firms* |
|---|---|---|---|---|
| Number of observations | 1,500 | 450 | 562 | 488 |
| Sample distribution (%) | 100 | 30 | 37 | 33 |
| Growth in sales (%) | 20.8 (95.8) | 28.3 (85.0) | –0.1 (82.1) | 41.2 (113.7) |
| Growth in unskilled labor (%) | 3.6 (50.6) | 10.1 (46.4) | –8.3 (52.1) | 13.9 (48.8) |
| Growth in skilled labor (%) | 5.2 (42.0) | 14.4 (46.5) | –8.8 (36.7) | 15.5 (39.1) |
| Growth in physical capital (%) | 22.8 (58.5) | 34.9 (64.3) | 10.6 (47.7) | 28.3 (63.0) |

Note
Mean of growth rate from 1998 to 2000 reported; standard deviation in parentheses.

488 firms are foreign firms, which constitute 33 percent of the whole sample. Without information on output, we use total sales value as a proxy. The current value of sales is converted to 1998 values using the GDP deflator from *The China Statistical Yearbook*, 2001.[3] Table 9.1 shows that sales grew by 20.8 percent on average in the full sample of 1,500 firms surveyed. Sales grew at 28.3 percent in private firms, 41.2 percent in foreign firms, and negatively in public firms.

Table 9.1 also reports growth rates of inputs of unskilled labor, skilled labor, and physical capital for the three ownership groups. The amount of skilled labor equals the number of engineering, technical, and managerial personnel. The amount of unskilled labor equals the number of basic production workers, auxiliary production workers, service personnel, and other employees. The amount of physical capital equals the book value of fixed assets including buildings, production machinery and equipment, office equipment, and vehicles; the value is converted to 1998 values using GDP deflators. As Table 9.1 shows, all three production factors increased significantly in private firms and foreign firms. In contrast, public firms saw an increase in physical capital input, but a decrease in both skilled and unskilled labor inputs.

## Estimation of production function

We start by assuming a production function $Y_i = A_i F(K_i, N_i)$ for firm $i$, where $Y$ denotes output, $K$ stands for physical capital, $N$ denotes total employment of labor, and $A$ is a productivity parameter. Applying a second-order Taylor approximation in logarithms yields the following translog production function:

$$\log Y_i = \log A_i + a_0 + a_1 \log K_i + a_2 \log N_i + 0.5a_3(\log K_i)^2 + 0.5a_4(\log N_i)^2 + a_5 \log K_i \log N_i$$

Taking the time difference (denoted by $\Delta$) and assuming that $\Delta \log A_i = \beta + \varepsilon_i$, we obtain the following regression equation:

$$\Delta \log Y_i = \beta + a_1 \Delta \log K_i + a_2 \Delta \log N_i + 0.5a_3 \Delta(\log K_i)^2 + 0.5a_4 \Delta(\log N_i)^2 + a_5 \Delta \log K_i \log N_i + \varepsilon_i.$$

The assumption $\Delta \log A_i = \beta + \varepsilon_i$ decomposes productivity growth into a general trend and a firm-specific component. Applying this regression equation to the full sample, we obtain the results displayed in regression (2.1) of Table 9.2.

Regression (2.1) indicates an estimated output elasticity of capital of 0.45, and an estimated output elasticity of labor of 0.68. All squared terms enter the regression with no statistical significance, suggesting that the production function takes the Cobb–Douglas form. In regression (2.2), we drop the squared terms and find that the estimated output elasticities become more statistically significant.

*Table 9.2* Regression results, ordinary least squares

|  | 2.1 | 2.2 | 2.3 | 2.4 | 2.5 | 2.6 |
|---|---|---|---|---|---|---|
| Sample | Full | Full | Full | Private | Public | Foreign |
| Constant | 7.67 | 7.58 | 9.19 | 10.50 | 2.86 | 14.39 |
|  | (2.51)*** | (2.50)*** | (2.64)*** | (5.35)** | (3.86) | (5.97)** |
| $\Delta \log K$ | 0.45 | 0.35 | 0.37 | 0.31 | 0.38 | 0.37 |
|  | (0.24)* | (0.06)*** | (0.08)*** | (0.11)*** | (0.11)*** | (0.15)** |
| $\Delta \log N$ | 0.68 | 0.81 |  |  |  |  |
|  | (0.38)* | (0.10)*** |  |  |  |  |
| $\Delta \log L$ |  |  | 0.33 | 0.51 | 0.09 | 0.73 |
|  |  |  | (0.11)*** | (0.20)*** | (0.11) | (0.24)*** |
| $\Delta \log H$ |  |  | 0.54 | 0.12 | 0.60 | 0.53 |
|  |  |  | (0.12)*** | (0.18) | (0.17)*** | (0.20)*** |
| $\Delta(\log K)^2$ | 0.01 |  |  |  |  |  |
|  | (0.02 |  |  |  |  |  |
| $\Delta(\log N)^2$ | 0.02 |  |  |  |  |  |
|  | (0.04 |  |  |  |  |  |
| $\Delta \log K \log N$ | −0.02 |  |  |  |  |  |
|  | (0.05) |  |  |  |  |  |
| R-squared | 0.23 | 0.23 | 0.23 | 0.21 | 0.23 | 0.28 |
| Observations | 1,261 | 1,261 | 1,103 | 291 | 467 | 345 |

Notes

$K$, physical capital; $N$, total labor; $L$, unskilled labor; $H$, skilled labor. The dependent variable is $\Delta \log Y = \ln Y(2000) - \ln Y(1998)$, where $Y =$ sales. All values are in 1998 prices.

Numbers in parentheses are heteroskedasticity-adjusted standard errors.

Statistical significance at the *** 1% level, ** 5% level, and * 10% level.

It should be noted that the implementation of the regressions assumes that the ordinary least squares (OLS) assumptions hold, which may not be true. Nevertheless, regression (2.2) provides the starting point of our investigation and is appealing for its simplicity. In regression (2.3), we introduce unskilled labor ($L$) and skilled labor ($H$) as two input variables instead of combining them as one input variable. The results show an estimated output elasticity of 0.37 for capital, 0.33 for unskilled labor, and 0.54 for skilled labor. One may interpret the results as suggesting increasing returns to scale, but we would adopt caution over such an interpretation because the sample contains very different firms, and the assumption of an identical production function for the whole sample is clearly an oversimplification, so the results here serve only as a reference.

Recognizing that ownership structure may result in firms using different production functions, we run regressions for the three ownership groups separately. Regression (2.4) reports the results from the sample of private firms. Both capital and unskilled labor show statistically significant effects, but the change in skilled labor shows no statistically significant effect on the change in output. Given that skilled labor increased by 14.4 percent in the period (Table 9.1), one would expect to see its effect on output. One interpretation of this result is that human capital affects output growth mainly through its effect on productivity rather than factor accumulation. In a widely known study, Benhabib and Spiegel (1994) find from cross-country data that human capital does not affect output as an ordinary production factor such as physical capital or unskilled labor. Rather, it affects output by facilitating technology absorption. This view implies that the production function should be specified as $Y = A(H)G(K, L)$ rather than $Y = AF(K, L, H)$. While we find some support for this view in our data, we do not intend to push this view too far in our interpretation of regression (2.4), as it may well be a result of data noise or the assumptions failing to hold.

Turning to the sample of public firms, we find in regression (2.5) that variations in capital and skilled labor help to explain the variation in output, but variation in unskilled labor does not. Our interpretation is that public firms in China are severely constrained in their decisions regarding the employment of unskilled workers. Thus, one would not be surprised to see that the variation in output is not correlated with the variation in unskilled labor employment. Again, this is a suggestive interpretation, and it may well be a result of data quality or regression mis-specification. Finally, we have regression (2.6), which features the sample of foreign firms. All three input variables are found to be statistically significant in this regression.

## Sample characteristics

Before exploring further with regression methods, it is useful to take a look at the characteristics of the firms in the sample. Table 9.3 reports capital intensity, skill intensity, research and development (R&D) intensity, and export intensity in 1998 and 2000 for the full sample and the three ownership groups. During this period, capital intensity, measured by the ratio of capital to sales, declined in all three

*Table 9.3* Sample characteristics

| | Full sample | Private firms | Public firms | Foreign firms |
|---|---|---|---|---|
| Capital intensity, 1998 | 3.81 | 1.08 | 3.15 | 7.01 |
| Capital intensity, 2000 | 2.85 | 1.04 | 3.11 | 4.01 |
| Skill intensity, 1998 | 0.97 | 1.12 | 0.91 | 0.92 |
| Skill intensity, 2000 | 1.02 | 1.18 | 0.90 | 1.04 |
| R&D intensity, 1998 | 0.07 | 0.04 | 0.06 | 0.13 |
| R&D intensity, 2000 | 0.07 | 0.05 | 0.04 | 0.15 |
| Export intensity, 1998 | 0.17 | 0.10 | 0.07 | 0.37 |
| Export intensity, 2000 | 0.18 | 0.12 | 0.08 | 0.37 |

Notes
Capital intensity = $K/Y$; skill intensity = $H/L$; R&D intensity = R&D expenditure/total sales; export intensity = export sales/total sales.

groups, with the largest decline in foreign firms. This suggests an increase in capital efficiency. Skill intensity, measured by the ratio of skilled labor to unskilled labor, increased in private firms and foreign firms, but stayed about the same in public firms. This may be reflecting the difficulty of public firms in reducing the employment of unskilled workers. R&D intensity, measured by the ratio of R&D expenditure to sales, increased in private firms and foreign firms, but decreased in public firms. Notice that private firms had the highest skill intensity, while foreign firms had significantly higher R&D intensity and capital intensity than private firms and public firms.

Table 9.3 shows that both private firms and public firms saw an increase in export intensity, measured by the share of export sales in total sales. Export intensity remained very high and stable at 37 percent for foreign firms in this period.

## R&D and exporting

So far we have used only changes in factor inputs to account for changes in output. Recall that the regression specification for Table 9.2 assumes that $\Delta \log A_i = \beta + \varepsilon_i$. To identify the variables that explain productivity changes, we assume that $\Delta \log A_i = \beta_0 + \beta_k X_k + \varepsilon_i$, where $X_k$ is a set of variables that explains productivity change.

According to economic theory, an important driving force of productivity growth is technical progress. A firm can achieve technical progress from innovating new technology or imitating existing technology, with the extent of technical progress depending largely on the firm's efforts in R&D. To capture this R&D

*Table 9.4* Regression results, ordinary least squares

|  | 4.1 | 4.2 | 4.3 | 4.4 | 4.5 | 4.6 |
|---|---|---|---|---|---|---|
| Sample | Private | Public | Foreign | Private | Public | Foreign |
| Constant | 9.50 | 2.85 | 14.81 | 5.50 | −1.08 | 10.64 |
|  | (5.38)* | (3.92) | (6.24)** | (6.09) | (4.29) | (9.25) |
| Δlog *K* | 0.30 | 0.36 | 0.33 | 0.30 | 0.37 | 0.33 |
|  | (0.11)*** | (0.11)*** | (0.16)** | (0.11)*** | (0.11)*** | (0.16)** |
| Δlog *L* | 0.54 | 0.08 | 0.74 | 0.54 | 0.09 | 0.74 |
|  | (0.20)*** | (0.11) | (0.25)*** | (0.20)*** | (0.11) | (0.25)*** |
| Δlog *H* | 0.08 | 0.60 | 0.53 | 0.09 | 0.60 | 0.53 |
|  | (0.17) | (0.17)*** | (0.21)** | (0.17) | (0.17)*** | (0.21)*** |
| R&D | 43.92 | −2.27 | 18.71 | 41.56 | −2.06 | 18.64 |
|  | (20.66)** | (0.93)** | (0.38)*** | (23.42)* | (0.92)** | (0.39)*** |
| Exporting |  |  |  | 18.19 | 19.45 | 6.68 |
|  |  |  |  | (10.26)* | (8.49)** | (10.36) |
| *R*-squared | 0.22 | 0.15 | 0.39 | 0.22 | 0.16 | 0.39 |
| Observations | 289 | 461 | 324 | 289 | 461 | 324 |

Notes
R&D, R&D intensity in 1998.
Exporting, a dummy variable that equals 1 if exporting in 1998 or 1999, and zero otherwise.
Statistical significance at the *** 1% level, ** 5% level, and * 10% level.

effect, we include an R&D variable in the regression and report the results in Table 9.4.[4]

As Table 9.4 shows, the R&D variable is statistically significant in all three ownership groups. In the sample of private firms and foreign firms, R&D intensity is positively correlated with output growth. The higher the R&D intensity, the faster is the output growth of a private firm or a foreign firm, which can be interpreted as R&D promoting productivity growth and, hence, output growth. Paradoxically, in the sample of public firms (regression 4.2), R&D intensity is *negatively* correlated with output growth. The higher the R&D intensity, the slower is the output growth of a public firm. What is the interpretation? We believe that this reflects the nature of public firms in China. State-owned firms in China have much better access to R&D funds than non-state-owned firms.[5] The firms with higher R&D intensity in our sample of public firms are mainly state-owned firms. The negative estimated coefficient on R&D suggests that those state-owned firms, while having a higher R&D-to-output ratio, are the ones with lower productivity growth. State owner-ship leads to both a higher R&D-to-output ratio and lower productivity growth; hence, the negative correlation between the two variables.

Next, we examine the role of export orientation. The economic literature is full of evidence that international trade is an important channel for technology diffu-sion.[6] Through exposure to the world market, exporters are able to absorb foreign technology better than non-exporters. Moreover, exposure to the world market adds competition and pushes exporters to improve production efficiency.

To see the role of exporting, we introduce a dummy variable that equals 1 if a firm exported in 1998 or 1999, and 0 otherwise. Table 9.4 reports the results. Regression (4.4) estimated that the sales of private exporting firms grew 18.7 percentage points faster than those of non-exporting firms. Recall that sales grew by 28.3 percent on average in the sample of private firms (Table 9.1), so this result is very significant. Export status is even more important for public firms. While sales grew negatively by 0.1 percent in the sample of public firms (Table 9.1), regression (4.5) estimated that sales of public exporting firms grew 19.5 percentage points faster than those of non-exporting firms. Regression (4.6) shows that export status does not matter for output growth of foreign firms. This is not surprising as foreign firms are already highly exposed to international competition, and their productivity growth is expected to be less sensitive to export status.

To gain more insight into the role of exporting, we display skill intensity and R&D intensity for exporting and non-exporting firms in Table 9.5. For all three ownership groups, exporting firms have lower skill intensity than non-exporting firms. This is consistent with the trade pattern of China in exporting unskilled labor-intensive goods. It is interesting to observe that R&D intensity is 0.20 for foreign exporting firms but only 0.03 for foreign non-exporting firms. R&D intensity is slightly higher for private exporting firms at 0.05 than for private non-exporting firms at 0.04. For public firms, R&D intensity is higher for non-exporting firms at 0.06 than for exporting firms at 0.02.

It should be noted that our results so far do not identify the causality between productivity growth and export status. The positive estimated coefficient on exporting may show that exposure to export markets enhances the productivity growth of firms, but may alternately show that firms with higher productivity growth choose to enter the export business.[7] The causality question is hard to answer with our limited data, but we will provide some evidence that exporting contributed to productivity growth in the following section.

*Table 9.5* Sample characteristics by export status

| Sample | Export status | Observations | Skill intensity | R&D intensity |
|--------|--------------|--------------|-----------------|---------------|
| Full | Exporting | 359 | 0.47 | 0.13 |
| | Non-exporting | 715 | 1.24 | 0.05 |
| Private | Exporting | 63 | 0.37 | 0.05 |
| | Non-exporting | 226 | 1.34 | 0.04 |
| Public | Exporting | 93 | 0.37 | 0.02 |
| | Non-exporting | 368 | 1.05 | 0.06 |
| Foreign | Exporting | 203 | 0.56 | 0.20 |
| | Non-exporting | 121 | 1.62 | 0.03 |

*Table 9.6* Regressions results, industry-specific effects

|  | 6.1 | 6.2 | 6.3 | 6.4 |
|---|---|---|---|---|
| Sample | Full | Private | Public | Foreign |
| Constant | 0.65 | −1.07 | 8.36 | −12.45 |
| $\Delta \log K$ | 0.35*** | 0.29*** | 0.39*** | 0.33** |
| $\Delta \log L$ | 0.31*** | 0.52*** | 0.10 | 0.73*** |
| $\Delta \log H$ | 0.54*** | 0.11 | 0.59*** | 0.60*** |
| R&D | 15.32*** | 27.67 | −1.90** | 17.77*** |
| Exporting | 19.08*** | 17.65 | 12.79 | 19.59 |
| Apparel and leather | Base | Base | Base | Base |
| Electronic components | 2.82 | 6.62 | −2.30 | 13.83 |
| Electronic equipment | 5.10 | 12.47 | 5.39 | −2.35 |
| Consumer products | −2.07 | 11.34 | −14.86 | 1.69 |
| Vehicles and parts | 8.94 | 11.36 | −12.23 | 40.67** |
| IT services | 3.09 | 32.06* | −15.29 | −3.15 |
| Communication services | −33.07*** | −46.20* | −33.35** | −13.62 |
| Financial services | 9.42 | 6.15 | −22.16 | 67.83 |
| Marketing services | 5.40 | 34.55* | −47.02* | 27.09 |
| Logistics services | 5.44 | −21.21 | −3.37 | 43.44** |
| *R*-squared | 0.28 | 0.26 | 0.18 | 0.41 |
| Observations | 1,074 | 289 | 461 | 324 |

Note
Standard errors are not reported to save space.
Statistical significance at the *** 1% level, ** 5% level, and * 10% level.

Besides R&D and exporting, there are other factors that impact on the productivity growth of firms in China. It is not difficult to imagine that institutional
factors must be playing an important role.[8] Unfortunately our data set does not
contain information on institutional variables other than ownership. Still, we may
obtain some indirect evidence on this. In Table 9.6, we report the results from
regressions that include industry dummies. The survey provides a classification
of ten industries. Using the apparel and leather industry as the base, we find that
the majority of the industry dummies are statistically insignificant.[9] Presuming
that the apparel and leather industry has a rather competitive market, we may
detect from Table 9.6 some interesting evidence on institutional effects. First,
the communication services industry has lower productivity growth than the base
industry. This is an industry with significant government monopoly power, which
may explain the lower productivity growth due to lack of competition. Second,
the marketing services industry shows an interesting pattern. Private firms in this

industry had higher productivity growth than the base industry, while public firms in this industry had lower productivity growth. One possible explanation is that the state-owned firms in this industry remain highly regulated, which gives private firms an edge. Notice that private information technology (IT) firms had a higher productivity growth rate than the base industry, which is consistent with the observation of spectacular growth of IT firms in China during this period. Private firms in the IT services industry had the highest R&D intensity among all private firms, which may explain why the estimated coefficient on R&D turns from statistically significant in regression (4.4) without industry dummies to statistically insignificant in regression (6.2) with industry dummies. In regression (6.4) of foreign firms, the industry of vehicles and vehicle parts and the industry of logistics services saw higher productivity growth than the base industry, probably because of their high technology levels not captured by the R&D intensity variable.

## Total factor productivity

Our investigation has been based on an assumed production function of the form $Y_i = A_i(X_k)F(K_i, L_i, H_i)$. We define $A_i(X_k) = Y_i/F(K_i, L_i, H_i)$ as total factor productivity (TFP). There are many issues regarding TFP construction. With the limited data we have, we can only compute TFP measures in a very rough way. Still, we hope that the rough estimates can shed some light on the productivity growth of Chinese firms.[10]

Specifically, we use estimated output elasticities of factor inputs from regressions (4.4), (4.5), and (4.6) to compute the TFP growth rate as the difference between output growth and the estimated contribution of input growth to output growth.[11] In so doing, we allow the three ownership groups to have different production functions, but assume that firms in each group share the same production function.

Table 9.7 displays the results from this computation. Notice first that TFP growth was 11.26 percent and contributed 41 percent to output growth in the sample of private firms; it was 17.26 percent and contributed 38 percent in the sample of foreign firms. In contrast, TFP growth was low at 2.72 percent in the sample of public firms, which saw a negative sales growth rate of −1.49 percent. The finding of strong TFP growth for China's private firms is encouraging.[12]

Exporting is very significant to TFP growth. Table 9.7 shows that TFP growth rates are 26.07 percent, 18.29 percent, and 20.91 percent for private firms, public firms, and foreign firms that exported. The fact that public exporting firms also enjoyed high TFP growth rates is worth noticing. The contribution of TFP growth to output growth is a high 67 percent for private exporting firms and 41 percent for foreign firms. Interestingly, while TFP growth is estimated to be 18.29 percent for public firms, the growth rate of sales from these firms is only 9.76 percent. One possible explanation is that the estimated output elasticities are based on the entire sample of public firms, which may be underestimates for the sample of public exporting firms and, hence, result in an overestimation of TFP contribution.

*Table 9.7* Results on total factor productivity (TFP)

| | TFP 1998 | TFP 2000 | TFP growth | Sales growth | TFP contribution | Observations |
|---|---|---|---|---|---|---|
| Private | 1.19 | 1.34 | 11.26 | 27.65 | 41% | 289 |
| Public | 0.53 | 0.53 | 2.72 | −1.49 | N/A | 461 |
| Foreign | 0.16 | 0.21 | 17.26 | 45.13 | 38% | 324 |
| *Exporting* | | | | | | |
| Private | 0.79 | 1.30 | 26.07 | 39.06 | 67% | 63 |
| Public | 0.43 | 0.49 | 18.29 | 9.76 | N/A | 93 |
| Foreign | 0.09 | 0.11 | 20.91 | 50.98 | 41% | 203 |
| *Non-exporting* | | | | | | |
| Private | 1.31 | 1.35 | 7.13 | 24.46 | 29% | 226 |
| Public | 0.55 | 0.54 | −1.22 | −4.33 | N/A | 368 |
| Foreign | 0.28 | 0.37 | 11.14 | 35.32 | 32% | 121 |
| *New exporting* | | | | | | |
| Private | 2.02 | 2.98 | 46.32 | 84.49 | 55% | 17 |
| Public | 0.31 | 0.41 | 37.24 | 42.11 | 88% | 14 |
| Foreign | 0.09 | 0.09 | 17.29 | 45.23 | 38% | 16 |

Notes
TFP computed based on regressions (4.4), (4.5), and (4.6).
TFP contribution is the ratio of TFP growth to sales growth; not applicable (N/A) if sales growth is negative.
New exporting firms are those that did not export in 1998, but exported in 1999 or 2000.

In sharp contrast, TFP growth rates are significantly lower for the sample of non-exporting firms compared with their exporting counterparts. TFP growth rates are negative for non-exporting public firms, largely because of the inefficient state-owned firms in the sample. This result is consistent with earlier studies that found the TFP growth of China's state-owned sector to be low. Notice that non-exporting firms had significantly higher TFP levels in 1998 than exporting firms in all three ownership groups, and the gap narrowed from 1998 to 2000. This supports the view that firms with higher TFP levels did not choose to be exporters; it is exporting that enhanced their TFP.

Finally, we examine a small sample of firms that were not exporting in 1998 but started to export in 1999 or 2000. This examination is intended to provide further evidence that exporting enhances productivity. Table 9.7 shows that the 17 private firms that did not export in 1998 had an average TFP level of 2.02, much higher than the average for all private firms (1.19). By becoming exporters, these firms experienced a TFP growth rate of 46.32 percent from 1998 to 2000, much higher than the average for all private firms (11.26 percent). Newly exporting public firms also had significantly higher TFP growth rate (37.24 percent) than the sample average (2.72 percent). We view this as evidence that exporting enhances productivity growth.

## Conclusion

In this chapter, we investigate the productivity growth of private firms in China. Based on a World Bank survey of 1,500 firms, we construct a sample of 450 private firms as well as a sample of 488 foreign firms and 562 public firms for comparison. The sample period is from 1998 to 2000. On average, private firms are less capital intensive, less R&D intensive, but slightly more skill intensive than other firms. While far less export intensive than foreign firms, private firms are more export intensive than public firms, and their export intensity increased over the sample period.

We estimate production functions for the three ownership groups separately. Using production function regressions, we identify R&D intensity and export status as two variables correlated with productivity growth. For private firms and foreign firms, higher R&D intensity is associated with higher productivity growth. We interpret this as reflecting the positive effect of R&D on technology absorption. For public firms, however, higher R&D intensity is associated with lower productivity growth. We interpret this as reflecting the inefficiency of state-owned firms, which implies higher R&D spending coexisting with lower productivity growth. Based on regressions with industry dummies, we obtain some indirect evidence on the impact of institutional constraints on market competition and productivity growth.

The main finding of the chapter is that exporting constitutes an important driver of productivity growth in both private firms and public firms in China. Exporting plays a much lesser role in the productivity growth of foreign firms in China. We estimate that exporting would raise a private firm's productivity growth rate by 18.19 percentage points over the sample period 1998–2000, and a public firm's productivity growth rate by 19.45 percentage points. While the regressions do not indicate the causality between exporting and productivity growth, we examine TFP estimates and find evidence that it is exporting that enhances productivity, rather than firms with higher productivity self-selecting to be exporters. Productivity levels of both private and public exporting firms were significantly lower than those of non-exporting firms in 1998, but the gap narrowed from 1998 to 2000. Firms that did not export in 1998 but became exporters in 1999 and 2000 had significantly higher TFP levels in 1998 than other firms; entering the export market makes them experience the highest productivity growth among all the firms in the sample.

Our results show optimism about China's economic growth in the coming years. As China's private sector continues to expand and become more involved in international trade, its productivity growth will become an important engine for the growth of the Chinese economy. While we do not have data to examine the link between the productivity growth of private firms and R&D spillovers from foreign firms, we suspect that the link exists and is strong. Despite low R&D

intensity at about 0.05, as shown in Table 9.3, the productivity growth of private firms benefited greatly from R&D investment (regression 4.4). Private firms may be effectively absorbing R&D spillovers from foreign firms, whose R&D intensity, as shown in Table 9.3, is three times higher than that of private firms.

## Notes

1  We thank the World Bank and the Davidson Data Center and Network (DDCN) for making the data available.
2  As pointed out in Asian Development Bank (2003: 1), "Exactly what comprises the 'private sector' in the PRC is murky, and a lack of clarity is evident in the data on economic performance provided by the State Statistical Office."
3  The GDP deflator is 0.978 for 1999 and 0.986 for 2000, with 1998 as the base year.
4  To avoid endogeneity, the R&D variable is R&D intensity in 1998.
5  See Brandt and Zhu (2004) for a study of the impact of financial constraint on technology absorption in a sample of Shanghai firms.
6  See the literature cited by Xu and Wang (2000).
7  Bernard and Jensen (1999) provide a discussion of the causality between exporting and productivity.
8  See Sachs and Woo (2000) for an excellent discussion of institutional factors in explaining China's economic performance.
9  We chose the apparel and leather industry as the base industry in the regression because it is arguably the industry with the most competitive market.
10  There is a large literature on measuring China's TFP. See Chow (1985, 1993), Chow and Li (2002), Gordon and Li (1995), and Li (1997), among many others.
11  Based on regressions (4.4) and (4.5), we use 0.09 as the estimated output elasticity of skilled labor for the sample of private firms and 0.09 as the estimated output elasticity of unskilled labor for the sample of public firms, despite their statistical insignificance. This practice has little impact on the results because the value of 0.09 is small.
12  These results regarding ownership impact on productivity are consistent with the findings of Zhang et al. (2001) who use a different data set.

## References

Asian Development Bank (2003) *People's Republic of China: The Development of Private Enterprise*, Manila: Asian Development Bank.
Benhabib, J. and M. Spiegel (1994) "The Roles of Human Capital in Economic Development: Evidence from Aggregate Cross-Country Data," *Journal of Monetary Economics*, 34: 143–73.
Bernard, A. and B. Jensen (1999) "Exceptional Exporter Performance: Cause, Effect, or Both," *Journal of International Economics*, 47: 1–25.
Brandt, L. and S.C. Zhu (2004) "Importing Technology: Evidence from Shanghai Firms," mimeo, Michigan State University.
Chow, G. (1985) "A Model of Chinese National Income Determination," *Journal of Political Economy*, 93: 782–92.
Chow, G. (1993) "Capital Formation and Economic Growth in China," *Quarterly Journal of Economics*, 108: 809–42.
Chow, G. and K.-W. Li (2002) "China's Economic Growth: 1952–2010," *Economic Development and Cultural Change*, 51: 247–56.

Gordon, R.H. and W. Li (1995) "The Change in Productivity of Chinese State Enterprises, 1983–1987," *Journal of Productivity Analysis*, 6: 5–26.

Huang, Y. (2003) *Selling China: Foreign Direct Investment During the Reform Era*, New York: Cambridge University Press.

International Finance Corporation (2000) *China's Emerging Private Enterprises: Prospects for the New Century*, Washington, DC: International Finance Corporation.

Li, W. (1997) "The Impact of Economic Reform on the Performance of Chinese State Enterprises, 1980–1989," *Journal of Political Economy*, 105: 1080–106.

Sachs, J.D. and W.T. Woo (2000) "Understanding China's Economic Performance," *Journal of Policy Reform*, 4: 1–50.

Xu, B. and J. Wang (2000) "Trade, FDI, and International Technology Diffusion," *Journal of Economic Integration*, 15: 585–601.

Zhang, A., Y. Zhang and R. Zhao (2001) "Impact of Ownership and Competition on the Productivity of Chinese Enterprises," *Journal of Comparative Economics*, 29: 327–46.

# 10 The demand for and supply of energy in China

## Implications for the private sector

*David F. Gates and Jason Z. Yin*

### Introduction

China's energy demand and the resources needed to meet that demand have become one of the most prominent issues in international discussions of energy. The emergence of China's energy demand commands academic and policy research, and even media coverage. In our earlier studies of China's energy demand as it relates to transportation and urbanization (Gates and Yin, 2002; Yin and Gates, 2002), we took more of a long-term view and raised the possibility that, even if China's economy continued to grow rather slowly – which was the prevailing perception at the time – there would still be a strong demand for car and truck fuel and for electricity and other clean energy resources for urban development, which would present major challenges. The economic expansion and the re-emergence of strong growth in energy demand over the past two years have clearly raised the level of interest in these topics. China's national oil companies now show up in all parts of the world aggressively looking for energy resources. Industry experts are now eager to quantify how much energy China is consuming today and whether the explosive growth of the recent past will continue or not.

This chapter intends to explore the fundamentals that underlie both the current situation and especially the longer term implications for the Chinese economy and the growth of the private sector. It begins with an overview of recent developments in China's energy demand and supply – including a discussion of what is known and what is still largely a matter of speculation regarding what has caused the recent surge in demand. It then analyzes the dynamics that underlie China's energy demand and supply, and what these imply for the sustainable growth of China's economy, and its efforts to protect its environment. The chapter concludes with a discussion of the implications for the private sector, including both private and foreign investments in the energy industries.

### The development of energy demand and supply

As is often the case, the most timely and credible evidence of what is happening with China's energy demand and supply is data on exports and imports of particular fuels. As China still produces most of its own energy – especially coal

– data on exports and imports of other fuels such as oil are certainly not the whole story, but they can provide a good early indication of what is happening. And as the international market for oil is much larger than the international market for coal, these data have the further advantage of providing an early indication of the impact of developments in China on the rest of the world.

Table 10.1 shows China's net imports – imports minus exports – of crude oil and refined products (gasoline, kerosene, diesel fuel, fuel oil, etc.) in millions of barrels a day from 2000 to 2005. These data are from monthly reports and are subject to the same problems as monthly data anywhere in the world. But, the totals and percentage changes are sufficient to begin to establish the point that, after a period of what appears to have been extremely low growth, energy demand appears to have grown more rapidly in 2002, and much more rapidly in 2004.

To put these numbers in perspective, according to the Paris-based International Energy Agency (IEA), the forecast for global oil demand in 2004 is about 82.4 million barrels per day, of which about 70 percent is traded internationally. According to the same agency, China's oil demand was just over 800,000 barrels a day in 2004 or just under 8 percent of total world demand (Figure 10.1). More importantly, the surging Chinese oil demand in 2004 contributed more than 30 percent of the growth in global oil demand (Behree, 2004).

Looking broadly at the total demand over time, China's share of world oil demand has been increasing steadily from 5.4 percent in 1997 to a projected 7.7 percent in 2004. And, more importantly, it made an even larger contribution to the growth in world oil demand over this period. Whether these developments are important or not probably depends on whether they are representative of what is happening with other fuels, and whether this is just a one-off event or something that can be expected to persist for some time. Clearly, if this surge in net imports of crude and refined products is simply a consequence of a rapid increase in the number of cars, as is sometimes suggested, the implications will be different than if the increase is more broadly based and reflective of ongoing changes in economic activity and changes in living conditions that will affect many if not most of the fuels that China currently uses, and not just oil or gasoline. In fact, the available evidence suggests that it is the latter, and that the current surge in demand is sufficiently broad based that it is affecting all fuels and not just oil, and certainly not just gasoline.

*Table 10.1* China's net imports of crude and refined products, 2002–05

|  | 2000 | 2001 | 2002 | 2003 | 2004 | 2005 |
|---|---|---|---|---|---|---|
| Total (MBD) | 1.3 | 1.4 | 1.6 | 2.2 | 2.9 | 3.0 |
| Percentage change |  | 4.0 | 18.6 | 32.7 | 36.1 | 0.7 |

Source: International Energy Agency, *Energy Statistics of Non-OECD Countries and Monthly Oil Data Service*, available electronically, by subscription, annually through 2003, 2005 and monthly thereafter, 2006.

Note
MBD, millions of barrels a day.

**Total Oil Demand**

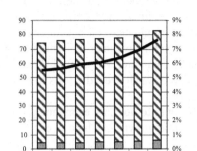

**Growth in Oil Demand**

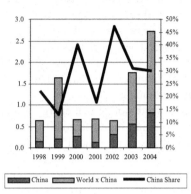

- China oil demand approaching 8% of world total
- China oil demand growth currently > 35% of world total

*Figure 10.1 China economic growth is increasingly important in world oil balances.*

This surging energy demand in China has raised two questions. What is causing this strong increase in energy demand and net imports? What are the implications for China and the rest of the world?

## Economic growth and energy demand

China is currently ranked as the second largest country in total energy consumption, following the US and ahead of Japan. In the early 1990s, China was self-sufficient in energy, consuming about 10 percent of the world's energy, while it accounted for about 10 percent of world energy production. However, beginning in the mid-1990s, China has become a net energy importer.

The strong growth of China's economy over the past 20 years has raised energy demand such that most observers expect that total energy demand will grow by something between 2.5 percent and 3.5 percent annually through 2015–25. The growth will be faster in the short term and slower in the long term. By comparison, the comparable growth for the industrialized countries would be more in the order of 1–1.5 percent – higher in North America and lower in western Europe and Japan (US Department of Energy, 2005). The rapid growth of energy demand and the lagging growth of energy production have raised concerns in a number of policy areas, including the availability and cost of energy supplies and the possibility of further adverse effects on the environment (Behree, 2004).

However, the relationships between economic activity, energy, and the environment in China are particularly complex. This complexity raises a number of questions: whether the data on economic growth published by the Chinese government are valid?; whether the historical relationships can be used as a guideline for future energy requirements?; and what is a reasonable assessment of the environmental consequences of those requirements? Overall, we want to know whether China is able to meet its energy requirements such that economic growth can be sustained and any adverse environmental consequences can be controlled. These questions (and the likely answers) have important implications for the role of the private sector, including foreign enterprises, in all aspects of China's future energy demand and supply and its much needed efforts to protect the environment.

It is worth noting that energy is a critical input to not only economic growth, but also rising living standards. Rapid economic growth in China over the past 25 years has clearly raised living standards with massive increases in energy use. Growth is expected to continue, and this is certain to require increases in energy, just as it will require increases in other factors of production. Too often, discussions of energy (especially among western experts) ignore or downplay these benefits as somehow unimportant. While the focus of the discussion that follows is how energy is used, how it is supplied, and what negative externalities it causes, it is essential to remember the benefits, especially as these relate to rising standards of living.

## Elasticity of energy demand and real GDP growth

From 1980 to 2000, total primary energy demand in China – basically direct use of coal, oil, and other energy sources plus energy used to produce electricity – increased by just over 11 million barrels of oil equivalent (MBDOE) or just over 90 percent versus the 12.1 MBDOE recorded in 1980. Over the same period, the adverse environmental consequences of energy production and use also increased substantially with emissions of $CO_2$, a "greenhouse gas" that figures prominently in the ongoing debate over climate change, likely to have increased at least as fast as total energy, and probably a bit faster.

Given the performance of China's economy, which saw an increase in real gross domestic product (GDP) of more than 500 percent over this same 20-year period, it is hardly surprising that energy demand and the emissions of $CO_2$ associated with energy use both increased sharply. But, in fact, as we shall see (as shown in Figure 10.2), what is perhaps most surprising is that the Chinese energy supply and the emission of $CO_2$ associated with energy consumption has not been growing anywhere near as fast as the overall economy – at least as both are measured in the government's estimates.

The traditional rule of thumb in forecasting the rate of growth of energy demand in emerging markets such as China is to assume an elasticity (or ratio of the rate of growth in energy to the rate of growth in real GDP) of about 1 or somewhat higher than 1. An elasticity of 1 means that each 1 percent increase in economic activity would require a 1 percent increase in total energy demand. The rule of thumb for energy elasticity in industrial counties is substantially less than 1 and, in many cases, 0.5 or even less. An elasticity of 0.5 means that each increase in

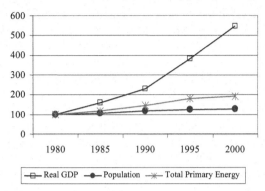

*Figure 10.2* Real GDP, population, and energy.

economic activity of 1 percent per year would require about half a percent increase in total energy demand.

Elasticity of emissions of $CO_2$ to economic growth are discussed less frequently, in part because these are usually calculated through a two-step process that looks first at energy by type of fuel and then applies carbon content factors to estimate emissions of $CO_2$ based on the volumes of the particular fossil fuels – coal, oil, and gas. Given the fundamentals, elasticity of emissions of $CO_2$ would generally be expected to be similar to those for total energy demand, except in countries with special circumstances or energy policies that have led, or are leading, to substantial shifts in the mix of fuels – fossil to non-fossil (hydro, nuclear, or at some point, solar or wind) or within the mix of fossil fuels – usually coal to oil and/or gas. France is one such country, which has aggressively promoted the use of nuclear as an alternative to fossil fuels for the generation of electric power and, as a result, has recorded a much lower elasticity of emissions of $CO_2$ to total energy or real GDP than other countries at a similar stage of economic development.

In China, the elasticity of energy demand and energy-associated emissions of $CO_2$ to real GDP are much lower than those in most other countries – certainly, most emerging market countries and, even more surprisingly, many industrial countries as well. Indeed, as evidenced by the growth rates presented above for the period from 1980 to 2000, the average elasticity of energy demand to real GDP in China was only about 0.37. The elasticity of energy-associated emissions of $CO_2$ to real GDP was probably a bit higher – but not that much higher – despite the fact that coal, the most carbon-intensive fossil fuel, has always accounted for a high percentage of China's energy requirements, and will remain the major energy resource in the foreseeable future.

Understanding what is behind these relationships is important because, even if China's economy grows more slowly in the future than it did in the mid-1990s, for instance, the increase in its requirements for energy and the implications of that increase for its environment will be extremely important for China and for the world. Given China's energy requirements and its energy-associated emissions of

$CO_2$ – and assuming that the average elasticity from the period from 1980 to 2000 continues into the future – each 8 percent per year increase in real GDP will mean a need to secure more than 0.8 MBDOE in additional energy supplies each year.

Any effort to understand the relationship between economic activity, energy demand, and emissions of $CO_2$ in China must first address three potential problems. Two of these problems involve the validity of China's estimates of economic growth and energy demand, while the third problem involves the adequacy of an elasticity approach to total energy and, by extension, emissions of $CO_2$, especially in an economy and energy system that is changing as rapidly as China's. Viewed in perspective, these problems do not undercut the analysis so much as provide a useful perspective on the importance of looking within the totals before making judgments on what is happening and what it means for the future.

Questions regarding the validity of China's estimates of economic growth have persisted for years in the literature. But what is notable about some of the recent discussions is the prominent role of estimates of energy demand growth in the arguments, that the government's estimates of economic growth are either too high, too low, or just about right. The starting point for these arguments is the relationships discussed above, which until recently revealed that total energy demand in China had been growing much more slowly than real GDP. Those who argued that the government's estimates of economic growth were too high pointed to slow growth in energy demand as evidence that economic growth was not growing as rapidly as the government was reporting. Those who insisted that the government's estimates of economic growth were about right then countered that slow growth in energy demand was simply an indication that improvements in energy efficiency were extremely high, and that this was responsible for most of the difference in the estimated rates of growth.

The truth is in the middle. Estimates of real GDP growth (like estimates of total energy demand) are rarely as rigorous as implied in government reports. Allowing for the size of the task in a country as large as China, the official estimates of the rate of growth in real GDP may not be much shakier than those of other countries. Whether these estimates are too high or, more recently, too low is effectively impossible to prove without a better system for collecting and analyzing the available data. However, there is also little question that improvements in energy conservation in China have been substantial. Indeed, even if GDP in China had grown at half the rate that the government has reported since economic reforms began, the reduction in energy consumed per unit of GDP would have been as fast or faster (the ratio of the rate of growth in energy demand to the rate of growth in real GDP as low or lower) than in other major countries.

## Energy elasticity in comparison

Figure 10.3 compares trends in the ratio of energy demand to real GDP in China, India, and the US, from 1980 to 2000. In 1980, China's economy consumed almost twice as much energy per unit of GDP as India, and nearly seven times as much energy per unit of GDP as the US. By 2000, using the government's estimates of economic activity, China's energy consumption per unit of GDP had fallen by almost two-thirds. This reduction enabled China to match India in terms of this particular measure, but still left its economy nearly four times as energy intensive as the US.

Expressed in terms of income elasticity (calculated as the rate of growth in total energy divided by the rate of growth in real GDP), China had an average elasticity over the period of 0.37 – exactly equal to that of the US. The comparable elasticity for India over this period was 0.66.

□uestions regarding the validity of China's energy statistics are usually more technical than those regarding the statistics on economic growth. But the arguments are not necessarily less spirited. Some of these questions relate to the fact that – like the economy – the number of transactions involving energy are too numerous and too diverse for anyone to be confident that the totals have been adequately captured through a multilevel government sampling and reporting system, which sometimes, at least, seems to place greater weight on compliance with government objectives (or concealing the actual situation) than anything else. An example of this problem is the statistics from the late 1990s, which showed a substantial fall off in coal production and consumption. The timing of the decline corresponded to what had been reported as an effort by the central government to close small and inefficient mines. With economic growth continuing, increases in production and consumption of alternatives to coal suggested that some cutbacks have actually occurred. But whether the actual cutbacks in coal were as large as those being reported – and how this was being accomplished with economic activity continuing to grow and, more recently, beginning to grow quite rapidly – is still being questioned. That this is more than a statistical exercise is clear from the fact that, if the official statistics are accurate and the usage of coal had actually fallen, this would imply that the inefficiency in coal use was actually higher than previously assumed. It would also be favorable for China's emissions

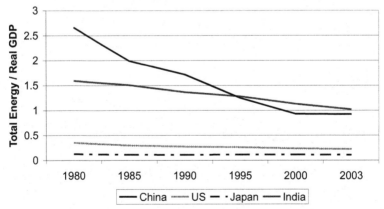

*Figure 10.3*  Trends in energy/GDP. Source: International Energy Agency (IEA), Energy Statistics of OECD Countries; Energy Statistics of Non-OECD Countries and Monthly Oil Data Service; all available electronically, by subscription; annual through 2003, 2005 and monthly thereafter, 2006.

of CO$_2$ as coal has a higher carbon content than other fossil fuels, that is oil and natural gas.

The final problem, the adequacy of an elasticity approach to understanding and forecasting total energy demand in an economic–energy system as diverse and complex as China, is valid, especially if the alternative is an approach that focuses on energy demand in particular end uses and draws upon other more specialized drivers of energy demand in addition to real GDP. But, before looking more closely at demand by end use, it is worth noting that a macro level elasticity approach can still have value where the intent is to compare one country with another, and where the differences are sufficiently great that any conclusions that are drawn will hold across wide variations in the underlying data. This would apply to most conclusions with respect to energy demand in China, where the differences are so clear and where the volumes are sufficiently great that growth at almost any rate will appear substantial in comparison with the rest of the world.

As a first step in the direction of understanding what is happening within the energy totals, Figure 10.4 shows the pattern of energy demand by end use in China in MBDOE from 1980 to 2000. The dotted line on the same chart shows the trend in real GDP over the same period.

According to most projections, there is an increasing gap between total energy demand (consumption) and production for the forthcoming years. Like most countries, total energy demand in China is a complex blend of end uses, some of which, such as industrial demand, are closely related to real GDP, but others, such as residential demand, are not. And, as noted above, elasticity calculations relating total energy demand and, by extension, various environmental indicators to real GDP can be useful for analysis including international comparisons, but only where there is at least some appreciation of the relative size of the various end uses and some understanding of what is going on in each.

We would like to highlight the key points regarding each of these end uses: (1)

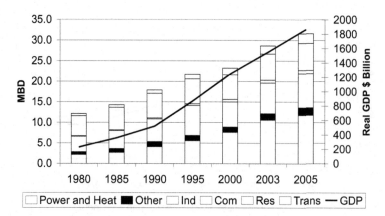

*Figure 10.4* China energy demand by end use and transformation. Source: International Energy Agency (IEA), Energy Statistics of Non-OECD Countries and Monthly Oil Data Service; available electronically, by subscription; annual through 2003, 2005. Authors' projections for 2005.

transformation and energy generation/distribution; (2) industrial use; (3) residential use; and (4) transportation use.

### Use for energy transformation

First, transformation and energy generation and distribution – fuel used in the generation of electricity and district heat – and other uses, such as fuel used to find and process coal, oil, and gas are the largest users of primary energy in China followed by industrial use and residential use. The continued emergence of utility fuel (and what is called energy industry own use) is important for a number of reasons, including the fact that it is tied directly to the growth in electricity demand, which is itself the fastest growing component of final consumption in each of the other end uses – except transportation, where electricity use is rather low – as it is in most countries.

For the period from 1980 to 2000, the elasticity of electricity output in China to real GDP was about 0.85. An elasticity of 0.85 would seem to be low by emerging market standards. But comparisons are complicated by changes in the availability of electricity in different countries and by differences in unauthorized usage, which tend to get recorded as transmission losses rather than end use.

### Industrial use

Industrial demand: China's second largest energy use would seem to be the most directly related to aggregate economic activity. Here, however, the specifics are strongly and importantly affected by real world considerations, including the validity of recent statistics on coal, shifts in the mix of economic activity in which the same monetary amount of real GDP may reflect substantially different requirements in terms of energy, and changes in the roles of state-owned and other entities in the management of industrial activity and supplies of industrial energy.

Using the same sources of statistics as above, the elasticity of industrial energy use in China from 1980 to 2000 was an extremely low 0.3. As noted, statistics on coal, especially in industrial uses, are a major factor in this outcome. This can also be seen by comparing the elasticity for the 20 years ending in 2000 (0.3) with the elasticity for the 15 years ending in 1995, which was 0.5.

But, whatever the actual situation in terms of industrial use of coal, the fact is that industrial energy has consistently grown rather slowly, especially in relation to the growth of the economy. There are several reasons for this. The first is that Chinese industrial activity was traditionally dominated by what would be characterized as heavy industry – iron and steel, heavy machinery, etc. – which required large amounts of furnace fuels, including coal and heavy fuel oil, and, over time, the mix of industrial activities has shifted toward lighter industry – electrical machinery and appliances – which require primarily electricity and more specialized fuels such as liquefied petroleum gas (LPG) and natural gas. This is sometimes called indirect conservation. The second is that the use of energy in all types of industry, but especially heavy industry, was very high historically in relation to output, and this has gradually improved over time as new facilities came online and as equipment wore out and was replaced in existing facilities. The latter is sometimes called direct conservation and reflects not so much the introduction of new "step out" technologies, but rather the introduction of modern, off-the-shelf equipment, often as a replacement for older equipment that, given the technology when it was introduced, was simply much less efficient. Two additional reasons, which operated behind and through the first two, included the gradual phase down of the share of industrial output controlled by state-owned enterprises (SOEs) and the gradual introduction of energy prices that were closer to market driven.

Looking to the future, the key point is that each of these factors – both types of conservation, the share of output controlled by SOEs, and the introduction of market prices – still have a long way to run. But the effects of some of these factors will likely diminish over time, and most will be affected by the rate at which the economy grows, by the rate at which reform proceeds, and the opportunities that China provides for non-state and foreign-participated enterprises. Strong growth would likely mean a faster shift in the mix of economic activities – with faster growth in lighter, less energy-intensive manufacturing. But, it would also mean faster growth in more traditional, more energy-intensive industries such as steel. Depending on how this sorts out, overall elasticity could rise, fall, or stay roughly the same – but the absolute volume of energy consumed will certainly be larger than if growth rates had remained relatively subdued.

### Residential use

Residential demand is currently China's third largest energy end use and accounts for close to one-third of energy consumption. This end use has traditionally been driven more by population, urbanization, and the availability of commercial energy (as distinguished from traditional energy such as wood and crop waste) than by GDP.

Looking ahead, the elasticity of residential demand to population and possibly even real GDP could actually begin to increase as urbanization continues and with it incomes, availability, and the use of household appliances, and access to commercial forms of energy. In this regard, stronger GDP growth will likely mean more rapid growth in urbanization, as well as stronger growth in disposable incomes. Much of the growth in residential use will be met by oil (LPG and kerosene), gas, and electricity, but most of the base will remain coal and traditional fuels such as biomass. These shifts are important for local air quality, but any positive implications for $CO_2$ will be tempered by the fact that much of the additional electricity will be produced from coal. Improvements in residential energy use are only part of the reason, but they are an indication that progress is beginning to be made in addressing the problem of local air quality, which by all accounts remains serious and is likely to lead to further changes in the mix of fuels, especially in urban areas.

### Transportation use

Transportation demand: China's fourth largest energy end use recorded a reasonably high elasticity in relation to real GDP (0.66) for the period 1980–2000. It is also noteworthy that, unlike most other end uses that may have been distorted by questionable data on coal, the elasticity of transportation energy actually jumped up toward the end of the period, averaging just less than 1 for the five years ending in 2000. Transportation energy demand in China is interesting for several reasons. For example, most transportation energy was associated with industrial uses – mainly the transportation of freight – where the relatively low elasticity likely reflected a combination of bulk shipments and excess capacity, especially in pre-reform rail and barge freight systems. Recent increases in the elasticity of transportation energy presumably reflect an increased reliance on trucking – and to some extent air – for industrial shipments and low, but growing amounts of personal transportation, increasingly involving cars.

In terms of fuels, transportation energy lines up fairly well by mode with trains, continuing to shift from coal and oil to electricity, barges continuing to shift from coal to oil, and trucks and cars pretty much staying with oil.

Finally, looking to the future, the elasticity of transportation energy demand is likely to remain close to 1 and could rise even higher, at least for a time. Consistent with the view that the elasticity could be something higher than 1, at least for a time, is the expected strong growth in specialized trucking and the expected strong growth in passenger car ownership. Tending to offset these trends, at least to some extent, is the possibility that miles driven and hence fuel per vehicle per year will tend to decline as the numbers of vehicles increases. Fuel efficiency is still relatively low and, while this should improve as the share of new vehicles increases, the rate of improvement is likely to be slowed by continuing concerns over the consistency of available fuels.

## Energy supply

Having considered the elasticity for each of the major end uses and the relationship of demand to ongoing changes in the performance of the Chinese economy, this next section will look at the supply side, i.e., the growth potential for each of the principal commercial fuel alternatives: (1) coal; (2) oil; (3) gas; (4) hydro; and (5) nuclear.

### Coal production

Coal makes up the bulk of China's primary energy consumption, and China is the largest consumer and producer of coal in the world. But, prospects for coal have become more questionable in recent years. In contrast to the goal of coal production of 1.4 billion short tons by 2000, China's actual coal production in 2000 was 1.27 billion short tons. By 2002, the shortfall was about 200 million tons, and the shortage is expected to continue in the future. Given where things stand today, any reduction in coal production/availability not caused by planned reductions in demand could have serious implications for future economic growth.[1] The reason is not that there are no alternatives to coal, but rather that, with China growing as fast as it is and with investments and time required to put these alternatives in place, any sudden reduction in supply is likely to result in a reduction in activity. The recent apparent shortages are reportedly due to depletion and also to restructuring of coal production, in which thousands of dangerous and inefficient small coal mines have been closed on economic or safety grounds in recent years. Meanwhile, coal exploration has been lagging.

In addition to the problem of supplies, coal, as the principal energy resource, creates severe pollution problems. Coal burning remains the leading cause of pollution in major cities. Major efforts have been made to reduce dependency on coal and to set targets for pollution control. For instance, Guangdong province announced its Blue Sky program in 2002, under which all coal- and oil-burning plants must install equipment to clean pollutants such as sulfur dioxide by 2010. Clearly, pollution control is quite often very expensive and time-consuming. Spending on pollution control, like other forms of investment spending, is counted in the GDP statistics but, if factories are shut down or decide to move rather than undertake that spending, growth will be lower.

### Oil production and importation

As to oil, China is already the world's second largest oil consumer, ahead of Japan and second only to the US. According to the US Energy Information Administration (EIA), China's consumption is expected to reach 10 million barrels per day by 2020 (IEA, 2003). Similar to coal, China's oil production has been basically flat at just over 3.0 million barrels per day in recent years. The gap between domestic oil output and its needs has been widening (Hirsch, 2004). Practically, the difference must be made up by imports, which, as noted, are already resulting in major changes in the activities of China's national oil companies and in China's approach to the world in general (EIA, 2005).

### Natural gas

Natural gas has not been a major fuel in China traditionally but, given China's domestic reserves of natural gas that were reported to be 48.3 trillion cubic feet (tcf) at the beginning of 2002, and recognizing the environmental benefits of using gas, China has embarked on a major expansion of its gas infrastructure. Until the 1990s, natural gas was used largely as a feedstock for fertilizer plants with little use for electricity generation. Gas currently accounts for only slightly more than 3 percent (3.3 percent) of total energy consumption. Consumption is expected to rise quite rapidly, but the share is likely to remain fairly low, at least for the next several years. Increases in consumption will require increases in domestic production and imports by pipeline and in the form of liquefied natural gas (LNG). Key steps in this process include the gas pipeline between the Ordos Basin in

Inner Mongolia and Beijing, which was completed in 1997, and the "west-to-east pipeline," which will connect gas deposits in western Xinjiang province to Shanghai. It also involves the joint venture projects to secure LNG supplies from Australia, Indonesia, and the Middle East, and possibly pipeline supplies from Russia. Two LNG receiving terminals and re-gasification projects are now under development – one in Guangdong and one in Fujian – and most experts expect to see several more – extending up the coastal provinces to Shanghai and beyond over the next several years.

### Hydropower generation

China's exploitable hydroelectric resources stand at 378 million kilowatts, equivalent to an annual power supply of 1.92 trillion kWh, topping the world and making up 16.7 percent of the world's total, according to the Ministry of Water Resources.[2] However, only 29 percent of China's hydropower resources have been exploited, far less than in some developed countries. Meanwhile, approximately 75 million rural people still have no access to power.[3]

The largest hydropower project currently under construction is the Three Gorges Dam. When fully completed in 2009, it will include 26 separate 700-MW generators, for a total of 18.2 GW. In March 2002, the Three Gorges project was reorganized into the China Three Gorges Electric Power Corporation. The corporation is seeking capital through an equity offering open to foreign investors, similar to those already carried out by the major Chinese oil companies. Developing hydropower stations is a significant part of China's sustainable energy initiative. In 2004, hydropower contributed 14 percent of total energy supplies in China, and it is expected that hydropower will contribute more clean energy to China's economy in the coming decades. However, China faces chronic water shortages, especially in the north, and social problems are caused by the need to relocate large numbers of people when rivers are dammed to create reservoirs for hydropower.

### Nuclear power generation

Currently, there are also developments involving nuclear power. China now runs 6.2 GW at eight nuclear generators, all on the east coast, and is building another three, which would bring total capacity to 8.8 GW by the end of 2005. China has recently drafted a preliminary plan to quadruple nuclear power capacity to more than 32 GW between 2005 and 2020, or roughly two plants a year to fill the energy supply gap. The expansion would boost the share of nuclear energy in China's power mix to 6 percent in 2020 from 1.4 percent in 2003. However, it is sharply below the wealthy nations' average of 30 percent of nuclear power in the total energy supply.

As discussed above, an important aspect of energy supply is to transform primary energy sources into more usable forms. Traditionally, power generation in China has been fueled by coal, which still accounts for about three-quarters of total power generation. Hydro is second at about 20 percent. For various reasons, including presumably the environmental policies of international lenders, China has been working to develop and implement alternatives to coal, including hydro and nuclear. Thus far, however, these efforts have not been sufficient to make much of a difference in terms of their shares in the total. Looking ahead, the best prospects for slowing the rate of growth of coal in power generation are hydro, as for example with the Three Gorges Project, nuclear, in selected areas especially around Hong Kong, and gas, especially in areas that are tributary to the west-to-east gas project, which will develop and transport gas from as far as the Tarim Basin in Xinjiang to Shanghai, and to the anticipated new LNG import projects from Australia and Indonesia in Guandong, Fujian, and beyond.

## Implications for public policy

Combining the analysis of elasticity of end uses and the growth potential of energy production and environmental concerns, the principal finding of this study is that, in the short term, the elasticity of total energy demand in China will not decline as rapidly as some studies suggest, and may actually edge upward. This, in turn, suggests that China will have to continue and even step up its efforts to develop additional volumes of energy to support economic growth, and continue to cope with any adverse consequences of that growth in terms of the environment.

Another important finding is that this additional energy will have to be far less coal intensive than it has been in the past if China is to avoid a further deterioration in local air quality, and possibly major complaints from the rest of the world on the subject of global warming.

Both these findings appear to have been recognized by the government, and appear to underlie a number of policy initiatives that began in the mid- to late 1990s, and include:

- The restructuring of the national oil companies (NOCs) followed by successful initial public offers (IPOs), designed at least in part to increase the exploration for and production of domestic oil and gas.
- More aggressive participation by the NOCs in the development of foreign oil and gas resources.
- Stepped up efforts to develop and transport domestic gas, as evidenced by the west-to-east gas pipeline project.
- Stepped up efforts to bring foreign LNG to coastal cities, especially those in the southeast, which are remote from domestic supplies of natural gas.
- Continuing efforts to develop hydro resources, as evidenced by the Three Gorges hydroelectric project.

The question then is not whether the government recognizes the need for action in each of these areas – clearly it does – but whether it is doing enough and whether there are additional steps that could be taken – especially involving the private sector – that could assure a more satisfactory outcome, even if the forces behind the elasticity of energy demand turn out to be different than what might be expected based on recent actual results. These issues are addressed in the next section.

### Implications for private and foreign investment

After privatization has taken place in many sectors such as agriculture, commercial appliances, and services, China's energy industries are still under strong central control. Little has been done to allow domestic private ownership and/or foreign ownership of China's assets in these industries. These industries are dominated by a few large state-owned corporations. The three largest petroleum companies are the Chinese National Petroleum Corporation (CNPC), Sinopec, and the China National Offshore Oil and Gas Corporation (CNOOC). Initially, CNPC was responsible for onshore exploration and production, Sinopec was responsible for refining, and CNOOC was responsible for offshore exploration and production. But, starting in the late 1990s, these responsibilities were changed, with CNPC and Sinopec integrating downstream and upstream, respectively – mainly through asset swaps – and CNOOC becoming involved in onshore LNG. Each of these companies also underwent major restructurings, in both operations and finance with each undertaking major and unprecedented, for them at least, IPOs.

Thus far, China has adopted a very limited form of privatization in the energy sectors for both Chinese private investment and foreign investment. The Chinese government has allowed privately and collectively owned enterprises to run small and low-grade coal mines and related semi-products, such as coking coal, but with insufficient financial, technological, and safety support. Most of these poorly equipped, small operations suffer from operating inefficiencies, heavy pollution, and safety problems. For instance, in Shanxi province, thousands of small coal mines emerged, but their recovery rate averaged only about 15 percent for the coal resources. More than 4,000 unauthorized coking plants were forced to shut down by the Shanxi provincial government after China began to restrict the scale of the coking coal industry.[4] Another recent case involved the government in ordering the seizure of thousands of private oil wells in northwest China.[5] Unfortunately, those closures were conducted without due process. Despite recent legal reforms, which strengthened the constitutional protection of private property, many private companies in China face an uphill battle in obtaining legal redress if there is infringement on their interests.

Recently, another format of private investment has emerged in the form of corporate groups – letting private companies buy shares in new ventures initiated by SOEs. For instance, China's largest coking coal-producing corporation – Shanxi Coking Coal Group Co. – signed a long-term cooperation pact with Shanxi Wulin Group Co., Ltd. According to the pact, the Shanxi Coking Coal Group Co. will organize a corporate group together with the Shanxi Wulin Group and another seven private companies, so as to conduct the coordinated development of major coking coal resources in Shanxi.[6] The collectiveness and large economic scale may offer better opportunities for private sectors to grow in the energy industries.

As to foreign capital participation in the energy industries, most foreign activity is in production-sharing contracts. China has recently emphasized exploration and development expenditures in western regions, particularly in the Xinjiang region of the northwest. Most onshore tracts offered to foreign investors in the three investment auctions are located in this area. The three major basins in the Xinjiang region are Tarim, Turpan-Hami, and Junggar. Experts have long believed that Tarim is the most promising as far as the possibility of finding "elephant-class" discoveries is concerned. However, Tarim's remoteness and lack of infrastructure have made it difficult for transportation facilities to keep up with discoveries, temporarily reducing production. To entice foreign companies who are concerned about getting their oil to market, China has launched a massive infrastructure expansion program in this region that will include pipelines, a trans-desert highway, parallel rail lines, and expanded storage.

A major issue for China's electric power industry is the distribution of generation among power plants. China's stated intention eventually is to create a unified national power grid, and to have a modern power market in which plants sell power to the grid at market-determined rates. In the short term, though, traditional arrangements still hold sway, and state-owned power plants tend to have a higher priority than independent private plants. Additionally, some private plants with "take-or-pay" contracts, which provide for guaranteed minimum sales amounts, have had trouble getting the provincial authorities running the local grids to honor those terms (IEA, 2002).

There has been some attempt at further reform in the coal industry. Mine ownership has been partially redistributed from the state to regional, collective, and private parties. Currently, approximately half of China's coal production comes from state-controlled mines and regional or local authorities. The other half is produced by collective or privately owned operations.

However, the coal industry is beginning to attract foreign participation. For instance, a cooperative agreement was announced between the government and an international consortium to construct a US$900 million underground coal slurry pipeline running from Shanxi province to coastal Shandong. It will be the largest and longest such installation in the world, and will have annual capacity of 15 million tons upon completion. Later, the project is to be expanded into an extensive coal slurry pipeline network. The project is one of the first major infrastructure projects in modern China to have western financial and management control. In addition, the BHP Mineral & Oil Company of Australia and two Chinese firms plan the joint development of coal-bed methane in northern China's Shanxi province.

Meeting China's future energy requirements in a way that will allow economic growth to continue while minimizing any adverse consequences for the local, regional, or world environment is a major challenge that will require a joint effort including both the government and the private sector. Traditionally, the government has had responsibility for most of the key decisions with respect to the development and allocation of energy resources, and this is not expected to change dramatically, at least any time soon. But, in recent years, the government's dominance in energy demand and supply has begun to ease as economic reform has proceeded. Examples include the freeing of the markets for crude oil and refined products, with crude oil prices being linked to world market prices in 1998 and refined products being linked to regional average prices in 2001.

The demand by private consumers, commercial establishments, and non-state industries is growing. These demand users have at least some degree of freedom to make their own decisions and arrangements with respect to energy supply. The entry of private producers into power generation, including the introduction of bidding procedures into dispatch decisions such that these private facilities can gain access to the publicly managed distribution system, is important.

In addition to energy production, the policy-makers should also consider allowing the private sector to participate in distribution markets such as gasoline and LPG retail operations. While some steps in this direction have been made, more can and should be done. It will help China move toward an optimal balance of energy demand, supply, and the environment. Note that none of these steps would require that the government fully remove itself from setting the framework in which energy is supplied or priced. But there are steps – mainly relating to setting the framework – that could be taken, and then left alone, while retaining the authority to make adjustments as might be required in the future.

## Notes

1  *The Economist*, London, 19 April 2003, p. 370.
2  *People's Daily Online*, 27 May 2004, available from www.people.com.cn.
3  *China Daily*, 10 October 2002.
4  *SinoCast China Business Daily News*, Dallas, 26 August 2004, p. 1.
5  *Asian Times Online*, 2 November 2004 (www.atimes.com).
6  *SinoCast China Business Daily News*, Dallas, 26 August 2004, p. 1.

## References

Behree, B. (2004) "Economy Improves, But Oil Prices Carry Risk: Extra Supply Won't Come in Time to Tame Impact of $50 Crude on Recovery," *Wall Street Journal* (eastern edition New York), 4 October: A.3.

Chen, A. (2004) "Chinese Increase Nuke Plans," *Reuter*, 18 February 2004.

EIA (The Energy Informtion Administration) (2005) *International Energy Outlook 2005*, Washington, DC: US Department of Energy, Office of Integrated Analysis and Forecasting.

Gates, D.F. and J.Z. Yin (2002) "Energy Development Strategy in China's Urbanization," in: Chen, J. and A. Chen (eds), *An Analysis of Urbanization in China*, Xaimen: Xiamen University Press, pp. 393–8 (in Chinese).

Hirsch, R.L. (2004) *Six Factors in Energy Planning*, Washington, DC: US Department of Energy, National Energy Technology Laboratory.

IEA (The International Energy Agency) (2002) "Privatization Report: China," Washington, DC: US Department of Energy.

IEA (The International Energy Agency) (2003) "China – An In-depth Study," *World Energy Outlook 2002*, Washington, DC: US Department of Energy.

World Bank (1997) *China 2020: Developing Challenges in the New Century*, Washington, DC: The World Bank.

Yin, J.Z. and D.F. Gates (2002) "Chapter 6: Automobile and Fuel Industries," in: Wen, J.G. and H. Zhou (eds), *The Globalization of the Chinese Economy*, Northampton, MA: Edward Elgar, pp. 82–99.

# 11 Legal protection of administrative regulations on private enterprises

*Hong Lu*

## Introduction

One of the major changes brought by the economic reforms of the 1980s in China is the gradual transformation from the planned economy and dominating state-owned enterprises (SOEs) to the market economy accompanied by emerging and rapidly expanding private enterprises. By all accounts, private and other non-state-owned enterprises have mushroomed under the reforms and the open door policy since the 1980s. In contrast to the monopoly status of the state or collective work units in the urban labor force prior to the reform, the post-reform era saw rapidly growing trends in the private sectors: those self-employed entrepreneurs, family or household enterprises, private firms that provide professional services such as law firms, and joint ventures including collaborative investments by oversees companies such as those from Hong Kong, Taiwan, and elsewhere. According to the Chinese State Statistical Bureau (2001), by the end of 2000, domestic private enterprises (including the self-employed) and joint ventures combined accounted for approximately 55 percent of the urban workforce, exceeding the state-owned and urban collective-owned units. This is especially striking when compared with only 3 percent in this sector at the start of the urban reforms in 1984.

Similar increasing trends in private enterprises can be observed in rural areas. While many rural people travel to the cities to find jobs, there has been a unique phenomenon in the Chinese urbanization process – the "invisible urbanization" or "latent urbanization" (Wang and Zhou, 1993). "Latent urbanization" refers to the kind of urbanization that is not officially recognized. In rural areas, this type of urbanization is mainly embodied by township and village enterprises (TVEs), in which members of the rural population are employed as workers in these private enterprises without having to leave their homes, social networks, and lifestyles in the rural area. For example, in Fujian province, the number of TVEs has increased almost 20-fold from 34,247 in 1978 to 667,385 in 1995, and the number of employees in these private sectors has increased eight-fold from 870,824 in 1978 to 4,709,956 in 1995 (Zhu, Y., 1999). Foreign investment in the city of Fuqing (one of the municipalities at the county level under the administration of the capital city of Fujian province – Fuzhou) had an average annual growth rate of 82.7 percent during the five-year period from 1990 to 1995 (Zhu, Y., 1999).

Despite the rapid and solid growth of private enterprises in the Chinese economy during the past two decades, there are many issues that, if not properly addressed, may hinder the healthy development of these private enterprises and their potential economic growth. One of the major issues is the legal protection of private property and rights. Although the existence of the private sector is legitimized as a result of economic reforms, these private enterprises by no means enjoy the same rights as SOEs. Discrimination in banking, taxation, and other governmental regulations, and possible abuse of power by governmental officials, may all pose a serious threat to the infringement of private rights. Whether and how the Chinese legal system protects private rights during the transitional economy is thus an important issue to be addressed.

Using annual court data presented in the *Law Yearbook of China* in the past decade and administrative court cases adjudicated in the 1990s, this chapter examines the claims, counterclaims, and the courts' rulings on disputes between private enterprises and government administrative agencies. Cases involving various issues are discussed, such as licensing, employment, contract and business transactions, and taxation and fines. Two inter-related research questions are addressed: (1) does the 1989 Administrative Law provide adequate coverage and protection for private rights?; (2) what are the patterns, if any, in the use of law by courts in adjudicating disputes between private entities and government agencies.

Study of "law in action" is important, especially in the Chinese context. While there has been extensive descriptive research on China's law and the legal system, the actual operations of the legal system are rarely examined with empirical data, with a few exceptions (Clarke, 1996; Pei, 1997; Lubman, 1999). As Pei (2000) pointed out, the lack of empirical study of the Chinese law is partly due to difficulties in accessing legal documents (e.g., court case judgments) and partly because of the background of those who engage in the study of law – most of them are legal scholars, not social scientists. "A lack of rigorous empirical studies of China's legal system is certainly a contributing factor to the poor understanding of how laws affect socioeconomic activities in a transition economy. It may also lead to incorrect assessment of the economic and political prospects of China" (Pei, 2000: 180).

## The Chinese legal context and the 1989 Administrative Law

Historically, the Chinese have disdained the law and stayed away from courts in dispute resolution. In accordance with ancient Confucian philosophy, that harmony, hierarchy, and societal obligations were given greater importance and value than confrontation, equality, and individual rights in Chinese society, the law was considered only as a last resort. In addition, Chinese laws were historically penal in nature (Bodde and Morris, 1973). Average citizens tried to avoid having any dealings with the legal system either as a defendant or as a plaintiff because of the design of the legal system, which was primarily punitive, rather than rewarding. Structurally, China had no separate judicial system, no legitimate system of legal representation, and few safeguards to prevent judicial corruption. Consequently, the certainty of legal outcomes was low and the rewards were limited, which discouraged average citizens from resorting to law for their grievances.

The culture and structure of the legal system have changed dramatically compared with those of ancient China, especially since the 1980s economic reforms. From the aspect of legal culture, Chinese citizens have gradually accepted the legitimacy of adjudication as an alternative for dispute resolution and become more "litigious." This is indicated by record numbers of civil and economic cases filed in the courts in the past two decades (*Law Yearbook of China*, 1988, 2001). The legal structure has been dramatically altered as a result of the passage of a number of landmark laws such as the substantive and procedural civil and criminal laws, the lawyer's law, the judge's law, and a host of business-related laws such as torts, contract, and copyright laws. Collectively, these substantive and procedural laws provide a new legal climate in which "injured" parties have an "open," "fair," and "regulated" arena to make claims and counterclaims about their "problems." More importantly, many of these "problems" have only been legitimized as legal issues since the economic reforms.

One of the most significant structural changes in the Chinese legal system involves increased legitimation and use of legal representation. For example, the 1996 Criminal Procedural Law (Luo, 2000) broadened the authority of the defense attorney in various areas such as earlier and more extensive involvement in criminal proceedings, opportunity to obtain bail, cross-examination, appeal, and mandatory legal representation for special groups of offenders and offences (e.g., death penalty cases). Although their effectiveness in achieving favorable legal outcomes for their clients is questionable (e.g., Lu and Miethe, 2002), the substantial increase in the number of professional attorneys and their involvement in various types of cases (see *Law Yearbook of China*, 1987–2001) suggests that their potential contribution to a "formalized" legal system cannot be overestimated.

## The 1989 Administrative Law

The impetus for the passage of the 1989 Administrative Litigation Law (ALL) was the economic reforms. The transformation from a planned economy to a market economy requires an orderly economic and social environment. Law provides the needed stability. To attract and sustain foreign investment, a legal system accessible by and acceptable to foreign business people is also deemed necessary to maintain the Chinese status as a major player in the global economy. Nevertheless, law is not just a tool used by the government to regulate and control the people, as was conceived in the traditional Chinese society. Law plays an increasingly vital role in protecting individual rights and private interests from the mighty, and sometimes corrupt, government. The problem of corruption has long been viewed by Deng Xiaoping as "critical" and "affecting the very survival of the Communist Party as the leading party in the PRC," quoted in 1979 before the economic reforms started (*People's Daily*, 2002). More recently, a high-ranking government official remarked that, if the Chinese Communist Party did not reform itself and address the issue of corruption, it would result in "self-destruction" (*Las Vegas Chinese News*, 7 December 2001: 8).

The ALL stipulates the legal rights of citizens and private entities to challenge the legality of specific administrative acts and their exercise of discretionary power in the courts. A variety of "punitive" or "negative" outcomes as a result of an administrative decision or act qualify for lawsuits under the ALL. For example, administrative sanctions such as deprivation of individual freedom by public security personnel, imposition of fines, termination of authorization of the use of land or property, interference with business operations, withholding or refusal of business licenses, confiscation of property, or excessive and unreasonable taxation (ALL, Article 11; see also Chen, 1999).

Judicial review of an administrative act includes the following aspects: (1) whether or not sufficient evidence existed when the specific decision or act was made; (2) whether or not, in the application of the substantive or procedural laws related to the decision or act, there were errors involved; (3) whether or not the process of decision-making violated the procedural requirements; or (4) whether or not the act or decision is an abuse of power (ALL, Article 54(2)).

While it is an important step that private citizens and groups can finally legitimately challenge decisions of the government, there are some limits. For example, only the concrete administrative act, not the abstract administrative act, can be challenged by judicial review. Although the concepts of "concrete" and "abstract" administrative acts are crucial in determining the scope of judicial review of the administrative acts, the ALL does not explicitly define these terms. Definitions of these terms, however, are offered in the Opinions of the Supreme People's Court on the Interpretation of the ALL (Section 1). More specifically, a concrete act is "a unilateral act undertaken by an administrative organ or its personnel, legally authorized organization, or organization or individual entrusted by an administrative organ, in exercising administrative authority in the process of administration, targeting at a specific citizen, legal person or other organization with regard to his rights and obligations" (cited in Lin, 1997: 76). In contrast, an abstract administrative act refers to administrative decisions and regulations that have general binding effects in an administrative jurisdiction (Lin, 1997). Based on these definitions, the legality of any administrative order or regulation cannot be challenged in court, unlike in western countries.

In addition, some specific administrative acts are excluded from legal review. For example, acts related to state defense and foreign affairs, normative orders, administrative personnel decisions, and final administrative decisions are not subject to challenge. Judicial review cannot interfere with the power of administrative bodies in interpreting their divisional regulations.

Procedurally, contrary to the widespread practice of in-court mediations sponsored, and often mandated, by the courts, mediation is prohibited in administrative cases (ALL, Article 50). In cases of withdrawal of cases by plaintiffs, approval of the court is required (ALL, Article 51). The primary reason for banning mediation and close monitoring of "reconciliation" between the parties by courts in administrative cases is concern with the imbalance of power between private groups and the government (Chen, 1998).

The burden of proof lies with the administrative decision-making bodies to substantiate the legality of the decision (ALL, Article 32). To safeguard the rights of the plaintiff and to protect the integrity of the case, the law specifically stipulates that government agencies are prohibited from collecting evidence from the plaintiff or witness; instead, the courts must gather the evidence (ALL, Articles 33 and 34).

## The extent and nature of administrative cases and the legal outcomes

Administrative cases have increased dramatically since the implementation of the ALL. According to the *Law Yearbook of China* (1990–2001), the total number of administrative cases tried by courts of first instance increased by almost tenfold, from 9,934 cases in 1989 to 85,760 cases in 2000 (see Table 11.1). Types of administrative cases have expanded from primarily disputes involving land use and public security in 1989 to increasing attention to urban constructions, commercial regulations, and taxation in 2000 (see Table 11.1). Commercial disputes between those who are regulated and the regulators have increased the fastest – by approximately 400 percent between 1993 and 2000.

Legal outcomes have changed over the years as well. As revealed by Table 11.2, in the years 1990, 1995, and 2000 the percentage of administrative decisions sustained by the court of first instance has declined significantly with the figures

*Table 11.1* Growth of litigation, 1989–96, 2000[a]

| Case type | 1989 | 1990 | 1991 | 1992 | 1993 | 1994 | 1995 | 1996 | 2000 |
|---|---|---|---|---|---|---|---|---|---|
| Land | 3,347 | 4,038 | 8,162 | 8,330 | 8,063 | 7,962 | 10,012 | 13,932 | 13,357 |
| Public security | 3,336 | 4,519 | 7,720 | 7,863 | 7,018 | 8,624 | 11,633 | 15,090 | 13,173 |
| Forest | | | | | 1,971 | 2,159 | 2,561 | 2,727 | 1,738 |
| Urban construction | | | | | 2,038 | 2,303 | 3,062 | 4,526 | 8,184 |
| Commercial | | | | | 571 | 886 | 1,556 | 1,486 | 2,897 |
| Public health | | | | | 456 | 601 | 916 | 1,388 | 1,144 |
| Transportation | | | | | | | 1,385 | 1,869 | 2,658 |
| Family planning | | | | | | | | | 1,372 |
| Taxation | | | | | | | | | 2,055 |
| Culture | | | | | | 58 | 72 | 190 | 423 |
| Other | 3,251 | 4,449 | 9,785 | 10,932 | 7,736 | 12,476 | 21,281 | 38,525 | 39,182 |
| Total | 9,934 | 13,006 | 25,667 | 27,125 | 27,911 | 35,083 | 52,596 | 79,966 | 85,760 |

Source: *Law Yearbook of China*, 1987–98.

Note
a   Cases accepted in courts of first instance at various ranks.

Table 11.2 Legal decisions by types of administrative cases in 1990, 1995, and 2000

| Type | Courts of first instance | | | | | | Second instance | |
|---|---|---|---|---|---|---|---|---|
| | No. of cases closed | Sustained (%) | Revoked (%) | Changed (%) | Withdrawn (%) | Other (%) | No. of cases | Sustained (%) |
| 1990 | | | | | | | | |
| Total | 12,040 | 36 | 17 | 3 | 36 | 8 | 3,431 | 64 |
| Land | 3,855 | 33 | 17 | 5 | 40 | 6 | | |
| Public security | 4,044 | 47 | 17 | 0 | 31 | 5 | | |
| Other | 4,141 | 28 | 16 | 5 | 38 | 13 | | |
| 1995 | | | | | | | | |
| Total | 51,370 | 17 | 15 | 1 | 51 | 16 | 9,694 | 63 |
| Land | 10,009 | 29 | 22 | 1 | 34 | 14 | | |
| Public security | 11,427 | 17 | 16 | 2 | 50 | 16 | | |
| Forest | 2,568 | 28 | 27 | 1 | 37 | 8 | | |
| Construction | 2,949 | 22 | 15 | 0 | 50 | 14 | | |
| Commercial | 1,388 | 30 | 17 | 0 | 40 | 12 | | |

| | | | | | | | |
|---|---|---|---|---|---|---|---|
| Public health | 892 | 19 | 11 | 1 | 53 | 17 | |
| Transportation | 1,275 | 10 | 5 | 0 | 70 | 15 | |
| Culture | 166 | 11 | 16 | 1 | 54 | 17 | |
| Other | 20,696 | 9 | 10 | 0 | 60 | 19 | |
| 2000 | | | | | | | |
| Total | 86,614 | 16 | 16 | 13 | 37 | 19 | 466,827 | 52 |
| Land | 13,640 | 19 | 22 | 14 | 28 | 17 | |
| Public security | 13,173 | 22 | 14 | 12 | 36 | 16 | |
| Forest | 1,757 | 19 | 27 | 6 | 39 | 8 | |
| Construction | 8,234 | 21 | 17 | 11 | 35 | 15 | |
| Commercial | 2,858 | 17 | 14 | 11 | 42 | 17 | |
| Public health | 1,182 | 14 | 18 | 16 | 35 | 17 | |
| Transportation | 2,650 | 12 | 9 | 8 | 43 | 28 | |
| Family planning | 1,372 | 14 | 13 | 10 | 43 | 20 | |
| Taxation | 2,025 | 8 | 9 | 8 | 59 | 16 | |
| Other | 39,723 | 11 | 14 | 14 | 38 | 22 | |

being 36 percent, 17 percent, and 16 percent respectively. More specifically, some types of cases experienced more dramatic decline in sustained decisions than others. For example, administrative decisions on land, public security, forest, and commercial issues were far less likely to be sustained by the courts in 2000 than in 1990. Similar trends can be observed from appealed cases. Over the past ten years, the percentage of cases tried by courts of second instance that resulted in corroboration of the lower courts' decisions have declined gradually from 64 percent and 63 percent to 52 percent in the years 1990, 1995, and 2000 respectively. Even though it may be argued that some of the sustained decisions by the appeals courts could be favorable to the plaintiff given the tradition of the Chinese judiciary system, the lower rates of affirming the lower courts' decisions by the appeals courts indicate greater judicial independence and intervention.

Only a small percentage of administrative decisions are revoked by courts, and the percentage is quite consistent over the years. The largest category of legal outcomes is the withdrawal of cases by plaintiffs. This rate has fluctuated each year and does not appear to show a clear trend. Some scholars argue that the greater number of withdrawn cases is a sign of judicial weakness in its intervention between an individual and the government (Chen, 1999). Others believe that the large number of withdrawals represent the success of the plaintiff in using legal redress as a means of deterring the government (Pei, 1997). The threat of litigation may be sufficient in some cases for the government agency to reconcile with the plaintiff. My interview with the President and Chief Judge of a district court in Jiangsu also suggests that, to save face, government agencies often voluntarily change their administrative decisions in exchange for the withdrawn lawsuit.

Recent data reported in the *Law Yearbook of China* (1998) suggested that the high rate of withdrawn cases may be indicative of both the weak protection of the court for private interests and the deterrence theory. This is because, in 1997, among the 50,735 withdrawn cases, approximately 56 percent of cases were voluntarily withdrawn by plaintiffs, and the remaining 44 percent of cases were withdrawn by plaintiffs after the government made concessions on original administrative decisions. The irony is that, while mediation is restricted in court for administrative cases due to concerns of imbalance of power between the individual and the government, out-of-court settlement is not prohibited by law. In fact, out-of-court settlements are acknowledged, and sometimes even encouraged, by the courts.

Previous studies also examined the profile of plaintiffs, the type of cases, and the presence of legal counsel. Using non-random court cases (a total of 236 cases) tried in the early 1990s, Pei (1997) reached a number of conclusions with regard to administrative cases and legal outcomes. These conclusions include: (1) the primary plaintiffs in administrative cases were SOEs and private entrepreneurs/firms; (2) while law enforcement and land use remained the two primary case types for administrative decisions, industrial and commercial cases seemed to be catching up; (3) a large proportion of cases brought by private entrepreneurs/firms and the SOEs were against industrial and commercial regulatory agencies, which was in direct contrast to the cases brought by urbanites for urban construction and zoning, rural people for land use, and individuals generally for the abuse of state authority by law enforcement; and (4) in terms of legal representation, SOEs and private entrepreneurs/firms were far more likely to hire an attorney in administrative cases than individuals.

In sum, there has been a proliferation of administrative litigation in China since the passage of the 1989 ALL. The nature of the lawsuits has changed quite dramatically, from previous cases on land use and public security to the more recent private enterprises challenging the legality of various administrative acts from taxation and commercial regulations to public health. While about one-third to one-half of the filed cases have been withdrawn by the plaintiffs over the years, there is a clear trend toward administrative decisions being less and less likely to be sustained by courts of both first instance and second instance. In other words, the ALL has served, to a certain degree, as an equalizer of power between the private entity and the government.

## The current study

This study takes a different approach to the study of the legal protection of private rights. While it is useful to systematically analyze a large number of cases with statistical techniques to delineate general patterns and relationships between major variables of concern, the aggregated analytical approach ignores the rich context and conditions of each dispute, especially given the lack of a systematic and random sample of court cases in China.

The current study focuses on specific administrative cases tried in the past five years in China. It examines additional dimensions and patterns of administrative cases and their legal decisions that were not examined in previous studies. This study explores, for example, the conditions under which a particular legal decision is made, beyond the traditional question as to whether or not a favorable legal outcome is more likely to occur for a particular type of plaintiff. More specifically, our primary interest is not whether private enterprises are more or less likely to win (e.g., in commercial disputes) over the governmental regulatory agencies. Instead, we are more concerned with whether private enterprises are more or less likely to win in these disputes where the challenged administrative decisions ultimately affect the government (e.g., taxation) or other private interests (e.g., wrongful dissolution of a joint-venture company).

We have examined a total of 95 administrative cases either being brought by private enterprises (including private companies, firms, joint-venture companies, and the self-employed) or whose outcome affected private enterprises. They were all adjudicated after 1995.

A survey of these latest administrative court cases reveals the following characteristics. First, administrative rulings, when applicable, tend to focus more on procedural propriety, not substantive justice. This point can be illustrated with case 1.

**Case 1**. Shenzhen Jinkeman Electrical Co., Ltd (hereafter Electrical Company) vs the Shenzhen State Taxation Bureau (hereafter Taxation Bureau) with regard to the Taxation Bureau's administrative decision on fines and taxation

Plaintiff, the Electrical Company, did not pay the full amount of taxes incurred through their business activities. The Taxation Bureau issued an administrative decision in 1994, citing several internal regulations, to order the Electrical Company to pay the taxes due in the amount of 491,955.56 renminbi (RMB) and fines in the amount of 100,391.10 RMB.

The Shenzhen Intermediate People's Court reached the following rulings. First, the legal authority of the Taxation Bureau's administrative decision was based on two internal departmental documents, which have never been disseminated to the public. Thus, the documents do not have a legally binding effect. Second, the fine in the amount of 100,391.10 RMB was substantially large. In accordance with the relevant stipulations of the Chinese Administrative Penalty Law, the plaintiff has a legal right to a hearing before the imposition of a "substantially large" amount of fines can be made. In this case, the plaintiff was not notified and the hearing did not take place. The imposition of the fine is therefore illegal. Third, the Taxation Bureau made a series of administrative decisions without conducting a thorough investigation and some facts of the case remained unclear. Thus, until the facts of the case are verified and the responsibility is clear, the current administrative decision shall be revoked. The court, however, did not make substantive rulings as to whether the Electrical Company should or should not pay the due amount in taxes and fines.

While it is certainly an improvement in the Chinese judicial system that "process" is recognized to be important for any decisions to have legitimacy, this new stipulation may have both positive and negative implications for private enterprises. On one hand, judicial review on "process" expands the scope of challenge of the government by private enterprises. On the other hand, the costs for private enterprises to seek both substantive and procedural justice may be higher because the same administrative agency may make a decision substantively unfavorable to the private entity after the trial for procedural impropriety. In the case of the Electrical Company vs the Taxation Bureau, the Electrical Company may very well be fined despite the current victory.

Second, administrative rulings tend to focus on the protection of social and public interests at the expense of private interests, especially when these two interests compete with each other. This pattern was observed in a number of cases, illustrated in cases 2–4.

**Case 2.** Hong Kong Hengda Trade Co. (hereafter Hong Kong) vs Shanghai Huangpu District Government (hereafter Government) with regard to its administrative decision to dissolve the agreement for the joint-venture enterprise (☐iao, 2000: case no. 54).

Hong Kong and Shanghai Metropolitan Co. (hereafter Metro) signed an agreement on 1 February 1994 to form a joint-venture enterprise, which was approved by the government on 24 March. The joint venture enterprise received the approval certificate from the Shanghai government on 27 April, and obtained the business license on 1 June 1994. According to the agreement, the total investment amount is US$70 million, of which Hong Kong is responsible for US$51million in the form of equipment and cash. It was agreed that the total amount of investment would be in place in four months after the business license was issued. In February 1997, Metro requested termination of the agreement because of inaction on the part of Hong Kong. Metro further requested that they should retain the project and try to find another business partner. The Government approved. By November 1997, the Metro had submitted a request to dissolve the company because of their failure to find a partner. In the same month, the Government issued a decision to dissolve the joint-venture program based on Hong Kong's failure to perform their duty and the failed attempt to find a new partner.

The Hong Kong sued this administrative decision of the Government by insisting that the decision violated the letter and the spirit of the joint-venture agreement that any major decisions, including dissolving the company, must be approved by the Board of Directors, and that the government's decision caused serious economic damage to the Hong Kong; they requested dismissal of the decision.

The Huangpu District Court, as the court of first instance, affirmed the Government's decision and ruled that the court filing fee of 100 RMB should be paid by the Hong Kong. The Shanghai No. 1 Middle Court, as the court of appeal, affirmed the lower court's decision.

**Case 3.** Shanghai Weilihuang Food Ltd Co. (hereafter Food Company) vs Shanghai Public Health Bureau (hereafter Health Bureau) with regard to health inspection public notice (☐iao, 2000: case no. 62).

In September 1998, the Health Bureau received several citizen complaints about dairies after consuming "moon cakes" produced by the Food Company. The Heath Bureau interviewed some of the complainants and someone from the Food Company, and inspected samples of their "moon cakes." The preliminary results suggested that the food poisoning incident was caused by added flavor enhancement chemicals that may have exceeded the amount specified by the related governmental regulation. The Health Bureau ordered the Food Company to recall those moon cakes already on the market and issued warnings through various news organizations to the public that "moon cakes" produced by the Food Company caused food poisoning.

The Food Company brought the suit against the Health Bureau by claiming that the Health Bureau's ruling that the food poisoning was caused by defective moon cakes was unfounded, and that their decision to order the Food Company to recall the product and publicly disseminating defamatory information about the Food Company was illegal and should be dismissed.

The Health Bureau argued that the reason why they decided to publicize the information was because the food poisoning incident occurred "right before the National Day" and, in order to "protect citizen's health" and "maintain order during this important holiday," they had to inform the public to take precautions. They further argued that a public announcement was not an administrative behavior and thus could not be challenged in the administrative court.

The court ruled that the Food Company had the right to sue in the administrative court because their interests were directly affected by the public announcement. The court further ruled that the Health Bureau performed its administrative duty by publicizing their preliminary findings of the food poisoning incident. Although "part of the announcement lacks factual bases," the administrative act was "legal" when looked at in its "totality" and its intent of "protecting the consumers' lawful rights."

**Case 4.** Jin Yinmin (hereafter Jin) vs Shanghai Xuhui Labor Bureau (hereafter Labor Bureau) with regard to an administrative decision on a labor dispute (□iao, 2000: case no. 65).

In February 1996, Jin signed an agreement with Shanghai Olympic Taxi Ltd Co. (hereafter Taxi Company) to contract a four-door passenger car for taxi services. The contracting period was from 1 March 1996 to 30 June 1998. The agreement stipulates that, if Jin operates outside the city limits, any traffic accidents and economic losses will be solely Jin's responsibility and not covered by company insurance. On 28 July 1996, Jin accepted two passengers' requests to take them to Zhejiang. Before leaving town, he went to buy food and then went home to let his family know about his long-distance travel. On the way back from his home to his car, he was hit by a car while crossing the street and subsequently diagnosed with a VII degree disability (e.g., loss of hearing in the left ear, some loss of hearing in the right ear, damage to his facial nerve and left shoulder).

The Labor Bureau ruled that Jin's traffic accident was not suffered during the course of his work, and thus was not covered by workers' compensation regulations. The decision that the accident had not occurred during the course of Jin's work was primarily based on two reasons: (1) Jin violated the company's regulation not to accept tasks requiring out-of-town services; and (2) Jin's accident occurred on the way from his home to his car, rather than in the car in the performance of his duties.

The court of first instance ruled that, given the unique working conditions of taxi drivers, the definition of "during the course of one's work" should be expanded to include on the way to and from work, having meals in between services, taking a break between services, and even going to a restroom. Given this broad interpretation of the definition of "during the course of one's work," the court ruled that Jin's accident occurred "during the course of his work" and should entitle him to appropriate compensation. The court further commented that, even though Jin had accepted work prohibited by the company, the work to be performed and the accident had no necessary connection. Therefore, the court ruled that the company was still responsible for Jin's accident. The appeal court affirmed the lower court's decision.

The commentator in the case pointed out that this case was unique in two aspects: (1) the interpretation of the existing regulations was very loose and broad; and (2) the intent of the loose interpretation of the laws was to protect the weaker party in this case.

There is no clear indication, from these three cases, that the courts were either systematically more likely to be in favor of private enterprises over the government, or were more likely to be in favor of the plaintiff over the defendant, or vice versa. However, what is clear is the intention of protecting the general public's interests –domestic interests when foreign join-venture programs such as the Hong Kong case were involved, consumers' interests when a potential outbreak of food poisoning such as the Food Company case was involved, and workers' interests when potential disabled workers' compensation and welfare such as the taxi driver Jin's case was involved. More importantly, in the context of upholding the interests of the general public and weaker individuals, it is the private enterprises, not the government, that are the ultimate "losers" in these cases.

Third, administrative rulings tend to enforce laws that protect national integrity and interests. This point is illuminated by the cases 5 and 6.

**Case 5.** Shanghai Jinma Advertising Co. Ltd (hereafter Advertising Company) vs Shanghai Nanshi District Commercial Administrative Management Bureau (hereafter Commercial Bureau) with regard to the administrative penalty for the management of advertisements (Zhu, M., 1999: case no. 16).

The Advertising Company is a joint-venture company. In March 1996, the Commercial Bureau spotted two advertising posters that contained the design of the Chinese RMB currency during a routine inspection in a shopping mall. In accordance with pertinent stipulations in the Chinese Advertising Law and the 1991 Notice of Prohibiting the Use of the Design of RMB, Foreign Currency, and Treasury Bond on Advertising Publications, the Commercial Bureau fined the Advertising Company 9,675 RMB for making these two commercials.

Shanghai Nanshi District Court reasoned that, in accordance with the national law's stipulations, RMB is the national legal currency. To maintain RMB's integrity and dignity, organizations and individuals must not use its design in advertisements, publications, and/or any other commercial goods. The court thus ruled to sustain the Commercial Bureau's administrative decision.

**Case 6.** Shanghai Aijian Advertising Co. (hereafter Advertising Company) vs Shanghai Changning Commercial Administrative Management Bureau (hereafter Commercial Bureau) with regard to the administrative penalty for the management of advertisements (Zhu, M., 1999: case no. 17).

In July 1994, the Advertising Company was retained by Shenzhen Bicycle Co. Ltd to design and make a bicycle advertisement. The advertisement was posted in a store and spotted during a routine inspection by the Commercial Bureau. The Commercial Bureau noticed that, on the advertisement, the design of the map of China did not include Taiwan and Hainan provinces. It orally advised the Advertising Company to revise the advertisement. The revised version showed an obvious mismatch of colors between the old design and the newly added design. The Commercial Bureau regarded the advertisement to be in serious violation of both the spirit and the letter of the Advertising Law, to have caused major political damage, and had negative effects on the national dignity and interests. In June 1996, the Commercial Bureau ruled that the fee the Advertising Company charged in making the commercial should be confiscated in the amount of 19,214.40, the company should be fined 76,857.60, and ordered to remove the advertisement.

The Advertising Company claimed that the advertisement was designed and completed on 25 July 1994, before the effective date (1 February 1995) of the Chinese Advertising Law. The Commercial Bureau's administrative decision was based on a law that does not have retrospective power, and thus should be regarded as a wrongful application of the law.

Shanghai Changning District Court reasoned that the Advertisement Law stipulated in its seventh article that advertisements must abide by public morality and professional ethics, and protect the national interests and dignity. It is a violation of the relevant stipulations of the Advertisement Law, that after the law's passage, the "defective" advertisement continued to be posted and, thus, the Advertising Company should share some responsibility. Accordingly, the court ruled to sustain the original administrative decision.

As revealed by cases 5 and 6, the courts' interpretation of business activities that damage national sovereignty and integrity can be very broad. Under these conditions, private interests may be marginalized because of the overwhelming consideration of national interests.

## Conclusions

Our analysis of the Administrative Litigation Law, its annual trend, and litigation outcomes of specific cases suggests both the benefits and the limitations of the law and its practice.

There is little doubt that the Administrative Litigation Law precipitates and transforms Chinese law from regulatory and penal to restitutive and compensatory functions. The law also facilitates the transformation of Chinese society from a duty-based, hierarchical ordered society to a rights-centered and horizontally structured society. Even though the structural and cultural aspects of Chinese society are still very different from their western counterparts, the step China has taken in the Administrative Litigation Law is unprecedented.

The actual use of the law has also proved that it is both symbolic and practical in nature. Since the implementation of the Law, annual rates of administrative cases prosecuted in courts have steadily increased. The final outcomes have also been gradually more favorable to the plaintiffs.

Despite these achievements, there are major limitations in terms of both the Law itself and its implementation. As discussed previously, the Law has fundamental limitations in its stipulation of the scope of litigated disputes over administrative decisions. The legality of an administrative regulation cannot be challenged in court unless it involves a specific administrative action. Class action-style lawsuits, common in western countries, are virtually impossible unless they challenge specific administrative acts. In addition, the existing inequality between the private enterprises and their regulatory governmental agencies, and the general lack of judicial independence in China, make it very unlikely that private rights are fully protected.

## References

Bodde, D. and C. Morris (1973) *Law in Imperial China*, Philadelphia, PA: University of Pennsylvania Press.

Chen, A.H.Y. (1998) *An Introduction to the Legal System of the People's Republic of China*, Butterworths Asia.

Chen, J. (1999) *Chinese Law – Towards an Understanding of Chinese Law, its Nature, and Development*, London: Kluwer Law International.

*China Statistical Yearbook* (2001) *China Statistical Yearbook*, Beijing: China Statistics Press.

Clarke, D. (1996) "Power and Politics in the Chinese Court System: The Enforcement of Civil Judgments," *Columbia Journal of Asian Law*, Spring, 10: 1–92.

*Las Vegas Chinese News* (2001) "Controversies over the speech of Li Reihuan," *Las Vegas Chinese News*, 7 December: 8.

*Law Yearbook of China* (1987–2001) *Law Yearbook of China*, Beijing: Law Yearbook of China Publishing House.

Lin, F. (1997) "Administrative Law," in: Wang, C. and X. Zhang (eds), *Introduction to Chinese Law*, Hong Kong: Sweet & Maxwell, pp. 75–106.

Lu, H. and T.D. Miethe (2002) "Legal Representation and Criminal Processing in China," *British Journal of Criminology*, 42: 267–80.

Lubman, S. (1997) "Dispute Resolution in China after Deng Xiaoping: Mao and Mediation Revisited," *Columbia Journal of Asian Law*, 11: 229–392.

Luo, W. (2000) *The Amended Criminal Procedure Law and the Criminal Court Rules of the People's Republic of China*, Buffalo, NY: William S. Hein & Co.

Pei, M. (1997) "Citizens v. Mandarins: Administrative Litigation in China," *China Quarterly*, 152: 831–62.

Pei, M. (2000) "Does Legal Reform Protect Economic Transactions? Commercial Disputes in China," in: Murrell, P. (ed.), *Assessing the Value of Law in Transition Economies*, Ann Arbor, MI: The University of Michigan Press, pp. 180–210.

*People's Daily* (2002) "On the Correct Recognition of Anti-Corruption Campaign," *People's Daily*, 27 June.

☐iao, X. (2000) *Shanghai Courts Case Collection*, Shanghai: Shanghai People's Publishing House.

State Statistical Bureau (2001) *China Statistical Yearbook*, Beijing: China Statistical Publishing House.

Wang, S.J. and Z.G. Zhou (1993) "The Investigation on Invisible Urbanization in the Rural Areas and the Estimate on its Level," *Population and Economics*, 1: 16–24.

Zhu M. (1999) *Zhongguo Adjudicated Case Collection*, Beijing: China People's University.

Zhu, Y. (1999) *New Paths to Urbanization in China: Seeking More Balanced Patterns*, Commack, NY: Nova Science Publications.

# Part IV

# Private enterprises, employment, and earnings

# 12 Policy reforms, private enterprise development, and rural household earnings

*Dennis Tao Yang and Vivian W. Chen*

## Introduction

Policy reforms in rural China have achieved remarkable success. Since the inception of reforms in 1978, real rural per capita income has increased about fivefold; earnings were nearly tripled between 1978 and 1985, followed by a period of continued growth (see Figure 12.1). These rapid increases in income are closely associated with several specific policy measures. The adoption of the household responsibility system (HRS) and increases in state procurement prices created a profound one-time effect on earnings through increased labor effort and price incentives; they were the major sources of income growth prior to 1985 (McMillan *et al.*, 1989; Lin, 1992). Agricultural research and technological change have also raised crop yields (Huang and Rozelle, 1996; Fan and Pardey, 1997). While the coverage of these studies extends to the collectivization period, they are primarily concerned with productivity gains within agriculture, especially during the early period of reforms. Since 1985, the growth rate of real rural per capita income still averaged around 4 percent per year, despite the fact that the influence of the HRS and price adjustments has abated. What are the major factors contributing to the continued income growth?

In this chapter, we examine the sources of sustained income growth between 1986 and 1995 in a broader context of the rural economy, including non-agricultural development.[1] The focus is on farmers' responses to factor market liberalization as they reallocated productive inputs and expanded non-farm production. Starting in 1983, the government announced a series of policies that encouraged the development of private enterprises in rural China and loosened restrictions on labor mobility out of agriculture. The regulatory changes, including permission for long-distance transport, marketing of commodities, and employment in small towns, encouraged farmers to establish non-farm businesses and seek off-farm jobs with better pay. At the same time, farm households also diverted funds and capital equipment to industrial and service activities for higher returns. During this ten-year period, the percentage of the rural labor force employed in township and village enterprises (TVEs) increased from 12.8 percent to 22.2 percent (State Statistical Bureau of China, 1996). In 1986, the gross output value of TVEs was about 88 percent of the gross value of agriculture but, in 1995, the former was more than three times the latter. These industrial developments resulting from optimization behaviors of the farm households are a major force behind rapid income growth in rural China.

To investigate the linkage between factor market liberalization, private enterprise development, and rural household earnings, we consider a framework of profit maximization in which the households engage in agricultural and non-agricultural activities.[2] Under central planning, which emphasized local grain self-sufficiency, factors of production were devoted excessively to agriculture, resulting in resource misallocations with higher input returns in the non-agricultural sector. Therefore, as restrictions on factor mobility were relaxed during the reforms, rural families increasingly reallocated inputs toward non-farm production. This adjustment process was facilitated by the education of family members, which enhances the ability of farmers to perceive and interpret market information in order to better respond to economic disequilibria (see e.g., Schultz, 1975).

The empirical analysis in this chapter uses household-level panel data between 1986 and 1995 from the Sichuan province to analyze how resource reallocation to non-farm activities contributed to profit and how households determined intersectoral input utilization. The panel data are constructed from the Rural Household Survey collected by China's State Statistical Bureau. The rich structure of the data enables control for household fixed effects, region- and time-specific factors, and endogeneity associated with idiosyncratic shocks to individual households. The empirical findings in this chapter indicate that, during this period, less-than-optimum levels of labor and capital were allocated to non-agricultural uses. More importantly, the data suggest that the expansions in non-farm activities, which were facilitated by schooling attainment, account for approximately 43.6 percent of the total farm income growth between 1986 and 1995.

The rest of the chapter is organized as follows: the next section provides an overview of policy changes in rural China during the early reform period, followed by specification of profit and input demand functions by which we can assess the effects of factor market liberalization on farm profit and input allocations

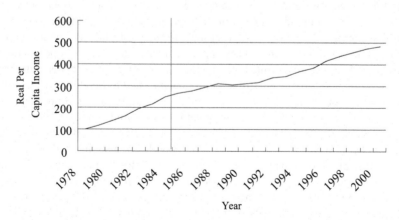

*Figure 12.1 Rural per capita income, 1978–2000.*

across agricultural and non-agricultural production. The next section describes the data and reports the estimation results, followed by concluding remarks.

## Policy reforms in China

Prior to the start of reforms in 1978, there were massive distortions in the allocation of resources in China's centrally planned system. The cumulative effects of pursuing a heavy industry-oriented development strategy since the 1950s resulted in excessive allocation of capital assets in urban areas, and a large percentage of the labor force being concentrated in the countryside.[3] Within the rural sector, this national policy stressed agricultural production and local grain self-sufficiency, a strategy rigorously pursued by prominent leaders ever since the tragic experience of the Great Leap Forward famine between 1959 and 1961. Before the reforms, rural industrial activities concentrated on a narrow range of products, emphasizing "five small" industries: iron and steel, cement, chemical fertilizer, hydroelectric power, and farm implements. Enterprises in the countryside were not oriented toward market and consumer products and remained subsidiary to agriculture (Findlay *et al.*, 1994; Naughton, 1996). In 1978, only about 7 percent of the rural labor force nationwide was in non-agricultural employment, generating approximately 7 percent of rural household earnings (State Statistical Bureau of China, 1988–1998), a level far below that of other comparable developing countries (Anderson and Leiserson, 1980). Owing to restrictions on non-farm production, capital and labor were scarce, and their returns were high in that sector, creating opportunities for rapid expansion along with policy reforms.

Market-oriented development in rural China started with a package of three reforms: the replacement of production teams with households as units of basic production (HRS), official increases in agricultural product prices, and the liberalization of markets for rural products. These reforms provided the necessary conditions for the boom in rural industrial development starting in the mid-1980s.

The change from communes to a household-based farm system began in 1979 and was essentially completed by the end of 1983. This institutional change induced strong family work effort, thus reducing the demand for workers on small Chinese farms. More importantly, the HRS enabled individuals to have increased command over their productive resources. During the same period, the government also implemented reforms in production planning, in which the state reduced the number of production planning targets (or categories). Of the remaining targets, few were mandatory, and many were guided by complementary prices and incentive schemes (Sicular, 1988). Therefore, farmers not only had incentives, but also certain freedoms in relocating labor and capital to non-farm uses.

In 1979, the government also implemented large increases in state procurement prices for agricultural products. □uota prices for grain, oil crops, cotton, sugar crops, and pork were increased by an average of 17.1 percent. In addition, the premium paid for above-quota sales of grain and oil crops was raised from 30 percent to 50 percent of the quota prices. The weighted average increase was 22.1 percent for all agricultural products.[4] In effect, these price adjustments injected large quantities of funds into the rural economy, which created a demand for industrial products and supplied the flow of funds for capital investment, especially in non-farm production. Finally, the liberalization of rural markets not only accommodated the sales of non-farm products, but also facilitated the purchase of inputs for non-agricultural activities. It is evident that these three reforms were inter-related; each helped to reinforce the impact of the others.

Consequently, by the mid-1980s, the economic basis for accelerated growth in rural industries was already embedded in China's rural economy. Input and output markets had emerged; households were conscious of their alternative opportunities, and had incentives to quickly allocate resources to non-agricultural activities that would generate higher returns than those from farming. This view is supported by the empirical findings of Putterman (1993), who analyzed intersectoral factor allocation in five production teams of Dahe Township in Hebei province. The study suggests that, in 1985, the marginal productivity of capital and labor in the non-crop sector exceeded the levels in the cropping sector, indicating "overal-location" of resources in agriculture.

The catalyst for the rapid expansion in non-farm production was a series of policies that loosened restrictions on labor mobility and the operation of rural enterprises. The policy's evolution can be briefly described as follows.

1983: Document No. 1 of the Central Committee of the Chinese Communist Party (CCP) provided general guidelines that encouraged the emergence of specialized households and praised their effectiveness in making the best use of limited funds and labor. Skilled workers and craftsmen were permitted to leave farming and engage in a variety of non-agricultural activities, including long-distance transport and the marketing of commodities. In addition, the document allowed cooperative ventures, as well as rural industrial and commercial households, to employ labor (Ash, 1988). In accordance with these liberalization measures, the state continued to narrow the range of products for compulsory procurement. It was after the inception of this document that some farmers began to quit farming to take up jobs in product transport, goods retailing, or business and handicrafts.

1984: In March, the Central Committee of the CCP and the State Council issued the "Report on Creating a New Situation in Commune and Brigade-run Enterprises," which outlined a new development strategy that targeted industry as the focus of future rural development. Industrial development was expected to provide inputs for agriculture, absorb rural labor, and help to raise rural earnings (Findlay *et al.*, 1994). This strategy sharply contrasted with the old policy of local grain self-sufficiency, in which rural industries had only a subsidiary role to agriculture.

1985: Document No. 1 permitted farmers to seek employment and establish businesses in nearby towns, if they could provide their own food grain and were financially capable of running a business. This landmark deregulation officially relaxed the controls on labor mobility within rural regimes; in the past, farmers had to live and work in the villages where they held household registration.

In addition to the relaxation of controls on labor mobility, a major reform in agricultural production and procurement helped to trigger the rapid growth of rural industries. At the beginning of 1985, after consecutive years of good crop harvests, the state announced that it would no longer set any mandatory production plans in agriculture and that obligatory procurement quotas were to be replaced by purchasing contracts negotiated between the state and farmers (Lin, 1992). The loosening of farming constraints, together with the increased freedom in allocative decisions, prompted farmers to adjust their productive activities in accordance with profit margins. In 1985, the grain-sown area at the national level fell by 4 percent, output by 7 percent, cotton-sown area by 26 percent, and cotton output by 34 percent (Sicular, 1988). In contrast, the number of TVEs more than doubled in the same year, and their total labor force increased by more than 30 percent, following a year of strong growth in 1984 (State Statistical Bureau of China, 1988–1998). These dramatic changes in policies and in farmers' responses marked the beginning of a sustained expansion in non-agricultural activities.[5]

## Empirical specification

To better understand the mechanisms through which state interventions led to distortions in factor allocations and how farmers responded to policy changes, we consider an empirical framework in which the household engages in two activities, agricultural and non-agricultural production. Before policy reforms in the mid-1980s, productive inputs were overly concentrated in farming, so that the marginal productivity of these inputs would be higher in rural industries. Consequently, with factor market liberalization, households started to reallocate capital and labor toward non-farm activities in order to close the inefficiency gap in resource allocation.

In order to quantitatively assess the extent of distortions with imperfect input markets and how resource reallocation contributes to household income growth, we estimate the following profit function:

$$
\begin{aligned}
\ln V_{it} = &\ \alpha_d \ln d_{it} + \alpha_l \ln l_{it} + \theta_l \ln \delta_{lit}^n + \alpha_k \ln k_{it} + \theta_k \ln \delta_{kit}^n \\
&+ \sum_c \beta_{sh}^c s_{hit}^c + \beta_{sa} s_{ait} + \beta_x x_{ait} + \sum_a \gamma_g^a g_{it}^a + \gamma_f f_{it} \\
&+ \sum_r \gamma_d^r D_t^r + m_i + \mu_{it}
\end{aligned}
\tag{12.1}
$$

The subscript "*it*" refers to household *i* in year *t*. $V_{it}$ denotes profit, which is defined as total sales minus expenditure on variable inputs; $\{d_{it}, l_{it}, k_{it}\}$ are quasi-fixed aggregate land, labor, and capital endowments, respectively, for household *i* in year *t*; land is used exclusively in agriculture and $\{\delta_{lit}^n, \delta_{kit}^n\}$ are shares of labor and capital devoted to non-agricultural production; $s_{hit}^c$ are dummy variables relating to the completion level for the most educated family worker: $c = \{$elementary, secondary, high school and plus$\}$, with elementary school as the reference group;[6] $s_{ait}$ is the average completion level of schooling for other family workers; and $x_{ait}$ is the average work experience for all family workers. The dummy variables $s_{hit}^c$ represent geographic areas: $a = \{$plain, hilly, mountainous regions$\}$, with plain areas as the reference group. The variable $f_{it}$ stands for compulsory fees imposed on farming by the government. This estimation equation also includes household fixed effects ($m_i$) relating to factors such as unobserved managerial ability and land quality, as well as region- and time-specific effects ($D_t^r$) relating to factors such as time-varying weather shocks at the region level and likely price variations over both time and space.[7] The superscript $r$ in $D_t^r$ indexes 23 prefectures from which the sample households were drawn. The error term $u_{it}$ is assumed to represent the effects of the remaining omitted variables, which are independent of the explanatory variables and are independently and identically distributed. $\{\alpha_d, \alpha_l, \alpha_k, \theta_l, \theta_k, \beta_{sh}^c, \beta_{sa}, \beta_x, \gamma_g^a, \gamma_f, \gamma_d^r\}$ are parameters to be estimated.

This profit function encompasses the idea that factor allocation may affect farm profits. More specifically, when allocations of labor and capital are already at the optimum across the two sectors, marginal changes in the shares of labor and capital around their sample means would have no implications for profits, i.e., $\theta_l = \theta_k = 0$. However, if, because of policy distortions, capital and labor are below the optimal level in non-farm production, and the households are still making adjustments by devoting more of these inputs to the non-farm sector, we would expect $\{\theta_l, \theta_k\} > 0$. As $\{\delta_{lit}^n, \delta_{kit}^n\}$ are choice variables, proper treatment for endogeneity is called for in empirical implementation.

While $\{\theta_l, \theta_k\}$ indicates systematic misallocations of labor and capital to the non-farm sector, it would be interesting to examine further whether the extent of inefficiency declines with the deepening of economic reforms. We expect that, *ceteris paribus*, the estimated parameters will become smaller over time as the gaps in distortion are gradually closed up with adjustments. But, if non-farm opportunities improve continuously with rapid growth and structural transformation, the need for input relocation toward that sector may persist for an extended period. To investigate the efficiency of factor allocations over time, we will add to the basic model in Eq. (1) interaction terms for the time periods (1986–89 and 1991–95 for which we have data) with $\ln \delta_{lit}^n$ and $\ln \delta_{kit}^n$, thus allowing different parameter estimates across the two panels. If the estimated parameters are positive but smaller for the latter panel, they would imply improvements in intersectoral factor utilization with market liberalization.

Given the structure of the model, the two factor shares are endogenous variables, e.g., idiosyncratic shocks to individual households (such as being lucky in landing a non-farm job) would affect both factor shares and household profit, violating the orthogonality condition of the error term. Therefore, it is necessary to estimate Eq. (1) using instrumental variables. From the model specifications, it is also evident that lagged factor shares may affect input allocation decisions for the current period, but not the current profit level of the household. Therefore, we use factor shares lagged by one period as instruments. Consequently, in addition to controlling for family fixed effects ($m_i$) and region/time-specific effects ($D_t^r$), the predicted factor shares from the first-stage equations will be used in estimating Eq. (1).

The parameters for the education variables $\{\beta_{sh}^c, \beta_{sa}\}$ would imply the productive value of education in the profit function. We make the distinction between the highest education attainment of family workers, approximating for the skills of making allocative decisions, and the average education of other family workers, approximating the quality of labor inputs (Yang, 1997). The allocative decisions, for instance, may include the choice of using fertilizers, whether or not to adopt modern seed varieties, and sales of farm products. The quality of labor affects the efficiency of carrying out routine tasks. When these two parameters are positive, education contributes to farm household earnings.

Equation (1) provides a framework for analyzing sources of household income growth. Taking total derivative of $\ln V_{it}$ with respect to time, we can infer that the contribution to income from reallocating capital and labor to non-farm activities is $\hat{\theta}_l \partial \ln \delta_{lit}^n / \partial t + \hat{\theta}_k \partial \ln \delta_{kit}^n / \partial t$, where $\{\hat{\theta}_l, \hat{\theta}_k\}$ are parameter estimates. Consequently, for the specific time period of our study, 1986–95, the percentage contribution to total income growth attributable to factor reallocation can be expressed as:

$$\% \text{ contribution} = \frac{\hat{\theta}_l (\partial \ln \delta_{lit}^n / \partial t) + \hat{\theta}_k (\partial \ln \delta_{kit}^n / \partial t)}{d \ln V_{it} / dt}, \tag{12.2}$$

where $d\ln V_{it}/dt$ is the observed average percentage change in household earnings for the sample.

To trace out the farm households' factor allocation decisions embedded in $\{\delta_{lit}^n, \delta_{kit}^n\}$, we also estimate input allocation functions for labor and capital to non-agricultural activities, using the following specification:

$$\ln \Omega_{it} = \alpha_d^\Omega \ln d_{it} + \alpha_l^\Omega \ln l_{it} + \alpha_k^\Omega \ln k_{it} + \sum_c \beta_{sh}^{\Omega c} s_{hit}^c + \beta_{sa}^\Omega s_{ait} +$$
$$\beta_x^\Omega x_{ait} + \sum_a \gamma_g^{\Omega a} g_{it}^a + \gamma_f^\Omega f_{it} + \sum_r \gamma_d^{\Omega r} D_t^r + m_i + \varepsilon_{it}, \tag{12.3}$$

where $\Omega_{it} \in \{l_{it}^n, k_{it}^n\}$ and $\Omega \in \{l^n, k^n\}$ denote input-specific parameters. To simplify the notation, we remove the superscript "$n$" from $\{l^n, k^n\}$ in the following analysis, given the fact that the corresponding parameters are for input demand functions for the non-farm sector.[8]

The two activity-specific factor demand functions will be estimated conditional on total factor endowments for the household in each period, namely land, labor, and capital. Accordingly, the parameter estimates would yield meaningful economic interpretations. For instance, the parameter $\alpha_k^k$ would represent the propensity to invest in non-farm production: $\alpha_k^k = 1$ is associated with a neutral strategy, while $\alpha_k^k > 1$ implies a high propensity of investment, i.e., for a given percentage increase in total capital, a higher percentage will be allocated to the non-farm sector. Similar interpretations also apply to $\alpha_l^l$. Moreover, as land is only used in agriculture, and if land is a complementary factor to capital and labor, we would expect $\{\alpha_d^l, \alpha_d^k\} < 0$, implying that abundant land endowment would have the effect of retaining the other two inputs in agriculture.

The estimation results will also shed light on the effect of educational attainment on factor allocations to non-agricultural activities. If the highest level of schooling in the household ($s_{hit}^c$) is a reasonable proxy for allocative skills, and education facilitates a narrowing of the inefficiency gaps during the adjustment period, we would expect $\{\beta_{sh}^{lc}, \beta_{sh}^{kc}\} > 0$, i.e., families with middle and high school education systematically to make better input decisions than families with a primary school education (see Yang, 2004). We would also expect the policy variable $f_{it} > 0$, indicating that the heavy levies on agriculture would divert the resource to non-agricultural production.

## Data and empirical results

The data used for this study, which were collected by China's State Statistical Bureau (SSB), are from the Rural Household Survey (RHS) for the Sichuan province for 1986–95.[9] Sichuan, the most populous province in inland China, is historically praised as the "land of fish and rice" because of its favorable climatic conditions for farming. The survey rotates a fraction of the sampled households each year. The data consist of two panels, one for 1986–89 and the other for 1991–95, that are constructed from the original, complete sample.[10] A number of adjustments were required in order to make the data suitable for this study. See the Data Appendix in Yang (2004) for detailed information on sources and adjustments. Here, we report only a summary description of the data set.

In this study, agricultural activities include cropping, animal husbandry, forestry, fishery, and sideline production, a breakdown that is consistent with the standard definition of "agriculture" in Chinese statistics. Non-agricultural activities consist of a variety of production, ranging from industry to handicrafts. The profit from each line of production is equal to revenue minus variable costs. Wage employment in non-agricultural activities is special because it does not incur variable costs. To our advantage, the RHS records the utilization of capital and labor by industry. Therefore, we can aggregate the factor allocations into agricultural and non-agricultural activities.

Table 12.1 reports summary statistics of income and major inputs owned by the farm households. Real per capita income for the sample rose from 501 yuan in 1986 to 710 yuan in 1995, indicating sustained growth after the initial burst in earnings between 1978 and 1985.[11] Despite the small scale of Chinese agriculture, land per farm declined during the period, while the number of workers per family stayed constant. In contrast, the value of capital equipment increased over time, a fact consistent with the national trend.

The RHS reports the level of schooling completion for rural workers instead of years of schooling attained. We organize the completion levels into four categories: illiterate and semi-illiterate (level 1), elementary school (level 2), secondary school (level 3), and high school and above (level 4). It is evident from Table 12.1 that the average education of the workers is around the elementary school level, with an increasing trend over the ten-year period. Within each subperiod, there were some changes in the highest and average levels of schooling within households. For the 1986–89 period, 21 percent of the households reported changes in the highest level of schooling, while 57 percent of the households had changes in average schooling. For the 1991–95 period, the corresponding percentages were

24 percent and 59 percent. Also note that the average schooling, reported by the level of completion, is significantly below the average highest level of education of the households, indicating schooling variability within families. The average experience of the labor force, defined as (age–schooling–7), is stable over time.

The two panel data sets have approximately 800 and 1,500 households for statistical analysis. Owing to missing information for some families in certain years, the number of observations is not exactly the same for each of the years, because the year-specific observations with missing information are deleted. The number of observations reported in column (8) of Table 12.1 is the sample used for the following empirical analysis.

The figures reported in Table 12.2 on activity-specific allocations of inputs reveal that, in general, the households devoted increasingly more labor and capital to non-agricultural activities over time. During the ten-year period, the share of labor with non-agricultural work as its main occupation increased by about 10 percentage points. Accordingly, the share of capital equipment for non-farm uses also increased by close to 10 percent. It appears that non-agricultural production is much more capital intensive than farming.[12]

For empirical analysis, we will also examine whether geographic environments influence factor allocations and household income growth. Table 12.3 contains information on the geographic features of the sample (plain, hilly areas versus mountainous regions) and compulsory levies on agriculture, which reflect policy environments for the households. It should be noted that, for each subperiod, the small variations in the percentage of households belonging to a geographic type reflect the fact that the number of observations is not exactly the same for each year. Some families with missing year-specific information are deleted from the sample for the corresponding years. Moreover, note that the second panel draws a higher percentage of households from plain areas, which in part explains the differences in sample characteristics across the two time periods as revealed in Tables 12.1 and 12.2. Therefore, caution is needed when making across-panel comparisons.

Table 12.4 reports estimation results for the profit function in Equation 12.1 and its two variant specifications. The model in column (1) is a baseline case excluding labor and capital shares, and the model in column (3) includes interaction terms of the two time periods with factor shares in order to investigate changes in resource misallocation over time. As the factor shares are choice variables, their lagged values are used as instruments for models (2) and (3). In the first-stage regression, the lagged factor shares have strong explanatory power for the current period factor allocations.[13] For comparison purposes, we first fit the profit function with a random-effects procedure based on the assumption that the effects of unobserved characteristics, such as household managerial skills and time/region fluctuations in weather and prices, are independent of the included explanatory variables. Then, to be consistent with the analytical model presented earlier, we estimate the function with a fixed-effects procedure, controlling for both household ($m_i$) and time/region ($d_t^r$) heterogeneity. These two procedures yield quite different estimates. To select appropriate specifications, the results of

Table 12.1 Summary statistics of real per capita income and major inputs

| Year | Real per capita income (yuan) | Land per farm (mu) | Labor force per family | Capital stock per family (yuan) | Level of average education | Level of highest education | Average work experience | Number of observations |
|---|---|---|---|---|---|---|---|---|
| | (1) | (2) | (3) | (4) | (5) | (6) | (7) | (8) |
| 1986 | 501 (187) | 7.7 (8.9) | 2.6 (1.1) | 502 (643) | 1.9 (0.5) | 2.5 (0.7) | 23.1 (6.5) | 809 |
| 1987 | 507 (198) | 6.9 (5.6) | 2.6 (1.0) | 551 (697) | 1.9 (0.5) | 2.5 (0.7) | 23.3 (6.4) | 798 |
| 1988 | 509 (224) | 6.5 (4.9) | 2.6 (1.1) | 590 (1,058) | 2.0 (0.5) | 2.5 (0.7) | 23.3 (6.7) | 770 |
| 1989 | 486 (186) | 6.6 (5.4) | 2.7 (1.1) | 646 (1,181) | 2.0 (0.5) | 2.5 (0.7) | 23.4 (6.5) | 788 |
| 1991 | 653 (288) | 6.2 (4.8) | 2.6 (0.9) | 1,046 (1,359) | 2.2 (0.5) | 2.7 (0.7) | 21.2 (6.7) | 1,519 |
| 1992 | 674 (305) | 6.1 (4.7) | 2.6 (1.0) | 1,101 (1,682) | 2.2 (0.5) | 2.7 (0.7) | 21.6 (6.7) | 1,516 |
| 1993 | 620 (337) | 6.2 (4.9) | 2.6 (1.0) | 1,337 (2,124) | 2.3 (0.5) | 2.7 (0.7) | 21.9 (6.5) | 1,511 |
| 1994 | 661 (343) | 6.1 (5.0) | 2.6 (1.0) | 1,554 (2,466) | 2.3 (0.5) | 2.8 (0.7) | 22.5 (6.8) | 1,516 |
| 1995 | 710 (368) | 5.9 (4.9) | 2.6 (1.0) | 1,613 (2,520) | 2.3 (0.5) | 2.8 (0.7) | 23.5 (7.2) | 1,518 |

Notes

Figures in column 1 are in 1986 prices. The deflator used is the consumer price index of rural residents (State Statistical Bureau of China, 1996). 1 yuan = US$0.125. In column 2, 1 mu = 0.165 acre.

Figures in column 4 are in nominal prices because of no appropriate price deflator.

Schooling attainment reported in columns 5 ☐

primary school as 2, middle school as 3, and high school and above as 4.

Experience in column 7 is approximated as (age–schooling years–7).

Figures in parentheses are standard deviations.

Data for 1990 are not available; see endnote 10 for explanations.

the Hausman test strongly reject the random-effects models, suggesting that the unobserved household and time/region effects are dependent on the explanatory variables. Therefore, the following discussions will concentrate on the independent variable (IV) fixed-effects estimates.

In column (2), family-owned assets – land, labor, and capital – all contribute to household earnings, although the coefficient for capital is not statistically significant. Controlling for the level of these quasi-fixed factors, if labor and capital are already optimally allocated across the two uses, any intersectoral redistribution, as reflected in $\{\delta_l^n, \delta_k^n\}$, would have no effect on profits. The positive and statistically significant coefficients estimated for these parameters indicate that, during the period of adjustment in rural China, the allocations of the two inputs have not yet reached the optimum. In particular, *ceteris paribus*, a 10 percent increase in the share of labor in non-farm activities would raise household incomes by 1.8 percent, whereas a 10 percent increase in the share of capital in non-farm activities would raise incomes by 2.2 percent. These findings provide evidence that less than optimal levels of capital and labor were allocated to rural industries and services during the period of transition. Consequently, factor adjustments to the non-farm sector raised family earnings.

Schooling variables are included directly in the profit function to capture their effects on earnings. However, these coefficients are not statistically significant. We also find that experience contributes to income through a concave schedule. Controlling average experience at zero, the marginal value of one year of experience is 2.2 percent of annual household profit; at the sample mean level of experience, the marginal value is 0.6 percent of the profit.

Conditional on family endowments and resource allocations, households who live in hilly and mountainous regions are no more disadvantaged than households living in plain areas, according to the data. This finding could be sample specific, however, as a large percentage of farm households in the Sichuan province (see Table 12.3) live in hilly and mountainous areas where the climate and soil conditions are generally good. Consistent with expectations, compulsory taxation on farming unambiguously reduces overall household earnings.

Column (3) in Table 12.4 presents the results of interacting factor shares in non-agricultural activities with the two time periods, thus allowing changes in the extent of resource misallocation over time. The estimated coefficients for all variables remain stable, and the estimates for the factor shares are both positive and significant, confirming the existence of resource misallocation. More specifically, the estimates show that the elasticity of profit with respect to capital shares in non-agricultural activities is reduced considerably. In the first period (1986–89), *ceteris paribus*, a 10 percent increase in the share of capital in non-farm production would raise total income by 3.1 percent, but this was lowered to 1.9 percent in the second period (1991–95). This result implies that policy reforms had reduced the severity of capital misallocation over time. For the labor shares, the coefficients for the two periods are not statistically different. This result is consistent with the possibility that rapid economic structural changes taking place in rural China during transition may have created continued demand for labor in the non-farm

Table 12.2 Allocation of labor and capital in agricultural and non-agricultural activities (household average)

| Year | No. of workers in agricultural activities (1) | No. of workers in non-agricultural activities (2) | Labor share in non-agricultural activities (3) | Capital in agricultural activities (4) | Capital in non-agricultural activities (5) | Capital share in non-agricultural activities (6) |
|---|---|---|---|---|---|---|
| 1986 | 2.35 (1.04) | 0.28 (0.44) | 10.8 | 178.6 (360.0) | 323.0 (501.8) | 64.4 |
| 1987 | 2.25 (0.96) | 0.34 (0.49) | 13.0 | 181.8 (214.0) | 368.8 (630.6) | 67.0 |
| 1988 | 2.27 (1.01) | 0.35 (0.49) | 13.3 | 171.7 (254.8) | 419.2 (997.7) | 71.0 |
| 1989 | 2.35 (1.07) | 0.32 (0.46) | 12.0 | 184.7 (254.3) | 461.5 (1,121.5) | 71.4 |
| 1990 | – | – | – | – | – | – |
| 1991 | 2.23 (0.94) | 0.34 (0.49) | 13.1 | 286.4 (454.7) | 770.6 (1,156.5) | 72.9 |
| 1992 | 2.21 (0.96) | 0.37 (0.53) | 14.2 | 289.5 (483.6) | 819.4 (1,513.0) | 73.9 |
| 1993 | 2.19 (1.01) | 0.44 (0.60) | 16.8 | 306.3 (461.0) | 1031.6 (2,015.8) | 77.1 |
| 1994 | 2.09 (1.01) | 0.54 (0.67) | 20.6 | 367.1 (650.0) | 1187.2 (2,282.0) | 76.4 |
| 1995 | 2.10 (0.98) | 0.52 (0.65) | 19.8 | 423.0 (1,089.2) | 1192.0 (2,225.6) | 73.0 |

*Table 12.3* Summary statistics of geographic and policy variables

| | Geographic features of sample households (%) | | | Compulsory levies on farming (yuan) |
|---|---|---|---|---|
| | Plain areas | Hilly areas | Mountainous areas | |
| Year | (1) | (2) | (3) | (4) |
| 1986 | 6.3 | 60.1 | 33.4 | 31.9 (27.8) |
| 1987 | 5.7 | 61.4 | 32.8 | 40.8 (33.2) |
| 1988 | 5.9 | 62.0 | 31.9 | 47.7 (60.2) |
| 1989 | 5.8 | 61.6 | 32.4 | 63.9 (56.3) |
| 1990 | – | – | – | – |
| 1991 | 16.5 | 55.8 | 27.6 | 103.6 (103.4) |
| 1992 | 15.8 | 56.1 | 27.9 | 107.6 (117.6) |
| 1993 | 16.4 | 55.1 | 28.4 | 103.6 (144.8) |
| 1994 | 16.4 | 54.3 | 29.2 | 139.9 (179.3) |
| 1995 | 16.4 | 53.8 | 29.7 | 155.1 (173.7) |

sector, and that the adjustments had not fully responded to the changes. It would be interesting to investigate the changes over a longer period of time.

Table 12.5 reports fixed-effects estimates of input demand functions for the allocations of capital and labor to non-agricultural activities based on the pooled data from the 1986–89 and 1991–95 panels. Specification tests are also performed in which the Hausman test statistics strongly reject the random-effects model in favor of the alternative fixed-effects specification. Therefore, the following discussions will concentrate on the fixed-effects results.

The negative coefficients estimated for the land variable are consistent with the

*Table 12.4* Estimates of profit functions

| | Dependent variable = ln(household net profit) | | |
|---|---|---|---|
| | Fixed effects | Independent variable fixed effects | Independent variable fixed effects |
| Explanatory variables | (1) | (2) | (3) |
| ln(total land) | 0.105** | 0.137** | 0.135** |
| | (0.017) | (0.018) | (0.019) |
| ln(total labor) | 0.185** | 0.138** | 0.136** |
| | (0.031) | (0.037) | (0.037) |
| ln(labor share in non-agriculture) | – | 0.178** | – |
| | | (0.038) | |
| ln(labor share in non-agriculture) × first period | – | – | 0.182** |
| | | | (0.044) |

*Table 12.4* continued

| Explanatory variables | Fixed effects (1) | Independent variable fixed effects (2) | Independent variable fixed effects (3) |
|---|---|---|---|
| | *Dependent variable = ln(household net profit)* | | |
| ln(labor share in non-agriculture) × second period | – | – | 0.179** |
| | | | (0.038) |
| ln(total capital) | 0.084** | 0.027 | 0.035 |
| | (0.029) | (0.030) | (0.043) |
| ln(capital share in non-agriculture) | – | 0.215** | – |
| | | (0.048) | |
| ln(capital share in non-agriculture) × first period | – | – | 0.309** |
| | | | (0.071) |
| ln(capital share in non-agriculture) × second period | – | – | 0.193** |
| | | | (0.049) |
| Middle school, highest | 0.030 | 0.019 | 0.018 |
| | (0.023) | (0.023) | (0.023) |
| High school and above, highest | 0.014 | –0.043 | –0.040 |
| | (0.041) | (0.042) | (0.042) |
| Average education | –0.007 | –0.000 | 0.003 |
| | (0.017) | (0.017) | (0.016) |
| Average experience | 0.016** | 0.022** | 0.022** |
| | (0.006) | (0.006) | (0.005) |
| Average experience$^2$ (× 1,000) | –0.339** | –0.352** | –0.344** |
| | (0.103) | (0.103) | (0.102) |
| Hilly areas | 0.062 | 0.103 | 0.107 |
| | (0.070) | (0.073) | (0.072) |
| Mountainous areas | 0.137* | 0.152 | 0.149 |
| | (0.082) | (0.091) | (0.091) |
| Levies on agriculture (× 1,000) | –0.197** | –0.269** | –0.265** |
| | (0.047) | (0.049) | (0.048) |
| $R^2$ | 0.719 | 0.722 | 0.722 |

Notes
All regressions include household and region/time dummies. Sample size is 8,480.
* Significant at the 10% level.
** Significant at the 5% level.
Standard errors are given in parentheses.

view that land endowment raises the productivity of capital and labor in agriculture, thus reducing the outflow of these two inputs from farming. The elasticity of capital investment in non-farm activities, as represented by $\alpha_k^{\tilde{k}} = \partial \ln k^n / \partial \ln k$, indicates that a 1 percent increase in total capital is associated with a 1.38 percent increase in non-agricultural uses. Therefore, new capital is increasingly being directed toward rural industries and services. Agriculture still appears to be the main sector for labor employment, as the elasticity of non-agricultural labor allocation, $\alpha_l^l = \partial \ln l^n / \partial \ln l$, is 0.52.

With regard to education, the findings provide evidence that allocations of capital and labor to the non-farm sector are positively related to the schooling attainment of the household. Using the highest level of education as a proxy for household allocative skills and controlling for household aggregate capital assets, the middle-schooled families devote 10 percent more capital to non-farm uses than the reference group, the primary-schooled households. Households having members with a high school or college education invest even more capital in non-farm uses: 17.7 percent higher than the primary-schooled households and 7.7 percent higher than the middle-schooled households. Moreover, the data yield evidence that households having high school- and college-educated members allocate 13.1 percent more labor to non-farm activities relative to the reference group, although middle-schooled families do not appear to allocate more workers away from agriculture. There is also evidence of centralized decision-making on the farms supported by the fact that the average education of family workers, excluding the highest attainment, does not contribute significantly to either capital or labor allocations. Moreover, the results indicate that, while the experience of workers does not significantly influence the intersectoral distribution of capital, older farmers with more general work experience are less likely to participate in non-farm work. This finding is consistent with the standard implications of human capital theory.

With regard to geographic and policy variables, the estimates indicate that levies on agriculture discourage farming activities, thus having the effect of encouraging factor allocations to non-farm uses, although the coefficient for capital does not reach the conventional level of significance. Geographic location also has a significant impact on sectoral input allocation. Being in hilly and mountainous regions increases capital investment in non-farm uses, a result that is consistent with the view that adverse geographic characteristics may have relatively less negative effect on returns for capital in the non-farm sector. In contrast, being in hilly and mountainous regions is associated with less labor utilization in non-agricultural activities, which may reflect the fact that geographically disadvantaged locations present fewer non-farm opportunities.

Finally, we can use parameters presented in Table 12.4 to estimate the contribution of intersectoral input allocations to rural household income growth between 1986 and 1995, as suggested in Equation 12.2. Data reported in Table 12.2 indicate that labor shares in non-farm activities increased by 83.8 percent from 10.8 to 19.8, and capital shares increased by 14.5 percent from 64.4 to 73.8. Based on estimates presented in column (2) of Table 12.4, these changes in intersectoral input allocations would result in an 18 percent increase in farm household earnings. Therefore, the rapid expansion in non-farm activities would account for approximately 43.6 percent of the total farm income growth, as real earnings grew by 41.2 percent in this ten-year period (see Table 12.1). While caution must be given to these estimates, because of the fact noted earlier that there is

*Table 12.5* Estimates of input demand functions for capital and labor in non-agricultural activities

| | Dependent variables | |
| --- | --- | --- |
| | *ln(capital in non-agriculture)* Fixed-effects estimates | *ln(labor in non-agriculture)* Fixed-effects estimates |
| *Explanatory variables* | *(1)* | *(2)* |
| ln(land) | −0.190** (0.869) | −0.058* (0.032) |
| ln(total labor) | −0.306** (0.073) | 0.523** (0.056) |
| ln(total capital) | 1.383** (0.024) | 0.048** (0.018) |
| Middle school, highest | 0.100* (0.055) | −0.025 (0.043) |
| High school and above, highest | 0.177* (0.099) | 0.131* (0.077) |
| Average education | 0.017 (0.039) | −0.003 (0.031) |
| Average experience | −0.005 (0.013) | −0.029** (0.010) |
| Average experience$^2$ (× 1,000) | −0.018 (0.243) | 0.239 (0.190) |
| Hilly areas | 0.373** (0.169) | −0.269** (0.132) |
| Mountainous areas | 0.879** (0.198) | −0.457** (0.155) |
| Levies on agriculture (× 1,000) | 0.117 (0.111) | 0.299** (0.086) |
| $R^2$ | 0.747 | 0.721 |

Notes
Both regressions include household and region/time dummies. Sample size is 8,480.
*   Significant at the 10% level.
**  Significant at the 5% level.
Standard errors are given in parentheses.

an issue of data comparability between the two panels, these sample estimates are nevertheless broadly consistent with provincial level information.[14] Although the model and the results presented in the chapter are not suited to tracing out many dynamic effects of the changes, the mechanisms concerning the contribution of rural non-farm production to household income growth are clearly revealed. With relaxation of policy controls, farm households devoted more factor inputs to non-farm activities, and the development of agricultural industries increased farm household income.

## Concluding remarks

This chapter uses panel data with rich economic and demographic information to investigate the sources and determinants of sustained income growth in rural China between 1986 and 1995. This was a period of market adjustment when the relaxation of factor market controls induced rural families to reallocate their productive inputs from agriculture to non-agricultural activities. The findings suggest that the development of private non-farm production was an important contributor to the sustained income growth in rural China.

The above findings have wider implications than simply understanding a special period of income growth in rural China. The centrally planned system created massive misallocation of resources both within the rural sector and across rural–urban regions. While past reforms have greatly improved allocative efficiency within the rural economy, China is still facing long-term, arduous structural adjustments across the rural and urban sectors.[15] Mobility of resources will be a key determinant of efficiency during this process. To a large extent, this study shows that lifting policy restrictions on factor mobility may induce optimal resource allocations of households across sectors. The increased efficiency resulting from input utilization may play a critical role in raising overall growth in the economy.

## Acknowledgments

The authors are grateful to Xian Zude, Sheng Laiyun, Wang Pingping, and other researchers at the Rural Survey Organization of China's State Statistical Bureau for providing data support, and Xiaoyuan Dong for helpful comments on an earlier version of this chapter.

## Notes

1  We cannot extend the coverage to the years after 1995 because of data availability. However, the method of analysis should be applicable to other time periods.
2  This framework is based on a model developed by Yang (2004), who analyzes the effect of education on household income growth during rural reforms in China.
3  The main enforcement mechanisms include the state control of agricultural production and procurement, and restrictions on rural-to-urban migration via a household registration system. See Yang and Zhou (1999) for discussions on resource allocation across rural and urban sectors.

4   For details of these price changes, and agricultural price adjustments in the following years of reforms, see Sicular (1988).

5   It should be noted that obstacles to rural labor mobility still exist today despite continued improvements since the early years of reforms. For instance, a rural worker currently employed in the enterprise of another village does not receive the allocation of homestead or other housing arrangements, even if the job is permanent, thus incurring high costs to the migrants. As reported by Yao (1999), local protectionism is also a significant issue, in which village workers often earn much higher wages than outsiders. In addition, in some regions, local government has continued to implement voluntary production contracts with a certain degree of coercion. Clearly, much has been improved regarding labor mobility, but further reforms are needed.

6   The illiterate and semi-illiterate group is merged with the group with elementary education because the percentage of households belonging to the former category is low, around 7 percent for the 1986–89 panel and dropping below 3 percent for the 1991–95 panel. Therefore, the following analysis focuses on the efficiency of the households with elementary education relative to the secondary and high school and above groups.

7   This treatment for price variations is necessary because the survey data do not contain price information for various agricultural and non-agricultural products. The approach taken is consistent with the fact that there likely exist competitive markets in local regions, but not necessarily across regions.

8   Therefore, for both Eqs (1) and (2), the superscript to a parameter indicates association with a particular dependent variable. School completion level $c$, geographic type indicator $a$, and region index $r$ are also included in the superscript. The subscripts refer to the independent variables associated with the parameters.

9   This national survey, started in 1952, consists of large random samples and records of detailed diary information on production, incomes, and expenditures. Data since 1986 are in computer-usable form, but they have not been released to the public. I have limited access to the Sichuan data through a collaborative project with researchers at the State Statistical Bureau.

10  The two separate panels reflect the fact that the State Statistical Bureau started a completely new sample in 1991, and the 1990 data received from the State Statistical Bureau was corrupt. A second attempt to restore the data by a different means of data transfer was also not successful.

11  For Sichuan, rural real per capita income rose by 115.7 percent between 1978 and 1985; and it accomplished 40.8 percent of growth between 1986 and 1995 (State Statistical Bureau of China, 1996). The increase of 41.7 percent in real income for the sample households between 1986 and 1995 is representative of the provincial income growth, despite the fact that there is noticeable discontinuity across the two panels.

12  The statement is subject to one caveat: the definition adopted for occupation may under-report the extent of labor participation in non-agricultural activities. A worker is classified as non-agricultural if, according to the survey, his or her "main occupation" is a non-farm industry. This definition systematically under-represents part-time participation in non-farm activities for some farmers. Unfortunately, there is no other information in RHS that could remedy this data limitation.

13  The $F$-values are $F(2,6190) = 18.13$ in the capital share function and $F(2,6190) = 11.11$ in the labor share function, both rejecting the null hypotheses at the 1 percent significance level that the two coefficients for the instruments are jointly zero.

14  At the provincial level, rural labor shares in non-farm activities increased from 12.8 percent in 1986 to 22.2 percent in 1995, an increase of 73.18 percent (State Statistical Bureau of China, 1996). In addition, the growth in real per capita income of the sample is comparable with the provincial level growth (see footnote 16). Unfortunately, aggregate statistics do not contain sufficient information for computing capital utilization devoted to agriculture versus non-agriculture.

15  For instance, Johnson (2000) forecasts that the agricultural labor force in China will likely fall by as much as 63 percent between 1997 and 2030. Therefore, the rural non-farm sector and urban regions will face a long-term challenge of absorbing large number of workers released from agriculture.

# References

Anderson, D. and M.W. Leiserson (1980) "Rural Non-farm Employment in Developing Countries," *Economic Development and Cultural Change*, 28: 227–48.

Ash, R.F. (1988) "The Evolution of Agricultural Policy," *China Quarterly*, 116: 529–55.

Fan, S.G. and P.G. Pardey (1997) "Research, Productivity, and Output Growth in Chinese Agriculture," *Journal of Development Economics*, 53: 115–37.

Findlay, C., A. Watson, and H.X. Wu (1994) *Rural Enterprises in China*, New York: St. Martin's Press.

Huang, J.K. and S. Rozelle (1996) "Technological Change: Rediscovering the Engine of Productivity Growth in China's Rural Economy," *Journal of Development Economics*, 49: 337–169.

Johnson, D.G. (2000) "Agricultural Adjustment in China: Problems and Prospects," *Population and Development Review*, 26: 319–34.

Lin, J.Y. (1992) "Rural Reforms and Agricultural Growth in China," *American Economic Review*, 82: 34–51.

McMillan, J.W. and L.J. Zhu (1988) "The Impact of China's Economic Reforms on Agricultural Productivity Growth," *Journal of Political Economy*, 97: 781–807.

Naughton, B. (1996) *Growing Out of the Plan: Chinese Economic Reform 1978–1993*, Cambridge: Cambridge University Press.

Putterman, L. (1993) *Continuity and Change in China's Rural Development: Collective and Reform Eras in Perspective*, New York: Oxford University Press.

Schultz, T.W. (1975) "The Value of Ability to Deal with Disequilibria," *Journal of Economic Literature*, 13: 827–46.

Sicular, T. (1988) "Agricultural Planning and Pricing in the Post-Mao Period," *China Quarterly*, 116: 671–705.

State Statistical Bureau of China (1988–1998) *The Statistical Yearbook of China*, Beijing: China Statistical Publisher.

State Statistical Bureau of China (1996) *China Regional Economy: A Profile of 17 Years of Reforms and Opening-up*, Beijing: China Statistical Publisher.

Yang, D.T. (1997) "Education in Production: Measuring Labor Quality and Management," *American Journal of Agricultural Economics*, 79: 764–72.

Yang, D.T. (2004) "Education and Allocative Efficiency: Household Income Growth During Rural Reforms in China," *Journal of Development Economics*, 74: 137–62.

Yang, D.T. and H. Zhou (1999) "Rural–Urban Disparity and Sectoral Labor Allocation in China," *Journal of Development Studies*, 35: 105–33.

Yao, Y. (1999) "Rural Industry and Labor Market Integration in Eastern China," *Journal of Development Economics*, 59: 463–96.

Zhao, Y.H. (1997) "Labor Migration and Returns to Rural Education in China," *American Journal of Agricultural Economics*, 79: 1278–87.

# 13 Effects of privatization on employment in transitional China

*Gene Hsin Chang*

## Introduction

It is generally agreed that privatization of China's state-owned enterprises (SOEs) would improve economic efficiency, but may have an adverse impact on employment. In the process of privatization, the newly privatized enterprises would cut their redundant staff in order to maximize profits, which would inevitably aggravate the high unemployment pressure in China. While liberal economists insist that privatization is the key to reform, many Chinese scholars and government policy-makers reject any suggestion of a rapid privatization process out of concern over unemployment.

In 1990, the Chinese Economist Society held its annual conference in Davis, CA, USA. One particular subject debated at the conference was privatization. At the conference, Professor Jiang Xuemo, a very respected economist in China, who attended the conference as an invited scholar, objected to privatization mainly out of concern for the large number of layoffs from SOEs. However, most attendees who received their economics training in the west naturally disagreed with Jiang. Although the disagreement between the two sides reflects the difference in economic training and beliefs, it also reflects the difference in what the two sides observe on a daily basis.

An economist observing a mature market economy would hardly believe that privatization *per se* can be a cause of unemployment on a nationwide scale. However, a person living in China, observing his neighbor being laid off from an SOE, and watching the reports and movies about similar stories from local TV channels and newspapers, may believe that increasing privatization is a major reason for the current high unemployment in China. In fact, the relationship between privatization and unemployment in China is more complicated than a single statement. For China, a developing country in transition from an old planning system to a market economy, privatization can affect employment in different directions and different ways.

The debate piqued my interest, and I started developing a theoretical model to explain the effect of privatization on employment. We all learned that, even in the early days of industrialization, workers in the west protested about automation and technology advancement on a massive scale because they feared losing their jobs. Only at a much later time, when the industrial revolution had benefited the entire society and raised the living standards of all residents, including the workers, to an unprecedented level did the protests cease. Similarly, the effects of privatization on the community utility can be complicated. Although western-trained economists are privatization advocates, we need a theoretical model to address all these positive and negative effects of privatization and provide a cogent answer to the concerns.

There have been many empirical and case studies on the effects of privatization on employment in developing economies: Glad (1991), Naqvi and Kemal (1994), and Cook *et al.* (1998). In particular, Sanjeev *et al.* (2001) investigate the different effects of privatization on employment in different situations in the former centrally planned economies in their transition to the market system. They consider that privatization may cause job losses in many situations in the short run, and offer policies to mitigate the adverse effects. Although these studies provide empirical evidence of the complicated relationship between privatization and employment, they do not offer a theoretical model.

There have been well-developed theoretical models of the effects on employment in western economics literature; these models are generally built on the classical, Keynesian, or neoclassical frameworks. Yet these models do not study the effect of privatization on employment in a transitional economy. These models do not consider the following two main characteristics of a transitional developing economy such as China. The first characteristic is the Lewis dual economic structure. China has an estimated 150 million units of surplus labor from rural areas (Gao, 2002). They form an unlimited labor supply at subsistence wage rates.[1] When the surplus labor is allowed to move to urban areas, it transforms the previously disguised rural underemployment into open unemployment nationwide. The second characteristic is the large number of layoffs from previously overstaffed SOEs as privatization proceeds. Any model that misses these two major characteristics would be outwith the context of China.

Hence, to describe how privatization would affect employment and what policy options are available to create more jobs during privatization, the model should capture the main characteristics of China and include all the main relevant variables. In addition, the model needs to be simple to stay focused on the main issue and to be easily manipulated to allow empirical testing. In what follows, I will propose a model to describe the relationship between privatization and unemployment.

## Model

The main shortcoming of the neoclassical model is that it assumes perfect substitution among factors, thus implying full employment of the factors. This is particularly unrealistic for a developing country with Lewis unlimited surplus labor. In our model, the production function is assumed to be of the Leontief type. After normalizing the units of input so the coefficients become unity and thus vanish, we have:

$$y^s = \min\{K, E\} \tag{13.1}$$

where $y$ is the national output, which can be conventionally thought of as gross domestic product (GDP). $y^s$ is the quantity supplied, $K$ is the capital stock, and $E$ is the effective labor input.

Each effective labor input $E$ is a product of physical input $L$ and productivity coefficient $e$. That is, $E = eL$, where $e$ is the productivity per physical labor input, representing efficiency. Privatization will raise the productivity of each physical unit of labor through better management, cutting redundant staff, raising the output of each worker through the incentive mechanism, etc. Let $s$ stand for the privatization index. Hence, $e$ is a function of privatization: $e = e(s)$. And, the partial derivative $e'(s) > 0$. So we have:

$$E = e(s)L \tag{13.2}$$

$$y^s = \min\{K(s), e(s)L\} \tag{13.3}$$

Mathematically, $e$ looks like the labor-augmenting technology in the Solow model but, in this case, it is explained by a different force, privatization, rather than the change in technology as in the Solow model.

The set-up of the production function implies that output is constrained by the existing capital. In developing countries, insufficient capital is the major reason for the large amount of surplus labor in rural areas and informal urban sectors. Privatization will encourage domestic private investment and foreign direct investment, which will raise $K$. Another reason for privatization to increase $K$ is that privatization will improve the investment efficiency, improving capital formation from a given amount of yuan of investment. Hence, $K$ is a function of $s$ and $K'(s) > 0$.

China's output can also be constrained by insufficient effective demand, as described by the Keynesian model. This is evidenced by the fact that, during the period 1997 through 2002. So the actual output is the minimum of the quantity supplied and the quantity demanded:

$$y = \min\{y^s, y^d\} \tag{13.4}$$

The demand $y^d$ is $y^d = MV/P$, where $M$ is the money supply, $P$ the price, and $V$ the velocity. In China, money supply is directly affected by the banks' credits and loans, which play a critical role in the economic boom. $M$ is also affected by foreign direct investment and capital flows into China. This is evident from the credit expansion in 2003 and 2004. The foreign capital inflow forced the government to increase the yuan supply, a result of maintaining a fixed peg of yuan to the US dollar.

The velocity $V$ is also strongly influenced by changes in a set of variables that may affect the saving behavior of households and the loan behavior of banks. The variables include the inflation rate, interest rate, the government policy regulating bank loans and credits, government's deficits, fixed investment, and people's expectations about the economy. When the government increases fixed capital investment by deficit financing, velocity increases for two reasons. First, it would raise the interest rate in the official and private financial markets; second, it would mobilize the otherwise idle money in the economy. The latter reason is probably more important in the case of China. So $V$ is a function of government spending $G$, and $V'(G) > 0$. We observe that $V$ changed substantially in the past two decades as inflation and deflation alternated during the period.

Hence, the actual national output can be expressed as follows:

$$y = \min\{y^s,\ y^d\}$$
$$= \min\{\min\{K,\ eL\},\ \frac{MV}{P}\} \tag{13.5}$$

Privatization will encourage competition, thus lowering prices. Hence, $P$ is a function of $s$, and the partial derivative $P'(s) < 0$. Privatization will also make the use of funds more efficient, often through the official and private financial markets. Therefore, privatization also raises $V$, so $V(s) > 0$. Privatization will also encourage foreign capital inflow, which will also affect $M$. For simplicity, we assume here that $M$ is a money supply controlled by the central bank of China, but not directly affected by $s$.

Next, we notice that China has unlimited labor supply (at equal to or above subsistence wages); hence, labor input $L$ is unconstrained, even at a very low productivity coefficient $e$. This assumption is quite reasonable for China, as there has always been surplus labor regardless of how low $e$ is. For instance, during Mao's era, there were not enough jobs for students graduating from middle schools, although overstaffing was prevalent in cities, and surplus labor was tremendous in the countryside. That is still true nowadays, although to a lesser extent. Because $L^s$ is not constrained, $y^s = K$, which means that the quantity supplied is determined only by the capital stock in China.[2] So we simplify the output equation as follows:

$$y = \min\{\min\{K,\ eL\},\ \frac{MV(s)}{P(s)}\}$$
$$= \min\{\min\{K(s),\ e(s)L\},\ \frac{MV(s)}{P(s)}\} \tag{13.6}$$
$$= \min\{\ K(s),\ \frac{MV(s)}{P(s)}\}$$

The actual output $y$ determines the use of capital $K$ and effective labor unit $E$. Let $E^d$ denote the use of labor $E$, or demand for $E$. From the production function, we know that $E^d = y$. Let $L^d$ stand for the use of the physical units of labor, or demand for labor, in employment. We have:

$$L^d = \frac{E^d}{e(s)} = \frac{y}{e(s)} = \frac{\min\{ K(s), \dfrac{MV(s)}{P(s)}\}}{e(s)} \tag{13.7}$$

The unemployment in China is thus the difference between the labor supply $L^s$ and $L^d$:

$$\text{unemployment} = L^s - L^d = L^s - \frac{\min\{ K(s), \dfrac{MV(s)}{P(s)}\}}{e(s)} \tag{13.8}$$

## Analysis and policy implications

Equation 13.7 provides a simple model to analyze the effects of privatization on employment in China with policy implications. Equation 13.8 reiterates the same result in terms of unemployment. Let us consider the following cases.

We consider first a case in which the output is constrained by the capital stock. This describes what happened in the red hot economic periods in 1992–94 and 2003 to date. In this case, employment is determined by:

$$L^d = \frac{K}{e} = \frac{K(s)}{e(s)} \tag{13.9}$$

Privatization will increase efficiency $e$, thus causing $L^d$ to decrease if other things are held constant. This explains the layoffs taking place when efficiency increases during privatization. Privatization may increase capital, thus creating new jobs in the private sector and foreign capital sectors (i.e., the "*Sanzi*" enterprises). The net result of privatization on employment is determined by the relative magnitudes of the two opposing effects. Differentiating $L^d$ with respect to $s$, we have:

$$\frac{\partial L^d}{\partial s} = \frac{K'(s) - e'(s)}{e^2} \tag{13.10}$$

It can be seen that the sign is determined by the numerator, which is in turn determined by the relative magnitudes of $K'$ and $e'$.

Next, we consider a case in which the output is constrained by the effective aggregate demand. This describes what happened in the period 1997–2002, when the economy was constrained by insufficient aggregate demand. In this case, employment is determined by:

$$L^d = \frac{1}{e(s)} \frac{MV(s)}{P(s)} \tag{13.11}$$

Here, there are several factors. The first fraction to the right of the equation says that the increasing efficiency due to privatization reduces employment. Yet, the second fraction indicates that privatization would raise employment. This is because privatization would increase aggregate demand through more efficient use of financial capital, and it would lower the price level because of promoting competition. In general, these two effects described by the second fraction tend to be relatively weak. First, change in velocity is normally limited. Second, price may be rigid downwards. Hence, the impact of *s* on the second fraction is limited. This implies that, if *M* is held constant, privatization may cause a net decrease in employment, when the macroeconomic situation is of insufficient aggregate demand.

What are the major conclusions and policy implications that we can draw from this model?

First, privatization will raise the potential national output through increasing the capital stock. When the effective aggregate demand is not constrained, privatization will raise the actual national output. This is because the output is $y = \min\{K(s), e(s)L\}$. Because labor supply is not constrained in China, an increase in the privatization index *s* will lead to an increase in *K*, thus increasing *y*.

An increase in GDP will make a country as a whole richer. Given the population size, privatization will lead to an increase in average output; that is, the GDP per capita. Of course, we are speaking of the average income. The model is an aggregate one; thus, it does not rule out the possibility that certain groups of the population may become worse off during privatization. However, only when the size of the cake becomes bigger does it then become possible that the government can enable the entire population to receive the benefits of increased wealth through redistribution schemes.

Next, we will discuss employment policy. If the capital stock is the constraint on creating more jobs, the key to creating more jobs lies in increasing the capital stock. This can be more factories, but it can also be more stores, clinics, and other service facilities. These are all capital stocks that are complements to the labor input. Because capital formation takes time, it will be a long-run process for the increasing stock to absorb all the surplus labor in China. It thus suggests that we should search for effective policies to sustain the growth of the capital stock, particularly in labor-absorbing sectors.

If effective demand is the constraint to creating more jobs, the model suggests that the government should adopt an expansionary monetary and fiscal policy. By expanding money and credit, which will cause *M* to increase, combined with an expansionary fiscal policy, which will increase velocity *V*, this would raise effective demand and create more jobs.

## Conclusion

This chapter develops a model to describe the effects of privatization on employment for a developing country in a transitional period from a planning system to a market system. It is comprehensive enough to include all the factors concerned, but also straightforward and intuitively appealing. The model shows that, while privatization may reduce the labor input demand, thus aggravating the unemployment situation, it can also create more jobs if proper macroeconomic and employment policies are implemented. After all, the ultimate determinant of a higher living standard is higher GDP per capita, which in turn depends on the growth of labor productivity. Privatization is a key determinant of productivity. Hence, the right policy is a continuous acceleration of privatization, while implementing proper policies in the macroeconomy, employment, and redistribution.

## Acknowledgments

The author appreciates the support of the Chinese Economists' Society (CES) in the research and thanks the participants of the CES Beijing Conference on privatization in transitional economies for their helpful comments.

## Notes

1   Although there was a temporary labor shortage in some areas in China in 2004, it was mainly caused by the fall in real wages below the subsistence level, as a result of inflation. There is no indication that the huge surplus labor in rural areas will vanish in the near future. See "Survey of Labor Shortage in Some Areas" by the Labor and Social Security Department, State Council, 2004. A brief summary is given at http://news.sina.com.cn/c/2004-09-08/05343612560s.shtml.

2   Modern management personnel and certain skills can also be constraints for China's output. To take account of the constraint on certain human capital, we can consider that human capital is included in $K$ rather than $L$.

## References

Cook, P., K. Colin, and N. Frederick (eds) (1998) *Privatization, Enterprise Development and Economic Reform: Experiences of Developing and Transitional Economies*, Cheltenham: Elgar.

Gao, H. (2002) "Job Demands Urgent Attention," *Business Weekly*, 13 August.

Glade, W. (1991) "Privatization, Employment and Migration," in: Diaz-Briquets, S. and S. Weintraub (eds), *Migration Impacts of Trade and Foreign Investment: Mexico and Caribbean Basin Countries*, Series on Development and International Migration in Mexico, Central America, and the Caribbean Basin, vol. 3, Boulder, CO: Westview Press, pp. 279–97.

Naqvi, S. and A.R. Kemal (1994) "Structural Adjustment, Privatisation and Employment in Pakistan," in: Islam, R. (ed.), *Social Dimensions of Economic Reforms in Asia*, New Delhi: International Labour Organization, South Asia Multidisciplinary Advisory Team, pp. 191–214.

Sanjeev, G., C. Schiller, H. Ma, and E. Tiongson (2001) "Privatization, Labor, and Social Safety Nets," *Journal of Economic Surveys*, 15: 647–69.

# 14 The effect of education and wage determination in China's rural industry

*Haizheng Li and Aselia Urmanbetova*

## Introduction

There has been a growing interest in studying education and human capital invest-ment in China (see Heckman, 2002; *Wall Street Journal*, 2003).[1] At the core of this issue is how an individual's earnings capacity is affected by education. This so-called private return to education, measured by increased earnings, is related to a number of important policy issues. Based on Heckman (2002), if the return to human capital investment is higher than that of physical capital investment, the Chinese government should raise its spending on education. On the other hand, the return to schooling is also critical for an individual's decision to invest in his/ her own education. Therefore, the effect of education on earnings has important implications for both public and private investment in education. Furthermore, given the widespread wage compression in the old planning economy (Fleisher and Wang, 2004a), the extent to which education is rewarded is also an important indicator of the overall development of the Chinese labor market.

There are numerous studies investigating the return to education in China. However, most of these studies have focused on the urban labor market (some recent studies include, for example, Zhang and Zhao, 2002; Giles *et al.*, 2003; Li, 2003; Fleisher and Wang, 2004a). Moreover, almost all studies using recent data have shown that the return to education has been rising in urban areas. They find that, for example, the rate of return to schooling has risen from 2–3 percent in the 1980s to 6–9 percent in the middle and late 1990s.

In contrast, very few studies exist about the effect of education on earnings in the rural labor market in China. Moreover, studies using rural data from the 1990s or later are especially limited. There are only two studies on wage determination focusing on rural industry. Meng (1996) used the data on rural enterprises from four provinces in China in 1985.[2] Given the rapid changes in rural China, it is desirable to investigate wage determination using more recent data. Zhang *et al.* (2002) used data from 1996, with a sample that covers only one province, Jiangsu. As Jiangsu province is a relatively developed province in China, the sample is unlikely to be representative of rural industry.

Additionally, Meng (1996) estimated the rate of return to schooling to be about 1.1 percent, while Zhang *et al.* (2002) reported a return above 5 percent based on data from one province. Given the well-documented rising returns to schooling in China's urban areas, it is of interest to examine whether the overall rural labor market has experienced a similar upward trend to that in the urban labor market.

There are two other studies on rural wage determination. Johnson and Chow (1997) estimated a return of 4.02 percent based on data from 1988, and Wei *et al.* (1999) found a return of 4.8 percent using data from 1991. These two studies, however, do not exclude farm workers and farming income from their estimations. As farming activities are mostly family based in China, the effect of education on farming income is less indicative of the development of the rural labor market. In Wei *et al.* (1999), for example, only 5 percent of the sample represented rural industry. Hence, their results do not reflect the wage structure that is specific to the industrial sector in rural areas.

Wage determination in rural industry and the extent to which education is rewarded will have important implications for attracting and retaining talented people in rural industry and for the long-term growth of the rural economy. In this chapter, we investigate the effect of education on wages in rural industry using household survey data collected in 1996. The data covers 34,739 individuals in 19 provinces of China. In addition to the national representative sample, one unique feature of the data is that we can calculate hourly wage rates, which is a better measure of the return to education. Most existing studies on the rural labor market in China rely on annual or monthly earnings in calculating the rate of return. As earnings are influenced by both wage rates and hours worked, the estimated returns will suffer from unobserved heterogeneity caused by the omitted work hours. Additionally, our data also provide information on individuals' non-farming work experience, which should be more relevant in wage determination in rural industry than the general experience.

Our results show that, in contrast to the urban labor market, the return to education in rural industry in 1995 is not higher than the estimates using the data from ten years earlier. Based on the generalized least squares (GLS) estimation, which controls for unknown forms of heteroskedasticity, the overall return is 1.2 percent. Second, our analyses indicate that the low estimated return cannot be attributed to the attenuation bias caused by reporting errors, which have commonly been found to cause substantial downward bias in ordinary least squares (OLS)-type estimation. Moreover, we find that education is still rewarded in terms of occupational attainment, but only those with professional/technical school or college education receive returns. Graduates from upper and lower middle schools, who make up the majority of the rural industry workforce, do not earn any more than those with education at the elementary school level. Finally, our results indicate that the oversupply of middle school graduates relative to the demand, as well as the rudimentary technology employed in rural industry, has contributed to the low return to schooling.

It is worth noting that, as we focus on workers in rural industry and exclude those who migrate to urban areas and those who engage mostly in farm work, there are potential selection biases in estimating a Mincerian-type earnings model. It is possible that there is a different type of return to education in the form of more potential non-farming job opportunities. In other words, education may increase the probability of finding a job in urban areas (Zhao, 1999) and the probability of finding a non-farming job in rural areas (Yang, 1997). Because we omitted these two groups in our estimation, the net effect of potential bias is unknown. In order to compare with the existing studies, in this study, we ignore the potential selection bias and focus on the Mincerian earnings function.

The rest of the chapter is organized as follows. The next section discusses the data, followed by presentation of the OLS results. Then potential attenuation bias caused by reporting errors is investigated, followed by an exploration of the factors that may have contributed to the low return to education and our conclusions.

## China's rural industry and data description

Since the economic reforms started in 1978, the Chinese rural sector has undergone a substantial transformation. The most notable changes are the implementation of the household responsibility system (HRS) and the creation of township and village enterprises (TVEs), both of which are believed to be economic propellers of the Chinese countryside.

The success of TVEs is one of the most distinctive institutional features of China's economic transition. Nationally, the output of TVEs, defined as all rural collectively owned enterprises, grew more than sixfold in real terms between 1985 and 1997 (Park and Shen, 2003). TVE employment grew at an average rate of 13 percent during the 1980s and 7 percent from 1990 to 1995.[3] Additionally, the rural off-farm labor force has expanded steadily since the early 1980s. Based on the work of De Brauw *et al.* (2002: 333–5), off-farm rural employment rose from less than 40 million workers in 1981 (around 15 percent of the total rural labor force) to more than 150 million workers in 1995 (32 percent of the total rural labor force). Furthermore, in 2000, more than 200 million rural workers worked off the farm, representing 43 percent of the total rural labor force.

Our data are from the second wave of the Chinese Household Income Project that was conducted in 1996 (CHIP-95). The first wave of the project, CHIP-88, was conducted in 1989.[4] CHIP-95, like CHIP-88, consists of two parts – an urban household survey and a rural household survey.[5] In this study, we use the rural household survey, which contains data for 34,739 individuals from 19 provinces.[6]

In order to study wage determination in rural industry, we restrict our sample to those workers who were involved in non-agricultural jobs as their primary activity with reported work hours and regular monthly income (including wages and bonuses) from the work unit.[7] In addition, we exclude those whose non-farming income was earned in an urban area through temporary migration.[8] The resulting sample consists of 1,182 workers, of whom 36.6 percent are females and the average schooling level is 8.28 years.[9] Descriptive statistics are reported in Table 14.1.

We measure the rate of return to schooling in terms of the hourly wage rate, which is calculated based on reported monthly income (including wages, bonuses, etc. from the work unit) and reported average monthly work hours (estimated from the average number of work hours per day and the average number of work days per week).[10] The average hourly wage rate is 3.11 yuan with a standard deviation of 3.95 yuan. Previous studies used either annual or monthly income. A potential problem is that annual or monthly income depends on hours of work, and hours worked are correlated with educational attainment in China. Generally, workers with less education work longer hours. In our sample, the simple correlation coefficient between years of schooling and monthly work hours is –0.12 and highly significant. Thus, those with less education earn additional income from extra hours of work. As a result, OLS estimation will suffer from omitted variable bias (actual working hours) and will underestimate the true returns.

In the data, individuals reported both their years of schooling and their educational qualifications achieved. In the sample, 0.17 percent of individuals have a college education, 1.69 percent have a professional school degree (Dazhuan, three-year college), and 7.28 percent have attended a middle-level professional, technical, or vocational school. Given the small number of observations in each group, we combine these three categories into one and call it "professional school education or above." For the same reason, we also combine the categories including different years of elementary school (four or more years; one to three years) as well as illiterate and semi-illiterate into one category called "elementary school or below," which accounts for 20 percent of the sample.

Based on the human capital theory, experience is a proxy of human capital acquired through on-the-job training. Thus, non-farming experience should be most relevant in wage determination in rural industry. In our data, individuals reported their non-farming experience. The average non-farming experience is about six years. Some previous studies used experience estimated with age and years of schooling, such as Johnson and Chow (1997) and Wei *et al.* (1999), or simply used age as a proxy for experience, such as Zhang *et al.* (2002). However, experience estimated in such a way is generally inaccurate, and it does not differentiate between farming and non-farming work.

## The rate of return to education

The most commonly used empirical model for estimating returns to schooling is the following Mincerian-type (Mincer, 1974) earnings function:

$$\text{Log } Y_i = \beta_0 + \beta_1 S_i + \beta_2 Exp_i + \beta_3 Exp_i^2 + \varepsilon_i,$$

where $Y_i$ is the earnings, $S_i$ is years of schooling, and $Exp_i$ is years of labor market experience. Based on human capital theory, wages are determined by investment in human capital. Schooling and on-the-job training are major types of investment. Wages will reach their peak when human capital is at its greatest. As experience (age) increases, human capital depreciation will eventually dominate accu-

*Table 14.1* Descriptive statistics

| Variable | Mean | Standard deviation | Minimum value | Maximum value |
|---|---|---|---|---|
| Age | 33.81 | 11.31 | 15 | 80 |
| Females | 0.37 | 0.48 | | |
| Ethnic minority | 0.023 | 0.15 | | |
| Monthly income (in yuan) | 553.13 | 659.86 | 16 | 5,000 |
| Hourly wage (yuan/hour) | 3.11 | 3.95 | 0.083 | 31.25 |
| Reported years of schooling | 8.28 | 2.75 | 0 | 16 |
| Professional school or above[a] | 0.091 | 0.29 | | |
| Upper middle school | 0.20 | 0.40 | | |
| Lower middle school | 0.51 | 0.50 | | |
| Elementary or illiterate | 0.20 | 0.40 | | |
| Non-farming experience (years) | 5.82 | 6.51 | 0 | 38 |
| TVE ownership | 0.54 | 0.50 | | |
| SOE ownership | 0.23 | 0.42 | | |
| Other collectives | 0.069 | 0.25 | | |
| Other ownership[b] | 0.15 | 0.36 | | |

Notes
a  Because very few individuals have education at middle-level professional school, technical
   school, professional school (three-year college), and college, we combined all these categories
   into "Professional school or above."
b  "Other ownership" includes private enterprises, individual enterprises, foreign-owned, Sino-
   foreign enterprises, and others.
SOE, state-owned enterprise; TVE, township and village enterprise.
The number of observations is 1,182.

mulation, and wage rates will decline. Thus, the wage–experience profile should be concave.

The commonly used estimation method is the OLS. However, it is well known that the OLS estimation will generally suffer from omitted ability bias and attenuation bias caused by measurement errors. Measurement errors are commonly found in reported schooling levels (Card, 1999, 2001). As these two biases head in opposite directions, the omitted ability bias will tend to overestimate the true return, while the attenuation bias will underestimate it; the net bias of an OLS estimation is unknown *ex ante*. However, studies have shown that the attenuation bias often dominates, and the resulting OLS estimation usually causes substantial downward bias (for example, Griliches, 1977; Angrist and Krueger, 1991; Ashenfelter and Krueger, 1994).

We first estimate the model using OLS and then investigate the possible attenuation bias caused by measurement errors. The OLS results are reported in Table 14.2. The estimated overall rate of return to education is 1.4 percent and is almost significant at the 5 percent level. This estimated return is very low, and is almost in the same range as the 1.1 percent reported by Meng (1996), which was based on data from 1985.

The estimated effect of experience supports the prediction based on the human capital theory, although the quadratic term of experience is very small and not significant at the 10 percent level. For new workers, an additional year of experience has greater impact on their earnings than their education. At ten years of experience, the return to experience is almost identical to the effect of education. Other variables have expected signs: women earn less than men after controlling for education and experience; ethnic minorities tend to have lower wages, but the effect is statistically insignificant.

It is somewhat surprising that the estimated returns for 1995 are in the same range as the estimates for 1985. A natural question is whether our estimation method and model specification have caused underestimation. We first investigate whether heteroskedasticity, a problem that commonly occurs for cross-sectional data, has contributed to the low estimate. It is known that, in the presence of heteroskedasticity, the OLS estimation will be inefficient. Although most previous studies ignored this issue, our tests, both the Breusch–Pagan test (the resulting $F$-statistic is 22.62 and the $P$-value is 0.0004) and the White test (the corresponding $F$-statistic is 39.97 and the $P$-value is 0.0017) strongly reject the hypothesis of homoskedasticity.

In order to improve efficiency, we apply the GLS estimation. In our treatment, we assume that heteroskedasticity is of unknown form, but is affected by all the explanatory variables included in the model. More specifically, we assume that the variance of regression error $var(\varepsilon_i \,|\, x)$ is a function of $x$, $h(x_i)$, where $x_i$ is the vector of all explanatory variables. For generality, we define $h(x_i) = exp(x_i'\delta)$ to estimate $h(x_i)$ and then apply the weighted least squares with the weight $\sqrt{h(x)}$.[11] Based on the above feasible GLS procedure, the estimated return becomes 1. 2 percent and is significant at the 10 percent level, close to the OLS estimate. The GLS estimates for other variables are also close to the original OLS estimate. It appears that heteroskedasticity does not significantly lower the estimated return.

Next, we estimate the model by controlling for ownership.[12] The resulting estimated return (reported in model III) becomes even lower (0.8 percent and insignificant). Among different ownership sectors, the SOEs seem to pay the highest wages. Wages in the other three ownership sectors do not differ significantly.

Finally, we test whether our use of the hourly wage rate instead of annual/ monthly income contributes to the low estimated rate of return. We estimate a model using monthly income as the dependent variable (model IV in Table 14.2). In this case, the estimated return becomes 0.68 percent, much smaller than that based on wages, and is statistically insignificant. As discussed above, the use of income typically lowers the return because of the omitted hours of work.

Clearly, the low estimated rate of return to education in rural industry is robust to model specifications and technical assumptions. The remaining question is whether the OLS-type estimation results in a substantial downward bias. As discussed above, if there are measurement errors in the reported years of schooling,

Table 14.2 Ordinary least squares estimation of returns to education

| Variable | I<br>Wages | II<br>Wages<br>(heteroskedasticity<br>corrected) | III<br>Wages | IV<br>Monthly<br>income |
|---|---|---|---|---|
| Years of schooling | 0.014*<br>(1.94) | 0.012*<br>(1.65) | 0.0083<br>(1.07) | 0.0068<br>(1.02) |
| Non-farming<br>experience | 0.022**<br>(2.66) | 0.024**<br>(2.87) | 0.021**<br>(2.50) | 0.025**<br>(3.10) |
| Non-farming<br>experience squared | −0.00049<br>(−1.54) | −0.00049<br>(−1.43) | −0.0005<br>(−1.57) | −0.00071**<br>(−2.38) |
| Female | −0.14**<br>(−3.16) | −0.14**<br>(−3.34) | −0.15**<br>(−3.24) | −0.14**<br>(−3.17) |
| Ethnic minority | 0.069<br>(0.29) | 0.066<br>(0.21) | 0.042<br>(0.18) | −0.077<br>(−0.33) |
| TVE ownership | | | 0.077<br>(1.05) | |
| SOE ownership | | | 0.18**<br>(2.13) | |
| Other collective | | | −0.085<br>(−0.96) | |
| Sample size | 1,182 | 1,182 | 1,182 | 1,182 |
| *F*-value | 7.02 | 8.03 | 5.74 | 5.69 |
| Adjusted *R*-squared | 0.025 | 0.029 | 0.031 | 0.019 |

Notes
The constant term is not reported; the heteroskedasticity robust *t*-statistics are in parentheses.
*    Significant at the 10% level.
**   Significant at the 5% level.
Wages are hourly wage rates.
The omitted ownership group is "Other ownership."
SOE, state-owned enterprise; TVE, township and village enterprise.

the OLS estimation will suffer from attenuation bias. In the next section, we will investigate the extent of measurement errors in the reported years of schooling and corresponding bias.

## Assessment of the effect of measurement errors

In order to assess the effect of measurement errors in the reported levels of schooling, a second measure of schooling is generally needed. For example, Ashenfelter and Krueger (1994) obtained the second education measure by asking twins to report on both their own and their twin's schooling level. In our data, individuals reported both years of schooling and educational achievements obtained. The latter enables us to estimate an individual's years of schooling based on the Chinese education system. Therefore, we can obtain two measures of years of schooling; the first is reported directly, and the second is converted from educational degrees.[13]

It is possible that each schooling measure contains measurement errors. The errors for the first one could stem from an individual's misreporting; while for the second one, measure errors could arise from converting reported educational categories into the relevant number of years. In particular, the number of years spent obtaining the same degree may vary across individuals. For example, an individual can enroll in a middle-level professional school either after finishing a lower middle school or after completing an upper middle school, or an individual may spend an additional year in the upper middle school. In this case, although both schooling measures contain measurement errors, the errors are likely to be uncorrelated due to their different nature.[14]

If we write $S_1 = S + v_1$ and $S_2 = S + v_2$, where $S$ is the true schooling years, $S_1$ is reported schooling years, and $S_2$ is converted schooling years, then $v_i$ ($i = 1$, 2) are measurement errors. For $S_1$, the mean is 8.28 years with a standard deviation of 2.75 years and, for $S_2$, the mean is 8.92 years with a standard deviation of 2.94 years. It can be shown that, for the true rate of return to education $\beta_1$, the OLS estimator $b_1$ will be biased when schooling is measured with error, i.e., $plim(b_1) = \beta_1 \cdot [\sigma_u^2/(\sigma_u^2 + \sigma_v^2)]$, where $\sigma_v^2$ is the variance of the measurement error, and $\sigma_u^2$ is the variance of the population error in regressing schooling on other regressors in the earnings equation. Clearly, the higher the variance of the measurement error, the larger the attenuation bias. As $\beta_1$ should be positive, the attenuation bias will result in an underestimation of the effect of education.

As the converted schooling, $S_2$ should generally be less accurate than the reported schooling, $S_1$, the measurement error in $S_2$ will have a higher variance, and will thus cause a larger attenuation bias. The estimated return will be smaller than that based on $S_1$. This is confirmed by the results reported in Table 14.3: the estimated return based on $S_2$ is 0.71 percent, which is much lower than the 1.4 percent based on the reported years of schooling $S_1$.

If we assume that individuals do not misreport their years of schooling and their educational achievements in a systematic way, then the correlation between measurement errors in the two schooling measures should be negligible. If the measurement errors in both schooling measures are uncorrelated with $S$ and with each other, the correlation between $S_1$ and $S_2$ is $Var(S)/[Var(S_1) \cdot Var(S_2)]^{0.5}$. This ratio is sometimes called the "reliability ratio." In our sample, the reliability ratio is 0.87, which indicates that 13 percent of the measured variance in schooling is attributed to error. Therefore, in our sample, the extent to which the years of schooling are misreported appears to be small.

A simple approach to reducing attenuation bias is to use the average of the two measures, $S_a$, to estimate the model. In general, if there are sizeable measurement errors in $S_1$ and $S_2$, the variance of measurement errors in $S_a$ should be smaller than the variance of measurement errors in either $S_1$ or $S_2$, and hence the attenuation bias using $S_a$ should also be smaller. On the other hand, if there are measurement errors in $S_2$ but not in $S_1$, then the estimate based on $S_a$ will be attenuated while the estimate based on $S_1$ will not. In this case, the estimated rate of return based on $S_a$ should be between the two estimates based on $S_1$ and $S_2$.

Therefore, although $S_a$ does not eliminate measurement errors, the relative magnitude of the estimated returns based on all three measures ($S_1$, $S_2$, and $S_a$) will provide some indication of the extent of attenuation bias. As shown in Table 14.3, the resulting estimate using $S_a$ is 1.1 percent, which is larger than that using $S_2$ (0.7 percent) and smaller than that based on $S_1$ (1.4 percent). This result indicates that measurement errors in the reported years of schooling ($S_1$) are small and do not cause large attenuation bias.[15]

In order to remove the attenuation bias caused by measurement errors, instrument variable estimation is generally applied using one measure of schooling as an instrument for the other.[16] When $S_1$ is used as an instrument for $S_2$, the resulting IV estimation gives a return of 1.5 percent (model IV in Table 14.3), higher than the OLS estimate based on $S_2$. This result is very close to the OLS estimation using $S_1$ as a regressor. On the other hand, when we use $S_2$ as an instrument for $S_1$, the resulting estimated return becomes statistically insignificant with the value of 0.87 percent (model III in Table 14.3). Clearly, if $S_1$ is not measured with errors, the OLS estimation will be efficient and preferred. Thus, the change in the estimated return in this case is likely to be caused by the inefficiency of the IV estimation.

All the above results suggest that the extent to which the years of schooling are misreported is negligible. Hence, with the years of schooling reported directly by each individual, the OLS estimation does not suffer from a significant attenuation bias.

However, another potential bias may stem from the omitted ability in the OLS estimation. As the omitted ability bias causes only overestimation of the return, then the actual rate of return to education in rural China may be even lower than the current OLS estimates. Given the already low estimated returns, it is not important to search for additional upward bias caused by omitted ability variables in OLS estimation. Hence, we turn to investigate the possible causes of the low returns to education in China's rural industry.

## Further investigation of the returns to schooling

Based on the results above, the returns to education in rural industry in China are not higher compared with the estimates using earlier data. This result differs dramatically from that in urban areas. The divergence in development in urban and rural labor markets raises many important questions. In this section, we explore some explanations for the extremely low estimates found in our data.

We examine first the average wage for each educational degree. As can be seen in Table 14.4, the average wages for those who graduated from upper middle school, lower middle school, and those with elementary education or below are almost the same, although their corresponding years of schooling differ

*Table 14.3* The effect of measurement error

| Variable | I OLS | II OLS | III 2SLS Instrument: converted years of schooling | IV 2SLS Instrument: reported years of schooling |
|---|---|---|---|---|
| Reported years of schooling | | | 0.0087 (0.99) | |
| Converted years of schooling | 0.0071 (1.01) | | | 0.015*** (1.84) |
| Average years of schooling | | 0.011 (1.49) | | |
| Non-farming experience | 0.022** (2.61) | 0.022** (2.63) | 0.022** (2.67) | 0.022** (2.62) |
| Non-farming experience squared | −0.00047 (−1.49) | −0.00050 (−1.51) | −0.00048 (−1.45) | −0.00047 (−1.42) |
| Female | −0.14** (−3.17) | −0.14** (−3.14) | −0.15** (−3.26) | −0.14** (−3.00) |
| Ethnic minority | 0.066 (0.28) | 0.066 (0.28) | 0.070 (0.50) | 0.060 (0.43) |
| Sample size | 1,182 | 1,182 | 1,182 | 1,182 |
| F-value | 6.52 | 6.76 | 6.53 | 7.00 |
| Adjusted $R$-squared | 0.023 | 0.024 | | |

Notes
The constant term is not reported; the heteroskedasticity robust $t$-statistics are in parentheses.
** Significant at the 5% level.
*** Significant at the 10% level.
In column I, returns are estimated using the converted years of schooling; in column II, returns are estimated using the average of the reported years of schooling and converted years of schooling.
In column III, reported years of schooling is used as a regressor, and converted years of schooling is used as an instrument; in column IV, converted years of schooling is used as a regressor, and reported years of schooling is used as an instrument.
OLS, ordinary least squares; 2SLS, two-stage least squares.

significantly. In fact, only those with education at the level of professional school or above earned higher wages.

The regression analysis confirms this finding when we estimate a model with dummy variables on educational levels (reported in Table 14.5). As can be seen, graduates from professional school, including college, professional school (three-year college), or middle-level professional or technical school, earn 24.8 percent more than those at an elementary school level, and the effect is significant at the 1 percent level.[17] However, this wage difference is much smaller than that found in the urban area. Based on the findings of Li (2003), urban graduates from middle-level professional schools or above earn 62–93 percent more than those with elementary education or below.

It appears that rural graduates from both upper and lower middle schools do not earn higher wages than those with elementary education. As those who graduated from professional schools or above account for only 9 percent of the sample, a vast majority (70 percent of the sample) of workers in the rural industry are graduates from middle schools. If this majority of the population is not rewarded for their additional education above the elementary level, then the overall rate of return will undoubtedly be very low.

The next question is why the additional years of schooling above the elementary school (three years for lower middle school and an additional three years for upper middle school) level do not result in higher earnings. Some studies argue that, in rural industry, all jobs are unskilled, and thus education does not increase productivity. As a result, education does not reap rewards (Meng, 1996). If this is the case, then why do graduates from professional schools still receive rewards for their education?

In order to answer this question, we turn to the analysis of education by skills and types of occupation. In our sample, the distribution of occupations in the rural industry is: unskilled workers, 72.1 percent; skilled/technical workers, 10.7 percent; and manager-type workers, 17.2 percent.[18] However, if we look at wage and education distribution across the occupations reported in Table 14.6, it is clear that skilled workers and managers are paid much more on average. For example, the average wage of a skilled worker is about 71 percent higher than that of the unskilled workers, and managers earn about 32 percent more than unskilled workers. The fact that skilled workers are paid more than managers (about 29 percent more) indicates that there are still some jobs in rural industry that require skills, and that those skills are highly valued. However, the proportion of skilled/technical jobs is the lowest.

Moreover, skilled workers and managers generally have higher education, and the years of schooling increase from unskilled worker to skilled worker and to managers. In this sense, education is still rewarded in terms of occupational distribution. However, as can be seen from Table 14.7, the managerial positions, which have the highest average schooling, are shared almost equally (around 30 percent) by the three education levels above elementary school. This distribution shows that managerial positions can be taken by anyone with education above

*Table 14.4* Years of schooling and wage by education levels

| Education level | Average years of schooling | Average wage | Standard deviation of wage | Number of observations |
|---|---|---|---|---|
| Professional school or above | 11.75 | 3.74 | 4.36 | 108 |
| Upper middle school | 10.77 | 3.00 | 3.84 | 230 |
| Lower middle school | 8.24 | 3.10 | 3.97 | 607 |
| Elementary or illiterate | 4.41 | 2.98 | 3.81 | 237 |

the elementary level. Thus, the education requirement for a manager is generally higher, but not strict. The same observation applies to skilled workers. Most
skilled workers (about 58 percent) are graduates from lower middle school.

Some plausible explanations come from both demand and supply sides. On the
demand side, even skilled and managerial jobs do not require education above the
lower middle school. Thus, the technology and management requirements seem
to be quite low in rural industry, although skilled workers are still well valued. On
the supply side, many well-educated individuals are limited to taking unskilled
jobs. As can be seen from Table 14.7, around 61 percent of graduates from upper
middle school take unskilled jobs, and even 25 percent of those with professional
or higher education also work in unskilled jobs. Given the fact that most upper
middle school graduates take unskilled jobs and most skilled jobs are occupied by
graduates from lower middle school (about 58 percent), it is possible that upper
middle school education may not enhance productivity in most skilled jobs in
rural industry. In China, students in upper middle school are generally pressed to

*Table 14.5* Returns to education levels

| Variable | I<br>All workers | II<br>Females | III<br>Males | IV<br>TVE | V<br>SOE |
|---|---|---|---|---|---|
| Professional school | 0.22**<br>(2.92) | 0.40**<br>(3.50) | 0.16***<br>(1.67) | 0.20<br>(0.87) | −0.14<br>(−0.80) |
| Upper middle | −0.02<br>(−0.32) | 0.074<br>(0.66) | −0.057<br>(−0.72) | 0.055<br>(0.73) | −0.48**<br>(−2.69) |
| Lower middle | −0.012<br>(−0.23) | −0.044<br>(−0.54) | 0.01<br>(0.15) | 0.056<br>(0.96) | −0.38**<br>(−2.10) |
| Non-farming experience | 0.022**<br>(2.59) | 0.051**<br>(2.98) | 0.0098<br>(0.99) | 0.045**<br>(3.21) | 0.016<br>(1.06) |
| Non-farming experience squared | −0.00056***<br>(−1.75) | −0.0015**<br>(−2.03) | −0.00015<br>(−0.43) | −0.0016**<br>(−2.15) | −0.0005<br>(−0.96) |
| Female | −0.15**<br>(−3.29) | | | −0.18**<br>(−3.36) | 0.032<br>(0.30) |
| Sample size | 1182 | 433 | 749 | 642 | 277 |
| *F*-value | 6.94 | 5.03 | 1.83 | 5.54 | 2.42 |
| Adjusted *R*-squared | 0.029 | 0.045 | 0.0055 | 0.041 | 0.03 |

Notes
The constant term is not reported; heteroskedasticity robust *t*-statistics are in parentheses.
** Significant at the 5% level.
*** Significant at the 10% level.
The omitted school level is elementary school or below.
SOE, state-owned enterprise; TVE, township and village enterprise.

pass the national entrance examinations to enter college, and thus their studies do not focus on pragmatic knowledge.

The demand and supply structure offers some explanations for our findings that the overall return to schooling is extremely low, and only those who graduated from professional schools are rewarded for their education. In particular, based on Table 14.7, 75 percent of those who graduated from professional schools or above take jobs as skilled/technical workers or managers, and they receive higher wages. Therefore, the return to this educational level should be higher. On the other hand, as most graduates from upper and lower middle schools share the pool of unskilled jobs with those workers who have only elementary or even lower education, the wage differences between those education levels will be suppressed. As a result, the overall rate of return to schooling will be lower.

In addition, as reported in Table 14.5, wage determination for men and women follows almost the same pattern. However, the return is much higher for women with professional or higher education. Women in this group earn 49 percent more than those with elementary education, while the wage for men is higher by only 17 percent. For women, the overall rate of return is 2.1 percent, which is still much lower than the 7 percent found for urban female workers (Li, 2003). Interestingly, women's wage experience profile follows the prediction of the human capital theory, and their non-farming experience has a strong effect on their wages. For men, however, the effect of non-farming experience is both economically and statistically insignificant.

It is a stylized fact that the return to schooling for women is higher than for men because of the scarcity of educated women (Psacharopoulos, 1994). In our sample, women account for only 37 percent of non-farming rural workers, and their education level is lower than that of male workers. More specifically, among those with education at elementary school level or lower, the proportion of men and women is almost the same. However, at the lower middle school level, women workers account for only 37 percent and, at the upper middle school level, women account for 29 percent. For those with education at professional school or above, only 27 percent of workers are women. Therefore, because of the relative scarcity of educated women in rural industry, they receive higher rewards than men for their investment in education.

A body of existing research attributes the low private returns to schooling in China to the persistence of labor market monopsony (Dong and Putterman, 1996). However, Fleisher and Wang (2004b) found that rural enterprises overpaid production workers relative to a monopsony profit-maximizing benchmark, while

*Table 14.6* Wages and schooling by occupation (yuan/hour)

| Occupation | Average wage | Average years of schooling | Number of observations |
|---|---|---|---|
| Unskilled workers | 2.75 | 7.82 | 852 |
| Skilled workers | 4.70 | 8.88 | 127 |
| Managers | 3.64 | 9.86 | 203 |

*Table 14.7* Occupation and education

| Occupation | Unskilled | Skilled | Managerial | Number of observations |
|---|---|---|---|---|
| *Education distribution for each occupation* | | | | |
| Professional school or above | 3.17 | 15.75 | 30.05 | |
| Upper middle school | 16.55 | 16.54 | 33.50 | |
| Lower middle school | 55.28 | 58.27 | 30.54 | |
| Elementary or illiterate | 25.00 | 9.45 | 5.91 | |
| Number of observations | 852 | 127 | 203 | |
| *Occupation distribution for each educational level* | | | | |
| Professional school or above | 25.00 | 18.52 | 56.48 | 108 |
| Upper middle school | 61.30 | 9.13 | 29.57 | 230 |
| Lower middle school | 77.59 | 12.19 | 10.21 | 607 |
| Elementary or illiterate | 89.87 | 5.06 | 5.06 | 237 |

there was extreme underpayment of skilled workers relative to the monopsony profit-maximizing amount. They explain the low private returns to schooling using this relatively large "exploitation" of skilled workers. The question is why rural enterprises overpay unskilled workers when, with the apparent higher degree of oversupply of unskilled labor, such workers can easily be underpaid. A possible explanation is that profit maximization may not be the only objective of rural enterprises. Some studies (for example, Dong, 1998) find that rural enterprises pursue profit as well as "pro-employment" goals, which in fact result in wage equalization behavior. Li and Zhang (1998) show that greater distributional equality in rural industry reduces individuals' returns to education.

Although our results do not directly contradict the findings in these studies, they suggest that the direct reason for the low return to schooling in rural industry can also be attributed to the oversupply of upper middle school graduates relative to the demand, as most of these graduates are engaged in unskilled jobs. The scarcity of industrial enterprises relative to the labor supply is aggravated by the relative labor immobility, or inability of rural workers to seek better employment opportunities elsewhere. The best alternative is to migrate to urban cities to find jobs. However, the economic and physical costs are high for temporary migration. In fact, based on the work of Li and Zahniser (2002), the proportion of temporary migrants from rural to urban areas is not substantial; in 1995, about 10 percent of individuals aged 16–35 took part in temporary migration. Therefore, although migration represents an opportunity for young rural workers, the effect of migration on the demand–supply structure in the rural labor market is still limited.

As a result, most middle school graduates are limited to unskilled jobs in rural industry. They are paid lower wages, either because their jobs do not need such education or because they are not more productive than those with lower education. In either case, the low return to their schooling is neither necessarily indicative of the monopsony power of enterprises in the rural labor market nor necessarily indicative of the relative underpayment of educated workers, as was suggested by other studies.

Finally, in order to investigate the behavioral differences in wage determination by ownership types, we estimate models for SOEs and TVEs separately.[19] TVEs generally operate in a more market-oriented manner than SOEs. Hence, the two enterprise types should have different wage structures. The results reported in Table 14.5 confirm this hypothesis. For TVEs, earnings generally increase with education (although statistically insignificant), and the effect of experience is significant and follows the prediction of the human capital theory. It appears that experience is more important than education, suggesting that wages in the TVE sector are still closely connected to seniority. For SOEs, however, all education variables appear to have the wrong sign. Moreover, middle school graduates seem to earn considerably less than elementary school graduates (statistically significant). The experience variables do not appear to have any significant effect. Additionally, as evidenced by the negative signs of the education variables in the SOE regression, it is clear that the wage structure in SOEs also contributes to the generally low returns to schooling in rural industry.

## Conclusions

In this study, we investigate the effect of education on wage determination in rural industry in China. We find that the return to schooling in rural industry in 1995 was not higher than the return ten years earlier. Our estimated overall return to schooling based on the GLS estimation is 1.2 percent. The low estimated return is robust to model specifications and estimation methods. Our results also demonstrate that the low estimated return is not attributed to the downward attenuation bias in OLS estimation caused by reporting errors. Moreover, we find that only graduates from middle-level professional school, technical school, or college receive economic rewards for their education, while those with education at the middle school level earn the same as workers with elementary education. These results are substantially different from the findings in the urban labor market, where the returns to education are much higher and have been increasing since the early 1990s.

We also find that education is still rewarded in occupational distribution. Skilled/technical jobs and managerial jobs are more likely to be taken by those with higher education, and generally pay more. Additionally, the wage structure in the TVE sector appears to be closer to a market system than in the SOE sector, although rewards to education are still very low. Finally, experience appears to be more important than education in wage determination.

We find that the low return to schooling is attributable to the relative oversupply of middle school graduates in the rural labor market and the rudimentary technology employed in rural industry. As a result, most of the graduates from upper and lower middle school are limited to unskilled jobs and are paid a low wage. As the majority of rural industry workers have a middle school education and are not rewarded for their schooling, the overall rate of return must be low. In addition, given the fact that the majority of skilled jobs are taken by graduates from lower middle school and most graduates from upper middle school work in unskilled jobs, it is possible that an upper middle school education does not enhance the productivity in those jobs. Instead, experience plays a more important role in productivity.

Although some studies attribute the low return to education and wage compression to the monopsony nature of the rural labor market and the non-profit objectives of rural enterprises, we believe that these results can occur even if the rural labor market is competitive and rural enterprises pursue profit maximization. Many studies (for example, Sachs and Woo, 1997) suggested the transformation of TVEs into normal private enterprises in order to improve efficiency. Since 1995, millions of TVEs have been transformed into private enterprises (Dong *et al.*, 2002). However, the effect of this transformation on the return to schooling will still depend on relative demand and supply in the rural labor market. If technology and management requirements in rural industry remain at a low level and if the supply of middle school graduates to non-farming jobs increases at a faster rate, the return to education in the rural labor market may remain low.

In order to increase the reward for human capital investment in rural China, the Chinese government should adopt policies geared toward improving technology in rural industry, and offering incentives for rural enterprises to grow and thus to increase demand for workers. On the other hand, it is also important to remove the obstacles to rural-to-rural and rural-to-urban migration, thereby reducing the costs of labor mobility. With improved technology, higher demand, and increased labor mobility, the rural labor market will become more efficient in allocating labor resources and in compensating workers according to their human capital investment.

## Acknowledgments

We would like to thank session participants at the Chinese Economists' Society Conference in Beijing 2004, especially Dennis Yang, for helpful comments.

## Notes

1 "The People's Republic May Neglect People By Starving Schools," by David Wessel, *Wall Street Journal*, 23 October 2003.
2 Two other related studies, Gregory and Meng (1995) and Meng (1998), used the same data as Meng (1996) and found similar results on the effect of education.
3 Percentage changes are calculated with the data from *The Statistical Yearbook of China* (2001).
4 The Chinese Household Income Project (CHIP) was conducted with the support of the Ford Foundation, the Chinese Academy of Social Science, and a number of other institutes. Both CHIP-88 and CHIP-95 are available to the public at the Inter-university Consortium for Political and Social Research (ICPSR).

5 The rural household survey of CHIP-88 has been used in studying the return to education in rural China by Johnson and Chow (1997).

6 The provinces covered in CHIP-95 include Beijing, Hebei, Shanxi, Liaoling, Jilin, Jiangsu, Zhejiang, Anhui, Jiangxi, Shangdong, Henan, Hubei, Hunan, Guangdong, Sichuan, Guizhou, Yunnan, Shaanxi, and Gansu.

7 In CHIP-95, these questions are asked for those who were involved in non-agricultural activities for three months or more in 1995.

8 We exclude those reported to be working in a city for at least one month in 1995, but do not exclude those migrants who work in another rural area.

9 We also dropped nine observations with reported monthly incomes above 5,000 yuan, which is about eight standard deviations away from the mean. These individuals could be enterprise owners, and their reported wages may include profits.

10 Monthly work hours = average work hours/day × average work days/week × 4.

11 The weight can be estimated by regressing $\log(\varepsilon_i^2)$ on $x_i'\delta$ to estimate $\delta$, where $\varepsilon_i$ is the OLS residual from the original equation.

12 Ownership is divided into four main categories: (1) township and village enterprises (TVEs); (2) state-owned enterprises (SOEs); (3) other collective forms of ownership; and (4) other types of ownership including private enterprises, Sino–foreign joint ventures, foreign-owned enterprises, and others.

13 Following other studies, the corresponding number of years for different education levels are estimated as follows: (1) college or above, 16 years; (2) professional school, 15 years; (3) middle-level professional, technical, or vocational school, 12 years; (4) upper middle school, 12 years; (5) lower middle school, 9 years; (6) 4 or more years of elementary education, 5 years; (7) 1–3 years of elementary education, 2 years; and (8) illiterate or semi-illiterate, 0 years.

14 However, if an individual deliberately exaggerates the years of schooling and educational achievements obtained, the measurement errors in the two schooling measures could be correlated.

15 It is possible to get similar results if the measurement errors in the two schooling measures are both very large and highly positively correlated. This should be unlikely given the possible sources of errors in the two schooling measures.

16 We follow the classic approach to error-in-variables. For a non-classic approach to assessing the effect of measurement error in estimating the effect of education, see a recent study by Kane *et al.* (1999).

17 For dummy variables, the percentage change in wage $d_i$ for group $i$ relative to the base group can be calculated by $d_i = e^{\beta_i} - 1$, where the $\beta_i$ is the coefficient for the dummy variable for group $i$.

18 In the survey, the manager-type occupations include manager, village cadre, official of the party or a government office, and ordinary cadre in an enterprise.

19 We also estimate models for other collective enterprises as well as private enterprises. Owing to the small sample sizes, the results are statistically insignificant.

# References

Angrist, J.D. and A.B. Krueger (1991) "Does Compulsory School Attendance Affect Schooling and Earnings," *Quarterly Journal of Economics*, 106: 979–1014.

Ashenfelter, O. and A.B. Krueger (1994) "Estimates of Economic Return to Schooling for A New Sample of Twins," *Quarterly Journal of Economics*, 113: 253–84.

Ashenfelter, O. and D. Zimmerman (1997) "Estimating of Return to Schooling from Sibling Data: Fathers, Sons and Brothers," *Review of Economics and Statistics*, 79: 1–9.

Butcher, K.F. and A. Case (1994) "The Effects of Sibling Composition on Women's Education and Earnings," *Quarterly Journal of Economics*, 109: 443–50.

Card, D. (1993) "Using Geographic Variation in College Proximity to Estimate the Return to Schooling," *NBER Working Paper no. 4483*, available at: http://papers.nber.org/papers/w4483.pdf.

Card, D. (1995) "Using Geographic Variation in College Proximity to Estimate the Return to Schooling," in: Christofides, L.N., E.K. Grant, and R. Swidinsky (eds), *Aspects of Labour Market Behavior: Essays in Honor of John Vanderkamp*, Toronto: University of Toronto, pp. 201–22.

Card, D. (1999) "The Causal Effect of Education on Earnings," in: Ashenfelter, O. and D. Card (eds), *Handbook of Labor Economics*, North Holland-Elsevier Science, 3A: 1801–63.

Card, D. (2001) "Estimating the Return to Schooling: Progress on Some Persistent Econometric Problems," *Econometrica*, 69: 1127–60.

De Brauw, A., J. Huang, S. Rozelle, L. Zhang, and Y. Zhang (2002) "The Evolution of China's Rural Labor Markets During the Reforms," *Journal of Comparative Economics*, 30: 329–53.

Dong, X.-Y. (1998) "Employment and Wage Determination in China's Rural Industry: Investigation Using 1984–1990 Panel Data," *Journal of Comparative Economics*, 26: 485–501.

Dong, X.-Y. and L. Putterman (1996) "China's Rural Industry and Monopsony: An Exploration," *Pacific Economic Review*, 1: 59–78.

Dong, X.-Y., P. Bowles, and S. Ho (2002) "The Determinants of Employee Ownership in China's Privatized Rural Industry: Evidence from Jiangsu and Shandong," *Journal of Comparative Economics*, 30: 415–37.

Fleisher, M.B. and X. Wang (2004a) "Returns to Schooling in China Under Planning and Reform," paper presented at the Allied Social Science Association annual meeting, 2004, San Diego.

Fleisher, M.B. and X. Wang (2004b) "Skill Differentials, Return to Schooling, and Market Segmentation in a Transition Economy: The Case of Mainland China," *Journal of Development Economics*, 73: 315–28.

Giles, J., A. Park, and J. Zhang (2003) "The Great Proletarian Cultural Revolution, Disruption to Education, and Returns to Schooling in Urban China," *Working Paper*, Department of Economics, Michigan State University.

Gregory, R.G. and X. Meng (1995) "Wage Determination and Occupational Attainment in the Rural Industrial Sector of China," *Journal of Comparative Economics*, 21: 353–74.

Griliches, Z. (1977) "Estimating the Returns to Schooling: Some Econometric Problems," *Econometrica*, 45: 1–22.

Heckman, J.J. (2002) "China's Investment in Human Capital," *NBER Working Paper no. 9296*, available at: http://www.nber.org/papers/w9296.pdf.

Johnson, E.N. and G.C. Chow (1997) "Rates of Return to Schooling in China," *Pacific Economic Review*, 2: 101–13.

Kane, T., C.E. Rouse, and D. Staiger (1999) "Estimating Returns to Schooling When Schooling is Misreported," *Working Paper no. 419*, Industrial Relations Section, Princeton University.

Li, H. (2003) "Economic Transition and Returns to Education in China," *Economics of Education Review*, 22: 317–28.

Li, H. and S. Zahniser (2002) "The Determinants of China's Temporary Rural–Urban Migration," *Urban Studies*, 39: 2219–35.

Li, T. and J. Zhang (1998) "Returns to Education under Collective and Household Farming in China," *Journal of Development Economics*, 56: 307–35.

Meng, X. (1996) "An Examination of Wage Determination in China's Rural Industrial Sector," *Applied Economics*, 28: 715–24.

Meng, X. (1998) "Male–Female Wage Determination and Gender Wage Discrimination in China's Rural Industrial Sector," *Labour Economics*, 5: 67–89.

Mincer, J. (1974) *Schooling, Experience and Earnings*, New York: Columbia University Press for the National Bureau of Economic Research.

National Bureau of Statistics of the People's Republic of China (2001) *The Statistical Yearbook of China*, Beijing: China Statistical Publishing House.

Park, A. and M. Shen (2003) "Joint Liability Lending and the Rise and Fall of China's Township and Village Enterprises," *Journal of Development Economics*, 71: 497–531.

Psacharopoulos, G. (1994) "Returns to Investment in Education: A Global Update," *World Development*, 22: 1325–43.

Sachs, J.D. and W.-T. Woo (1997) "Chinese Economic Growth: Explanations and the Tasks Ahead," in: Joint Economic Committee, Congress of the United States (ed.), *China's Economic Future – Challenges to US Policy*, pp. 70–85.

Wei, X., M.C. Tsang, W. Xu, and L.-K. Chen (1999) "Education and Earnings in Rural China," *Education Economics*, 7: 167–87.

Yang, D.T. (1997) "Education and Off-farm Work," *Economic Development and Cultural Change*, 45: 613–32.

Zhang, J. and Y. Zhao (2002) "Economic Returns to Schooling in Urban China, 1988–1999," paper presented at the 2002 meeting of the Allied Social Sciences Association, Washington, DC.

Zhang, L., J. Huang, and S. Rozelle (2002) "Employment, Emerging Labor Markets, and the Role of Education in Rural China," *China Economic Review*, 13: 313–28.

Zhao, Y. (1999) "Labor Migration and Earnings Differences: The Case of Rural China," *Economic Development and Cultural Change*, 47: 613–32.

# 15 Privatization and rising earnings inequality in China's rural industries

## Evidence from Shandong and Jiangsu

*Xiao-yuan Dong*

### Introduction

In the late 1990s, China's rural industry underwent radical property rights reforms with millions of township and village enterprises (TVEs) being privatized. While the methods and speed of reform varied widely between regions, the privatization of TVEs was achieved mainly through the transfer of ownership rights from local governments to enterprise insiders, i.e., managers and employees. As in other transition economies, the goal of privatization of TVEs is primarily to increase economic efficiency; however, the ownership restructuring has important distributional consequences. Studies have shown that privatization in transition economies is often accompanied by significant increases in income inequality (see Aghion and Commander, 1999). The rise in inequality has raised social tensions, posing a threat to social stability. In this chapter, we examine the impact of the privatization of TVEs on earnings inequality using a unique data set from Jiangsu and Shandong provinces.

Privatization is likely to affect income distribution through two main channels. The first is the redistribution of public wealth from local government to new private investors that was associated with the divestiture of a collective enterprise. Our field survey shows that the privatization of TVEs has resulted in a high degree of ownership concentration in management and a skewed distribution of shareholdings among employees (see Dong *et al.*, 2002). The unequal distribution of share ownership is expected to influence the distribution of earnings among employees, as dividend payments have become an important source of income after privatization. The second channel by which privatization may affect distributional equity is through changes in the wage-setting behavior of privatized enterprises. As the changed ownership structure may lead to a higher priority being placed on enterprise profits, a rise in wage inequality, associated with increased returns to human capital and widening gender wage gaps, is likely to occur.

Understanding the causes of earnings inequality is important for the design of sound income policies, because different types of income disparity affect resource allocation differently. Increasing returns to education may be regarded as a reflection of scarcity values of skilled labor and, hence, a necessary accompaniment of transition to a market economy, whereas the rise in inequality resulting from increased gender discrimination is undesirable both economically and politically. In this chapter, we examine the effect of privatization on earnings inequality with a regression-based inequality decomposition technique. We find that the privatization of TVEs has led to a sharp increase in earnings inequality and that unequal distribution of share ownership among employees, increased returns to human capital, and widened gender wage gaps are among the major factors contributing to the rise in earnings inequality. The next section provides an overview of the data used in this chapter, followed by a description of some of the main characteristics of the privatization process and a discussion of the distributional consequences of privatization in the sample counties. The results of the earnings regressions and regression-based inequality decomposition are followed by a brief conclusion.

## Data and the sample counties

The data used in this chapter are derived from the fieldwork we undertook in Jiangsu and Shandong in 1999 and 2000. Both provinces had been leaders in the development of collective rural industries prior to the radical property rights reform instigated in the late 1990s. However, for a variety of reasons, including slowing output and employment growth and increased competition from the private sector, the local governments, in conformity with national policy, undertook major privatization programs of their TVEs in the period 1996–98 (see Ho *et al.*, 2002). A study of the sample from the two provinces illuminates how privatization has occurred in the heartland of the rural collective sector.

The data on which our empirical analysis is based were gathered from 45 enterprises and more than 1,000 workers (mainly production workers, but also some technical, sales, and mid-ranking managerial personnel) using questionnaire instruments.[2] The sample enterprises are located in three counties, 13 in Penglai and 14 in Yanzhou, Shandong, and 18 in Wujin, Jiangsu. While all three counties are above the national and their respective provincial average per capita income levels, the income levels of the three counties nevertheless vary widely, with Wujin being the highest and Yanzhou the lowest. All the enterprises are engaged in industrial production, and most of them produce light consumer goods. At the time of the survey, 39 sample enterprises had been privatized and six remained owned by their local governments. Among the 39 privatized enterprises, two were privatized in 1994, 17 in 1996, 17 in 1997, and three in 1998, and all were sold to enterprise insiders, i.e., managers and workers. Enterprise data included information on the ownership structure, enterprise size, and profitability. Employee data were collected from approximately 25 workers in each enterprise and covered a number of variables such as income from enterprises in the forms of wages, bonuses, interest and dividend payments, share ownership, and personal characteristics such as age, sex, education, and work experience. All data were obtained for a number of years.[3] The empirical analysis in this chapter is based on the data for the 39 privatized enterprises. Table 15.1 presents summary statistics for the firm and individual characteristics that are relevant to the empirical analysis.

*Table 15.1* Descriptive statistics of the sample

| Enterprise characteristics | |
|---|---|
| No. of enterprises | 39 |
| Employment | 241.8 |
| (employees) | (135.2) |
| Assets | 1,374.6 |
| (10,000 yuan) | (1,590.8) |
| *% of shares held by* | |
| Managers | 52.6 |
| Other board members | 24.9 |
| Employees | 17.9 |
| Local government | 2.9 |
| Others | 1.7 |
| *Employee characteristics* | |
| Male | 0.587 |
| | (0.493) |
| Experience (years) | 9.2 |
| | (5.6) |
| Education (years) | 9.08 |
| | (2.19) |
| *Percentage of the sample employees in* | |
| Yanzhou, Shandong | 0.33 |
| Penglai, Shandong | 0.36 |
| Wujin, Jiangsu | 0.31 |

Note
Figures in parentheses are standard deviations.

## Privatization and rising inequality

We gathered the information on the privatization process from in-person interviews with enterprise managers and with local leaders at the county, township, and village levels in three counties. From these interviews, we found that the leaders in all three counties were mostly concerned about managerial incentive problems and, hence, the primary economic goal of TVE privatization was to provide adequate incentives to the managers by making the managers the majority owners of privatized TVEs ("*changzhangchidagu*"). In each of the counties, there was a strong desire to privatize TVEs quickly so as to prevent further asset stripping and loss of managerial talent.[1] Typically, TVEs were privatized over a two-year period with the focus on township enterprises in the first year and on village enterprises in the second year.

To achieve the objective of transferring TVE assets to enterprise managers, two main divestiture techniques were adopted.[2] The first was selling the enterprise outright to its manager or to a small group of senior employees led by the manager. Usually, this method was used to privatize small enterprises. The net value of enterprise assets was assessed by the local government's assessment agency, and managers were typically asked to pay 70–90 percent of the assessed value. The actual purchase price was usually determined through negotiation between the buyer, typically the original manager, and the local government. In a few rare instances, the price was determined through public auction. Payments were in installments usually spread over a three-year period.

The second method, called "*xianshou hougu*," involved selling the enterprise to a legal person, usually represented by the original enterprise manager, who then reorganized the enterprise into a shareholding company. This method was used to privatize most of the larger enterprises. To entice buyers and ensure a speedy sale, shares representing up to 30 percent of the net value of the enterprise, based largely on the assessment of the township government's assessment agency, although the value was subject to some negotiation, were offered for "free distribution." However, free shares were distributed only to those who also purchased shares. In other words, buyers of enterprises were given up to 30 percent discounts. The enterprise manager was given the responsibility of raising funds for the rest of the net value of the enterprise, again usually to be paid in installments over a three-year period. Therefore, enterprise managers were able to decide, depending on their own personal financial situations and their assessments of the enterprise, how many of the shares to buy themselves, how many to sell to others, and to whom to sell. However, the manager's decision on these matters was usually made in consultation with, or jointly with, the local government, although the degree of government involvement varied among the three localities.

When shares were sold to employees, free shares were usually distributed in proportion to the shares purchased. To offer greater incentives to the managerial and technical staff, we were told that the allocation of purchased, and hence free, shares was often rationed, with senior managers, sales and technical staff permitted to purchase more shares than production workers. In many enterprises, migrant workers were not eligible to purchase shares and, in some enterprises, local workers were also not given the opportunity to purchase shares. Unlike managers, who were allowed to pay for their shares in installments and use working capital and retained profits to finance their purchase, other employees were usually required to pay cash for their shares, typically financed by personal savings or money borrowed from relatives and friends. In one enterprise, shares were distributed to workers to compensate them for unpaid wages.

As a result of these divestiture procedures, the privatization of TVEs in all three counties led to a high level of concentration of shares in the hands of management. Of the 45 enterprises surveyed, 39 were privatized and six remain government owned. Of the 39 privatized TVEs, only 16 had sold shares to their employees. In 33 of the privatized enterprises, the manager or the managerial group, i.e., the manager plus other board members, held 50 percent or more of the shares. Employees were majority shareholders in only six of the privatized enterprises. For all 39 privatized TVEs, 77 percent of the shares were held by managers and other board members, 17.9 percent by employees, 2.9 percent by local governments, and 1.7 percent by private investors from outside the enterprise (Table 15.1).

This distribution of share ownership reflects the fact that local cadres were in a strong position to influence the outcome of privatization, as were enterprise managers, given their relative scarcity and the objectives of the local leaders. Workers in rural enterprises were in a much less powerful position. Typically, workers in rural enterprises lack the organizational ability and historic privileges that have been conferred upon their counterparts in state-owned enterprises (SOEs). Given this lack of bargaining power, the limited role of workers in the privatization process should not come as a surprise.

About a third of the privatized TVEs in the sample did give their employees the option to buy shares. However, the distribution of share ownership by employees in these enterprises was often highly skewed. Table 15.2 reports descriptive statistics of employee shareholdings from the employee sample that was taken from those who, together, owned the aforementioned 17.9 percent of the privatized TVEs in the sample.[3] As reported in Table 15.2, about one-third of the workers in the sample held some shares. The average value of shareholdings was 3,812.8 yuan for all the observations and 11,649 yuan among the shareholders, with a large variation, as reflected by the respective squared coefficient of variation and Gini coefficient. The distribution of employee shareholdings was skewed toward those who were male, local residents, in managerial positions, and wealthier (Table 15.3). About 75 percent of the shareholders received dividend payments in 1998. The rate of return to share ownership was quite respectable, 11.6 percent for shareholders who received dividend payments and 8.6 percent for all shareholders in the sample. With the high rates of return to the majority of shareholders, the unequal distribution of share ownership became an important source of rising income inequality in the post-privatization rural enterprises.

Ownership restructuring has also led to noticeable changes in the employment and wage-setting behavior of the privatized enterprises, as the new owners placed a greater weight on profits in the objectives of the enterprises. As elsewhere, the privatization of TVEs was accompanied by drastic downsizing of the workforce. Among the 39 privatized enterprises, 20 enterprises laid off workers, with an average rate of 31 percent reduction in the existing workforce. Two types of workers seem to have commonly been the target of retrenchment. First, elimination of administrative jobs, jobs that were typically held by women, seems to have been high. Second, several enterprises told us that "those who were too old, too weak, too sick, or disabled were dismissed." The pattern of labor restructuring is expected to depress the wage levels of women relative to those of men and widen wage disparity between different age groups. Moreover, many enterprises took measures to further strengthen the link between rewards and the performance of individual workers.[4] These measures are likely to increase wage differentials among workers with different productive characteristics.

The rising wage disparity after privatization is evident in our sample. Table 15.4 reports changes in wage inequality between different gender, education, and age groups and between different regions after privatization.[5] Calculated as the ratio of the mean wage between groups, the gender wage gap was widening with the ratio of male to female wages rising by six percentage points in the post-privatization period. Educational differentials between workers with post-secondary degrees and graduates from senior high schools, from junior high schools and workers with grade school education or lower had gone up by approximately 15.6, 20, and 26 percentage points. These estimates show a clear trend of rising returns to education. The wage ratios of the age group 50–60 years to the group aged 25–49 years and to the group aged 16–24 years decreased, whereas the wage differential between the middle-aged and young groups went up. Returns to experience therefore decreased for the oldest workers but increased for middle-aged workers, indicating a non-linearity in the changes in the returns to experience as a result of privatization. Privatization has also been associated with widening of regional wage differentials, as all three wage ratios between localities went up by an appreciable amount in the post-privatization period.

To provide an overall picture of the impact of privatization on earnings and earnings inequality, we present, in Table 15.5, the means and the Gini coefficients for total earnings and labor and non-labor income before and after privatization. To assess the statistical significance of changes in earnings inequality, we compute the standard errors for Gini coefficients using the Jacknife technique. Then, the Gini coefficient is decomposed by income sources using the procedures given by Shorrocks (1982). The earnings statistics from our sample indicate that the privatization of TVEs did not result in earnings depression. In fact, total earnings increased by 25.3 percent between the two comparison periods, with an average growth rate of 8.5 percent per year. As a result of the introduction of employee shareholding, the share of property income, i.e., dividends and interest

*Table 15.2* The distribution of share ownership in the employee sample

|  | Total | Shareholder | Non-shareholder |
| --- | --- | --- | --- |
| No. of employees | 883 | 289 | 594 |
| (%) | 100.0 | 32.7 | 67.3 |
| Mean value of shares (yuan/employee) | 3,812.8 | 11,649.0 | 0.0 |
| Standard deviation | 17,402.9 | 28,912.1 | – |
| Minimum | 0.0 | 500.0 | |
| Maximum | 320,000.0 | 320,000.0 | |
| $CV^2$ | 20.83 | 6.16 | |
| Gini coefficient | 0.874 | 0.615 | – |

Notes
The statistics are derived from the employee survey for 39 privatized township and village enterprises (TVEs). The values of shares, dividends, and total earnings are measured in 1998 current yuan.
$CV^2$, squared coefficient of variation.

*Table 15.3* Between-group differentials in shareholdings

| (1) | Male | Female | Ratio of male to female |
|---|---|---|---|
| Mean value (yuan/employee) | 5,440.6 | 1,638.1 | 3.3 |
| (2) | Local resident | Migrant | Ratio of local to migrant |
| Mean value (yuan/employee) | 4,024.9 | 500.0 | 8.0 |
| (3) | Managerial staff | Production worker | Ratio of managerial to production workers |
| Mean value (yuan/employee) | 7,605.8 | 2,339.8 | 3.3 |
| (4) | Top 20% of family income | Bottom 40% of family income | Ratio of top 20% to bottom 40% |
| Mean value (yuan/employee) | 12,491.7 | 1,949.1 | 6.4 |

from shareholdings, rose from 0.3 percent of total earnings before privatization to 4.8 percent after privatization, and the relative importance of non-labor income in explaining total earnings inequality also rose sharply from 0.3 to 8.9 percent. The Gini indexes show that the inequality in total earnings and wages rose by an appreciable amount in the post-privatization period. In fact, over the short period 1995–98, the Gini coefficient for total earnings increased remarkably from 0.255 to 0.295, or by 15.7 percent. This change is statistically significant at the 10 percent level because the 90 percent confidence intervals of the Gini indexes for the two periods do not overlap. The magnitude of change in inequality is noteworthy given that the Gini coefficient is derived from a truncated sample because the earnings of senior managers and the income of laid-off workers are not part of the sample, and the inclusion of these observations at the upper and lower tails of the distribution would have led to an even larger increase in inequality. Having indicated that earnings inequality increased significantly after privatization, we now turn our attention to examining the underlying causes of the increase more systematically.

## Regression-based approach to inequality decomposition

The privatization of TVEs has led to a skewed distribution of share ownership, widened the wage gaps between different gender, education, and age groups, and increased regional income disparity. We now apply a regression-based inequality decomposition technique to estimate the contribution of each income determinant, such as shareholdings, gender, education, experience, and localities, to the rise in earnings inequality in the post-privatization period. As pointed out by Morduch and Sicular (1999), this regression-based approach provides an efficient, flexible,

*Table 15.4* Between-group changes in the wage structure

| Wages and bonuses | Before privatization (ratio) | After privatization (ratio) |
|---|---|---|
| Gender | | |
|   Male/female | 1.326 | 1.396 |
| Education | | |
|   Post-secondary/senior high | 1.117 | 1.261 |
|   Post-secondary/junior high | 1.333 | 1.553 |
|   Post-secondary/grade school | 1.264 | 1.524 |
| Age (years) | | |
|   50–60/25–49 | 1.359 | 1.104 |
|   50–60/16–24 | 1.714 | 1.446 |
|   25–49/16–24 | 1.261 | 1.308 |
| Region | | |
|   Penglai/Yanzhou | 1.272 | 1.343 |
|   Wujin/Yanzhou | 1.461 | 1.752 |
|   Wujin/Penglai | 1.148 | 1.305 |

Note
The numbers reported are the ratios of the means between the two groups.

and general method of quantifying the role of individual and community characteristics in a multivariate context.

### Decomposition procedure

The decomposition procedure begins with an earnings equation:[6]

$$Y = X\beta + \varepsilon$$

where $X$ is an $n \times K$ matrix of explanatory variables with the first column defined as an $n$-vector of one, $\beta$ is a $K$-vector of regression coefficients, and $\varepsilon$ is an $n$-vector of random disturbances. From the earnings equation, total earnings can be written as the sum of the income flows contributed by individual and community characteristics and the regression residuals, that is:

$$Y_i = \sum_{k=1}^{K+1} \hat{Y}_i^k \quad \text{for all } i$$

where $\hat{Y}_i^k = \hat{\beta}_k X_i^k$ for all $k = 1, \ldots, K$ and $\hat{Y}_i^{k+1} = \hat{\varepsilon}_i$ for $k = K + 1$.

The share of each of these estimated income flows in an inequality measure can then be calculated using the formula:

*Table 15.5* Earnings and earnings inequality

|  | Total earnings | Wages and bonuses | Dividends and interest |
|---|---|---|---|
| Before privatization | | | |
| Mean (yuan) | 3,145.6 | 3,134.6 | 11.0 |
| Standard deviation | (1,784.4) | (1,785.4) | (78.7) |
| Share (%) | 100.0 | 99.7 | 0.3 |
| Gini coefficient | 0.255 | 0.255 | 0.980 |
| Standard error | (0.009) | (0.009) | (0.004) |
| 90% CI | (0.240, 0.269) | (0.240, 0.269) | (0.973, 0.986) |
| Pseudo-Gini | 0.255 | 0.205 | |
| Share (%) | 100.0 | 99.7 | 0.3 |
| After privatization | | | |
| Mean (yuan) | 3,942.3 | 3,754.5 | 187.7 |
| Standard deviation | (3,034.8) | (2,912.5) | (566.1) |
| Share (%) | 100.0 | 95.2 | 4.8 |
| Gini coefficient | 0.295 | 0.286 | 0.877 |
| Standard error | (0.014) | (0.015) | (0.010) |
| 90% CI | (0.272, 0.318) | (0.261, 0.311) | (0.861, 0.893) |
| Pseudo-Gini | 0.282 | 0.554 | |
| Share (%) | 100.0 | 91.1 | 8.9 |

Notes
The statistics are derived from the employee survey for 39 privatized township and village enterprises (TVEs). The post-privatization year is 1998 for all enterprises. The pre-privatization year used is rescaled data for 1995. Earnings variables are measured in 1990 constant yuan.
CI, confidence interval.

$$s(Y^k) = \frac{\sum_{i=1}^{n} w_i(Y) \hat{\beta}_k X_i^k}{I(Y)} \quad \text{for } k = 1, \ldots, K$$

where $w_i(Y)$ is the weight of individual $i$ in overall inequality and $I(Y)$ is the inequality indicator. The standard error of $s(Y^k)$ is given as:

$$\sigma(s(Y^k)) = \sigma(\hat{\beta}_k)[\frac{\sum_{i=1}^{n} w_i(Y) X_i^k}{I(Y)}].$$

This regression-based decomposition procedure is applied to the Gini coefficients for the before- and after-privatization periods.[7]

### Empirical results

The empirical analysis begins with the estimation of an extended human capital equation where annual earnings are treated as a function of values of shareholdings, years of schooling, years of experience (and its square), a gender dummy for male workers, and location dummies for Penglai and Yanzhou. The dependent variable, annual earnings in yuan, is measured in linear form to facilitate inequality decomposition. The variable of shareholding, also measured in yuan, is introduced only for the post-privatization period. The earnings regressions are run separately by ordinary least squares (OLS) for the before-privatization and after-privatization periods, and the results are presented in Table 15.6. The introduction of values of shareholdings into the earnings equation may create a simultaneous bias. To test this possibility, the earnings equation for the post-privatization period is also estimated with the two-stage least squares (2SLS) method using age and

*Table 15.6* Regression results of linear earnings equation

|  | *Before privatization* | *After privatization* |
| --- | --- | --- |
| Shareholdings | – | 0.051 |
|  |  | (5.182)* |
| Male | 729.6 | 963.01 |
|  | (7.046)* | (7.210)* |
| Education | 150.32 | 254.0 |
|  | (4.175)* | (4.491)* |
| Experience | 35.42 | 100.31 |
|  | (3.158)* | (2.882)* |
| Experience$^2$ | 0.43 | −1.730 |
|  | (0.829) | (−1.735)*** |
| Penglai | −375.57 | −753.52 |
|  | (−3.018)* | (−4.364)* |
| Yanzhou | −1,186.21 | −,881.9 |
|  | (−8.701)* | (−9.939)* |
| Constant | 1,397.78 | 733.43 |
|  | (4.526)* | (1.163) |
| Adjusted $R^2$ | 0.203 | 0.272 |
| $F$-test (zero slopes) | 36.94 | 48.05 |
| $P$-value | 0.0 | 0.0 |
| Observations | 875 | 880 |

Notes
The table presents the ordinary least squares estimates of linear earnings equations with $t$-statistics reported in parentheses. The $t$-statistics are derived from heteroskedasticity-consistent standard errors.
*, **, and ***, significance levels of 1%, 5%, and 10%, respectively, for a two-tailed test.

marital and residential status as the instrumental variables. The Hausman test, based on a comparison of the OLS and 2SLS estimates, fails to reject the null hypothesis that share values are uncorrelated with the error terms of the earnings equation.[8] Thus, the OLS estimates of the earnings regressions in Table 15.5 are unbiased and consistent for both periods.

The estimates of the earnings equations show that shareholdings are a significant determinant of total earnings, with an average rate of return of 5.1 percent in the post-privatization period. For the other explanatory variables, the estimates for the post-privatization period increased noticeably. Specifically, the earnings differential between male and female workers increased from 729 to 963 yuan, a 13.5 percent increase over the mean value. The return to education rose from 150 yuan per year of schooling to 254 yuan, a 2.6 percent increase over the mean. The return to experience also went up, from 35 to 100 yuan for each year of work experience. Before the privatization, earnings increased monotonically according to the seniority of a worker. In contrast, the return to experience increased, but at a decreasing rate in the post-privatization period. Thus, for a worker who entered the labor force at the age of 16, his/her earnings would peak in the year of retirement under the pay structure before privatization, but at the age of 45 under the post-privatization pay structure. The privatization also widened the earnings gaps between regions.

Table 15.7 reports the shares of the Gini coefficient of the income flows contributed by shareholdings, human capital characteristics, and regional factors estimated by the earnings regression for the before- and after-privatization periods. Except for squared experience, the shares of the inequality components are all significant at the 1 percent level. Prior to privatization, human capital, gender discrimination, and regional segmentations together explained 27.1 percent of the earnings inequality in the sample. In the post-privatization period, the shares of these de-equalizing factors have all gone up, with an increase of 2.5 percentage points by education, 2.7 by experience in linear terms, 1 by gender gap, and 4 by spatial variations. Non-labor income from shareholdings represents a new de-equalizing component, contributing, remarkably, 9.1 percent of the earnings inequality in the post-privatization sample. As a result, the share of the explained earnings inequality rose to 41.4 percent.

## Conclusions

In this chapter, we have examined the distributional consequences of privatization using a small sample from China's rural industries. Our results indicate that the privatization of TVEs was associated with a sharp increase in earnings inequality over a short period of three years. We find that unequal distribution of share ownership has been an important source of the rise in earnings inequality after privatization. Looking at other causes of the increased income disparity, we find increased returns to education, increased returns to experience for middle-aged workers, a widened gender wage gap, and enlarged regional disparity.

*Table 15.7* Decomposition of Gini coefficients: estimated proportional shares

|  | *Before privatization* | *After privatization* |
| --- | --- | --- |
| Shareholdings | – | 0.091* |
| Standard error | 0.017 | |
| Education | 0.035 | 0.060* |
| Standard error | 0.008 | 0.013 |
| Experience | 0.048 | 0.075* |
| Standard error | 0.015 | 0.025 |
| Experience$^2$ | 0.014 | −0.036 |
| Standard error | 0.017 | 0.021 |
| Male | 0.065* | 0.074* |
| Standard error | 0.009 | 0.010 |
| Penglai | −0.007* | −0.005* |
| Standard error | 0.002 | 0.001 |
| Yanzhou | 0.116* | 0.155* |
| Standard error | 0.013 | 0.016 |
| Percentage explained | 0.271 | 0.414 |
| Percentage of residuals | 0.729 | 0.586 |
| Total | 1.00 | 1.00 |

Note
* Significance level of 1% for a two-tailed test.

While the results in this chapter are based on a limited sample, they have implications for our understanding of the transition process in China. While much attention has been focused on rural–urban and inter-regional trends in income inequality, our results suggest that privatization may also be an important contributing factor, as it has been in other transition economies. In rural China, where the welfare and redistributive functions of local government have become increasingly difficult to maintain in the reform period, increasing inequality from the privatization process is likely to contribute further to social fragmentation. The need for state-led redistributive policies is evident. Moreover, as mentioned above, the choice of privatization methods by local leaders has been made primarily through considerations of efficiency and concerns about managerial incentives. As our results show, however, the form of privatization affects income distribution; privatization methods associated with wealth concentration have undesirable distributional consequences. Hence, the issue of distributive equity must play a proper role in the design of privatization policies. The need to create managerial incentives cannot justify a massive giveaway of public assets to a few individuals from the standpoint of social justice.

## Acknowledgments

Paper prepared for the International Symposium on Equity and Social Justice in Transitional China, 11–12 July 2002. This research is part of the University of British Columbia Center for Chinese Research's project on rural change in the People's Republic of China, and was carried out with aid of a grant from the International Development Research Center, Ottawa, Canada. I wish to thank my collaborators on the project, Samuel Ho, Paul Bowles, and Fiona MacPhail, for their input to this chapter.

## Notes

1  The enterprises were selected from a list of enterprises provided to us by the local Bureau of Township–Village Enterprises, as it is not possible to survey TVEs without the approval and cooperation of the local government. The employees in each enterprise were selected randomly from the payroll list subject to the following constraints: (1) five of the selected employees must be mid-ranked managerial or technical personnel; and (2) all of the selected employees must have worked at the enterprise both before and after ownership reform.

2  Enterprise data were obtained from enterprise records. However, employee data for past years were based upon employee recall. As such, they may be subject to error. We were able to compare our data with a small sample of official wage data for previous years and are confident, based on this comparison, that our data are of an acceptable level of accuracy.

3  For the analysis of the determination of share ownership by employees, see Dong *et al.* (2002).

4  There was also evidence of more primitive forms of labor discipline being introduced. For example, one local cadre told us approvingly of how productivity had been increased in one enterprise. Here, the "*mowei taotai zi*" method of labor discipline had been introduced. This involved ranking all employees' performance each year and dismissing the bottom 5 percent. The ranking was made on the basis of employees' votes on each others' performance, the assessment of the supervisor, and a set of measures on absenteeism and product quality.

5  To facilitate comparison, the rescaled data for 1995 are to represent the pre-privatization year, while 1998 is used as the post-privatization year. All wages are measured in 1990 constant yuan. The price deflators are obtained from the 1999 editions of the *Jiangsu Statistical Yearbook* (pp. 45–46 and 128) and the *Shandong Statistical Yearbook* (pp. 111–15).

6  For the details of this decomposition procedure, see Morduch and Sicular (1999).

7  As pointed out by Morduch and Sicular (1999), while the Gini decomposition does not satisfy the property of uniform addition, "it remains by far the most popular method in the literature, and it is often used exclusively."

8  The Hausman test value is 2.01 and its $P$-value is 0.95. The value of the instrument validity test is 1.76 and its $P$-value is 0.99.

## References

Aghion, P. and S. Commander (1999) "On the Dynamics of Inequality in the Transition," *Economics of Transition*, 7: 275–98.

Dong, X.-Y., P. Bowles and S. Ho (2002) "The Determinants of Employee Ownership in

China's Privatized Rural Industry: Evidence from Jiangsu and Shandong," *Journal of Comparative Economics*, 30, 415–37.

Ho, S., P. Bowles, and X.-Y. Dong (2002) " 'Letting Go of the Small': The Political Economy of Privatizing Rural Enterprises in Shandong and Jiangsu," *Journal of Development Studies*, forthcoming.

Morduch, J. (1999) "Rethinking Inequality Decomposition with Evidence from Rural China," unpublished manuscript.

National Bureau of Statistics (various issues) *China Statistical Yearbook*, Beijing: Zhongguo Tongi Chubanshe.

National Bureau of Statistics, (1999) *Statistical Yearbook of Jiangsu Province (Jiangsu Tongji Nianjian)*, Beijing: Zhongguo Tongi Chubanshe.

National Bureau of Statistics (1999) *Statistical Yearbook of Shandong Province (Shandong Tongji Nianjian)*, Beijing: Zhongguo Tongi Chubanshe.

Shorrocks, A.F. (1982) "Inequality Decomposition by Factor Components," *Econometrica*, 50: 193–211.

# Index